MORRIS PUBLIC LIBRARY

3 3460 11680 0126

P9-CQA-953

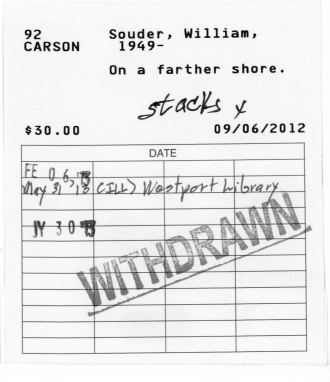

92
CARSON

Souder, William,
1949-

On a farther shore.

stacks ✗

$30.00   09/06/2012

DATE		
FE 06	CILL) Westport Library	
May 31 '13		
JY 30		

WITHDRAWN

MORRIS PUBLIC LIBRARY
4 North Street
Morris, CT 06763
(860) 567-7440

4/15 mended   Mended-1/17

BAKER & TAYLOR

MORRIS PUBLIC LIBRARY
4 North Street
Morris, CT 06763
(860) 567-7440

On a
Farther
Shore

Also by William Souder

A Plague of Frogs

Under a Wild Sky

The Life and Legacy
of **Rachel Carson**

On a
Farther
Shore

William Souder

Crown Publishers • New York

Copyright © 2012 by William Souder

All rights reserved.

Published in the United States by Crown Publishers, an imprint of the Crown Publishing
Group, a division of Random House, Inc., New York.

www.crownpublishing.com

CROWN and the Crown colophon are registered trademarks of Random House, Inc.

Grateful acknowledgment is made to Frances Collin, literary agent, for permission
to reprint excerpts from the following books by Rachel Carson: *Under the Sea-Wind,*
copyright © 1941 by Rachel L. Carson (New York: Simon and Schuster, 1941); *The Sea
Around Us,* copyright © 1950 by Rachel L. Carson (Oxford: Oxford University Press,
1950); *The Edge of the Sea,* copyright © 1955 by Rachel L. Carson (Boston: Houghton
Mifflin Co., 1955); *Silent Spring,* copyright © 1962 by Rachel L. Carson (Boston:
Houghton Mifflin Co., 1962); *Always, Rachel* edited by Martha Freeman, copyright ©
1995 by Roger Allen Christie (Boston: Beacon Press, 1998); *Lost Woods: The Discovered
Writing of Rachel Carson,* copyright © 1998 by Roger Allen Christie (Boston: Beacon
Press); and unpublished Rachel Carson material copyright © 2012 by Roger A. Christie.
Reprinted by permission of Frances Collin, Trustee.
Excerpt from "The Dry Salvages" from *Four Quartets* by T. S. Eliot;
copyright © renewed 1969 by Esme Valerie Eliot. Reprinted by permission of
Houghton Mifflin Harcourt Publishing Company.
All rights reserved.
Dorothy Freeman's letters and other writings quoted by permission of Stanley Freeman Jr.
and Martha Freeman.

Library of Congress Cataloging-in-Publication Data
Souder, William
On a farther shore : the life and legacy of Rachel Carson /
William Souder.—1st ed.
p. cm.
Includes bibliographical references and index.
1. Carson, Rachel, 1907–1964. 2. Carson, Rachel, 1907–1964. Silent Spring. 3. Carson,
Rachel, 1907–1964—Influence. 4. Marine biologists—United States—
Biography. 5. Naturalists—United States—Biography. 6. Environmentalists—United
States—Biography. 7. Science writers—United States—Biography. 8. Pesticides—
Environmental aspects—United States—History. 9. Environmentalism—United States—
History. 10. Environmental ethics—United States—History. I. Title.
QH31.C33S68 2012
508.092—dc23
[B]   2012003077

ISBN 978-0-307-46220-6
eISBN 978-0-307-46222-0

Printed in the United States of America

Book design by Maria Elias
Frontispiece photograph: *Rachel Carson,* 1951, by Irving Penn.
Copyright © 1951 (renewed 1979) Condé Nast Publications Inc.
Jacket design by Janet Hansen
Jacket photograph: Alfred Eisenstaedt/Time Life Pictures/Getty Images

1   3   5   7   9   10   8   6   4   2

First Edition

For Susan

Rachel Carson, 1951, by Irving Penn

In that hollow of space and brightness, in that ceaseless travail of wind and sand and ocean, the world one sees is still the world unharassed of man, a place of the instancy and eternity of creation and the noble ritual of the burning year.

—Henry Beston

Here between the hither and the farther shore
While time is withdrawn, consider the future
And the past with an equal mind.

—T. S. Eliot

Contents

On a
Farther
Shore

PART ONE

Water World

ONE

Miss Carson's Book

L ate in the summer of 1962, extreme weather visited both ends of the United States. In the West it was so hot that women wore swimsuits on the streets of San Francisco, and the smog levels in that city were the highest ever recorded. On the East Coast, Hurricane Alma churned northward, interrupting a pleasant spell as it neared the tip of Long Island. On August 28 the edge of the storm ended play at Yankee Stadium one inning after Mickey Mantle blasted what proved to be the game-winning home run to right centerfield through a driving rain. The next morning it was sunny and warm in the nation's capital, where the *Washington Post*'s weather section reported daily radiation levels of just three micromicrocuries per cubic meter of air—unchanged from the day before and not bad given the recent pace of atmospheric nuclear weapons tests by both the United States and the Soviet Union.

That same day, President John F. Kennedy appeared at the State Department at four in the afternoon for the forty-second press conference of his year and a half in office. The president began by announcing Felix Frankfurter's retirement from the U.S. Supreme

Court. He then fielded questions about farm policy, tensions in Berlin, and whether he would meet with Nikita Khrushchev during the Soviet premier's upcoming visit to the United Nations. Kennedy also answered several vaguely portentous queries about an apparent increase in Soviet shipping traffic to Cuba. Near the end, Kennedy took an unusual question. "Mr. President, there appears to be a growing concern among scientists as to the possibility of dangerous long-range side effects from the widespread use of DDT and other pesticides. Have you considered asking the Department of Agriculture or the Public Health Service to take a closer look at this?"

If he was surprised, Kennedy did not miss a beat. "Yes," he said quickly, "and I know that they already are. I think, particularly, of course, since Miss Carson's book, but they are examining the issue."

In this brief exchange something new came into the world, for this was a cleaving point—the moment when the gentle, optimistic proposition called "conservation" began its transformation into the bitterly divisive idea that would come to be known as "environmentalism." Kennedy's promise of a government investigation into the contamination of the environment by a widely used and economically important class of products had no precedent. And because the government itself used pesticides extensively, any such inquiry necessarily had to look in the mirror. Compared with the other matters Kennedy had discussed that day—policies that would evolve, situations that would change and fade away—a problem with the health of the environment became by definition a problem with the totality of human existence. At issue was humanity's place in the natural order of a world increasingly subservient to the human species. Who but us could devise so perfect a way to contend with ourselves?

The president's reference to "Miss Carson's book" would now be opaque to the several generations of Americans who have come of age in the intervening years—Rachel Carson is unknown to almost anyone under the age of fifty. But in 1962 no elaboration was needed.

Carson was the bestselling author of three books about the oceans and by any measure one of America's most respected and beloved writers. Or so she had been. The new book to which Kennedy referred, *Silent Spring,* was a bristling polemic about the indiscriminate use of pesticides. It was unlike anything Carson had previously written. Although not yet actually a book—it wouldn't be published for another month—in June three long excerpts from *Silent Spring* had appeared in consecutive issues of the *New Yorker.* By the time of Kennedy's press conference, the *New Yorker* articles had raised public alarm in the United States and abroad and prompted the chemicals industry to launch an angry and concerted effort to discredit *Silent Spring* and destroy its author.

The woman at the center of this firestorm scarcely seemed capable of becoming such a polarizing figure. Now fifty-five years old, Rachel Carson had spent most of her adult life in the company of her mother—writing, bird-watching, and visiting the seashore. Petite, soft-spoken, and nearly apolitical, she lived quietly in a leafy suburb of Silver Spring, Maryland, with a cat and her orphaned ten-year-old grandnephew, Roger Christie, whom she had adopted. Carson had earned a master's degree in zoology at Johns Hopkins University but had never worked as a scientist. In the gloom of the Great Depression, she instead found a job as an information specialist with the federal government's Bureau of Fisheries, an agency later merged with the Biological Survey to form the U.S. Fish and Wildlife Service.

In 1951 her book *The Sea Around Us* made Carson's literary reputation—it stood atop the *New York Times* bestseller list for thirty-nine weeks and won the National Book Award—and she left government service. Every spring Carson and Roger drove north to Southport Island on the Maine coast, where she owned a cottage on a rocky bluff overlooking Sheepscot Bay. Here Carson passed her summers in reflection, gazing at the ebb and flow of the sea, collecting marine specimens in the tidal pools along the shore, and visiting, often deep into the fog-shrouded nights, with her neighbors Dorothy and Stanley Freeman. In the fall, she went home.

Carson's writings about the sea were characterized—solemnly and without fail—as "poetic," a term invoked by reviewers as a way of saying that she wrote with a grace that was unexpected given her subject. The living, evolving nature of the open ocean and the intertidal zones on its threshold were unfamiliar to most readers—as were the lessons in geology and physics and biology that Carson poured into her narratives. Her knack for gentle explanation beguiled critics and readers alike, even those who could have never imagined caring about science or the strange water world that so fascinated Carson.

Critics remarked, time and again, that there was something bracing and surprising in the fact that a woman should have such a profound understanding of the physical environment. They also believed her to be a heroic correspondent regularly at sea on research vessels hurtling through storms, or swimming among the fish teeming on the coral reefs of the tropics—a false impression that she never bothered to correct. A friend who once drew a caricature of Carson's public persona had depicted her as an Amazon towering at the edge of a stormy sea, a harpoon in one hand and a writhing octopus in the other. Carson, who would have been more accurately shown hunched over a microscope or in the library surrounded by piles of books, thought the drawing hilarious.

A slow writer who revised endlessly, Carson had worked on *Silent Spring* for almost four years—though she had worried for much longer than that over the new pesticides developed at the outset of World War II and in the years immediately after it. One of the best known and most widely used of these compounds was a molecule of chlorinated hydrocarbon called dichloro-diphenyl-trichloroethane— DDT. Although it had been first synthesized in 1874, nobody found a practical application for DDT until 1939, when a forty-year-old chemist named Paul Müller, who worked for the J. R. Geigy Company in Basel, Switzerland, discovered that it killed insects. DDT was immediately deployed against an outbreak of potato beetles in Switzerland, where it proved astonishingly effective. DDT's long-lasting fatal properties lingered on anything it touched. And because doses that killed insects appeared to be harmless to warm-blooded animals, including humans, DDT became the overnight weapon of choice in fighting lice, ticks, and mosquitoes that transmitted human diseases. Production of DDT expanded rapidly during World War II to speed it to combat zones for use as a delousing agent, particularly on refugees streaming out of Nazi-occupied territories. When the U.S. Army sprayed more than a million civilians with DDT and successfully halted a 1943 typhus epidemic in Naples, a conviction that the new pesticide would be a panacea against insect-borne diseases gained wide acceptance. In 1948, Paul Müller won the Nobel Prize in Physiology or Medicine. At the award ceremony, DDT was declared a major discovery that illustrated the "wondrous ways of science."

Not everyone believed that.

On June 5, 1945, an FWS airplane flew back and forth just above the treetops of a 117-acre tract of forest in the sprawling Patuxent Research Refuge in Prince George's County, Maryland, not far from Washington, D.C. The plane sprayed the woods with DDT dissolved in xylene and fuel oil. The mixture drifted down through the forest canopy unevenly, riding updrafts and crosswinds, and arrived on the ground in varying concentrations as the pilot, navigating by sight, passed over some areas more than once and missed other places entirely. Some of the toxic cloud landed on a nearly mile-long section of the Patuxent River, a small, muddy stream that was home to twenty species of fish.

In the days and weeks after the spraying, researchers monitored what became of the mammals, birds, frogs, and fish exposed to the pesticide. In their later report, the scientists noted that the initial general enthusiasm for DDT should be tempered by "grave concern." The investigators cautioned that while most poisons affect living organisms in different ways—such selectivity is a fundamental requirement for any pesticide—all poisons are "a two-edged sword," and one as toxic as DDT would likely cause collateral damage to wildlife. The Patuxent experiment, which had been undertaken after exploratory tests by several federal agencies in 1943 and 1944 hinted at problems with DDT, confirmed as much. Although the airborne DDT appeared to cause no significant harm to mammals, birds, or amphibians, dead fish began collecting in a net stretched across the Patuxent River fewer than ten hours after the spraying. Subsequent tests in carefully maintained artificial ponds showed that, even at concentrations much weaker than were used in the forest spraying, DDT caused extensive mortality in fish.

Further laboratory studies launched as part of the same investigation hinted that the animals that escaped poisoning in the aerial spraying might have just been lucky or simply weren't exposed to high doses. When mammals and birds were fed DDT, or when it was put into aquariums with developing tadpoles, every species tested was sickened, and many of the animals died. The final report described how death occurred in birds, but noted that the effects of DDT were much the same in all of the animals tested: "excessive nervousness, loss of appetite, tremors, muscular twitching, and persistent rigidity of the leg muscles, the last continuing through death." On August 22, 1945, the FWS issued a press release describing the results of the DDT tests and warning that the pesticide should be used with extreme caution. The agency advised anyone observing "unusual reactions" in wildlife following an exposure to DDT to report it at once.

These troubling findings led to a series of investigations of DDT at Patuxent that would continue for years. By 1947, Patuxent had a staff biologist whose sole responsibility was to investigate "DDT problems." That same year, one of the spring visitors to Patuxent was a woman from the Fish and Wildlife Division of Information who signed the guest log as Rachel L. Carson and who was already a step ahead of the emerging science.

Carson routinely read the scientific reports out of Patuxent and would end up editing many of them dealing with DDT. She had misgivings about the popular new insecticide even before the first results from the testing were known. In July 1945, while the investigators were still at work, Carson had proposed a story to *Reader's Digest*. She began breezily enough, but ended on a frightening note:

"Practically at my backdoor here in Maryland, an experiment of more than ordinary interest and importance is going on," she wrote. "We have all heard a lot about what DDT will soon do for us by wiping out insect pests. The experiments at Patuxent have been planned to show what other effects DDT may have if applied to wide areas; what it will do to insects that are beneficial or even essential; how it may affect waterfowl, or birds that depend on insect food; whether it may upset the whole delicate balance of nature if unwisely used."

The *Reader's Digest*, lacking Carson's vision, passed.

But Carson never stopped thinking about DDT, even as the questions about its safety raised in the Patuxent testing were largely ignored. DDT quickly gained wide acceptance as an agricultural and commercial product, thanks to its low cost, its deadly persistence wherever and however it was used, and a wildly successful campaign to portray the poison as a miraculous answer to the long struggle against the insects that decimated crops and forests, plagued livestock, and brought disease and misery to millions of people every year.

The uses for DDT seemed endless. It could be applied in powders or dusts, in assorted liquid sprays and emulsions, and in aerosol "bombs" that housewives began purchasing in department stores as early as 1945. The bombs used Freon (later found to be destructive of the ozone layer) as a propellant and were claimed to treat an average-sized room in as little as six seconds. DDT was sold in hardware and grocery stores in products such as soap, furniture polish, shelf paper, paint, and fabric treatments. DDT could be applied to lawns by means of a fogging device that attached to the muffler of a lawn mower, dispersing a hot, poisonous cloud as the grass was cut. Airplanes sprayed DDT over millions of acres of forest to kill woodland insects such as the spruce budworm and the gypsy moth. It was sprayed in hospital kitchens and in residential neighborhoods hit by Dutch elm disease. In the South children played in the murk behind DDT fogging trucks that cruised the streets during encephalitis outbreaks. In the fall of

1945, an intrepid pilot sprayed the Yale Bowl to eliminate mosquitoes for an upcoming concert. DDT helped finish the campaign to wipe out the vestiges of malaria in Europe and in North America, and in 1955 the World Health Organization launched a global effort to eradicate the disease—with DDT as its main weapon. By 1959, some eighty million pounds of DDT were being used annually in the United States alone.

In early 1958, Carson learned that *Reader's Digest* planned a favorable article about the use of aerial DDT spraying for gypsy moths—and she wrote to the magazine's editor warning him there was another side to the story. About that same time, she also heard about a group of landowners on Long Island who were suing the state of New York to halt a gypsy moth control effort in which their homes and property were being aerially sprayed with DDT. Carson, disinclined toward journalism, tried to persuade the *New Yorker's* E. B. White—author of the classic children's books *Stuart Little* and *Charlotte's Web*—to cover the trial. He suggested instead that she write something. By spring, Carson had signed a contract with her publisher, Houghton Mifflin, for a book about pesticides tentatively titled "The Control of Nature" that would also appear in installments in the *New Yorker*.

In 1945, as the U.S. Fish and Wildlife Service began discovering the danger to wildlife from DDT, the United States exploded three nuclear devices—one at Alamogordo, New Mexico, in the test of a bomb called "Trinity," and two in Japan, where the cities of Hiroshima and Nagasaki were leveled and somewhere between 150,000 and 250,000 people died. During the Cold War of the 1950s and early '60s, a number of countries—but principally the United States and the Soviet Union—continued to conduct atmospheric tests of nuclear weapons. A moratorium was agreed to in 1958, and such tests were suspended until the summer of 1961, when the Soviet Union announced it would resume its atmospheric program.

Over the course of the next three months, the Russians exploded thirty-one nuclear devices, including one 3,300 times more powerful than "Little Boy," which had been dropped on Hiroshima. Fearful of the Soviets gaining an advantage and under pressure from Congress and the public, President Kennedy, who had campaigned on a pledge to enact a permanent ban on testing, reluctantly restarted American tests. Between April and November 1962, at sites in the Marshall Islands in the South Pacific, the United States exploded thirty-five nuclear devices in the atmosphere—approximately one every five days. When a comprehensive ban ended the era of atmospheric testing in August 1963, more than five hundred nuclear devices had been exploded aboveground—about two hundred of them by the United States.

A by-product of these tests was the debris carried on high-altitude winds that eventually returned to earth as radioactive fallout—notably the isotopes strontium 90 and iodine 131. High concentrations came down in the central United States, where people, especially children, were exposed through the consumption of milk from cows that were pastured in areas where fallout landed. Radiation exposure was understood to be a potential health hazard, but for years there was no scientific agreement as to how serious it might be. In 1957 a group of prominent scientists who believed radioactive fallout had as yet done little harm to humans nonetheless urged the United Nations to seek an international limit on atmospheric testing. The U.S. Atomic Energy Commission disagreed. The government's position was that atmospheric testing could continue as it had for decades without—in the words of the *New York Times*—"posing any danger to mankind." Then came the spate of testing in 1962, and by the following spring strontium 90 levels in milk had doubled in some areas.

Invisible and ubiquitous, undetectable without special instruments, radioactive fallout was a strange and terrifying thing—a poison whose effects might not be experienced for years or even decades following exposure. The same held true for DDT, which was also discovered in milk. Carson recognized an "exact and inescapable" parallel between pesticides and radioactive fallout that had profound implications. Our species, Carson reasoned, having evolved over thousands of millennia, was well adapted to the natural world but was biologically defenseless in an unnaturally altered one. Pesticides and radiation, apart from their acute toxicities, were also mutagenic—capable of damaging the genetic material that guides the machinery of living cells and provides the blueprint for each succeeding generation. Carson believed that widely dispersed and persistent substances such as DDT and radioactive fallout—which contaminated the environment not in isolated, specific places, but throughout the global ecosystem—were the inevitable and potentially lethal developments of the modern age, each one a consequence, as she put it bluntly in *Silent Spring,* of the "impetuous and heedless pace of man rather than the deliberate pace of nature." ·

The furor over *Silent Spring* began at once. In the weeks following publication of the first excerpts in the *New Yorker,* moody stories expressing shock and outrage began appearing in newspapers across the country. Some compared the book to *Uncle Tom's Cabin* and predicted an earthquake of change in the way pesticides were used. Most reports nervously welcomed Carson's dire warning about chemical contamination of the environment, although many also acknowledged a rapidly building counterattack from trade groups and a chemicals industry that decried Carson's book as unscientific and one-sided, arguing that she took no account of the economic and health benefits achieved through the use of pesticides.

Some of Carson's detractors imagined her in league with a lunatic fringe that included food faddists, anti-fluoridationists, organic farmers, and soft-headed nature lovers. A major pesticide manufacturer threatened Carson's publisher, Houghton Mifflin, with a lawsuit if *Silent Spring* was issued without changes, saying they believed and would attempt to prove that Carson was a front for "sinister influences" in the Soviet Union and its Eastern European satellites that were intent on undermining America. The U.S. Department of Agriculture meanwhile told the *New York Times* it was being deluged with letters from citizens expressing "horror and amazement" that the agency permitted the wide use of such deadly poisons. The Book-of-the-Month Club announced that *Silent Spring* would be its main selection for October 1962, proof that Carson was still expected to be popular even though she'd hit a nerve. A newspaper in London reported that "a 55-year old spinster has written a book that is causing more heart-searching in America than any book since Upton Sinclair's *The Jungle* forced Chicago to clean up its abattoirs."

Everyone remarked on the sharp and fatalistic tone of *Silent Spring*—including, as Carson enjoyed noting, people who had not read it. From its opening pages the book was a harrowing excursion through a chemically strangled world. Carson made no attempt to soften her vision of the future. At stake in the unrestrained use of chemical pesticides was nothing less than human existence itself:

> Along with the possibility of the extinction of mankind by nuclear war, the central problem of our age has therefore become the contamination of man's total environment with such substances of incredible potential for harm—substances that accumulate in the tissues of plants and animals and even penetrate the germ cells to shatter or alter the very material of heredity upon which the shape of the future depends.

Silent Spring arrived at a time when there was already unease about the unanticipated ways that science and medicine could betray the public welfare. In 1959, just days before Thanksgiving, the government had abruptly halted the sale of cranberries after discovering that the crop was contaminated with residues of an herbicide known to cause cancer. The "cranberry scare" caused economic hardship for cranberry growers and created a never-before-seen loss of consumer confidence in the safety of the American food supply. Then, in 1961, came devastating news from Great Britain—where some seven thousand babies had been born with appalling deformities. The birth defects were caused by the sedative thalidomide, which had been prescribed for pregnant women to alleviate morning sickness. Thalidomide was thought to be safe even for expectant mothers and it was—except, as was learned after the damage had been done, for a sixteen-day period during pregnancy. Many women who consumed even a single dose during that fateful window of time gave birth to babies with abnormalities, including a condition called phocomelia, in which the long bones of the arms, and sometimes both the arms and legs, were drastically shortened, so that stubby hands and feet appeared to grow directly out of the torso—like the flippers on a seal. The U.S. maker of thalidomide had asked permission to market it in this country and had been prevented from doing so only through the perseverance of a lone scientist at the Food and Drug Administration who had reservations and had managed to stall an approval until the problems with the drug were discovered. When a reporter questioned Carson about thalidomide she unhesitatingly connected it to the pesticide issue. "It's all of a piece," Carson said. "Thalidomide and pesticides—they represent our willingness to rush ahead and use something new without knowing what the results will be."

As *Silent Spring* was being set into type, everyone's attention had turned back to the overriding fear of the times: the prospect of nuclear war and the unknown dangers of the fallout raining from the skies as the United States and the Soviet Union waged dueling programs in the perfection of mass destruction. When President Kennedy responded at his press conference to a question about the possible "long range" risks of pesticide use, many listeners felt an uncomfortable prickle, as the term was more commonly used to describe the intercontinental ballistic missiles that America and Russia had arrayed against each other—Armageddon at the push of a button.

In October 1962, just after *Silent Spring* arrived in bookstores, American intelligence discovered that the Soviet ships recently traveling to Cuba in large numbers were delivering missiles, launch equipment, and the personnel needed for construction of a base capable of initiating a nuclear strike against the United States from only ninety miles away. By the time *Silent Spring* had made it to number one on the *New York Times* bestseller list on October 28, Cuba was under a naval blockade and the United States and the Soviet Union were on the brink of war. Eventually the Soviets backed down in the face of U.S. resolve and removed the weapons from Cuba—but public anxiety about the nuclear age remained high, joined now by a new worry about chemicals contaminating the environment.

President Kennedy's announcement that the government would look into the pesticide issue was reassuring—but it hid a more complicated reaction to *Silent Spring* forming behind the scenes in Washington and all along the web of connections that linked the government to agricultural and industrial interests. The day after his press conference, Kennedy appointed a special commission, headed by his science adviser Jerome Wiesner, to conduct a thorough review of pesticide use. It also came to light that the DDT studies begun in the mid-1940s at Patuxent had continued at a cost that had risen to $3 million a year, despite little public attention and scant changes in the way pesticides were used. Joining the Wiesner panel to evaluate pesticide safety would be representatives from several federal agencies that were themselves heavy users of DDT and other pesticides, and whose lack of regard for the consequences had been pitilessly described in *Silent Spring*. Meanwhile, the FBI did what the FBI usually did in such cases and quietly launched an investigation of Carson that just happened to coincide with the accusation that she was a Communist front.

Elsewhere within the administration a simmering hostility toward Rachel Carson and *Silent Spring* was shaping a different side to the government's response. Immediately following the *New Yorker* serialization, Secretary of Agriculture Orville Freeman ordered his inner circle to begin developing plans for attacking the articles, apparently on the reflexive assumption that his job was to oppose anything inimical to the interests of farmers and agrichemical companies. But Freeman wavered. Beleaguered over what to do about the milk supply in his home state of Minnesota, where strontium 90 contamination was approaching unsafe levels, Freeman simultaneously suggested that, as an alternative to fighting with Carson, the agency could consider how it might explain to the public the benefits of pesticide use and the steps the government was taking to head off the kind of long-term environmental problems she predicted. Freeman apparently did not contemplate what to do if it simply turned out that Carson was right.

And so the terms of the long, partisan struggle to come were established. They stand to this day. On one side were the voices raised in the name of science and the defense of nature. On the other was the unbreakable coalition of government and industry, the massed might of the establishment.

Aware of the controversy swirling around her, Carson remained unfazed by it. What did surprise her was how well *Silent Spring* was selling—some 65,000 copies in just the first two weeks. And the Book-of-the-Month Club edition, with an initial printing of 150,000 copies, was coming with an urgent endorsement from U.S. Supreme Court Justice William O. Douglas, who thought the book tremendously important. As with her previous books, Carson was swamped with fan mail that she found gratifying and overwhelming. She answered mainly with form letters, but she often took time to make personal responses to students who wrote asking for help with assignments or debates.

Carson complained of "drowning," as she put it, in clippings from newspapers running pieces on *Silent Spring*. A steady flow of speaking requests also arrived—most of which she turned down—as she routinely did with inquiries from reporters offering to do stories on her. Carson did say yes to a few of these, however. One notable request she initially rejected came from *Life* magazine, which proposed a portrait in words and photographs. Carson hated the idea. She knew all about *Life* profiles, she said, and didn't care for their "tone," which amounted to an invasion of privacy. But Carson relented—after having it pointed out to her that the chemicals industry would never turn down a chance at such high-profile publicity—though only after extracting a promise that the piece would focus on the writing of *Silent Spring* and not on "silly personal details."

Carson never specified exactly what kind of information was too personal for public consumption. She was used to the grudging acceptance accorded a woman writing knowingly and well about the challenging subjects she chose. And she was accustomed to, if not happy about, being identified in print as a "spinster." Carson had no problem with being famous. It was something she relished, since for as long as she could remember no title had ever seemed more worthy to her than "author."

But Carson was hiding one specific piece of information from everyone but a handful of her most intimate friends. In early 1960, while in the middle of writing *Silent Spring*, Carson had suffered through a succession of illnesses. First, it was a duodenal ulcer. She had barely recovered from that when she contracted pneumonia and had to stop working for a time. Then in the spring, just as she was finishing up two chapters on the link between pesticides and cancer, Carson discovered two masses in her left breast, which she was advised to have taken out. She thought these would be like a cyst she'd had removed in a minor procedure ten years earlier. They weren't. Carson required a radical mastectomy, though she was led to believe afterward that it had been done mainly as a precaution because of an ambiguous pathology report. At the time, no further treatment had been recommended.

Carson eventually discovered this was all a lie—that not only was one of the masses in her breast malignant, but it had already metastasized at least as far as her lymph nodes. Over the next two years, as she struggled to finish *Silent Spring*, Carson endured the cancer's steady spread and a series of brutal radiation treatments that at times seemed to slow but could not halt the progress of the disease. When the *Life* magazine piece came out in early October 1962, Carson, who had never been sturdy looking, appeared haggard and elderly. *Life* glossed over this, describing her look as "gentle."

Earlier that year Carson had been approached about appearing on *CBS Reports,* a popular and highly regarded hour-long TV news-magazine devoted to in-depth reporting on significant issues. The program had caused a sensation two years previously with an installment by Edward R. Murrow called "Harvest of Shame," which exposed the slavelike conditions of migrant farmworkers. CBS wanted to make *Silent Spring* and its author—along with some of her supporters and critics—the focus of an episode. The on-air reporter for the show was going to be the debonair former war correspondent Eric Sevareid. Carson and Houghton Mifflin thought this was a great idea, but delays and postponements throughout the summer had them worried that whoever had been found to represent the chemicals industry in the program's pro-and-con format was spending time sharpening their criticism of *Silent Spring.* When a producer and cameraman finally arrived at Carson's cottage on Southport Island in September to shoot background scenes of her in Maine, they were the ones who became concerned. Carson appeared seriously ill and seemed impatient to get on with the actual interview.

In late November 1962, after Carson had returned to Silver Spring, Sevareid and a film crew visited Carson's home and began interview sessions that lasted for two days. Carson looked terrible. Seated before the camera in an armchair, she wore a frumpy dark suit. On a shelf behind her were a typewriter and a starfish—a graceful touch in an otherwise inert, slightly claustrophobic setting. A heavy black wig hiding the hair loss caused by her radiation therapy made Carson vaguely resemble Lady Bird Johnson. Visibly uncomfortable—the long sessions seated under the lights must have been agony—Carson rolled her head slowly from side to side, sometimes resting it on an upraised hand, as if she were weary beyond words.

But all of that went away when she spoke. Her voice steady and precise, Carson's flat mid-Atlantic accent suited her chilling message, which could only be described as relentlessly rational and at odds with the character assassinations that had branded her a kook. Carson's virtuoso performance was more forceful for seeming anything but a performance. Afterward, Sevareid confided to his producer that he hoped they'd get the story on the air while their leading lady was still alive.

A few days later, Carson wrote to her friend Dorothy Freeman. Carson had already told Freeman that she felt she'd never had any choice but to write *Silent Spring,* that it had been an obligation of the kind Abraham Lincoln meant when he'd said that "to sin by silence when they should protest makes cowards of men." Now that it was done, she told Dorothy, she felt a mixture of pride and an indescribably heavy exhaustion, as if she had come to the end of a long and difficult road.

"I'm just beginning to find out how much I wanted sleep," Carson wrote. "It is delicious to give in to it."

TWO

Bright as the Midday Sun

As winter gave way to spring in 1932, the already grim economic situation in America continued to worsen. Since the stock market crash in 1929, thirteen million people had lost their jobs and by year's end unemployment would stand at nearly 24 percent. Some ten thousand banks had failed—about four of every ten—and the value of farmland was less than half of what it had been. Among the dispossessed were thousands of World War I veterans. In 1924, Congress had promised the veterans a deferred bonus, payable with interest in 1945. Now the veterans were pleading for an immediate payout. When a small group of veterans from Portland, Oregon, went to Washington, D.C., to promote the cause, they were spontaneously joined by forty-five thousand others who streamed to the capital from across the country. Some hitchhiked and others hopped freight trains. They called themselves the Bonus Army.

The veterans ended up hunkered down in several encampments, including a large shantytown on the Anacostia Flats, a dismal low-lying area just across the Anacostia River from the city proper. The camp was so big it had its own streets, sanitation, and law enforcement. Some of the veterans living there were accompanied by their families. They all said they wouldn't leave without their bonuses. On July 28, 1932, after an initial skirmish with police in which two veterans were killed, President Herbert Hoover ordered the army to expel the veterans from the city. That afternoon, regular regiments of infantry and cavalry, led by General Douglas MacArthur and Major George Patton, using tanks, tear gas, and fixed bayonets, drove the veterans out of the downtown area as office workers and shopkeepers looked on in horror. MacArthur pursued the fleeing vets across the river to their main base on the Anacostia Flats, where he ignored Hoover's order to stop and instead burned the encampment to the ground. The country was shocked, and four months later Hoover was defeated by Franklin Delano Roosevelt, who arrived in office with an ambitious plan to reinvigorate the shattered economy by making the government America's foremost going concern. For the country at large, the New Deal held the prospect of a gradual return to stability and growth; for those who joined it, Roosevelt's program was an immediate lifeline.

The new president packed his cabinet with reformers, including a lawyer from Chicago named Harold Ickes, who became secretary of the interior. One of Ickes's first orders of business in spite of the troubled times was to plan and oversee the construction of a new headquarters building for the Interior Department. Ickes and Roosevelt thought the building should make a statement. The result, a monument to a great country and a vast continent, cost $12.7 million and was finished in 1937. Built of granite and limestone, it stood seven glistening stories high, contained 2,200 rooms, and covered two city blocks just south and west of the White House. Enormous murals on the walls inside its long, ornate hallways depicted the sprawling diversity of peoples and lands for which the Interior Department was responsible. It was the first federal building to have escalators and among the first to be air-conditioned. By any measure it was then, and is now, one of the most beautiful and inspiring buildings in Washington.

In May 1942, an assistant aquatic biologist named Rachel Carson, newly assigned to the Fishery Biology section of the Interior Department's Fish and Wildlife Service, went to work in the building. Carson had an office on the third floor, room 3127, that had a south-facing window from which she could see trees and birds and the skies that hung over Washington as economic depression retreated and the nation found itself again at war.

At thirty-five, Carson had worked for the government for seven years, until then at field stations in Baltimore and College Park, Maryland. A pretty young woman with blue eyes and light brown hair that she wore short and tightly waved, Carson had fine features, stood five feet, four inches tall, and weighed 120 pounds. Colleagues, most of them men, recognized her approach from the familiar clack of her high heels in the hallway. If Carson socialized with anyone outside the office, it went unremarked. Each day she took her lunch in the employee cafeteria, and at night rode the streetcar home to the house she shared with her mother, Maria Carson, on Flower Avenue in Silver Spring.

Carson's job title was misleading. She did not work on aquatic biology or perform any other kind of investigative duty. She wrote pamphlets and press releases, and edited scientific papers generated by other Fish and Wildlife staff—most of whom thought she was the best at what she did. Like all federal employees, Carson was subject to the Hatch Act of 1939 and had to declare, in writing, that she did not belong to any political party or group whose purpose included the overthrow of the U.S. government by force or violence. She also had to periodically acknowledge that she had no right to go on strike or to organize her fellow workers in a union. Not that any of those ideas would have occurred to her. Carson had been more than glad to have a good job and a regular paycheck during the Depression. When she moved to the Interior Department headquarters in 1942, Carson was earning $2,600 a year.

Carson's employment file did include one unusual item. In 1941, Simon and Schuster had published a book she'd written called *Under the Sea-Wind*. Hardly anyone had ever heard of it.

She always wanted to be a writer. In 1918, at the age of eleven, Carson published her first article in the *St. Nicholas* magazine, a publication for boys and girls that featured a special section for young contributors. "A Battle in the Clouds," told in a single, suspenseful paragraph, recounted the story of a Canadian flyer who, through bravery and imagination, survived a harrowing dogfight in the skies over France—only to die in a training accident. The "main facts" of these faraway wartime events, young Miss Carson reported, had come to her in a letter from her older brother, Robert, who'd recently enlisted in the Army Air Service. Carson's well-told story was awarded a silver medal by the magazine.

News of this accomplishment arrived at a small white clapboard-sided home in Springdale, Pennsylvania, a hardscrabble town on the Allegheny River fourteen miles northeast of Pittsburgh. The house, a two-over-two design with a parlor and a dining room on the first floor and two small bedrooms on the second, stood plain and boxlike on sixty-five acres of woodland and open fields on the face of a high, steep hill that sloped to the south toward the river a mile away. There was a squat lean-to kitchen attached to the back of the house, and two outhouses, also in the back, were a short walk up the hill. Beyond the outhouses was an apple orchard sheltered beneath the hilltop. A porch overlooking the river valley ran along the length of the front of the house. In the yard there was a springhouse and, off to the side, a shed where a horse could be stabled. The house had no electricity or indoor plumbing, and was heated by small coal-grate fireplaces in each room.

Rachel Louise Carson entered the world in one of the upstairs bedrooms at one thirty in the morning on May 27, 1907. At three weeks, little Rachel began regularly napping in a hammock on the front porch. When she was five months old, she contracted a severe case of chicken pox. By the time she was eight months old, according to her mother, Maria, Rachel had begun to talk and, when told not to put something in her mouth, would respond with a "roguish look." As an older child, Rachel loved reading and being outdoors, regularly wandering the family property and looking at animals and birds, usually with her mother. It was a lovely setting, though, of course, a gray coating of ash from the steel mills downriver covered everything exposed to the sky.

The Carson house was crowded. In addition to her brother, Robert, Rachel had an older sister named Marian. Robert sometimes lived in a tent in the backyard. Neither Robert nor Marian finished high school. Robert's air unit went to fight in France; he came home in 1919. Marian had gotten married at the age of eighteen, and for a time the couple lived with the Carsons. But Marian's husband deserted her after a few months. She later divorced him and quickly remarried.

The family's financial situation was always precarious. Rachel's father, a loving but distant man also named Robert, had bought the Springdale house and property in 1900 for $11,000. Although he at different times held jobs as an electrician, an insurance salesman, and a night watchman, Mr. Carson never earned a salary sufficient to support the family. His main hope was to develop a residential neighborhood on their land. In 1910 he advertised "large level lots" for $300 each, in cash or by installments. The lots sold poorly, and never for what the Carsons hoped they were worth. Maria supplemented their income by giving piano lessons.

Rachel continued submitting stories to *St. Nicholas* magazine, which published several. Springdale's school went only as far as the tenth grade, so Rachel spent her final two years of school at nearby Parnassus High, graduating in 1925. Famous with her classmates as a voracious reader and a superb writer, Rachel was an exceptional student, as evidenced by the inscription to her in the yearbook during her senior year:

> *Rachel's like the mid-day sun,*
> *Always very bright,*
> *Never stops her studying,*
> *'Till she gets it right*

It was also said of Rachel that her mother awakened her every day to hear the birds singing in the morning sunlight, and that Rachel spoke to them as she headed off to school.

Rachel's senior thesis, a sober, reproachful consideration of human potential titled "Intellectual Dissipation," argued that a "thinking, reasoning mind" was our most valuable possession. Carson linked the cultivation of an active, educated intelligence to the conservation of natural resources. This didn't track perfectly—Carson thought young people were overly concerned about "minerals and lumber" or the desire for "a stronger and more perfect body" at the expense of their intellectual development, without explaining how any of these concerns were exclusive of one another. But at the center of the essay was a celebratory passage on the importance of books—not just any books, but the very best kind of books, the kind that stayed with you forever. Like everyone who loves books, Carson felt at once awed and aggrieved that there was more to read than could ever be read, and that to choose to read one book was to forsake the chance to read a different one. "If you read this, you cannot read that," Carson wrote. "The hour you spent today on the latest best seller can never be recalled." How much better it would be, Carson continued, to spend that hour reading "real literature, something that would raise you a little higher than you were yesterday, something that would make you willing and able for your part in the work of the world."

• • •

Pennsylvania College for Women—commonly known as PCW—
was like an island, hidden away in the wealthy enclave of Woodland
Road among the steep, ash-covered hillsides on the edge of Pittsburgh's East End. Founded in 1869, PCW by the 1920s occupied
nearly half of a horseshoe-shaped ridge that overlooked Fifth Avenue, where electric streetcars ran to and from the city proper for five
cents a ride. The base of the high ground on which the college stood
formed a natural, wooded amphitheater. An expansive view to the
north took in the gothic steeple of the Third Presbyterian Church,
which rose sharply into the sky against a background of distant bluffs
marking the Allegheny valley. The verdant campus featured neatly
mowed lawns and well-tended walkways.

The college itself comprised a handful of buildings, of which the
most imposing was Berry Hall, where Rachel Carson came to live as
a freshman. Formerly a private mansion, the palatial structure, with
its soaring ceilings on the inside and a dizzying profusion of peaked
gables and crenellated walls on the outside, had sixty rooms, many
still richly appointed with carpets and fine furniture. Said to have at
one time been the largest residence in the county, it had been subsequently enlarged and connected by a covered passageway with Dilworth Hall, a vine-entombed brick building with heavy arches that
had been the college's first major addition when it opened in 1889.
To Carson, coming from a house without even running water, her
new home must have seemed opulent beyond belief. She arrived on
September 15, 1925, accompanied by her father and mother, in a borrowed Ford Model T.

Carson had won a $100 scholarship in a statewide competition,
and her parents planned to help pay her college expenses by continuing to sell off—and borrow against—the Springdale property. Tuition
in Carson's freshman year was $200, room and board another $575.
Later, tuition rose to $300. The Carsons managed to keep up for a
couple of years, but eventually they fell behind, and Rachel would
spend the second half of her college years accumulating knowledge

and debt in equal measures. When one of Rachel's classmates visited the Carson home, she noticed their dishes were the kind given out as premiums with rolled-oats cereal, the good china having been sold off to help pay the bills at PCW.

There were eighty-eight women in Carson's freshman class. Half lived on campus; the others were "day students" who lived at home. Students were not allowed to live on their own in apartments off campus and were not permitted to get married while in school— though this rule was sometimes broken, causing no end of delicious scandal within the student body, where such liaisons were regarded as adventurous and romantic, and were reliably kept secret from the faculty and administration. There were regular teas and luncheons, and a formal prom that was held at the swank Schenley Hotel early in the second semester each year. Attendees wore long gowns and white kid gloves. Students were expected to go to Sunday morning services at a church of their choosing, and attendance at Sunday evening vespers on campus was mandatory.

The curriculum at PCW aligned with what would have been found at any liberal arts college, though it was understood that the main aim of a young woman at PCW was to marry and become a homemaker—perhaps after working a year or two as a teacher—and that a higher education was for the purpose of personal growth and enrichment that would someday make one a better wife and mother. Students at PCW studied English, history, science, math, foreign languages, and music. Everyone had to take physical education, and most of the girls played intramural sports. Carson, dressed in blue bloomers, black stockings, and white tennis shoes, played goalie on a field hockey team that won three consecutive class championships. At one game the cheering students had to share the spectators' area with two goats and several dogs loitering on the scene. A later report had it that at least one of the goats had come from the Carson home in Springdale. In a team photograph, Carson appeared trim, athletic, and firm-jawed.

Carson suffered from acne, which at times covered her face and shoulders. She had only a few, unusually plain dresses, all of them sewn by her mother. Like most of the other girls, she wore a bobbed hairstyle, sometimes with a tight Marcel wave put in with a hot iron, so that her hair fit the shape of her head like a helmet. Never shy in class, never unprepared, Carson always knew the answer to any question and was eager to give it. A few girls who got to know her a little discovered that Carson also had a subtle wit, was alert to pretense or shallowness, and could be slyly observant of her classmates. But this was a side of her personality she rarely showed off. Mostly invisible, Carson came off as a quiet, awkward girl who usually skipped social events and was thought to be either a recluse or a studious bore. Some students resented her academic skills and the earnest impression she made on her instructors.

Maria Carson made regular weekend visits to PCW. She'd show up at Rachel's dormitory room and spend hours talking and reading and typing papers for her talented daughter. Rachel's classmates saw Mrs. Carson as a doting mother who was determined to see her daughter succeed academically. Maria had an education beyond what the meager circumstances of the Carson family might have suggested—and that was not typical of women at the time. Before she'd met Rachel's father, Maria had graduated with honors in Latin from the Washington Female Seminary in 1887. Now approaching sixty, Maria was older than most of the other students' mothers. She was friendly enough but seemed to have no interest in anyone other than Rachel. One of Rachel's friends would later recall that Mrs. Carson was without pretense—and said that if the queen of England had called on Rachel's mother she would have answered the door in an "old calico housedress." Mrs. Carson spent so much time with Rachel that other girls in the dorm—who found Maria's frequent presence there inappropriate—joked that Carson's mother ought to have been paying tuition herself. Rachel heard but ignored these criticisms and seemed not to mind her mother's visits.

Carson's assignment to write about herself in her first-year English class resulted in a strange, impenetrable essay that suggested she had great expectations without explicitly saying what they were. It opened moodily, with Carson describing herself as "a girl of eighteen" who loved the outdoors and who could never be happier than when in the glow of a campfire with the stars overhead. She continued, less gracefully, to explain her special relationship with that world: "I love all the beautiful things of nature, and the wild creatures are my friends. What could be more wonderful than the thrill of having some little furry animal creep closer and closer to you, with wondering but unafraid eyes?"

Carson went on to say that she was an avid reader and named some of her favorite writers, including Shakespeare, Milton, Dickens, and Mark Twain, the last for his "hatred of hypocrisy." She said she didn't care for contemporary writers, as the "realism in modern literature does not appeal to me." Near the close of the essay, Carson's tone turned pious. She wrote that she was an "idealist" and hinted at an ambition so lofty that it would ultimately bring her near God: "Sometimes I lose sight of my goal, then again it flashes into view, filling me with a new determination to keep the 'vision splendid' before my eyes. I may never come to a full realization of my dreams, but 'a man's reach must exceed his grasp, or what's a heaven for?'"

Carson concluded by saying that she'd chosen PCW because it was a Christian college, "founded on ideals of service and honor," where she could reach a "fuller realization of my self" and thus play her part on "the stage of life."

Although Carson would never back away from her childlike fascination with cute, furry animals—it was something she hung on to for life—her choice of the words "vision splendid" was startling. It's possible, though unlikely, that Carson simply invented the phrase for her essay and put it in quotes for emphasis—or that it was something she'd heard or read without remembering where. What seems more probable is that she was referencing a thoroughly religious book of poems titled *The Vision Splendid,* published in 1917 and written by John Oxenham, a pen name for the English writer William Arthur Dunkerley. The title poem was a meditation on the parallel Oxenham saw between the terrible cost of victory in World War I—at the time still not yet in hand—and Christ's death on the cross. It began like this:

Here—or hereafter—you shall see it ended,
This mighty work to which your souls are set;
If from beyond—then, with the vision splendid,
You shall smile back and never know regret

Carson had grown up during the war, heard her brother's stories, felt the normal patriotic allegiance to America's commitment in the cause. But how a dead soldier's gaze from heaven could have had any bearing on her hopes of becoming a writer was a mystery. If the vision splendid was a view of the world from the afterlife then what good was it in the here and now? Maybe Carson simply liked the words without knowing what they meant. For her next theme, Carson wrote about field hockey. She earned a B+ on both papers.

Carson entered college as an English major. She skipped taking a science class her freshman year, when most PCW students got that requirement out of the way. In her sophomore year she signed up for biology—the entry-level class in a program in the midst of an upheaval. In the fall of 1925, the department had offered only three courses: general biology, botany, and human physiology. By Carson's senior year, there would be ten courses, including advanced botany, general zoology, invertebrate and vertebrate zoology, histology, microbiology, genetics, and embryology. The force behind this change was one of the most compelling figures on campus and head of the biology department—she was actually the entire biology department—Professor Mary Scott Skinker.

Miss Skinker was an object of fascination among the students, who thought her uncommonly beautiful and almost ethereal in her bearing—she exuded an airy, incorporeal remoteness that may have been due to the fact that she was nearsighted and refused to wear glasses. Slender and graceful, Skinker had dark eyes and wore her hair in a loose swirl atop her head. At PCW, everyone dressed for dinner, meeting in the chandeliered dining room of Berry Hall before taking their places at tables set with linen and silver, where faculty members guided the conversation and provided the occasional instruction on proper etiquette. Mary Scott Skinker's stylish wardrobe, which usually included a rose pinned at her left shoulder, was always closely watched at dinner. For a time rumors of a serious suitor circulated, as boxes of flowers arrived for Miss Skinker every few days, though eventually these stopped coming. Skinker later told one of her former students that she had given up on the idea of getting married while she was at PCW.

A dynamic and demanding teacher, Skinker was not averse to handing out a low grade when it was deserved. People were curious as to whether even a clever, hardworking girl like Rachel Carson could get an A in her class. What nobody anticipated was that Carson would be transformed by biology and by Miss Skinker. Not only did she earn A's, Carson began to think about changing her major to biology. She mulled this decision carefully, and for a time would contemplate only adding biology as a minor. As a junior, she found herself happily spending more and more time in the cramped little laboratory on the top floor of Dilworth Hall, which always smelled of formaldehyde. Sometimes Carson and her lab partner would go back after dinner to dissect specimens in the wan light given off by the tungsten-filament bulbs that hung on wires from the ceiling and swayed when the winter wind was up.

The field of biology was then in a primitive state relative to what it would become during Carson's lifetime. DNA wouldn't be fully described for another three decades and little was known about the molecular basis of life. A living cell was described as a membrane containing "protoplasm," a fluid, unstable jumble of varied substances and structures believed by some biologists to be composed of filaments or fibers, while others thought it was more like a mass of bubbles. All living things were known to be made of cells, and processes within cells were understood to regulate metabolism and heredity. Biologists were keenly interested in chromosomes, distinct structures within cells whose precise separations during cell division were visible in a light microscope. It had been proposed that specific segments of chromosomes called "genes" were involved in heredity. But how this worked remained a mystery.

Biology in the 1920s encompassed tangential subjects—including hygiene, food safety, agronomy, public health, nutrition, and sanitation—that reflected an intersection between science and home economics, a prominent feature in the education of women. Standard biology texts also explored the concept of eugenics, a frankly racist and xenophobic field that proposed to improve the human species by means of selective reproduction. The idea was that "race improvement" could be achieved by encouraging persons with superior physical, mental, and moral attributes to marry and mate—while discouraging inferior people from breeding. One popular textbook suggested that eugenics should be the official policy of the state and that anyone wanting a marriage license should have to pass a physical examination first. Immigrants, the book advised, should be rigorously screened to exclude those with undesirable characteristics, and it would be prudent for "feeble minded" persons to be confined to government-run work camps.

Much in vogue after the turn of the century, eugenics flourished—as an idea if not as a policy—until Nazi Germany extended the concept to its logical conclusion in the Holocaust.

Evolution figured prominently in biology instruction in the 1920s, although some high school programs downplayed or excised Darwin's theory following the 1925 conviction of a schoolteacher named John Scopes in the so-called Monkey Trial in Tennessee, where it was illegal to teach evolution. For Skinker and her students, evolution was settled science. The earth was then estimated to be about three billion years old—it's closer to four and a half billion—and all living forms were believed to have descended from earlier organisms, although no one could answer how life had arisen in the first place. Carson learned these lessons well, as evolutionary theory would later be central to her writing about the sea.

Skinker taught that all life was interconnected, and seen in the light of evolution this meant, as Carson came to realize, that every day in the world offered evidence of all the years of the world that had come before. Skinker naturally saw extinction as an inevitable aspect of evolution, and she was alert to the fact that human carelessness about the environment could sometimes hasten the disappearance of species that might not otherwise be endangered. This holistic view of the living world—and our place in it—was already being called "ecology," though the term wasn't yet in common use and didn't figure in Skinker's teaching as an identifiable discipline.

The prospects for anyone determined to live as a writer were then—as now—uncertain. But for a woman, a career in science was an even more daunting undertaking. Women had a hard time earning advanced degrees in science, and those who did often ended up teaching at women's colleges that—like PCW—had limited programs that perpetuated the underrepresentation of women in science. In 1925, the National Academy of Sciences—America's most elite scientific organization—elected its first-ever woman member when Florence Rena Sabin, a physiologist from Johns Hopkins, joined the 229 men in the group. Even the gifted Miss Skinker had gotten only as far as a master's degree from Columbia and now spent much of her time arguing for more rigorous academic standards at PCW while dreaming of perhaps one day earning her doctorate.

Carson, who never seemed to consider the advantages or disadvantages of any career choice, continued to write. She worked as a reporter for the *Arrow*, a twice-monthly campus magazine. In the spring of her sophomore year, she won a prize for a short story called "Broken Lamps," a dark, formulaic tale about a young civil engineer disenchanted with his life and his wife, but who is redeemed when the wife suddenly falls desperately ill, causing him to see that he truly loves her. In 1928 she published a fine—if dubiously spelled—poem in the *Arrow*:

March

I know a marsh-girt hill where brown paths cross
And intermingle till they touch the sky.
There troops of shadows pitch their tents among
The thorn trees, guant [sic] and gnarled before the blast.
In sombre [sic] dun and green the moss entwines
Slow figures on the crags that face the dawn,
Where wind-tossed geese in shadow squadron sail,
And beat their wings against the foam-flecked sky.

But by then, Carson had fallen under Miss Skinker's spell. One night in the lab, Carson confessed to a friend that she'd begun to think about how to merge her two interests. "I have always wanted to write," Carson said, "but I don't have much imagination. Biology has given me something to write about." In late February 1928, Carson told Skinker she was going to declare biology as her new major. Skinker was shocked, and insisted on discussing the decision at length, though in the end, as Carson told a friend, she'd been a "peach" about it.

There'd been a heavy snowfall the weekend before, and that night, with Orion ablaze in the black sky above, the girls of PCW had a sledding party—mostly on aluminum trays liberated from the dining hall. Carson and another girl riding together on one breakneck downhill run hit a bump that pitched them off and sent them tumbling through clouds of snow. Their knickers and sweaters soaked, the girls finally came in, showered, and then, dressed in pajamas, sat before the enormous fireplace in Woodland Hall, eating sandwiches and potato salad. Then they turned off the lights and by the firelight sang songs until the clock on the mantel chimed midnight. Carson was deliriously happy.

Carson and another girl in biology started privately referring to Skinker as "the big boss." Carson said that she felt "safe" with her affairs now firmly in Skinker's hands, but she was rudely questioned by her classmates, who disapproved of the change from English to biology. Their complaints, Carson said, were monotonous. She amused herself by dissecting a dogfish, which was terrific fun, though it made Carson and everything she touched smell awful. She could hardly wait to begin embryology in her senior year.

In March 1928, friends arranged a date for Carson to attend the annual PCW prom. The young man, named Bob Frye, was a junior at nearby Westminster College. Carson bought silver slippers a size too small—all the girls did this—and spent a few days trying to break them in before the dance. In a letter to a friend after the event, Carson declared that she'd had a "glorious time" and that she had enjoyed the dim lighting and the mirrored walls at the Schenley Hotel. More memorable than anything else, though, was one of the chaperones, the radiant Mary Scott Skinker: "Miss Skinker was a perfect knockout at the Prom," she wrote. "She wore a peach colored chiffon-velvet, with the skirt shirred just about 8 inches in front and a rhinestone pin at the waist. Then she wore a choker necklace of rhinestones and two longer ones of tiny pearls."

Evidently, there was nothing relevant to report about Bob, though she mentioned going with him to a basketball game the next day and said that it had been an "awfully nice weekend."

Carson saw Bob Frye at least one more time that spring. And then she never dated again.

Not long after Carson finalized her decision to switch to biology, Miss Skinker said she had something important to tell Rachel. She said she couldn't discuss it yet, but assured Carson that she would be among the first to know. A few weeks later, Carson learned that Miss Skinker planned to take a leave of absence to complete work on her PhD and would not be at PCW for Carson's senior year. Skinker would spend the summer studying at the Marine Biological Laboratory at Woods Hole, Massachusetts, and then go to either Johns Hopkins or Cornell for her doctorate.

Disconsolate, Carson for a while imagined she might transfer to Johns Hopkins herself. She applied for admission to the graduate program in zoology at Hopkins and was promptly accepted. But in the end Carson realized that her scholarship and the money she already owed to PCW would keep her there. By the middle of her senior year, Carson owed PCW close to $1,400, an impossible sum. She proposed taking a mortgage on two of her father's lots but was told by the bank that mortgages on vacant land were hard to obtain, and even if she could get one it was unlikely to reflect the true value of the property. Instead, she was advised to offer the two lots directly to PCW as collateral and to arrange a payment plan she could manage by installments after graduating and finding work. To Carson's relief, PCW agreed to this. Carson signed the formal agreement on January 28, 1929, nine months before the American economy collapsed.

Skinker was replaced by a woman named Anna Whiting. Whiting held a PhD in genetics from Iowa State University, where she'd concentrated on cattle breeding. She was thrilled to have a job at PCW because her husband was a professor at the University of Pittsburgh. But Whiting turned out to be unqualified to teach any of the advanced biology coursework Carson had signed up for, and she was inept in the lab. Carson and her classmates felt they knew more about the material than their professor, and Carson spent her senior year wondering if she would learn enough to survive in graduate school if she ever got to attend one. To keep their spirits up, Carson and a couple of her friends organized a science club and named it Mu Sigma Sigma—in tribute to Mary Scott Skinker.

Carson's thoughts about life after PCW were also shaped by a singular experience—a moment of profound insight—that had come to her one night while going over an English assignment. The reading was Alfred, Lord Tennyson's long and complicated poem "Locksley Hall." It was late, and outside the dorm a fierce thunderstorm swept over the darkened campus. As rain beat against her window and thunder rocked the hillsides, Carson sat straight up as she came to the poem's closing lines, in which the narrator tells of a storm advancing over the moors toward the ocean:

Comes a vapour from the margin, blackening over heath and holt,
Cramming all the blast before it, in its breast a thunderbolt.

Let it fall on Locksley Hall, with rain or hail, or fire or snow;
For the mighty wind arises, roaring seaward, and I go.

Carson, who had never laid eyes on the sea, felt a sudden, powerful conviction that it was, in fact, in her destiny—the place to which her newfound love of science would one day lead. Here, she realized, was the thing she longed to write about, even though she had yet to make its acquaintance.

Now again, as she had with the "vision splendid," Carson took inspiration from an unlikely source. Although it's possible to interpret Tennyson's ending as a call to adventure at sea—as Carson did—the consensus reading of those lines is that the narrator is on his way to join the British army. When the poem was published in 1842 that same army was engaged in imperialistic enterprises around the world that are agreeably—some would say sickeningly—referenced earlier in the poem. In fact, "Locksley Hall" is a disturbing, racially intolerant tale in which the narrator, desperate to obliterate the pain of a failed love affair, imagines himself traveling to some wild place within reach of the empire where he can conquer the "savage" natives.

The poem's much better remembered line—*In the spring a young man's fancy lightly turns to thoughts of love*—has the amiable connotation usually given it only when considered outside the context of Tennyson's dark verses. It's hard to understand how Carson could have read "Locksley Hall" without perceiving the narrator's torment and feeling the violent twist of his emotions—even if she cared not for the fancies of young men. To be moved by just a handful of beguiling lines in a poem so otherwise brutal, so much bigger and more ominous, required a rare ability to focus only on a detail that interested her while setting aside a whole world of bewildering complexities.

And yet that is exactly what Carson did. This kind of tunnel vision would prove to be a defining trait.

THREE

Biologizing

The Marine Biological Laboratory at Woods Hole, Massachusetts—a quiet seaside village on the inner arm of Cape Cod once known mainly for its guano fertilizer works—was America's preeminent scientific field station. Established in 1888, the MBL by the mid-1920s had become a regular summer gathering place for scientists and students to pursue research—either in the many nearby inshore marine environments or at one of the coveted benches in the Crane laboratory, a massive redbrick building that also housed a tremendous and ever-expanding library.

During her time at PCW, Mary Scott Skinker had spent summers doing research in protozoology (an outdated term that formerly referenced a diverse group of aquatic single-celled animals) at the MBL. As Carson prepared to begin her senior year, Miss Skinker encouraged her to consider an MBL summer research fellowship after graduation. It was a thrilling prospect. At PCW, biology students worked mostly on pickled specimens—fish and reptiles and, worst of all, cats, whose stiff, gruesome corpses smelled awful. At Woods Hole, students collected live specimens along the shoreline, in the marshes, and from boats out on the waters of Buzzards Bay. And the immersion in biology there was total—Skinker had written one of her other students at PCW that there were no distractions at Woods Hole, nothing beyond "the biological world." Skinker sent Carson clippings from a Woods Hole weekly newsletter, the *Collecting Net,* which Carson told a friend made her "crazier than ever to go there." Woods Hole, Carson said, "must be a biologist's paradise." Plus, it was on the ocean.

Carson, with a recommendation from Miss Skinker, had reapplied to Johns Hopkins and earned a full scholarship. In June, she graduated magna cum laude from PCW. That summer, again with help from Skinker, Carson also earned a scholarship to study at the MBL during the month of August. She went first to Baltimore, where it was unusually hot, and spent a day exploring the Johns Hopkins campus. Then she caught a bus for Luray, Virginia, at the foot of the Blue Ridge Mountains, a half day away. Miss Skinker had invited Carson to join her on vacation at Skyland, a rustic turn-of-the-century resort perched atop a four-thousand-foot peak with commanding views of the Shenandoah Valley.

Cars could not ascend the difficult road to the summit, so Carson went up on horseback. It took about an hour, during which she was delighted by the forest and the birds, including a turkey that scuttled away as she approached. The best part, she said later, was reaching the resort and finding Miss Skinker coming up the path to meet her. The two women spent their days riding horses and playing tennis. Carson thought Skinker, who claimed to be a poor player but wasn't, helped her game some. They passed their evenings sitting by a fire in their cabin and talking.

The oppressive heat had not abated back in Washington, D.C., where Carson went next to catch a train from Union Station to New York City. She spent a day sightseeing, riding a tour bus around Manhattan, lunching at a German restaurant, and taking the subway up to Columbia to climb the steps of the library. It was raining late in the day when she boarded a boat for New Bedford, Massachusetts. The boat passed the Statue of Liberty, just visible in the storm, and turned east, following along the coastline of Long Island. Carson—looking for the first time at the sea and breathing salt air—said it was pleasant out on the deck later that evening, even more so after the boat passed Montauk and they were out of sight of land. Before dawn the next day Carson changed boats at New Bedford. Carson said the sixteen-mile trip across Buzzards Bay as the sun came up had been "glorious," although the sea was running and it was rough.

Carson found Woods Hole and the MBL complex completely wonderful, better than she'd expected in every way. The apartment she shared with another researcher from PCW had hot and cold running water and was located just across the street from Crane lab, where her table was. She was especially taken with the library, which beckoned to her and seemed to have "everything." And she discovered that no matter where you went, you were never far from the water. She loved this. The sea was all around her.

Carson wrote to a friend that Woods Hole was a "delightful place to biologize" and said she could see herself returning every summer. Researchers worked hard but also took time to enjoy the ocean and the beach. Carson said she was trying to learn to swim the crawl. She'd also had an adventure after a beach party on one of the islands in the bay when the boat she was on became lost in the fog on the return and had nearly been swept out into the open ocean. Carson particularly liked exploring rocky sections of shoreline when the tide was low and examining the marine life that teemed in the tidal pools. Sea anemones and urchins fascinated her, and she became acutely aware of the power of the ocean currents, as these sometimes brought in unexpected treasures such as Sargasso weed or jellyfishes from warmer regions far away. Delicately fair-skinned, Carson said these hours on the shore and under the sun had at last convinced her she would never get a tan, though she believed that she had acquired a "weathered" look and a fresh set of freckles. The U.S. Bureau of Fisheries had a sizable contingent of researchers at Woods Hole, and

Carson got to know them. One day they took her aboard their research ship for a day of collecting.

Carson also enjoyed collecting trips aboard the MBL's "little dredging boat" on which they would steam up and down the waters of Buzzards Bay and sometimes the Vineyard Sound, seining the bottom to inspect the plants and animals of the sea floor. It was often a wild ride as the boat lurched against the weight of the net in rolling seas. But Carson loved discovering what came up from under the water: Mixed in with rocks and shells was a profusion of species— crustaceans and seaweeds, invertebrates and small fish—an embassy of living things she had never seen before, from a place she was just beginning to imagine.

She allowed her thoughts to "go down through the water," so that what was unseen below gradually came clear to her and she could at last "see the whole life of those creatures as they lived them in that strange sea world." The great variety of life in the sea impressed upon Carson that every living thing belonged to a larger diverse community of life that was sustained by interdependence and perpetuated across the vastness of time. Of all the lessons she'd learned well, this was the one she learned best.

But Carson's two months of study at the MBL were not entirely happy. For the first time in her life she struggled. In the lab, Carson couldn't decide what to work on. Even though she was surrounded by the marine environment that she felt destined to study and write about, Carson initially investigated the terminal nerve in reptiles. The terminal nerve, which belongs to the subset of the central nervous system known collectively as the cranial nerves, is associated with the sense of smell. At the time olfaction hadn't been thoroughly described in reptiles and so Carson felt she might break new ground by studying it in lizards and snakes, and possibly crocodiles. She also remained interested in turtles, which had intrigued her at PCW. But this left her once again working on embalmed inland specimens, slicing and staining tissue sections for microscopic examination—the very same laboratory subjects and techniques Carson felt she had been inadequately trained in after Miss Skinker's departure from PCW. She was still heartsick over the way things had ended at PCW, which she described as a "near tragedy." She wrote to a friend that she'd spent much of her time at Woods Hole trying to overcome the feeling that her last year at PCW had left her unready for real biological research work.

"We thought we realized what it was doing to us," Carson said of the classes at PCW with Anna Whiting, "but we didn't. We couldn't, there. I tell you frankly, I was a near-wreck the first week I was here. Didn't know what I wanted to do, and had no ambition to do it! But I'm slowly recovering, and beginning to come to life mentally once more."

Woods Hole was an intimidating place, the working retreat of many of the country's leading scientists. Still woozy after four cloistered years at PCW, Carson had moved on to one of the main stages of American biology. And she had done so just as biology was becoming a more experimental science. Until the turn of the century, biology had been mostly about natural history, an "organismal" discipline that was mainly concerned with comparative anatomy, morphology, taxonomy, behavior, and, more recently, evolution.

In describing and differentiating species, biology was in many ways not that different from what it had been for Aristotle—a science that served mainly to enumerate and catalog the living world. Then, in the early part of the twentieth century, a number of researchers rediscovered the work of Gregor Mendel, the Austrian monk whose study of dominant and recessive hereditary traits in pea plants had led to his formulation of the laws of inheritance. Published in 1866, Mendel's laws languished for three decades before becoming the basis of the new study of genetics. Biologists began putting less emphasis on characterizing "wild type" organisms found in the field, and more on exploring functional biology through experiments with captive colonies of species that bred rapidly and were easy to maintain: rats, salamanders, and, most significantly, a tiny prolific insect called *Drosophila melanogaster*—the fruit fly. Carson's interest in dissecting wild specimens to see how they were made was, if not yet quaint, at least musty—the back end of science rather than the cutting edge.

The MBL had always been generous in its acceptance of female students and researchers, though they were usually noticeably outnumbered by men. Of the twenty-three students in an embryology class in 1897, six were women—one of whom was Gertrude Stein. Ann Haven Morgan, arguably the country's foremost freshwater ecologist when Carson was still at PCW, had taught at the MBL in the summers before the publication in 1930 of her classic *Field Book of Ponds and Streams*. Morgan's little blue book with the red-edged pages—it was the same size and shape as a modern-day Audubon field guide—demonstrated a curiosity about nature and a competence in depicting it that suggested there ought to be no limits on what women could do in the field. But Carson had never shared lab space with men, who arrived at the MBL better trained, and she marveled at how adept they were. She found that she had trouble distinguishing important features of the tissues she painstakingly sectioned from her specimens. It wouldn't be until months later, back in Baltimore at Johns Hopkins, that Carson would begin to make tentative progress on her slides from Woods Hole. Meanwhile, long hours at the microscope hurt her eyes.

Carson's story was a familiar one in biology, where even brilliant students sometimes falter when it comes to actually doing hands-on science. Some are clumsy; others are careless or indifferent to the precision required in carrying out a well-controlled experiment. Or they lack the insight needed to formulate hypotheses that can be experimentally tested—the essence of the modern scientific method. Carson's admission that she would be content working in the library contained a whiff of self-recognition. It was, in fact, an allusion to what would become for her both a refuge and a lifelong wellspring of inspiration.

As she hit one dead end after another Carson could not make up her mind whether the problem was her or her subject. At Johns Hopkins she briefly narrowed her focus to snakes, and at one point got curious about the pit organ sensory system in vipers. Sometimes her specimens were delivered alive, and one day she took a friend to the lab to see a crate full of rattlesnakes. As the two women peered in through the mesh top of the container, several thick-bodied specimens disengaged themselves from the tangled mass on the floor of the cage and, tongues flicking, slowly raised their heads.

The next several years saw a winding-down of one phase of Carson's life and a halting transition into the next. At Johns Hopkins, Carson again assumed her favorite role, that of the hardworking student. Her days were long, beginning just after seven with breakfast at the university cafeteria and often continuing into the evening. Carson estimated that class time and lab research occupied almost fifty hours every week, with the balance of her waking moments left to studying. Organic chemistry was her most demanding class, while botany, a subject that didn't interest her, nonetheless provided the welcome diversion of an occasional field trip. Carson eventually earned a hard-won B in chemistry and surprised herself with an exemplary performance in physiology. She told a friend that she liked living in Baltimore, which had a pleasant climate and seemed to be slightly better off economically than Pittsburgh. The atmosphere at Johns Hopkins was decidedly southern, and Carson loved listening to the accents of her classmates.

As absorbing as her studies were, Carson was not insulated from the hard times besetting the country. In her second year at Hopkins she became a half-time student and found work as a lab assistant in the medical school, where she helped maintain colonies of rats and fruit flies. Carson hoped to earn enough to make payments on what she still owed to PCW—and to help support her family, most of whom came to live with her early in 1930. They rented a large three-story house outside of Baltimore in the remote, mostly rural area of Stemmers Run. The house had no central heat but did have indoor plumbing and a big fireplace. A handsome grove of oaks sprawled over the property, and a two-mile hike through the woods brought you to Chesapeake Bay. The house also featured—incongruously—a tennis court, a step up from the homestead back in Springdale. But life at Stemmers Run could hardly have been comfortable. Carson's father was in poor health, weak and quiet and spent. Carson's sister, Marian, divorced again, lived there, too, accompanied by her two energetic young daughters. Mrs. Carson, forever at Rachel's side, seemed content to encourage her daughter's studies and happily type her papers. It was apparent to everyone who saw them together how close Carson and her mother were.

Not surprisingly, with Carson the only wage earner in the household, PCW didn't get the money still owed on her undergraduate studies. In 1932, after many missed payments, Carson settled with the school by signing over the title to the pair of her father's lots she'd offered as collateral back in 1929. Much later, a neighbor at Stemmers Run would recall stopping in at the Carsons' early one evening and finding the family seated at the table with only a bowl of apples for dinner.

In the lab, Carson's problems multiplied. She gave up on snakes and at one point tried to study embryonic development in squirrels. But she couldn't get the animals to breed. She complained to a friend, "I don't have time to think any more." Between working part-time and going to school part-time, she wasn't making any progress at all. She began to worry that she was running out of time for an ambitious study. Eventually Carson's adviser suggested that she work on the pronephros in catfish—a project interesting to Carson mainly because it could be done quickly. The pronephros is an embryonic precursor of the kidney, and at the time it was unknown whether it was retained as a functional excretory organ in the adult fish. Carson concluded that it wasn't, and in June 1932, a full year behind schedule, she submitted a mostly descriptive one-hundred-page master's thesis featuring drawings and photographs of histological sections. It wasn't breakthrough science—but it was done.

When Carson later received letters of recommendation from her professors at Johns Hopkins, they all expressed confidence in her teaching abilities but were tepid about the prospect that she would do meaningful scientific research. Whether they'd have thought differently had Carson had the resources to finish her degree on time, or that it was simply the case that she lacked a talent for research, Carson would never know. As the months and then years unspooled at Johns Hopkins, Carson's fascination with biology remained intact, but her commitment to it as a career waned.

Through graduate school, Carson had steadily increased her efforts to earn money. She started teaching biology in the summers at Johns Hopkins and worked as a lab assistant and zoology instructor at the University of Maryland in College Park, which was a long ride from Stemmers Run by bus or train that Carson made several times each week. In the fall of 1932, Carson began work at Johns Hopkins toward her PhD. She would not complete this degree, but she did fall in love with an animal she studied for the first time: the American eel.

Carson had an enormous aquarium in her lab that was filled with eels, and contemplating their dark undulations as they glided from one end of the tank to the other made her think. Eels are migratory and have a complex life history that Carson found beguiling. Born in the open ocean, larval eels drift on currents toward the continental shelf, where they metamorphose into elvers, finger-sized and serpentine and so transparent they appear to be made of glass. The elvers move up through estuaries and eventually into freshwater streams and ponds, where they undergo a maturation that takes many years. As adults they return to the ocean for the long journey back to their breeding areas in and around the Sargasso Sea in the middle Atlantic. Carson could not stop thinking about the story of the eel.

Migrations like that of the eel are one of nature's most literal examples of the continuity of life. In the same lab where she studied her eels, Carson also kept some amoebas that caused her to think about this in a different context. As almost every student of biology comes to realize, amoebas—and indeed, all single-celled animals that reproduce by simply dividing in two—have a kind of eternal life. Although they can be killed, amoebas do not senesce and die, but rather divide and live on. So every amoeba is arguably not an individual with a singular identity, but is rather part of the first amoeba—and thus an organism whose life originated in the mists of time and that might exist for as long as there are amoebas. Carson thought another way to picture it was to imagine that within such species there must be "infinitesimally small molecular aggregates" that had been "alive" for millions of years and would be perpetuated indefinitely. Carson told all this to a friend, admitting that it was "a curious train of thought."

Robert Carson collapsed and died one morning in the backyard at Stemmers Run in July 1935. He was seventy-one. Rachel, whose brother lived on his own in Baltimore, was now truly the head of the household at the age of twenty-eight. She had left the doctoral program at Johns Hopkins a year and a half earlier and continued with her several part-time academic jobs. At the urging of Mary Scott Skinker, who had completed her PhD and gone to work for the U.S. Department of Agriculture, Carson in early 1935 had taken and passed civil service examinations in parasitology, wildlife biology, and aquatic biology. In October she was hired as a field aide by the U.S. Bureau of Fisheries in their Baltimore office. Her job entailed "assembling information for public distribution on the natural history and conservation of the fishes of the Atlantic Coast." These duties consisted mainly of writing short scripts for a radio program called *Romance Under the Waters,* which the bureau produced in partnership with the CBS Radio Network. The job was, as Carson later reported, "intermittent." When she worked, Carson earned $6.50 a day. On a personnel form that asked her to list the number and ages of any dependents living with her, Carson stubbornly answered that she had "1 totally; 3 partially" and left it at that.

The Bureau of Fisheries had come into existence partly by accident. In the mid-1800s, commercial fishermen in New England noticed a decline in fish numbers in coastal waters. In response, Congress in 1871 created the U.S. Commission of Fish and Fisheries—but did not limit its charter to the problems in the New England fishery. With no deadline to report on or resolve the issue, the commission became by default a permanent federal agency—the first one whose mission was the conservation of wildlife.

The commission initially made fishery surveys using navy vessels or revenue cutters borrowed from the Treasury Department, but by 1883 was operating two of its own ships, the first vessels ever designed for the purpose of marine research. The *Fish Hawk,* a 157-foot steam-and-sail powered schooner, conducted dredging and trawling operations along the eastern seaboard and served as a mobile hatchery. The *Albatross,* a majestic, white-hulled behemoth, was a 234-foot brigantine with twin two-hundred-horsepower steam engines and could carry more than 7,500 square feet of sail.

With a cruising speed of nearly ten knots the *Albatross* could go anywhere in the world, and it did. The first government vessel equipped with electric lighting from stem to stern—Thomas Edison designed the generator—it also carried submersible electric lights for attracting marine life at night. There were two well-equipped laboratories on board and dredging gear on deck that could collect specimens from the depths of the open ocean. The *Albatross* made collecting expeditions along the East Coast, out into the Atlantic, down through the Caribbean and the Gulf of Mexico, and into the Pacific. The ship traveled to the Galápagos Islands, Alaska, the Philippines, and into the Sea of Japan. Over a span of several decades, research done onboard the *Albatross* laid the foundation of modern marine biology. *Oceanic Ichthyology,* the 1895 classic on deep-sea fish by George Brown Goode and Tarleton H. Bean, was based mainly on collections made aboard the *Albatross.*

The commission continued to grow. It added the maintenance of food fish in inland waters to its duties and eventually established ninety stocking hatcheries around the country. In 1887, the Commission of Fish and Fisheries established a Division of Scientific Inquiry, and in 1902 the commission itself was reorganized as the U.S. Bureau of Fisheries and moved into the Department of Commerce. In 1911 the bureau landed its most far-flung responsibility: jurisdiction over the Pribilof Islands, a tiny volcanic archipelago two hundred miles west of Alaska in the Bering Sea that was home to a few hundred people of Russian descent, about two hundred thousand fur seals, and an economy based almost entirely on seal hunting. Through prudent management of both the people and the seals, the seal population had steadily risen to more than 1.5 million by the time Carson joined the bureau in 1935.

Carson's boss was Elmer Higgins, who headed what was by then called the Division of Scientific Inquiry Respecting Food Fishes. Every year, Higgins prepared a long report on the research activities of bureau personnel, including studies and findings published by the bureau itself, as well as papers and articles written for scholarly journals and the general press. In the mid-1930s, Higgins's reports usually lamented the limited resources that curtailed all research activities and shut some down entirely. During the Depression, the bureau had come to depend increasingly on cooperative research programs with various state agencies and academic institutions. In 1936 the total budget for Higgins's division was $109,000, about half of which was spent directly on field and lab investigations.

The annual summary emphasized emerging knowledge and the importance of conservation in promoting sustainable commercial and sport fishing. Higgins even occasionally used the still uncommon term "ecology" in discussing the study of specific marine environments—although the bureau did not hold all of the life forms composing such communities in equal regard, as some that preyed on commercially valuable species were regarded as "pests." Between 1935 and 1937, for example, the bureau received a special appropriation of $125,000—more than its entire budget for a single year—to develop a chemical poison for the "eradication" of starfish in oyster farming operations.

Efforts to control or eliminate predatory species were consistent with the bureau's mission as Higgins construed it—a mission that did not differ from the quest to understand and then subdue and dominate nature that had existed since the dawn of civilization. In his 1936 report, Higgins explained that the "mastery and utilization of the forces of nature" arose from the knowledge gained through research that did not necessarily have such utilitarian purposes to begin with. Knowledge, he wrote, permits nature to be "harnessed, controlled, and directed to economic advantage." When the practical applications of marine research aren't immediately apparent, Higgins said, such knowledge nonetheless makes "permanent contributions to social progress" even if it takes time to figure out what those contributions are.

Carson seems to have looked upon the great wealth of scientific research suddenly at her fingertips in a completely different way. For one thing, her assignment—how glorious to have one again—was to write about science. What could be better? It was like getting paid to do homework, the very thing she was best at. As she went about the work of writing short, easily consumed radio scripts, the storyteller inside her came alive again. In early 1936, just months after starting at the bureau, after having her mother neatly type up the manuscript, Carson sent off a long, loosely written piece on Chesapeake Bay shad fishing to the *Baltimore Sun*—which promptly bought it. Carson's first newspaper story, "It'll Be Shad Time Soon," ran in the *Baltimore Sun Sunday Magazine* on March 1, 1936. Carson got a check for twenty dollars.

Over the next four years, Carson became a frequent contributor to the *Sun,* writing on a variety of wildlife subjects and being paid ten or twenty dollars for each. These stories involved little conventional journalism—Carson was not an interviewer or investigator by nature—and were more often than not about places she had never been and things she had never witnessed. She wrote about tuna fishing off Nova Scotia and oyster farming in the Chesapeake Bay. She wrote about how duck numbers were gradually increasing after years of wetland drainage and how overhunting had decimated waterfowl populations. She wrote about problems with starlings overwintering in the Baltimore area. Returning to one of her favorite subjects, Carson wrote a piece about eels and their incomprehensible migration from the Sargasso Sea to the very same coastal bays and streams from which their parents had come, but which the new generation could recognize only by instinct. "Chesapeake Eels Seek the Sargasso Sea" ran in the Sunday *Sun* on October 9, 1938.

Carson also sold a couple of stories to the *Richmond Times-Dispatch Sunday Magazine*. In "Fight for Wildlife Pushes Ahead," an ambitious, sweeping piece about the former abundance of North American wildlife before European settlement and the long, steady decline in animal populations that had followed, Carson's consideration of these losses and the efforts then under way to reverse the trend hinted at the depth of her affection for the natural world:

> But what of wildlife today? Government services whose business it is to know conditions paint a general picture of scarcity and depletion. The last heath hen perished on the island of Martha's Vineyard in 1933, and the passenger pigeon is now a creature of legend. Salmon are virtually gone from the rivers of New England, and the Atlantic coast shad fisheries have declined some 80 percent within a half a century. Waterfowl flights fell to their lowest point in all their history in 1933 and 1934, and although government regulations plus the establishment of sanctuaries have resulted in some improvement, the plight of certain species, notably canvasback and redhead duck, remains serious. The ranks of elk were so thinned by 1904 that domestication was urged as the only means of preventing their extinction. Although pronghorn antelope are now on the increase within refuges and reservations, they are reduced from some 30,000,000 or 40,000,000 to about 60,000. Mountain goats, moose, and Grizzly bear are also on the wane.

In July 1936, Carson was appointed to a full-time position at the bureau as a junior aquatic biologist, and she was sworn in the following month. The job mainly involved writing reports on fisheries conservation issues—but also included some lab work in making age determinations of fish. Carson's salary was $2,000 a year.

FOUR

The English Connection
and the Ocean Deep

Christmas Eve 1914 was clear and cold in Flanders. Frost glittered on the no-man's-land that lay between the opposing lines forming the western front, a quagmire of mud and barbed wire and stalemate that ran from near Dunkirk on the English Channel south to a point fifty miles northeast of Paris, then east toward the German border. On one side were the British, backed by Belgian and French soldiers. On the other side, in many places close enough so that the men in the trenches could call out to their enemies, were German and Prussian forces.

As the holiday season approached there had been talk of a cessation of hostilities, but leaders on both sides worried this would destroy fighting morale and undertook to prevent fraternization between the combatants. In mid-December, the British command had put forward a series of attacks along the line in hopes of heating up the stalled conflict, but these mainly produced shocking casualties—many by friendly fire—that only furthered the misery and doubt in the trenches. Then, on the night before Christmas, the fighting stopped. Up and down the lines, candles were lit on the German side, and makeshift Christmas trees appeared on the parapets. The Germans began singing carols, and the British joined in. Before sunrise the artillery batteries were unattended, rifles had been laid down, and soldiers from both sides armed only with food and cigarettes and liquor had emerged from the trenches to meet in no-man's-land, where they sang together and exchanged gifts. Handwritten signs went up with the words "You no fight, we no fight." So it went through Christmas Day and, in some places on the front, for several more days after that.

And then the war resumed.

Among the participants in what came to be known as the Christmas Truce was a gangly nineteen-year-old private from suburban London named Henry Williamson. The son of a stern bank clerk, Williamson was a sensitive young man. He had large eyes and sometimes wore a trim mustache that ended at the corners of his mouth. Williamson had been at the front for just over a month and had witnessed, as he put it in a letter home, "a bitter and bloody struggle" that added up to "some of the most desperate fighting of the war." The brief pause in hostilities at Christmas caused Williamson to question the war, which suddenly seemed to him futile. Having met the enemy on friendly terms—Williamson had shaken hands with his German counterparts and merrily smoked a cigar with them—he discovered that soldiers on both sides were much the same: expendable pawns in a game played by politicians and generals. Many of the German soldiers Williamson met seemed to be waiters in civilian life. They were like himself, Williamson thought, inasmuch as they believed in their cause and yet could see its folly. Eventually, Williamson would be convinced that peace, not war, should be the natural state of the European community of nations—a conviction that would lead him down divergent paths, one into the English countryside and the other into the darkest realms of politics.

The trenches on the front—which in some areas had been dug into reclaimed swampland that was below sea level—were watery lagoons of filth, mud, and rotting flesh. Soldiers sometimes had to sleep standing up. Only a few weeks after the Christmas Truce, Williamson came down with dysentery and had to be shipped home to England. By March he was better, though he remained weak and admitted to nerves that left him feeling "joggy." That spring Williamson got accepted for training as an officer, and in March 1917 he returned to the front as a lieutenant in the machine gun corps. Williamson again saw heavy fighting, and after being injured and falling ill during two months of artillery bombardments and poison gas attacks, Williamson was again evacuated back to England. He recovered and was returned to the war once more in the spring of 1918. It's unclear what happened to him during his final three weeks of fighting back at the front, but he was "shaky" when he was sent home to convalesce again.

Williamson had begun a novel about his wartime experiences during one of his furloughs home, and after the war he devoted himself in equal measures to writing and tearing around the countryside on a Norton motorcycle, a passion that would later morph into a love of sporty motorcars. Sometime in the summer of 1919 Williamson discovered a slim memoir called *The Story of My Heart* by the English essayist and nature writer Richard Jefferies.

Raised on a farm halfway between London and Bristol, Jefferies from an early age indulged in frequent, solitary communion with the outdoors that began as an enthusiasm for hunting and tramping the countryside and evolved into a solemn reverence for nature. His reputation rested mainly on his nature essays, including the intense and revealing *Story of My Heart,* which he wrote as an autobiography. Published in 1883, just four years before Jefferies's death, the book is an account of the author's love of the natural world that is at times exquisite and in other places overripe with mystical mumbo jumbo. In the opening pages, Jefferies explains the connection to nature that illuminated his innermost feelings as a young man, when he would make a daily hike to the summit of a hilltop from which he could survey the English countryside:

> Lying down on the grass, I spoke in my soul to the earth, the sun, the air, and the distant sea far beyond sight. I thought of the earth's firmness—I felt it bear me up: through the grassy couch there came an influence as if I could feel the great earth speaking to me. I thought of the wandering air—its pureness, which is its beauty; the air touched me and gave me something of itself. I spoke to the sea: though so far, in my mind I saw it, green at the rim of the earth and blue in deeper ocean; I desired to have its strength, its mystery and glory.

And so on.

Jefferies was an odd man, tall but stooped, enthusiastic but humorless. As a youth, he grew his hair long and wandered about with his gun and his deepening thoughts, much to the consternation of his neighbors. By the time he came to write *The Story of My Heart* Jefferies had acquired a set of unusual beliefs. He thought that all accidents and diseases were preventable—that the innumerable tragedies that befall human beings were the result of carelessness and stupidity. He saw no reason why everyone should not live long past the age of one hundred. He did not believe in God. He did not believe that things "happen for the best."

On the contrary, Jefferies was stricken by the knowledge that good people often endure nightmarish lives, while those who do evil are just as often rewarded for their misdeeds. "Human suffering," he wrote, "is so great, so endless, so awful that I can hardly write of it." He hated being indoors and disliked all quotidian activities, which he thought useless. His natural companions, he wrote, were "the earth, and sun, and sea, and stars by night." Jefferies believed that we are on our own in the universe and that if human affairs could be properly directed it would be by some wise and benevolent dictator.

And yet, in a rapturous passage in *The Story of My Heart,* Jefferies confessed that despite the countless cruelties of existence, his hunger for life was insatiable and the one thing he wanted was *more* of it all: "I burn life like a torch. The hot light shot back from the sea scorches my cheek—my life is burning in me. The soul throbs like the sea for a larger life. No thought which I have ever had has satisfied my soul."

Some readers found *The Story of My Heart* inspiring, while others thought it irreverent and dangerous. For Henry Williamson, scarred in equal measures by the terror and the folly of war, *The Story of My Heart* was profound—a true search for meaning in life that was as right and noble as what had happened to him on a night before Christmas in Flanders. Reading the book was a transforming experience, one effect of which was to convince Williamson that he should commit himself to writing. And he did. In the coming years, Williamson's output swelled—by 1924 he had produced five books. He'd also been intrigued by a nature story he read during the same period, J. C. Tregarthen's *Life Story of an Otter.* Convinced he could do better and having moved to rural Devon—"Devonshire" some people still called it affectionately—on that southwestern arm of Britain that separates the Atlantic from the English Channel, Williamson began spending time with (of all things) an otter hunting club. In 1927 he published the book that would make him famous, *Tarka the Otter.*

A vivid and at times brutal portrayal of nature, *Tarka* was a peculiar book. Almost a genre unto itself—essentially the biography of a wild animal—*Tarka* offered a warm portrayal of the English countryside, brought to life by Williamson's powers of observation and a knack for imagining how the world might look and feel to an energetic and playful nonhuman being that divides its life between land and water. But the story is grim, too. Nature is remorseless, a beautiful world also filled with privation and loss, mortal enemies and ultimately death. Williamson did not stint in depicting the daunting situations that would confront an otter in its struggle to survive and raise another generation of otters. Not the least of these difficulties was the endless pursuit of Tarka by local hunting parties and their packs of dogs. In the story's harrowing climactic sequence, Tarka is chased for ten agonizing hours before being swept away by the river in a fight to the death.

A few months after *Tarka* was published, Williamson received an unusual critique of the book from one of Britain's strangest but most eminent public figures—the celebrated soldier, hero of Arabia, and author of *Seven Pillars of Wisdom,* T. E. Lawrence. Lawrence's message was in the form of a letter, more than four thousand words long and in handwriting that Williamson said was "smaller than ordinary typewriting." Lawrence, under the mistaken impression that this was Williamson's first book, thought *Tarka* was an exhilarating "achievement," but offered numerous page-by-page suggestions for improving Williamson's style, which Lawrence felt was overly dependent on local jargon and generally too abrupt and "staccato." Williamson, who might have taken offense, was instead grateful—and undoubtedly awed that such a famous man had taken an interest in his book. In a subsequent edition of *Tarka,* Williamson even made some of the changes that Lawrence had suggested—though he later thought better of this and returned future editions to the original language. Meanwhile, Williamson and Lawrence became friends, though they wrote letters far more often than they met face-to-face over the course of the next eight years.

Their long, affectionate correspondence ended on May 13, 1935, when Lawrence sent Williamson a telegram confirming a lunch date the two planned the following day. Leaving the telegraph office on his motorcycle, Lawrence swerved to avoid a bicyclist and crashed. He died of his injuries six days later. Williamson, in the middle of writing a new book that was proving difficult, buried himself in his work.

The new book had been inspired by the place Williamson, by now married and raising a family, had chosen to settle for a few years. It was a cottage named Shallowford, which was on an estate owned by the Earl of Fortescue, about twenty miles east of the town of

Georgeham, in Devonshire. Shallowford was two stories, with four bedrooms upstairs and four rooms on the main floor. Built of lime-washed cob—a mix of mud, straw, and water similar to adobe—the cottage had a thatched roof, came with a small garden, and stood near the banks of the River Bray. Clear and cold, the Bray rose in the Devon moors, passed through the earl's deer park, and thence flowed glitteringly beneath a lovely old triple-arched stone bridge that marked the upper boundary of a two-mile stretch of fishing rights included in the rent. On his first visit, Williamson had stood on the bridge and seen trout idling in the current. The Bray harbored native trout and seasonal spawning visits from sea-run trout and salmon, powerful fish that could be as big as a man's leg.

Williamson fell in love with Shallowford the moment he saw it. But he was anxious, too. He wondered if anything in ordinary life could ever match the fearsome thrill of war, which had been so horrific and yet so intense that, in a perverse way, he was afraid that he missed it. How could commonplace safety and security substitute for the action and camaraderie of soldiering? The world after the war had seemed to him a "poor and dispirited" place, the joys and passions of youth remote and possibly forever lost. Williamson felt unsure he had the imagination to reclaim his former happy life, and this was a "dark secret" he carried within himself. The Williamsons moved to Shallowford in the fall of 1929. Over the winter, Williamson decided that what would cheer him up was to go fishing come spring.

> So I rediscovered the delights of water and of fishing. Once the clang of the lodge gate was behind me, and I was hastening under the limes where the bees sought murmurously for honey, my new life was one of anticipation, for what trout might I not see from Humpy Bridge? The view from the grey stone parapet was becoming so familiar that I began to regard the deer park as my own. And on a morning in May, how quiet and peaceful it was, standing on the bridge.

As the days of fishing and watching and studying the river accumulated, Williamson started thinking about a book about a salmon, something that would be similar to *Tarka*. Finally, in January 1935, Williamson began the book he tentatively called "Salar the Leaper," but fortunately retitled *Salar the Salmon*. In the scientific name for the Atlantic salmon, which is *Salmo salar,* the word "salar" actually means "leaper."

Williamson's research consisted almost entirely of firsthand observation. He was on the river for hours at a time in every kind of weather. But for reasons he never explained, *Salar* became a misery to write. As he labored away in the upstairs writing room of his perfect, charming cottage, with the sounds of the river through his open window for company, Williamson held on grimly to the principle known to all writers—and ignored by many—that it matters not if you write only a little in a day as long as you write every day. Williamson would later recall that *Salar* had been a "continuous anguish to write," a chore he so bitterly resented that he spent forty minutes of every hour he worked on the book wishing he were doing anything else. In his last letter to Lawrence, Williamson confided that *Salar* was an "awful book" that was so "boring" and "dull" that it was dragging the life out of him. Lawrence's death that spring only deepened Williamson's melancholy. And yet by August 1935 the book was finished. Williamson admitted he'd cut the ending short, feeling that if the salmon didn't die he himself surely would.

None of this difficulty was apparent in the book itself, which was, in a word, brilliant. Williamson had entered into the watery realm of his protagonist—an animal that cannot speak or think or in any way comprehend its existence—and made that world come alive. *Salar* turned out to be a book as much about water as it was about a fish, a story of currents and colors and perceived pressures, about salt and fresh, deep and shallow, cold and warm, light and dark. Salar comes in from the moving, tide-swept ocean to the quieter but still ceaselessly changing river, where he takes his rest in quiet pools and works his way against the weight of water during the sudden floods called "spates," heading instinctively upstream to spawn and die. In one thrilling passage, Salar is hooked by a fisherman and a deadly contest ensues:

> Salar knew of neither the fisherman nor rod nor line. He swam down to the ledge of rock and tried to rub the painful thing in the corner of his mouth against it. But his head was pulled away from the rock. He saw the line, and was fearful of it. He bored down to his lodge at the base of the rock, to get away from the line, while the small brown trout swam behind his tail, curious to know what was happening.

Salar the Salmon was published in Britain in October 1935, and the following summer in the United States. Anita Moffett wrote a long, adoring review in the *New York Times,* calling it "a rare and beautiful book that should take its place as a classic among the few which are written at once with a poet's insight and a naturalist's knowledge."

Exhausted but happy to be done with *Salar,* Williamson went on holiday while the book was being readied for publication. The trip would be, like the Christmas Truce, a turning point in his life. In early September 1935, Williamson boarded the *Bremen* at Southampton and sailed for Bremerhaven, where he got on a train for Berlin to begin a tour of Germany. His itinerary included, by invitation, a stop at the annual National Socialist Rally at Nuremberg for a close look at the country's popular but controversial chancellor—and recently self-anointed "führer"—Adolf Hitler. Williamson's semiofficial visit, which joined up for a time with a more organized excursion of foreign press, had been arranged by an English friend connected with a couple of Nazi cultural ministers. On the train ride to Berlin, Williamson amused himself by looking at the sturdy black-and-white cows that browsed in the fields along the way.

The author of *Tarka* was well-known in Germany and got a warm reception. Many of Germany's leading writers had fled the country during Hitler's rise to power, and the lesser authors who remained were steering clear of social themes and devoting themselves instead to nature writing and idyllic depictions of rural life. An assortment of censoring authorities, including the Gestapo and the Interior Ministry, routinely raided bookstores and libraries to get rid of hundreds of banned titles.

Williamson's later accounts of this trip didn't make clear exactly how long it lasted, but he was evidently in Germany for at least a few weeks, through the Nuremberg rally that ended on September 16, 1935, and for a number of days after that. He traveled extensively through the country, accompanied by a rotating assortment of Nazi minders. The Nuremberg rally did not disappoint—something like a million people swelled the city, and the sky remained continually lit up with fireworks. On the first morning Hitler was to address the crowd, Williamson described a spectacle that was Wagnerian in scale and dramatic effect, set in a vast arena draped in swastikas.

The day was warm and sunny—Hitler weather, someone said. Williamson thought the führer's speech seemed calmer and more restrained than in the days during his rise to power. After Hitler's speech, Williamson was amused when Hermann Goering and Joseph Goebbels appeared before the crowd. Goering, Williamson said, was a "Falstaff-like figure," capering and laughing, waving to the crowd and stopping to be photographed with eager onlookers. Later on, Williamson admiringly noted Hitler's stamina as the führer stood in his open motorcar, right arm outstretched in salute for hours during a parade of regional Nazi organizations.

Wandering about after the review, Williamson found himself at the rally headquarters and was suddenly standing close to Hitler. He wondered anxiously what he would say if he were to be introduced. Hitler was impressive: "He was very quick in his head movements," Williamson wrote. "He spoke rapidly, I got the idea his natural pace is much swifter than the ordinary, his eyes falcon-like, remarkably full of life. A man of spiritual grace; he calls himself a medium; which means the small inner voice has been developed until it possesses the physical brain."

Before and after the Nuremberg rally, Williamson was much impressed by Germany under Nazi rule. Everything appeared crisp and orderly. Not a speck littered the streets. The people seemed happy, vigorous, optimistic—and contemptuous of any suggestion that Germany was preparing for war. In the countryside, gray-uniformed troops were on the march everywhere, and somehow their martial bearing struck Williamson as thrilling rather than threatening. Under the recently proposed Nuremberg Laws, Jews would soon lose their German citizenship. Just a month earlier, Nazi storm troopers had held truck parades in Munich and Berlin denouncing Jews as enemies of the state. German businesses now routinely posted signs banning Jews as customers—a practice that reminded Williamson of the "colored only" signage he had seen on a visit to the southern United States. Williamson said he'd arrived in Germany expecting to find Jews hidden away and cowering behind closed doors, even though he suspected the newspapers outside of Germany exaggerated Jewish persecution under the Reich. But this didn't seem to be the case at all. Williamson saw Jews on the streets, and he even ate at a large popular restaurant that was Jewish-owned—although his German escort declined to join him there. When someone told him that Hitler had said privately that if he had his way "there would not be a Jew alive in Germany today," Williamson said he didn't believe it.

As the tour went on, traveling from city to city, hotel to hotel, it took on a predictable rhythm of late dinners and still-later cocktail hours—followed by a drowsy start over sausages and wine late the next morning. Williamson was dazzled by the women he encountered in the bars, some of them bored and looking for company, others who were surely prostitutes. He discovered that his traveling companions among the foreign press were offended by his enthusiasm for Hitler, while his German escorts were chilly on this point for different reasons, apparently mistrusting the Englishman for coming on too strongly.

It was evidently expected that Williamson, on his return to England, would write some articles friendly to Germany for the British papers—a quid pro quo for what had been, after all, a propaganda junket. This didn't work out, as Williamson couldn't find any publication interested in a sympathetic view of Nazism. His new friends in Germany were disappointed but not surprised, as they were accustomed to the foreign press being more interested in news about concentration camps and ethnic violence than it was in the glories of the new Germany.

Williamson had been favorably disposed toward Hitler's Germany before he visited it. He felt a kinship with Hitler that was based on the hopeful feelings Williamson had about regular Germans after the Christmas Truce. He even thought it possible that he'd met Hitler as a young German soldier on that night. Williamson was convinced that Hitler was a man of peace, determined to avoid war while putting his country right—perhaps the sort of man Richard Jefferies had had in mind as The One to rule a better world. There was a renewal in Germany, in its cities and forests, on its farms and among its strong, happy people, that reminded Williamson of the world he wanted to live in—a linkage between fascism and the romanticism of his own work that he found undeniable.

Williamson believed, without the slightest evidence, that T. E. Lawrence, had he lived, would have felt the same way about Hitler. Both men so dominated Williamson's thoughts that he began to fantasize about what the three of them—Hitler, Lawrence, and Williamson—might have accomplished. In the spring of 1936, the *Dorset County Chronicle* picked up a report from a British radio magazine that could only have originated with Williamson himself. As the story went, Williamson had persuaded T. E. Lawrence that they should do a series of programs promoting world peace from the Albert Hall in London. These would be broadcast on the radio and would involve—the article didn't explain this part—the agreeable participation of Hitler.

How this demented idea gained enough traction to be picked up in the papers is hard to explain. Harder still is to understand how it was that Williamson gradually came to believe the story was true, and that Lawrence had died on his motorcycle after cabling his agreement to the plan. Whatever temporary luster this myth might have lent to Williamson's reputation vanished a year and a half later when Williamson joined the British Union of Fascists. He remained an unapologetic member even as Germany rained war across Europe. The group was outlawed in 1940.

An ocean away, Rachel Carson was busy. In the spring of 1936, Elmer Higgins asked Carson to write something "of a general sort" about the sea. Carson later recalled getting carried away with the assignment, as "the material rather took charge of the situation." The result, an elegant essay titled "The World of Waters," stunned Higgins, who immediately rejected it. The piece, he told Carson, was too good for a minor government production. He suggested that she submit it to the *Atlantic Monthly* magazine. This she did not do right away, concentrating instead on her freelancing assignments for local newspapers and her new full-time position at the bureau. In the spring, Carson entered "The World of Waters" in a writing contest sponsored by *Reader's Digest*. It didn't win.

Then, in early 1937, Carson's older sister, Marian, died of pneumonia, leaving Carson and her mother to care for Marian's two preteen daughters, Virginia and Marjorie—who were already living under the same roof. In June, Carson finally sent "The World of Waters" to the *Atlantic,* where it was immediately accepted. The magazine's editors thought the piece would "fire the imagination of the layman." They asked Carson for a few changes and to agree to a new title: "Undersea." In August, she received a check for $100.

"Undersea" appeared in the *Atlantic*'s September 1937 issue. Carson had the magazine use "R. L. Carson" as a byline, explaining that this was an identity she preferred at the Bureau of Fisheries to enhance her credibility by permitting readers to assume that she was a man. The essay was an animated distillation, just four magazine pages long, of seemingly everything that Carson knew firsthand or had learned from the scientific literature about the life that crowded the sea, from the water's edge at the high-tide mark to the depths of black chasms beneath the open ocean. Carson went beyond mere description of the lives of starfish and eels and crabs and fish into the deeper meanings of oceanic natural history. Here, in the tidal wash and beneath the waves, appeared nature's demonstration of the systemic biological forces that link all life in the present and through the ages—the myriad churning, interrelated existences that are the leading edge of evolutionary history:

> The ocean is a place of paradoxes. It is the home of the great white shark, two-thousand-pound killer of the seas, and the hundred-foot blue whale, the largest animal that ever lived. It is also the home of living things so small that your two hands might scoop up as many of them as there are stars in the Milky Way. And it is because of the flowering astronomical numbers of these diminutive plants, known as diatoms, that the surface waters of the ocean are in reality boundless pastures. Every marine animal from the smallest to the sharks and whales, is ultimately dependent for its food upon these microscopic entities of the vegetable life of the ocean. Within their fragile walls, the sea performs a vital alchemy that utilizes the sterile chemical elements dissolved in the water and welds them with the torch of sunlight into the stuff of life.

This was imprecise, though reflective of the limited range of scientific knowledge at the time. The sea does not literally operate inside the impermeable cell walls of diatoms, and the word "alchemy" has a supernatural connotation. Even the largest pair of hands could at most scoop up enough seawater to hold 100 million diatoms—a number that is a tiny fraction of the 200 to 400 billion stars that make up the Milky Way. But Carson's broad point, that life is a continuum in which every organism plays a role, was well made. Carson imagined for her readers the bottom of the ocean as if it were landscape one could journey over:

> If the underwater traveler might continue to explore the ocean floor, he would traverse miles of level prairie lands; he would ascend the sloping sides of hills; and he would skirt deep and ragged crevasses yawning suddenly at his feet. Through the gathering darkness, he would come at last to the edge of the continental shelf. The ceiling of the ocean would lie a hundred fathoms above him, and his feet would rest upon the brink of a slope that drops precipitously another mile, and then descends more gently into an inky void that is the abyss.

Carson's picture of the ocean was a modern one, based mostly on her scrupulous research into a body of knowledge that was still young and evolving. For most of human history little was known about what lay beneath the surface of the sea anywhere but in the near-shore shallows. Even after European exploration had filled in the coastal outlines of the world's oceans in the sixteenth and seventeenth centuries, it would be another two hundred years before answers began to emerge on two fundamental questions: How deep is the ocean, and what, if anything, lives in its depths?

For as long as humans had voyaged on the ocean, sailors had determined water depths by means of sounding lines—long ropes or cords that were marked at measured intervals and attached to weights that were plunged to the bottom. By the nineteenth century the conventional unit used to indicate depth was the fathom, which is equivalent to six feet. This system worked well enough in modest depths but was poorly suited to measuring the deep ocean. The "abysmal" depth of the ocean was unknown and perhaps impossible to find by sounding, as the longer the sounding line became the more its own weight tended to pull additional line toward the bottom. And no one had any idea how long a line would be needed even if that difficulty could be overcome. As early as 1521, while exploring the South Pacific on his circumnavigation, Ferdinand Magellan put down a sounding line of nearly 200 fathoms—1,200 feet. It did not touch bottom.

Early in 1840, during the British Antarctic Expedition, the first accurate abysmal soundings were made using a specially designed line attached to a seventy-six-pound weight. By observing the rate of the line's descent, it was possible to determine when the free-falling weight reached the bottom, even though the line then continued paying out on its own at a slower rate. The first of a series of measurements in the South Atlantic indicated a depth of 2,425 fathoms, or 14,550 feet—more than a third of a mile deeper than the 12,500 feet that was later found to be the mean depth of the ocean.

With advanced soundings came attempts to pick up samples of the ocean bottom. Nets and dredges were also used to collect sea life from various depths. In the mid-1800s it was proposed that, owing to the enormous pressure and absence of light, life could not exist at depths greater than 300 fathoms. But this was soon disproven—spectacularly in 1860 when a telegraph cable lying on the bottom of the Mediterranean Sea broke at a depth of 1,200 fathoms, or 7,200 feet down. When the cable was brought to the surface for repair live corals were found growing on it where it had parted, and a great assortment of other sea creatures clung to the cable along sections that had been in shallower water.

The picture of the world's oceans as deep and teeming with life was brought into clearer focus in the 1870s during one of the greatest scientific ventures ever undertaken: the four-year, around-the-world exploration cruise of the HMS *Challenger*. Sponsored by the Royal Society and the British Admiralty, the *Challenger* expedition was the first-ever true "oceanographic" voyage, a term that was actually invented for the enterprise. *Challenger,* a two-hundred-foot naval corvette powered by both sail and steam, with most of her guns removed and replaced by laboratories and storage areas, sailed from Portsmouth in December 1872. She carried a crew of 264 officers and men, plus six scientists. By the time she returned to England in the spring of 1876, *Challenger* had traveled nearly seventy thousand miles across the world's oceans, made hundreds of deep soundings, taken countless readings of currents, temperatures, and water chemistry, and amassed an extensive collection of bottom samples from the oozes and clays of the abyss.

Along the way, *Challenger* biologists discovered close to five thousand new species of marine life. The full published account of the *Challenger* expedition eventually ran to fifty volumes, a work that would remain a standard oceanographic reference. On March 23, 1875, as she rode the Pacific swell near Guam in the Mariana Islands, *Challenger* recorded the deepest sounding in the course of her voyage—almost 4,500 fathoms, about 27,000 feet. The "Challenger Deep," as this place was named, was later learned to be a section of the sea floor within the frigid darkness of the Mariana Trench, not far from its deepest point of more than 35,000 feet—the deepest place in all of the world's oceans.

By the time Rachel Carson endeavored to describe the world beneath the waves to the readers of the *Atlantic Monthly,* the topography of the ocean bottom was being mapped using an innovation called sonar, an echo-sounding device that was initially developed to help ships detect icebergs after the sinking of the *Titanic* in 1912. Sonar further revealed the vast plains and spectacular deeps, the jagged mountains and sheer valleys of the sea floor. Much of the bottom in the deep ocean is covered by a thick biologic ooze made up of the remains of trillions upon trillions of dead planktonic organisms.

Here, as Carson described it, is a place that is forever changing, renewed in perpetuity by the endless cycling of life and death and rebirth—and yet at the same time a region that is in a sense changeless: "In the silent deeps a glacial cold prevails, a bleak iciness which never varies, summer or winter, years melting into centuries, and centuries into ages of geologic time. There, too, darkness reigns—the blackness of primeval night in which the ocean came into being, unbroken, through aeons of succeeding time, by the gray light of dawn."

Carson closed the essay on a thought she'd had back in her lab at Johns Hopkins about the eternal nature of living matter—the blending and polymerization of atoms into the macromolecules that are exchanged and reused from one generation to the next in a majestic symphony of synthesis and decomposition and resynthesis:

> Individual elements are lost to view, only to reappear again and again in different incarnations in a kind of material immortality. Kindred forces to those which, in some period inconceivably remote, gave birth to that primeval bit of protoplasm tossing on the ancient seas continue their mighty and incomprehensible work. Against this cosmic background the life span of a particular plant or animal appears, not as a drama complete in itself, but only as a brief interlude in a panorama of endless change.

A writer cannot have better luck than to publish something both good and unexpected. "Undersea" was unlike anything Carson had previously written, and different from what the readers of the *Atlantic* were used to seeing in its pages. The piece caught the attention of an author named Hendrik van Loon. Van Loon, whose book *The Story of Mankind* had won the first Newbery Medal in 1922, was a Dutch-born writer of literature and history for children and young adults. He'd immigrated to the United States during World War I and, after working with several publishers, settled with Simon and Schuster. Van Loon conveyed his enthusiasm for "Undersea" to Simon and Schuster editor Quincy Howe. Howe wrote to Carson asking if she had ever considered writing a book. Carson, elated but unsure of herself, replied that she had no concrete plans at the moment—though she apparently offered some general thoughts about a book that Howe described to van Loon as "nebulous." Carson also indicated she'd be eager to consider any ideas that Howe and van Loon might have for her. Howe replied that he'd discuss this with van Loon.

While the September issue of the *Atlantic* was still on newsstands, van Loon wrote to Carson. His letter, posted from Grand Central Station in New York, arrived in an envelope on which van Loon—who illustrated his own books—had drawn a spouting whale cruising on a placid sea that appeared to be alive with sharks. Van Loon proved to be a quirky, jovial correspondent. He wrote out dates in Roman numerals, decorated his letters with small sketches, and composed his thoughts in a private syntax that was hilarious when he used a typewriter and that bordered on incomprehensible when he wrote in longhand. In his first letter to Carson, van Loon—who was in his midfifties—said he'd been curious about the sea since reading Jules Verne "sixty years ago," and that it was apparent to him that she was "the woman . . . or words to that effect" who could answer his questions.

Van Loon confessed that he was responsible for bringing her to the attention of Simon and Schuster and hoped she'd deliver them a fine book, as "the better they do with other people's books, the more they can afford to lose on mine." He proposed that Carson should take the train up to Connecticut to visit him at his home in Old Greenwich, where he would introduce her to Quincy Howe. He said he was sure the Bureau of Fisheries would give her time off for such a meeting, as the prospect of a book deal would "bring glory" to the department. Van Loon ended this generous note saying he was at Carson's service and that "Undersea" was a "swell article."

Through the fall, van Loon continued to press Carson to come to Connecticut. Carson, feeling unprepared, demurred, saying she was still engaged in a "preliminary browsing in the literature" to come up with ideas. In December 1937, van Loon told her the tides were such that she could go clamming three times daily—as long as she wouldn't expect him to eat any of them. Carson, furiously working to make her vague notion of a book coalesce into something definite, waited until after the holidays and finally went north in mid-January—where the full meaning of having been discovered settled on her. Van Loon—a great man, she realized—had opened a door into the refined and wonderful world of publishing, an exclusive club she longed to join. The author, as she now could not help but think of herself, walked boldly in. From that moment on, Carson belonged to something "exciting and fabulous."

By February 1938, Carson and Howe were in general agreement about a book that would describe life in the sea from the viewpoint of the creatures of the ocean. Explaining her plan to van Loon, Carson said she didn't want any human voice or insight in the narrative and that if any people appeared in the story they would be shown as a fish would perceive them—as predators and threats. Nor would she invent a plot as such. The story would emerge from the everyday lives and natural histories of her sea-dwelling protagonists, which she described as "always strange and sometimes incredible." These she would choose and divide into groups so as to capture the different habitats of the living ocean, from shoreline to the abyss. Carson said she now felt sure this was the right plan for the book and that she, in fact, had a specific narrative model in mind. Having thought long and hard, she said, she was convinced that the right thing to do would be something "in the manner of Henry Williamson's salmon book."

A delighted van Loon wrote back to say that he could not have come up with a better concept himself. Sensing that Carson was embarked on a special journey and yet in need of reassurance, he told her to seize her destiny confidently, as there were great things in her future.

"You have the ability," van Loon wrote. "You have started. And you are going to go to those places you want to go."

Carson hoped to replace the income she would at least temporarily forgo from writing newspaper pieces by selling chapters from her book in progress to the *Atlantic,* whose editors were initially receptive to the idea of a serialization. But when she sent a sample, the magazine's editors changed their mind, telling Carson that they were publishing a series of articles by the nature writer Donald Culross Peattie and that his work and hers were too similar for the *Atlantic* to do both. Carson and the editors discussed the possibility of using excerpts from her book at a later time, but this never came to pass.

Meanwhile, she wrote some book reviews for the *Atlantic,* earning fifteen dollars that spring for a piece on *Maritime Fishes of the Pacific Coast.* In April 1938, Carson implored the *Atlantic* to let her review *Goodbye, West Country,* the latest book by Henry Williamson. The magazine declined. Williamson's American publisher was the Atlantic Press, and the magazine tried to avoid the appearance of promoting its own authors. Plus, the book had been out for several months and sales were disappointing. But a month later they relented, and Carson was offered a short double review of *Goodbye, West Country* and Llewelyn Powys's tubercular memoir of life in Dorset, *Earth Memories.* Carson's letter to the magazine about the Williamson book was nearly as long as the review that eventually ran the following December and revealed the depth of her admiration for the English writer:

> I have been more impressed with Mr. Williamson's *Tarka* and *Salar* than any other pieces of nature writing that I can recall. The keen beauty of his prose is something anyone might envy. The first pages of *Salar* give me the feeling of the strange ocean world better than all 800 pages of that oceanographer's bible, *The Depths of the Ocean*—rank heresy on my part! But I can think of no one who has comparable powers of recreating the atmosphere of the aquatic world that moves through his books. I also admire his powers of observation, his sympathetic but never sentimental understanding of the creatures of which he writes, and his generally sound interpretation of what he sees. *Goodbye, West Country* is full of charming pages in itself and has made the otter and salmon books take on new meaning for me through its revelation of so much of their background.

In 1936, feeling dispirited with his life in Devonshire, Williamson had bought a farm on the other side of England, near the Norfolk coast on the North Sea. He spent the year improving the property and readying himself to become a farmer. *Goodbye, West Country* was a diarylike record of his final months in Devonshire and, as Carson said in her letter offering to review it, Williamson's daily comings and goings made pleasant reading. One day, not feeling like working, he'd gone down to the Bray with his fly rod and, after creeping to river's edge on hands and knees, hooked a magnificent nine-pound salmon. The great fish led him on a struggle upstream and down that produced a thrilling interlude over several pages in *Goodbye, West Country:*

> When most of the line was out, I knew I'd have to go into the water, else the trees and bushes on the bank below would make it a tug of war, when the weight of the fish with the current would break the gut immediately. I went into the river, hoping I wouldn't slip over in my nailed shoes as I waded downstream, water to my armpits. The bottom was uneven, sometimes gravel and then abruptly a pit through which I floundered half swimming, feeling this was the life.

A photograph of Williamson's eventual triumph over the fish was taken against the wall of Shallowford cottage. In it Williamson stands erect and sober, dressed in a coat and tie with woolen knickers, a fly rod in his right hand. His left, balled into a fist and held near his waist, hoists the giant fish by the tail, its nose nearly touching Williamson's shoe.

Carson's review of *Goodbye, West Country,* just three paragraphs long, took notice only of Williamson's close observations of nature, and she found in these a kindred spirit. As he had done in *Tarka* and *Salar,* books that Carson declared were at the "front rank of nature literature," Williamson showed his keen appreciation for the endless cycle of life and death and rebirth that animates the natural world. Carson felt that Williamson perceived the "whole life" of a creature he beheld even for a moment. She wrote that he was the sort of "sensitive person" who is simultaneously saddened by the mortality of all living things and yet keenly aware that this is nature's way.

These were themes that resonated with Carson and that she may have been alone in detecting as an essential feature of Williamson's journal of a country year. Whether *Goodbye, West Country* was a book mainly about nature was debatable. In fairness, the space for her review was so short that the list of things she had to leave out would have been long. And, just as the *Atlantic* did not want to be in the business of hyping one of its authors, neither would the magazine have likely run a thoroughly critical review. Short and favorable were the requirements, and Carson's desire to emphasize what she liked best about the book was understandable. But as anyone who read *Goodbye, West Country* would have noticed, Carson's review omitted even a mention of a long, detailed, and important section of the book—Williamson's enthusiastic recollection of his visit to Nazi Germany in the fall of 1935, a revealing account that unfolded over the course of some thirty pages and that emphasized Williamson's admiration for Hitler.

There are friendly allusions to Hitler and Germany elsewhere in *Goodbye, West Country,* and in one of these passages Williamson recalls with annoyance the response he'd gotten from the editor of an American literary journal after Williamson had written him a letter suggesting that people fearful of Germany had it all wrong: "'I am all with you when it comes to salmon and otter,' the editor wrote back, 'but violently opposed to your ideas of the great Mr. Hitler. He seems to me a disease of the times.'"

Why Carson didn't say something along those lines in her review is puzzling. Perhaps she read *Goodbye, West Country* as she had Tennyson's "Locksley Hall" back at PCW—blind to its darker meanings. Maybe she was simply uninterested in Williamson's thoughts about Europe and whether it was to be peace or war with Germany. Although she was happy enough working inside Roosevelt's New Deal administration and later in life hinted that she was a Democrat, Carson seems to have been at heart apolitical.

But evidence of Hitler's menace had been accruing for years, and while Americans were slow to realize what was happening in Germany under the Nazis, by 1938 when she reviewed *Goodbye, West Country,* Carson could not have been unaware that Williamson's politics were extreme. As early as 1933, in a review of Houghton Mifflin's American edition of *Mein Kampf*—a book everyone was curious about—the *New York Times* had suggested that the "Aryan" leader of Germany was a menace to other states in Europe and that fascism had evil "implications for the Jewish race." Throughout the 1930s, the news from Germany had grown steadily more alarming. In the summer of 1935, as Henry Williamson was finishing *Salar the Salmon* at Shallowford cottage, Jews were being harassed by Nazi storm troopers in Berlin, and at the Nuremberg rally Williamson attended that fall Hitler had announced new laws rescinding German citizenship for Jews, placing restrictions on where Jews could live and work, and forbidding intermarriage between Jews and gentiles.

By 1938, Hitler had annexed Austria; within months he would invade Poland and Czechoslovakia, and Britain and France would declare war on Germany. In December 1938, the month Carson's review appeared in the *Atlantic,* a sharp diplomatic dispute arose over Germany's formal protest of Interior Secretary Harold Ickes's public criticism of Hitler's regime in a speech he'd given in Cleveland. The papers in Germany spewed criticism of Ickes—they labeled him a gangster—and hinted at an imminent break in relations between the two countries. Two years later, Rachel Carson would be working for Ickes.

Carson may or may not have been aware that Henry Williamson had joined the British Union of Fascists in the fall of 1937—though it seems likely that the Atlantic Press, his American publishers, would have known as much. It's also unclear whether Carson understood how Williamson's nature writing and his interest in farming and rural life fit into a mythical narrative embraced by the Nazis in Germany, where so-called blood-and-soil literature celebrated racial purity and a working life close to the land. Writers in Germany were required to be members of the Reich Chamber of Literature, which exercised broad censorship powers through various subagencies. The blacklisting of "modern" and Jewish authors, along with public book burnings, were among the first official acts of the Nazis after Hitler came into power in 1933. Under National Socialism, German literature was expected to emphasize—as propaganda minister Goebbels put it—a "steely romanticism." This produced a steady supply of unimaginative novels portraying the sturdy rewards of rural life that were thought to be the pillars of Germany's renewal under Hitler—and which matched the führer's more general belief that all artistic endeavors should be aimed at the common man. In 1937, Hitler had decreed that German artists could paint only works that were comprehensible to the average German.

In *Goodbye, West Country*, Williamson—as steely a romantic as there could be—observed that city-dwelling modernists "growing up on sidewalks" suffered from too much "mental living" and had far too little experience of "the natural world, the world of men working their minds in harmony with their bodies." The by-products of the "nervous strain" of city life and of having "no roots in the soil," Williamson wrote, were "mental confusions." Carson, who had her own reservations about the implications of human progress, may well have agreed with Williamson on these points—without making the connection to fascist ideology. No doubt the evil that takes center stage for a big part of *Goodbye, West Country* is easier to see in hindsight, though this does not alter the fact that it was there.

What seems probable is that Carson dashed off a short review of *Goodbye, West Country* while she was thinking much more deeply about a different book by Henry Williamson—*Salar the Salmon*. Williamson's bitter complaint in *Goodbye, West Country* about the difficulty he had writing the salmon book did not dissuade Carson in her plan to model her own first book on *Salar*. Carson wrote to van Loon that she and Howe had agreed that the book should be about twelve chapters long, each one telling its own story of one group of sea dwellers, a mosaic that would ultimately yield a coherent picture of the total ocean habitat. In this respect it would differ from *Salar,* which featured a single fish as a protagonist. But Carson also longed to achieve the same sense of immersion—of taking the reader under and into the water—that Williamson had managed.

With that in mind, Carson asked van Loon for a favor, one that marked the beginning of what was to become a permanent feature of her approach to research and writing: She asked van Loon to introduce her to an expert, in this case a friend of his named William Beebe. Beebe, then in his early sixties, was the director of the Department of Tropical Research at the New York Zoological Society and one of the country's leading naturalists. By chance, Beebe was tall and thin and bore an uncanny resemblance to Henry Williamson.

Largely self-taught—he'd spent a few semesters at Columbia—Beebe was famous as an ornithologist and, more recently, for his underwater exploits as a helmet diver. Beebe's enthusiasm for the "sport" of helmet diving was boundless. He believed that within a few years, people would routinely tend to underwater gardens in the near-shore ocean, planting and visiting them with guests on diving parties to which everyone traveled by boat before going overboard in a metal helmet attached to an air hose tethered to a pump that would keep each reveler merrily alive and breathing at the comfortable depth of five fathoms, or thirty feet. Beebe himself had extensive diving experience, and once, while wandering over the ocean bottom off the coast of Haiti in his glass-fronted copper helmet at a depth of about ten fathoms, had come to a steep precipice. Staring down into the depths, Beebe had an urge to jump over the edge to see what lay below—but knew that he would quickly succumb to the added pressure of the water. The longing to visit that deeper world, which Beebe said was as unknown as the surface of Mars, stayed with him.

In 1929, Beebe met a man named Otis Barton who had built a deep-diving apparatus. In principle, it reminded Beebe of something he claimed had once been suggested to him by a young cavalry colonel named Theodore Roosevelt. It was a simple contraption, a steel sphere just under five feet in diameter, or large enough to hold two men seated next to each other. The wall of the sphere was an inch and a quarter thick and featured three heavy quartz windows, round like portholes and just big enough to peer out into the depths or to frame a human face within should anything swim by for a look. Access was through a small hatch that bolted in place and was so heavy it had to be removed or installed with a winch. Oxygen tanks and charcoal air scrubbers inside the capsule provided a breathable atmosphere. The whole apparatus, some 5,400 pounds of it, was lowered into the sea on a cable specially designed to prevent it from twisting and causing the capsule to spin. Other cables provided electricity for a searchlight and telephone communication with the surface. Beebe, looking for a name for Barton's invention, dubbed it the "bathysphere."

After making initial unmanned tests in the deep waters off Nonsuch Island in Bermuda, Beebe and Barton made a series of progressively deeper dives in the bathysphere. At the time, the depth record for a submarine was 383 feet. The lowest depth reached by any human being who had survived the experience was 525 feet, which had been set by a diver in an armored suit in a lake in Bavaria. The first manned dive in the bathysphere, on June 6, 1930, went to 800 feet. On August 15, 1934, Beebe and Barton took the bathysphere down to 3,028 feet. They might have gone a bit deeper, but the lift operator on the boat deck noticed that there was only a handful of turns left on the winch and feared the cable might break off if it came to the end. Later that year, Beebe published a lively book about his diving exploits called *Half Mile Down*.

Carson was certainly familiar with this book and its charming, evidently fearless author. In visiting so deep a part of the ocean, Beebe and Barton had gone to a place nobody had ever seen—and learned much about it in the process. Although many deepwater species had been retrieved in netting operations such as those of the *Challenger*, specimens were often damaged by the change in pressure when they were brought to the surface. Observing for the first time the unimaginably rich diversity of life far below the reach of sunlight, Beebe and Barton photographed and made drawings of a wild assortment of fish, eels, squid, and jellyfish. Some of these creatures produced their own glowing lights; others passed though the searchlight like transparent ghosts or dark, indistinct shadows. Beebe was surprised that a number of species that frequented the surface were also seen at great depths, demonstrating a previously unsuspected ability to navigate between regions of extreme pressure differentials.

The dangers inherent in this undertaking were never out of Beebe's thoughts during a dive. Every time the bathysphere was lifted from the boat deck and swung out over the water to begin a dive, Beebe was struck by how their journey down into the ocean always began with a ride twenty feet into the air. Once in the water and out of sight of the boat, their connection to the surface was almost an abstraction. Sometimes a wave would pass beneath the boat above them and the bathysphere, suspended motionless, would suddenly pitch disconcertingly. What happened? Had they broken free? Were they being hauled up for some reason—or sinking into the abyss? On their first dive the hatch had sprung a leak. As water trickled in and pooled around them, Beebe and Barton watched to see if the flow increased. When it didn't, Beebe ordered the bathysphere lowered more rapidly so as to complete the dive before the water got too high inside the bathysphere. Beebe knew that as they went deeper and the pressure outside the bathysphere increased, the result of any failure of the steel or the quartz windows would be something they'd take no notice of. "There was no possible chance of being drowned," Beebe wrote in *Half Mile Down*, "for the first few drops would have shot through flesh and bone like steel bullets."

On another occasion, the seal on one of the windows failed during an unmanned test dive to three thousand feet. When the bathysphere was brought back up and lowered onto the deck it was full of water that everyone realized was highly pressurized. The center wing bolt on the hatch was loosened—and the bathysphere hissed ominously. The deck was cleared and the wing bolt was cranked open until it exploded from the hatch, rocketing across the deck as if shot from a cannon, followed by a solid jet of water powerful enough to slice a man in two. A few days later, the same thing happened again on another test dive.

But against all risks was the immense reward of exploring the unknown, of shining a light into an ocean realm where light had never visited and where only the creatures that dwelled there had looked upon one another. Beebe wrote that the deep ocean made him feel small.

> Here, under a pressure which, if loosened, in a fraction of a second would make amorphous tissue of our bodies, breathing our own homemade atmosphere, sending a few comforting words chasing up and down a string of hose—here I was privileged to peer out and actually see the creatures which had evolved in the blackness of a blue midnight which, since the ocean was born, had known no following day; here I was privileged to sit and try to crystallize what I observed through inadequate eyes and interpret with a mind wholly unequal to the task.

Carson echoed this closely in "Undersea," in her description of the abysmal depths and their "blackness of primeval night in which the ocean came into being, unbroken, through aeons of succeeding time, by the gray light of dawn." Carson's picture of the topography of the sea floor, rendered as it might look to someone literally flying above it through the water, was also inspired at least partly by Beebe's observations in *Half Mile Down*.

Between their deepwater dives, Beebe and Barton had tried something they called "contour diving." The bathysphere, rather than simply being lowered into the ocean at a fixed location, was instead towed slowly behind the boat. Starting out in the shallows as close to shore as they dared, the bathysphere was dropped to within a few fathoms of the bottom and then slowly moved out to sea. Beebe watched the changing bottom and telephoned up to the winch operator to either raise or lower them. The bathysphere swam along the contours of the sea floor, rising over reefs, sinking down into holes, and aiming ever deeper as it traveled seaward. This was, in Beebe's estimation, much more dangerous that making a straight-down deep dive in the open ocean. If he were to miscalculate his distance or speed—or fail to notice some obstacle suddenly looming into their path—the bathysphere could snag and break loose. They had a few close calls. As Beebe dryly put it, "In spite of a constant watch ahead, accidents were on several occasions barely avoided." Although the bathysphere was sturdy and might have survived a collision with something on the bottom, smashing a window or becoming entangled in an outcropping of coral "would not have been so good," Beebe said.

Carson was beguiled by Beebe's adventures and observations. It's a little harder to imagine that she was tempted by them. Carson tolerated boats but did not really care for them. She never did become a competent swimmer and rarely ventured into water much deeper than her ankles. But as Carson began a more careful consideration of the book project, Elmer Higgins, her boss at the fisheries office, suggested that if she really wanted to get it right she needed to go "undersea" herself for a firsthand look. Bravely, Carson agreed that this was a good idea. A ride in a bathysphere presumably out of the question, Carson decided she should attempt helmet diving, preferably somewhere warm and inviting. When she wrote asking van Loon for an introduction to Beebe she told him she hoped Simon and Schuster might give her enough of an advance that she could "invest it in a trip to Bermuda or the Bahamas for this purpose." Carson wanted to talk with Beebe about how to go about all of this.

The business of an advance from her publisher was meanwhile a matter of concern to Carson, and she asked van Loon for advice. From the start, Carson proved to be a careful businesswoman when it came to every aspect of becoming an author; no detail was too small for her attention. By the spring of 1939 Carson had completed a chapter of the book. She sent it to Howe and asked if it was enough for Simon and Schuster to offer her an advance. Howe, who liked what he read, said he could give her $250 for an "option" on the book. This seemed reasonable to Carson and she told van Loon how much she liked and trusted Howe. But she also wondered what if, after writing more on the book, Simon and Schuster decided not to go forward with their option—or offered her final terms that were less than she might get from another publisher? And how long would the option period last? Carson said she felt "helpless" because she didn't know what a normal publishing contract looked like. Explaining these routine concerns to van Loon, Carson also confessed her deepest worry—one every author knows. When the book was done, would Simon and Schuster do its utmost to sell it?

"I suspect the best thing is just to go ahead and trust that everything will come out all right," Carson wrote, "especially since I do need some immediate cash so badly that I have no time to stop and bargain now. I should hate, however, to let them do the book if those who would have the job of putting it over are going to be luke-warm about it."

Carson and van Loon exchanged several letters about her arrangement with Simon and Schuster. Van Loon told her that a $250 advance was a good one, especially for a first-time author, and was better than he ever got "in the olden days." Rumors of publishers paying out big advances against royalties were just that, he said—except for a handful of bestselling writers whose work was all but guaranteed to do well. As for the eventual contract, van Loon said Carson could be confident she'd get the same royalty as everyone else in the business, as this was now all standard. Behind in his own work and testy about it, van Loon assured Carson that both he and Quincy Howe remained "101 percent" behind her. In a short, cranky note, he also lamented having wasted the better part of the past year "trying to make people understand the perils of Hitler." At the bottom of the page he drew a toothy, sharklike fish with a swastika on its flank.

Carson meanwhile completed an outline for the book to go along with the first chapter. She told van Loon she hoped it would cause Howe to increase his advance offer to $500.

• • •

Carson eventually agreed to the $250 advance—and Howe, in turn, said he'd pay her another $250 if Simon and Schuster exercised its option after seeing the first fifteen thousand words. Working evenings and weekends, Carson continued writing features for the *Baltimore Sun* while slaving away on the book. She apparently had no social life at all. In the summer of 1939, the Bureau of Fisheries was transferred from the Commerce Department to the Department of the Interior—a move that was part of Secretary Ickes's plan to concentrate conservation programs there. Carson's position and salary—which had recently increased to $2,300 a year—were unchanged. A year later, the bureau was merged with another unit at Interior, the Biological Survey, to form the U.S. Fish and Wildlife Service. Carson was transferred from Baltimore to a research laboratory at College Park, Maryland, where she continued editing technical reports and writing press releases and brochures.

Carson's ability to work invisibly into the small hours of the morning and her deliberate approach to research concealed an eagerness to gain the recognition and respect she believed was due any serious author. A year and a half elapsed after "Undersea" had come out before the first chapter of the book was done, and her letters to van Loon at the time made it seem that she was only barely started. This wasn't the case. In the fall of 1938, Carson, along with her mother and the girls, Virginia and Marjorie, had gone on what was a working vacation for Carson to the Bureau of Fisheries station at Beaufort, North Carolina.

A quiet and for much of the year steamy port city, Beaufort is near the southern end of the Outer Banks, a narrow two-hundred-mile-long chain of low barrier islands that lies just off the Carolina coast. On the islands' landward side are a series of sounds and protected bights that have long provided safe mooring for fishermen and seafarers. To seaward their shoals reach out for many miles beneath the waves—hazards that have wrecked ships and drowned sailors for more than four centuries, earning this treacherous edge of the ocean a nickname: the Graveyard of the Atlantic.

Beaufort is old, with some houses from the 1700s still standing. Its harbor is along Front Street, in a section of Taylor's Creek that opens onto a sound dotted with islands and salt marshes. The town breathes with the rhythms of the sea, its air heavy and salted, the boats lying at anchor in the harbor swinging first one way and then another with the changing tides. Although Beaufort is part of the mainland, a surrounding network of creeks and rivers made road access to the town circuitous until 1926, when a highway bridge finally joined a rail trestle in connecting it more directly to nearby Morehead City. In 1899, the U.S. Fish Commission had established a marine laboratory at Beaufort, in two buildings on Front Street. A year later, Congress made the research facility permanent—a southern sister of the station at Woods Hole. In 1902 a large, mansion-like laboratory was built on nearby Pivers Island, just west of the town proper. Its main floor housed an aquarium and a museum of mounted fish and marine exhibits.

Researchers at Beaufort conducted surveys of the local commercial fisheries and specialized in aquaculture experiments in an attempt to develop farming techniques for species such as mullet and oysters. For several decades the station raised thousands of diamondback terrapins in special pens that were continually refined to improve production. A small turtle that inhabits brackish marshlands where fresh and salt waters meet, the diamondback terrapin was a longtime food staple on the East Coast that came to be regarded as a delicacy as its numbers dwindled from overharvesting. Although the Beaufort studies demonstrated that the terrapins could be reared in captivity, nobody but the scientists took an interest, and terrapin farming never came to be.

Carson was intrigued by the terrapin project and the other work ongoing at the lab, but her real purpose in coming to Beaufort was to collect scenery for the story forming in her mind that yet needed a setting. From Pivers Island, Carson could observe the sand spits and tidal marshes of the inner sound, and on clear days could make out the black-and-white checkered 165-foot-high spire of the Cape

Lookout lighthouse. She found something to write about right next to the fisheries lab—an island of scrub and sand called Town Marsh that separated the channel of the Beaufort waterfront from a broad, shallow portion of the inner sound. In the distance beyond Town Marsh lay Shackleford Banks. A nine-mile ribbon of beach and dunes, it runs straight off to the northwest at a ninety-degree angle from the foot of Cape Lookout, which curves protectively around the tip of Shackleford. A century earlier it had been a whaling port. Long since deserted but for a few fishing shacks, it was now inhabited most noticeably by a herd of wild horses descended from Spanish stock that swam ashore from a shipwreck in the 1600s. The island is accessible only by boat; Carson probably hitched rides over to it with someone from the fisheries lab.

At no place on its length is Shackleford Banks more than a handful of feet above the high-tide line, but it changes the character of the sea just the same. On the outside the open ocean lashes at the beach, and contrary winds and fierce currents turn the waves into a confused and mighty froth. Along the inner shore the sound is calm. Carson, who likely stayed with her family in the nearby oceanfront community of Atlantic Beach, said the mistake most people make when they visit the shore is hanging close to the fishing piers and resorts—and thus to one another. Her preference, she said, was for the solitude found far away from such places. And nowhere had she felt this pull more powerfully than at Shackleford Banks, where half an hour's walk along the ocean side takes you out of sight of anything but the water before you, the sky above, and the long blinding rim of sand reaching off in either direction.

This "lovely stretch of wild ocean beach," as Carson thought of it, was to join Town Marsh in the opening of a book that, while as yet unwritten, had evolved from the ideas she'd initially discussed with Quincy Howe. Carson now thought she could give a "fairly complete picture of sea life" by dividing her story into three parts: one set at the shoreline, another on the open sea, and the third in the murk of the abyss. Each of these settings would feature one animal protagonist in a complex interplay with the ecosystem and its other inhabitants. Carson had a title in mind, too: *Under the Sea-Wind.* It was a phrase that had come to her from the same source that had inspired Henry Williamson—Richard Jefferies.

Like Williamson, Carson revered Jefferies. She was moved by the words "the wind, wandering over the sea" in his long prose poem *The Pageant of Summer.* This piece was for her a kind of sacred text, one that inspired a lifelong sense of wonder—a phrase she used often—for the natural world. Carson had a special affection for one passage near the end of the poem: "The exceeding beauty of the earth, in her splendour of life, yields a new thought with every petal. The hours when the mind is absorbed by beauty are the only hours when we really live. . . . This is real life, and all else is illusion, or mere endurance."

Surveying the sea or the sound from the dunes at Shackleford Banks or walking on the strand at the edge of the surf, Carson breathed in the sea wind and felt time slowing and everything but what was before her eyes melting away. She made notes and wrote out fragments of narrative, carrying with her each day a small spiral-bound notebook into which she poured her thoughts and observations. A careful and fastidious writer, Carson was much less orderly in her note taking and would flip open her notebook and begin writing on the first blank space she found, her thoughts becoming a random tangle of snippets that were interspersed with odd lists of expenses and items to pack.

Carson was attentive to colors and sounds, and to the endlessly shifting tones of light and shade under the temperate sun of the Carolina coastline. Looking down into a shallow pool where the tide had flooded the beach, Carson thought the lined ridges in the sand beneath the water looked as if the "shadows of surface ripples had dug deep and become permanent." She was struck by the way the tops of the sea oats in the dunes, bending before the wind to touch the earth, carved arcs in the sand as they swayed in the breeze. And always, her gaze was drawn to the sea: "The crests of the waves, just before they toppled, caught the gold of the setting sun then dissolved in a mist of silver. The sand in the path of each receding wave was amethyst, topaz, and blue black. A lone sanderling hunted the surf line, with busy probings of his bill. Two ghost crabs scurried about in the wet sand."

It is clear from her notes that Carson at this point thought *Under the Sea-Wind* would be a book for young readers. She wrote that it was important to make youngsters curious about the sea. More practically, she wondered in her notes what age of children would most appeal to publishers and how she might eventually describe the reading level the book required. Carson made lists of "things to include" and of potential "characters" in the story. Among these were squid, starfish, scallops, crabs, clams, and a big jellyfish. She thought she might make "a squid who lives in a wreck" the "villain" of the narrative. But she also wrote out long, technical discussions on subjects such as fish migration, and tried to imagine the phenological changes in the assemblage of birds that would occur on the shore in different seasons.

In the end, Carson ignored the question of who would read the book and simply wrote it the way she wanted to, in the voice that came most naturally to her. She drafted her manuscript in longhand on the backs of stationery bearing the letterhead "National Recovery Administration, Washington, D.C." By the spring of 1940 she'd finished five chapters, the first one-third of the book, and sent it off to Quincy Howe at Simon and Schuster where, as he told Carson a few weeks later, everyone loved it.

Shortly before the book's official publication on November 1, 1941, Carson sent a copy of *Under the Sea-Wind* to her editor at the *Baltimore Sun,* who wrote her a note saying how much he liked it except for the opening chapters that composed Book I, "Edge of the Sea." Carson would later admit that many readers felt the same way, though for her these five chapters about life along the threshold of the ocean—based

so much on her own observations at Beaufort and at Woods Hole—
had an inner meaning closest to the nature-as-spirit world of Richard
Jefferies and with an outer structure most like *Salar the Salmon*. In fact,
Carson began her book exactly as Williamson had his, near an island
close to shore where fishermen do their work and where the tides and
currents make a meeting place for many species of wildlife, including
the transitory visitors who stop there to hunt or breed or only rest on
their way to far-off destinations. Carson's island was based on Town
Marsh, and in a thank-you to the Bureau of Fisheries staff at Pivers
Island, the creatures she described there included a pair of diamondback terrapins.

Following Williamson's convention—and breaking her own vow
not to anthropomorphize—Carson gave names to some of her animal
characters, using a mix of scientific nomenclature and whimsical invention. A pair of sanderlings named Blackfoot and Silverbar are the
featured players in this opening section. The sanderling is a species of
sandpiper familiar to beachgoers for its entertaining habit of running
over the sand so close to the surf line that it seems to be chasing the
waves, though Carson had a different reason for putting them center stage. Sanderlings are long-range migrators, breeding among the
rocks and tundra of the high Arctic and overwintering on tidal flats
as far south as Patagonia. Carson was fascinated by migration, and by
the game of chance that takes place in the mass movement of animals
that breed in great numbers in one place and then succumb in waves
to predators and to hostile environments as they travel the earth on
their instinctive journeys.

Books II and III of *Under the Sea-Wind,* which tell the stories re-
spectively of a mackerel and an eel, were in mood and setting more
like "Undersea," watery and dark and densely packed with information about the diversity and tenuousness of life in the ocean. Unlike
what prevails in the frozen northern landscape, where the sanderlings
build cozy nests and guard their small clutches of hatchlings, here the
fish cast their unprotected offspring into the vast ocean by the thousands to begin life against odds so long that it would be accurate to

say that for each species, death is a way of life. Riding currents and swimming ahead of a ceaseless onslaught of hungry enemies, the fish and all their cousins of the sea—the spiny and the tentacled and the clawed—are a self-sustaining multitude in which every individual is both predator and prey, and whose numbers are winnowed every day.

Carson would later say that it was only in the writing of the book that she became aware that its true central character was the sea itself. As with "Undersea," she was at her best in describing that portion of the planet that is water:

> Between the Chesapeake Capes and the elbow of Cape Cod the place where the continent ends and the true sea begins lies from fifty to one hundred miles from the tide lines. It is not the distance from shore, but the depth, that marks the transition to the true sea; for wherever the gently sloping sea bottom feels the weight of a hundred fathoms of water above it, suddenly it begins to fall away in escarpments and steep palisades, descending abruptly from twilight into darkness.

Carson had high ambitions for *Under the Sea-Wind,* and as the reviews came out it appeared she had achieved something special. She was delighted when the book was named a selection of the Scientific Book Club, a recognition that it was as serious and as informed as it was entertaining. In a glowing review, the *New York Times* called *Under the Sea-Wind* a "beautiful and unusual book." The reviewer for the *Times,* Peter Monro Jack, explained that Carson was both a writer and government marine biologist. He thought the book's great strengths were its varied settings and the many creatures whose stories were told, especially the eel that breeds and dies in the open ocean but spends most of its life in inland freshwaters—an epic life history, Carson knew, that is the reverse of the salmon's.

A slightly more critical but still favorable review came from an important source—William Beebe. Writing in the *Saturday Review of Literature,* Beebe said that Carson had succeeded in making "the sea and its life a vivid reality." He "enjoyed every word" in the book, but complained that too many of them were technical and that the story was often overburdened with facts. Still, he added almost apologetically, the accuracy of Carson's science was never in doubt; the man who'd visited the depths of the ocean said he could not find a single error in *Under the Sea-Wind*. Beebe loved the "sureness and ease" with which Carson described life in the open sea, apparently unaware that the greater portion of her experience was with the shallows and the shoreline. A few years later, Beebe would include two chapters from *Under the Sea-Wind* in an anthology of writing by naturalists.

Despite the terrific notices, *Under the Sea-Wind* sold slowly at first—then hardly at all. Toward the end of January, *Under the Sea-Wind* had sold fewer than 1,300 copies, and weekly totals had dropped to only a handful. Carson was gratified when she learned the book would be translated into a Braille edition, but she was disappointed at learning there was no interest in publishing the book in England. In fact, Simon and Schuster's London agent relayed the complaint of one English publisher that the book was "poetical" and "broody" and full of fish names that would be unfamiliar to British readers. For those reasons and owing to "present conditions" in wartime London, *Under the Sea-Wind* would have no chance of success there.

Carson would later blame the failure of *Under the Sea-Wind* on the U.S. entry into World War II, which she believed obliterated readers' interest in books like hers. If she detected any irony in the poor wartime sales of a book that had been inspired by a Nazi sympathizer, she apparently kept such thoughts to herself. She always believed in the felicity of the literary lineage—Jefferies to Williamson to Carson—that was behind *Under the Sea-Wind*.

Two days after the Japanese attack on Pearl Harbor, Carson had gotten a letter from her PCW friend and mentor, Mary Scott Skinker. Skinker had followed developments on the publication of *Under the Sea-Wind* all through the fall and was immensely happy at her former star pupil's success. But now she conceded a preoccupation with a darker reality. "The world tonight is depressing," Skinker wrote, "and thoughts of friends in danger serve but to increase a sense of de-spair over the inevitable period of years we must face before we know anything resembling peace or security."

Whether *Under the Sea-Wind* was a casualty of war is impossible to know, but as Carson later put it, "the rush to the book store that is the author's dream never materialized." For a while, Carson held out hope that word of mouth would keep the book selling at a slow but steady pace. She kept close track of reviews, offered suggestions for serializing chapters of the book in magazines, and compiled lists of groups such as the Audubon Society and the American Fisheries Society that might be marketed to in direct-mailing campaigns. But a mailing to six hundred members of the latter resulted in only four or-ders. Carson also discussed with Simon and Schuster which category of the Pulitzer competition *Under the Sea-Wind* might be eligible for. Around the beginning of March 1942, Carson appeared on a Wash-ington, D.C., radio program about books and diligently provided its host—a woman uncannily named Mrs. Eales—with a ten-page memo detailing the origins and concepts behind *Under the Sea-Wind*. Shortly afterward, Carson was told by Simon and Schuster that their sales department now blamed the book's anemic performance at least in part on its title, which on reflection seemed too abstract and liter-ary. The publisher wondered whether she might consider changing it to something more like *Life Along the Atlantic Seaboard* for future editions—not that any were imminent.

For the better part of the next seven years *Under the Sea-Wind* languished. Sales never reached 1,700 copies. Carson complained to Simon and Schuster about what she saw as their halfhearted attempt to generate interest in the book—and what she believed was the pub-lisher's failure to attend to a long list of details that she worried over endlessly. Royalty statements. Reprint opportunities. The status of remaindered copies. At one point she argued with Simon and Schus-ter over whether *Under the Sea-Wind* was or was not still in print.

In the spring of 1948, she asked to be released from her contract with Simon and Schuster and requested that the publisher forgo its option on her next book. She wrote them a letter saying how disappointed she was that Simon and Schuster didn't have "wider interests and contacts in the field of nature writing" that could have maintained a "steady, continuing sale" of her book. She added that she felt this assessment was completely realistic. "Please understand," Carson wrote, "that I have never believed that *Under the Sea-Wind* would, under any circumstances, have been a run-away best seller; nor do I ever expect to want to write that kind of book."

Carson did not explain what she meant by "that kind of book." She later said that for a while she had doubted she'd ever write another book, period. She was wrong on both counts.

FIVE

This Beautiful
and Sublime World

arold Ickes, Franklin Roosevelt's strong-willed secretary of the interior, wanted to take over the Biological Survey and the Forest Service from the Department of Agriculture—along with Fisheries from Commerce and the Civilian Conservation Corps, which was being run by the army—and move them into his department. Ickes was a powerful New Deal figure. During Roosevelt's second term he was discussed as a potential future candidate for president. But there was resistance to his plans from the departments that would have to give up these agencies.

Ickes saw his chance in the fall of 1936, when the president informed him of an impending reorganization plan for most units of the federal government. He told Roosevelt what he wanted—and added that he'd like to rename his agency the Department of Conservation. Roosevelt liked the idea, but in the end opposition in Congress and from the USDA convinced the president to leave the name unchanged. Ickes got his new agencies all the same and soon combined

Fisheries and the Biological Survey in what amounted to a "conservation department" that lacked only the name.

It was a time when the abuse of the nation's resources had become evident across large areas of the heart of the country, where the great, flat American prairie was devastated. In the early 1930s the onset of a prolonged period of drought and intense heat scorched the over-tilled, exhausted landscape, turning its once rich, loamy topsoil to a powder that was borne aloft on the wind in roiling dust storms that could block out the sun. Some were so powerful that they drifted all the way to the East Coast, dropping dust and black rain on New York and Washington, D.C. One of the worst swept through the central United States, from Colorado through Kansas, and from South Dakota down to Oklahoma, on April 14, 1935—Black Sunday—carrying away three hundred thousand tons of topsoil, more dirt than had been dug out to build the Panama Canal. Five days later the storm reached Washington, D.C., where it darkened the early afternoon sky and interrupted a Senate hearing on soil erosion. Before the month ended Congress had passed the Soil Conservation Act, and twenty thousand Civilian Conservation Corps workers were moved from the Forest Service into the new Soil Conservation Service, where they would go to work establishing conservation districts and replanting sod.

President Roosevelt, enamored of the idea of planting trees in a part of the country that hadn't had many in the first place, pushed forward a plan to plant trees from the Canadian border to Texas. It was thought that trees would not only help to retain soil but would also increase rainfall. Some 220 million trees were planted, but most either died or were cut down by farmers when normal rainfall returned to the prairie years later and crops again covered the land from horizon to horizon.

Roosevelt's tree-planting scheme rested on the dubious premise that nature could be regulated on a large scale, and in this respect, it at least had a history—one that Harold Ickes was mindful of as he tried to consolidate conservation efforts within the Department of the Interior. The merger of the Bureau of Fisheries with the Bureau of Biological Survey in 1940 brought together two federal agencies with similar origins, but whose missions and methods had diverged. Both had been created by Congress for the purpose of maximizing economic resources through the monitoring and "control" of nature. Fisheries, the older of the two agencies, took a passing interest in aquatic pests such as starfish, which could destroy oyster beds, but was more actively engaged in rearing fish stocks in its network of hatcheries and in doing basic research as it did on the high seas from the *Albatross* and other vessels.

The Bureau of Biological Survey—fourteen years younger than Fisheries and originally called the Division of Economic Ornithology and Mammalogy—was set up mainly to advise farmers on the control of birds and animals that destroyed crops. In 1896, the agency changed its name to the Biological Survey to reflect a broader mandate in surveying wildlife—notably migratory birds—and establishing the geographic distribution of species that didn't always directly bear on agricultural output. But a decade later the bureau refocused its primary mission again on the control of agricultural pests—mainly birds and rodents that reduced crop production, and larger predators such as coyotes and wolves that threatened livestock. Survey managers were not ignorant of the fact that they were attempting to rebalance a natural order that had evolved over millions of years. After all, birds eat insects, which can also be harmful to crops, and coyotes and wolves eat gophers and mice. Whether nature could be made more friendly to modern man—that is, "controlled" through the selective culling of certain species—was unknown. They tried anyway.

The Biological Survey advised farmers and ranchers on several means of reducing coyote and wolf numbers, including shooting, trapping, and poisoning. But the agency more strongly promoted the "comparatively simple" and more effective technique of locating dens in the spring and killing the litters before they dispersed. Detailed instruction was offered in a circular that explained the pros and cons of various control methods. Attempting to shoot wolves or coyotes, for example, was generally a waste of time—unless a rancher happened to locate a den with pups where he might have a clear shot at one or both of the parents as they stood outside the den in the early morning or at dusk. Hunting the animals from horseback was even less likely to produce results, though the bureau acknowledged this could be "thrilling sport." Trapping and poisoning required careful attention. Traps had to be well disguised and either anchored in the ground or tied to a heavy rock that would exhaust a captured animal as it was dragged along over rough terrain. The preferred poison was strychnine, which was loaded into gelatin capsules available from druggists and then inserted into walnut-sized nuggets of beef suet—baits that could be set out along trails frequented by the animals. The rancher had to hope a wolf or coyote ingested a bait on an empty stomach, as the animal would then sicken and die in a matter of minutes— whereas if the poison was eaten after a full meal its action was slowed and the animal might travel a long distance and never be discovered. In 1907 more than 1,800 wolves and some 23,000 coyotes were destroyed across the country, a record. The Biological Survey estimated the economic value of livestock thus spared from predation at $2 million.

At other times, the bureau had engaged in pest control efforts that even then must have seemed implausible. In 1922 one of the agency's most experienced field agents undertook a bizarre experiment. Since the end of World War I, the bureau had been receiving inquiries from farmers about the possibility of reducing bird numbers through the use of poison gases developed for trench warfare. It was assumed that birds would be more susceptible to such toxic compounds and these could therefore be diluted to levels that would be safe for humans, livestock, and pets living near croplands. To increase the margin of safety, tests were undertaken to see if the gas could be applied to roosting areas, especially marshlands, which were usually somewhat removed from row crops. With assistance from the army's Chemical Warfare Service, several compounds were evaluated at the Edgewood Arsenal in Maryland. These included phosgene and chlorine gases, and dichloroethyl sulfide—mustard gas. The final report on mustard gas dryly summed up the whole effort: "Because of the dangers attendant with the distribution and subsequent exposure of 'mustard' gas in or near agricultural sections its use as a bird control agency must be greatly discounted." It turned out that mustard gas persisted in vegetated areas for days or even weeks and could be lethal to anyone who merely happened to walk through an area after it had been treated. It was also dangerous to handle and could be applied only from airplanes. Plus, poison gas didn't seem particularly more lethal to birds than it was for mammals. There was some hope for chlorine gas, which was fatal for birds at about one-sixth the dosage needed to kill a dog—but questions about how temperature and wind affected the dispersal of a "gas cloud" once it was loosed discouraged further testing.

By the end of the 1920s, the Biological Survey boasted that its predator-control efforts in stock-raising areas of the western United States—with the assistance of a number of other federal agencies—had routed a host of animals whose numbers had been dramatically reduced. For wolves, the agency declared, "the end is in sight." It was the same for cougars, lynx, and bobcat. Livestock depredation by these species was considered under control, and their ultimate eradication was thought to be "only a matter of time." Eradication, which in plainer language meant local extinction, remained a continuing goal. Strangely, the bureau did not regard bears as predators, even though bears are omnivores and occasionally dined on cattle, sheep, and even horses, and had to be dealt with to a "limited extent." Despite its best efforts, the bureau never did make much progress against coyotes. In 1927 federal sharpshooters and trappers killed thirty-eight thousand coyotes, and the agency estimated another fifty thousand succumbed to poisoning but were not found. This seemed to have little effect on the overall presence of coyotes.

Less noticed but having a greater economic return were the bureau's control efforts on "noxious" animals such as rats, mice, ground squirrels, and prairie dogs, which in 1929 were estimated to cause

$300 million in annual agricultural losses. After spending years try-
ing to find disease agents that could target rodents and small mammals, the bureau gave up on viruses and bacteria and concentrated
on poisoning programs. These worked but often had the unfortunate
side effect of increasing the populations of undesirable species in untreated areas adjacent to the poisoned ones.

The Bureau of Biological Survey also engaged in efforts to conserve species—especially waterfowl, upland game birds, and wading
birds prized for their plumages, all of which had been overexploited
by market hunting and lax game laws. In colonial America, as early
as the 1600s, there had been occasional efforts to regulate hunting
through local ordinances. These usually involved temporarily closed
seasons when game numbers appeared diminished, or prohibitions
against overzealous pursuits such as nighttime hunting. These laws
had little impact—in reality probably none—on game populations.

In the early 1800s, John James Audubon, the pioneer and bird
artist, spent several decades hunting and painting on the American
frontier. Working on his masterpiece, *The Birds of America,* Audubon
described a continent of unimaginable natural wealth. He believed
that American birds lived in such profusion that hunting could never
diminish their abundance. With a few exceptions—notably several
now-extinct species including the Carolina parakeet, the passenger
pigeon, the ivory-billed woodpecker, and the great auk—Audubon
was mostly right, although plume hunting eventually decimated
some species of wading birds, and market gunners did the same to
waterfowl.

Audubon—himself an enthusiastic hunter who posed the subjects of his paintings after first collecting them with his shotgun—
gradually came to recognize that a threat to American wildlife much
greater than hunting was the clearing of the forests and the conver-
sion of land to agricultural use. Once, while traveling down the Mississippi River to New Orleans in 1820, Audubon had been amazed
at the many acres of logs that had been floated downriver and were
waiting for the sawmills at Natchez and points south. He realized that

what he was seeing was the removal of a small part of the vast inland forest that harbored so many species of birds and animals. Audubon understood that American game had more to fear from sawyers and plowmen than it did from hunters.

In fact, it was hunters and explorers shortly after Audubon's time who first raised public concerns about wildlife conservation. The Boone and Crockett Club began organizing to promote sportsmen's interests in the late 1800s. One of the club's founding members was Theodore Roosevelt. In 1900, Congress passed America's first wildlife conservation measure, the Lacey Act. The bill banned market hunting and the interstate transport of game, and ended the importation of exotic species. In 1903, at the urging of the American Ornithologists' Union and the Audubon Society, then-president Theodore Roosevelt ordered the establishment of a federal bird sanctuary at Pelican Island on the east coast of Florida. He eventually added more than fifty game management areas around the country, precursors of the National Wildlife Refuge System.

In the nineteenth century there had been a dawning awareness that human encroachment and exploitation could threaten wildlife. No species demonstrated this more dramatically than the American bison. Before European settlement of North America, some thirty million bison roamed the Great Plains, and smaller numbers were found even in the eastern forests, all the way to the Atlantic coastline. But by the middle 1800s, the bison was vanishing.

Horses came to the New World with the earliest European explorers, and their eventual arrival on the Great Plains gave rise to a short-lived but intense equestrian hunting culture among the nomadic Indian tribes. The relationship between the American Indian hunters and the buffalo was mostly harmonious—although the Indians' respectful dependence on the animal was sometimes violated. In the early 1830s—the exact date is in dispute—several hundred Sioux buffalo hunters near Fort Pierre in South Dakota reportedly killed

1,500 bison in a single day. They cut out the tongues and traded them for whiskey.

But much greater depredations came at the hands of market hunters, both Indian and Euro-American, who shipped buffalo hides back east and down through the port of New Orleans by the tens of thousands, leaving the pale corpses from which they were stripped to rot on the plain. The destruction of the bison was also semi-official government policy. In the late 1860s, General William Tecumseh Sherman, the Civil War hero turned Indian fighter, encouraged commercial hunters in their pursuit of the rapidly diminishing herds in an effort to starve the Indians into submission so they could be removed to reservations. Uniformed cavalry troops were occasionally recruited for this purpose, too, and bison were sometimes fired on with artillery. By the 1870s, bison had all but disappeared from the southern parts of the Great Plains; a decade later it was the same in the North, where hunting excesses and drought brought the herds near to annihilation.

As early as 1832, the artist George Catlin, who'd traveled widely across the American West, had written that the bison was "so rapidly wasting from the world that its species must soon be extinguished." Catlin thought this might be prevented by the establishment of some kind of national park in the heart of the continent, where the buffalo and the Indian hunting culture could coexist in perpetuity. Decades passed, the buffalo dwindled, and nothing happened in the way of preserving natural areas. But in 1868, Congress approved Ulysses S. Grant's decision to protect and manage the fur seal population in the Pribilof Islands off Alaska. Then in 1872, Grant signed an act setting aside more than two million acres of northwestern Wyoming and prohibiting "settlement, occupancy, or sale" of the lands within its boundaries, which from that time forward would be reserved as a "public park or pleasuring ground for the benefit and enjoyment of the people."

The secretary of the interior was specifically charged with ensuring that there be no further disturbance to "timber, mineral deposits, natural curiosities, or wonders" within the park, which were instead to be maintained "in their natural condition." Congress, mainly concerned with protecting hot springs and geysers from opportunistic developers, mentioned in passing that there should be no "wanton destruction" of wildlife in what was to be called Yellowstone National Park. But within a decade a few hundred bison, remnants of the herds from the grassland plains to the east, were being harbored within the park's boundaries and Congress tightened wildlife protection measures at Yellowstone.

The federal government had also been brought into the business of conserving natural resources in California, where in 1864 the U.S. government ceded control of the Yosemite Valley to the state of California with the stipulation that it be preserved in a natural state. In the early 1900s, Yosemite was returned to the federal government and incorporated into a surrounding national park. In the interim a group of students and professors at the University of California, whose interest in the region went beyond wildlife, established a conservation group they called the Sierra Club, the purpose of which was "preserving the forests and other natural features of the Sierra Nevada Mountains." They enlisted the great naturalist and explorer John Muir as the club's first president.

In 1905, President Theodore Roosevelt established the U.S. Forest Service, an agency within the Department of Agriculture whose business was to oversee the country's rapidly expanding forest reserves. In a span of just four years, Roosevelt increased federal holdings of forest land from 63 million acres to more than 150 million. Field managers were needed to take charge of the government's sudden investment in this natural wealth, and among the best and brightest of the young recruits was a recent graduate of the forestry program at Yale University, twenty-two-year-old Aldo Leopold. In the summer of 1909, Leopold reported for duty at his first Forest Service posting, the Apache National Forest in the Arizona Territory. Arizona was not yet a state, and the Apache National Forest was so rugged and remote that there were no roads through it.

Though inexperienced—he bungled an initial three-month backcountry reconnaissance assignment—Leopold took to his work enthusiastically and in the coming years was promoted to several positions in the district. In 1915, worried about the vanishing game in the region, Leopold wrote a short treatise on the importance of conserving wildlife called the *Game and Fish Handbook.* At the time, the conservation movement had split between two opposing theories of proper resource management. On one side were the utilitarians, who believed that through "wise use" nature could be managed so as to maximize its productiveness, whether that meant planting and harvesting forests, or enforcing hunting laws and stocking game. On the other end of the argument were the preservationists, inspired by John Muir and the Sierra Club, who thought the only way to truly conserve wild lands and wildlife was to leave them alone—to set certain areas off to the side, permanently protected from human alteration. Like other recruits to the Forest Service, Leopold started out as a utilitarian. But he came to see that neither approach to conservation was perfect and that what was needed was a balance between wise use and preservation. In 1921, Leopold published a paper in the *Journal of Forestry* titled "The Wilderness and Its Place in Forest Recreation Policy." In so doing he introduced a new word into the vocabulary of conservation and offered a definition: "By 'wilderness' I mean a continuous stretch of country preserved in its natural state, open to lawful hunting and fishing, big enough to absorb a two-weeks' pack trip, and kept devoid of roads, artificial trails, cottages, or other works of man."

Leopold was not the first to appreciate the attraction of the wilderness. It had long been the subject of philosophical inquiry—Edmund Burke and Immanuel Kant both wrote essays arguing that people should not fear but rather adore the "beautiful and sublime" essence of nature, and eighteenth-century primitivists believed that the more civilized people became the less happy they were. The American wilderness had been irresistible to men such as Daniel Boone, whose "long hunts" out across the frontier had lasted years at a time, and

Henry David Thoreau, who professed a preference for wilderness over the city—though he wasn't entirely consistent on this point. The "wilderness" around Concord, Massachusetts, and at Walden Pond suited him, but when Thoreau traveled into the remote forests of northern Maine he was badly frightened by the "deep and intricate wilderness" that he thought could be endured only by men more like animals than other men. Such profound wilderness, he said, was "savage and dreary."

And yet it was that fearsomeness that made the wilderness so appealing to others—and all the more so as it disappeared. Theodore Roosevelt thought that an America without an untamed frontier was a country bereft of the thing that had given it a national character. Wilderness, Roosevelt said, was needed to sustain among the citizenry "that vigorous manliness" he believed to be the most essential virtue—and that was at risk as the country became more settled. When Roosevelt helped organize the Boone and Crockett Club in 1888, it was as much for the purpose of self-improvement as it was about promoting a shared passion for big-game hunting in the wilderness.

As more people came to live in larger, denser cities, the allure of wilderness increased. By the early twentieth century, the experience of wild places was seen as a restorative for agitated minds and city-bound souls—as it was thought to be by George Babbitt, the overfed, overstressed businessman in Sinclair Lewis's 1922 satirical novel, *Babbitt*. After escaping to Maine on a fishing trip with a friend, Babbitt comes home thinking himself a changed man. He felt "converted to serenity" and was convinced he could stop worrying about his business affairs and instead have more "interests," such as the theater and reading. Babbitt had, in fact, made only the most superficial contact with nature on his Maine sojourn, spending more time in the lodge playing cards and smoking cigars than he did fishing. But Lewis's point was that we *believe* in the healing powers of the natural world—whether we really experience it or not.

It was Aldo Leopold who articulated what real wilderness was and proposed incorporating wilderness preservation into the management of natural resources as matter of policy. Beguiled by the hunting and fishing on the headwaters of the Gila River in southwestern New Mexico, Leopold in 1924 helped establish the Gila Wilderness Area—the first protected tract of wilderness in the world. Leopold later left the Forest Service and moved to Madison, Wisconsin, where as a consultant to the Sporting Arms and Ammunition Manufacturers' Institute he continued doing survey work on game that further convinced him intelligent wildlife management could not be accomplished by hunting laws alone. More important, Leopold realized, was the protection of productive habitat that could sustain breeding, foraging, and migrating populations of game. In 1929, Leopold gave a series of lectures at the University of Wisconsin that would become the basis for his monumental and still influential book, *Game Management*. With its holistic approach to managing game by understanding and promoting a sustainable environment in which birds and animals could be hunted yet thrive, *Game Management* marked the true beginning of conservation biology and earned Leopold a professorship at the University of Wisconsin that he would hold for the rest of his life. In early 1934, Leopold was named to a three-man committee commissioned by the Bureau of Biological Survey and officially designated as the President's Committee on Wild Life Restoration— though it soon came to be known as the Beck Committee.

For years, the federal government had been looking for ways to stabilize and restore dwindling waterfowl numbers and to bring order to a chaotic system of state-based game laws that regulated hunting. Drought, habitat loss, and overhunting had decimated duck and goose populations. In 1918, Congress approved the Migratory Bird Treaty Act, an agreement between the United States and Canada that outlawed the taking of migratory bird species, except for a handful of game birds for which there were to be orderly hunting seasons and strictly enforced bag limits. But as Leopold had pointed out in *Game Management,* in the absence of habitat improvement waterfowl numbers would continue their downward trend while hunting seasons and bag limits, already being steadily constrained, would also continue to shrink.

The so-called Beck Committee was formed at the behest of a man named Thomas Beck, who was the editor of *Collier's* magazine, the president of a sportsmen's group called More Game Birds, and a personal friend of President Franklin Roosevelt. Beck and Leopold were joined on the committee by Jay "Ding" Darling, a popular and well-known editorial cartoonist with the *Des Moines Register* who'd won the Pulitzer Prize in 1924, and whose passion for conservation often found its way into his cartoons. The committee's job was to come up with a comprehensive wildlife conservation plan that would provide a framework for spending the $25 million the president had set aside for purchasing marginal agricultural land.

The deliberations turned contentious. Beck, whose main goal was to boost sagging waterfowl numbers, seemed preoccupied with the idea of setting up federal duck-rearing operations that he thought would do for migratory flyways what fish hatcheries had done for trout streams. Darling and Leopold were more interested in finding ways to improve waterfowl breeding habitats. After about a month, the committee submitted a plan that tilted toward land acquisition and restoration. Another month after that, Roosevelt named Darling—a conservative Republican—to replace the head of the Bureau of Biological Survey, who had abruptly resigned. Darling lasted only about a year and a half on the job, but in that time redirected the agency's conservation efforts toward habitat improvement in the refuge system. Darling also instituted a requirement that waterfowl hunters buy an annual duck stamp. He drew the first one himself.

In 1935 Aldo Leopold became one of the founding members of the Wilderness Society, a lobbying organization whose efforts eventually contributed to the passage of the Wilderness Act in 1964, a law that set aside nine million untouched acres of America.

• • •

Rachel Carson had been at work in the Interior building for only a couple of months when her group was transferred to offices rented for the FWS in Chicago. With the war under way, it seemed that official Washington was cramped for space. Carson, miserable about the move, reported there in August 1942. The relocation was mercifully short, and by May 1943, Carson was sent back to Washington with a $600 raise and shortly after arriving returned to the FWS offices at the Interior building. A year later, FWS created a new position—information specialist—and promoted Carson to it with another $600 a year raise. She now earned $3,800 annually. But while her career in government had been good to her, Carson longed for something different.

Sometime in early 1945, after William Beebe included two chapters of *Under the Sea-Wind* in an anthology of nature writing, Carson had written to her hero and told him she hoped they might meet sometime when she was in New York. Beebe wrote back that he'd be delighted. Apparently this meeting did not take place for several years, but in October 1945 Carson wrote to Beebe on a different matter. Might there be a job for her at the New York Zoological Society? Carson said she'd been thinking about this for months and that she had begun to doubt the wisdom of her current career path:

> As you may remember, I have been with the Fish and Wildlife Service as a biologist and writer for nearly ten years. Currently, I have been in charge of informational matters related to the wartime fisheries program. This specific assignment will soon come to an end. While I am offered a reasonably attractive future with the Service, for some time I have felt disinclined to continue longer in a Government agency. Frankly, I don't want my own thinking in regard to "living natural history" to become set in the molds which hard necessity sometimes imposes on Government conservationists! I cannot write about these things unless I can be sincere. So if a broader field is open I should certainly want to consider its possibilities.

Beebe wrote back to say he thought Carson would be a terrific addition to their staff and that he'd forwarded her inquiry to the president of the Zoological Society, Fairfield Osborn. Osborn answered that if Carson was truly "exceptional" they might be able to find a spot for her in the society's education department. Beebe forwarded this response to Carson, but said that such a position would be too modest for her talents and advised her against pursuing the matter. Carson followed this advice but made similar inquiries at *Reader's Digest* and the National Audubon Society—neither of which had a position to offer.

Meanwhile, she was impatient to get on with her writing and was always on the lookout for a likely subject. On November 12, 1944, Carson issued a press release reporting that an overwintering site for North American chimney swifts had been discovered in Peru. She promptly proposed an article on chimney swifts to *Reader's Digest,* which turned it down. That same month she published a story on bats and echolocation called "The Bat Knew It First" in *Collier's.* In April 1945, Carson's report on the Marine Studios aquarium at Marineland in Florida ran in a London magazine called *Transatlantic,* which specialized in stories from America. It was a challenging piece, as Carson had never laid eyes on the place. She had to do all of her reporting by letter, and at the time Marine Studios was actually closed because of wartime gas rationing. Carson somehow managed to track down enough key people in Florida to get her questions answered and to write a descriptive account of the aquarium, which was famous for its dolphin shows and the underwater viewing ports in the main tank that allowed visitors to watch helmet divers feeding the captive fish.

A few months later, Carson found a place for the rejected chimney swift story, selling "Ace of Nature's Aviators" to *Coronet,* which cut the piece extensively and paid Carson $55. In early 1946, Carson pitched a story about bird banding to a new magazine called *Holiday,* which had yet to bring out its first issue. Her first draft of the piece was a bloated 6,000 words long. She eventually cut it to 3,500 words—which *Holiday* accepted, paying her $500. Things were not always easy. Months before putting out an FWS press release about an outbreak of red tide on the Florida gulf coast, Carson tried to sell an article about it over the course of a few weeks to *Collier's, Reader's Digest,* and *Coronet.* They all said no.

Carson was friendly with two women, both younger than she was, who'd recently come to work at Fish and Wildlife. Kay Howe and Shirley Briggs were both graphic designers, photographers, and illustrators. They worked on FWS publications and shared an office next to Carson's. The three women were an island of femininity in the otherwise heavily masculine agency. Howe was pretty and had a sunny disposition; Briggs came off more sternly, though she bore a resemblance to Carson's beloved college professor, Mary Scott Skinker. The three of them sometimes lunched together, and they made "illegal" tea in an office closet almost every day. Briggs found Carson outwardly ladylike and soft-spoken, but learned that she had firm opinions about government publications and could be "pungent" in private.

Everyone liked Carson. Friends called her "Ray." Howe thought she seemed on the frail side—though she also noticed Carson's surprising stamina in the field. One time Carson had to spend a week in her friends' office when a group of FWS regional directors temporarily took over Carson's space for a conference. Briggs, in a letter to her mother, reported that the three women spent part of their time together trying to figure out how to clean up Carson's office when she got it back, as the men borrowing it smoked cigars constantly, dropping their ashes on the floor and "using strong language."

Carson was an avid bird-watcher. In the fall of 1945, she and Shirley Briggs joined a two-day Audubon Society excursion to Hawk Mountain in southeastern Pennsylvania. The "mountain" is only 1,506 feet in elevation, but the rocky outcroppings on its summit intercept the prevailing winds in such a way as to attract migrating eagles and hawks of all kinds. Once popular with hunters, Hawk Mountain was the first established refuge for raptors. During the fall flight, the great birds of prey flew by the mountaintop at close range, and they could be observed passing at eye level and sometimes even from above as they flew below the viewing area.

At the office, Carson's work was only a sometime source of inspiration. Most of the press releases she wrote did not suggest magazine stories and were usually routine updates about commercial fish and shellfish production. Carson also edited a steady stream of technical reports for the annual *Fishery Bulletin*. One of these papers, "Biology of the Atlantic Mackerel (*Scomber scombrus*) of North America," which concerned the fish's early life history, must have been a bitter reminder that she'd already told this story herself, more artfully but to no greater notice.

This dreary work—there are only so many ways to report the sardine harvest—was occasionally interrupted by something that caused Carson to take notice. In August 1945, Carson wrote the first of three press releases on DDT that left an indelible impression with her. On August 10, Carson issued a short but alarming notice to the operators of fish processing plants about the potential hazards of using DDT in their facilities. Carson reported that preliminary experiments indicated that DDT was toxic to animals and to humans when ingested, and its use in facilities where it could contaminate food products "might have serious consequences." Exactly what the fish processors were to do with this information was vague. Carson's release only advised them to "consult experts" about using DDT.

A couple of weeks later, on August 22, 1945, the FWS issued a much broader warning about DDT, this time including details of the latest findings from the ongoing DDT experiments at the Patuxent Research Refuge in Maryland. Carson didn't write this release, but she read it with concern. The need to protect armed forces in Europe and the Pacific from insect-borne diseases during the war had been so urgent, the report said, that "its effects on other organisms had to be overlooked." Now experiments showed that DDT killed birds and that even diluted amounts could be lethal to fish and other aquatic organisms. Still unknown was whether DDT was even more injurious to wildlife when it was used in the repeated applications that could be expected as the pesticide came into general use. Applying DDT to large areas or in concentrated amounts was, in light of the new evidence, considered "dangerous." In a telling passage, the release said flatly that natural enemies such as birds, small mammals, amphibians, and other insects were considered the "the cheapest, safest, and one of the best means of controlling insect pests." Replacing these with the unrestricted use of DDT "could conceivably do more damage than good."

Nine months later, in May 1946, Carson put out a longer and more detailed release on concerns the agency had about DDT. The U.S. Fish and Wildlife Service had compiled a new report intended to provide guidance for the safe use of DDT, though Carson's announcement of this was in language that hinted there might not be any such thing as "safe." The pesticide was likely to be injurious to wildlife, including commercially valuable species of fish and shellfish, unless it was applied only at "the lowest concentrations useful in insect control." And even then, the best that might be hoped for was "minimal" harm to nontargeted species.

In the spring of 1946, Carson and Shirley Briggs were sent to the Chincoteague National Wildlife Refuge, at the southern tip of Assateague Island on the Virginia coast, to begin work on the first in a series of ambitious pamphlets describing the natural histories of the federal refuges and explaining the work the U.S. Fish and Wildlife Service was doing in them. The series, titled Conservation in Action, was Carson's idea. As usual, her thoughts were expansive and literary. Conservation in Action would become a classic in the ordinarily unimaginative world of public information—and the high point of Carson's career as a government biologist and writer.

Over the course of several days, Carson and Briggs tramped and rode by car over the refuge and visited other areas by boat. Carson, as would be her habit on such expeditions, brought a copy of *Under the Sea-Wind* to give to the refuge manager. Chincoteague was a recent addition to the refuge system. The government had purchased its nine thousand acres, about one-third of Assateague Island, in 1942. The refuge, which looked across the narrow channel to Chincoteague Island, was established in 1945 as part of the FWS's plan for a system of staging and resting areas for waterfowl and other birds migrating along the Atlantic flyway on the eastern seaboard. Carson wanted everyone, whether they were visiting the refuge or only reading about it, to have a sense of why it was there and what it looked like, and early in *Chincoteague: A National Wildlife Refuge, Conservation in Action 1,* she offered a graceful description:

> Assateague is one of the barrier islands typical of the Middle Atlantic coast, never more than three miles from shore to shore, lying between Chincoteague Bay and the sea. Seen from the air, as the migrating waterfowl coming in from the north must see it, its eastern border is a wide ribbon of sand that curves around in a long arc at the southern end of the island to form a nearly enclosed harbor.
>
> Back from the beach the sand mounts into low dunes, and the hills of sand are little by little bound and restrained by the beach grasses and the low, succulent, sand-loving dune plants. As the vegetation increases, the dunes fall away into salt marshes, bordering the bay. Like islands standing out of the low marsh areas are the patches of firmer, higher ground, forested with pine and oak and carpeted with thickets of myrtle, bayberry, sumac, rose, and catbrier. Scattered through the marshes are ponds and potholes filled with wigeongrass and bordered with bulrushes and other good food for ducks and geese. This is waterfowl country. This is the kind of country the ducks knew in the old days, before the white man's civilization disturbed the face of the land. This is the kind of country that is rapidly disappearing except where it is preserved in wildlife sanctuaries.

Because Chincoteague was primarily a rest stop for many migrant species, its assemblage of wildlife was ever-changing. In cataloging the many birds that visited the refuge over the course of the year, Carson paid close attention to these seasonal shifts. Owing to its proximity to the sea, Chincoteague enjoyed mild winters, and some thirty thousand ducks—mostly black ducks, but also pintail, wigeon, mallard, teal, and others—stayed in the refuge through the cold time of the year, while another ten thousand or so sea ducks puttered in the ocean waiting for spring. These were joined by migrants arriving from the south in March, a month of transformation leading to April, when the shorebirds came in. Through spring and into summer, bird numbers fell, reaching their lowest point in midsummer, which Carson described as "the ebb between the flood tides of migration." Carson also wrote about oyster cultivation and clamming and about the special relationship between the refuge and its most famous inhabitants—the wild ponies of Chincoteague. No one knew how the ponies came to live there, but they were shaggy and rugged-looking as would befit animals that, as Carson put it, "live most of their lives within sight or sound of the surf." These small, sturdy, feral horses no longer lived on Chincoteague Island itself, but instead grazed within the refuge boundaries on Assateague Island by permit. Once a year the ponies were rounded up and made to swim over to Chincoteague Island at low tide, where they were corralled and the herd was culled in an annual pony auction. In the fall of 1946, while the first Conservation in Action pamphlet was still in production, Carson, this time accompanied by Kay Howe, was sent out again to start work on the next installment in the series.

The Merrimack River rises in New Hampshire and flows south to Lowell, Massachusetts, where it bends to the east and runs to the Atlantic Ocean. As the river nears the coast it comes to a series of small islands in the main channel. Just below these, on the south bank, stands a town, uncommonly charming even by New England standards, called Newburyport. The village is old but well preserved. Settled by English immigrants in 1635, it became a thriving port and ship-building center in colonial times. Its narrow streets are lined with Federalist-period houses and overlooked by the gleaming white steeple of the Church of the First Religious Society. In the heart of the town, at the confluence of three broader avenues, is Market Square, a commercial district flanked by rows of handsome three-story brick buildings that were built after a fire destroyed several blocks of the downtown area in 1811. At the end of the long waterfront by the river, the houses change over to shingle-sided saltboxes and ramshackle cottages as the Merrimack widens into a broad estuary. Two miles farther east at the river's mouth is the tip of Plum Island, a narrow wall of beach and high dunes that stretches along the coastline for eight miles to the south. Plum Island is separated from the mainland by a sound at its southern extremity and by a vast salt marsh closer to Newburyport on its northern end. The marsh, one of the most diverse and productive ecosystems on the Atlantic seaboard, is fed by the tides and by the Parker River, much smaller than the Merrimack, which comes into it from the west.

Since the earliest settlement in the area, Plum Island and the salt marsh had been an important resource for farmers, fishermen, clam diggers, sportsmen, and market gunners. Every summer farmers made several cuttings of marsh grass for hay. It was an unusual business, as the marsh was wet and soft and often inundated at high tide. The hay was dried by piling it in tall, domed stacks atop cedar posts driven into the mud. These "staddles," as the hay stands were called, rose above the marsh like thatched villages. Once dry, the hay was removed on flat-bottomed scows called "gundalows," or by dragging it out behind horses wearing "bog shoes," wooden saucers the size of dinner plates that were clamped to the horses' hooves and allowed the animals to walk over the muck. Fish camps and hunting shacks also dotted the island and the fringes of the marsh.

In 1929 a small, private bird sanctuary was established near the marsh. In 1942 the FWS acquired this tract and a large surrounding parcel, more than 4,600 acres in all, including the southern three-fourths of Plum Island, for the creation of a permanent refuge. This further erosion of hunting opportunities went down hard. The local residents, notably sportsmen and those who kept shacks on the island, were bitterly opposed to the establishment of the Parker River Wildlife Refuge, as it was designated. Meant to help restore duck numbers—which had plummeted in the 1930s and '40s—the refuge was seen as an unwarranted seizure of a natural asset that belonged to the people who used it.

The situation at Parker River demonstrated that the idea of natural resource conservation was still a long way from general acceptance. When Carson and Howe boarded the train to head north to begin work on *Parker River: A National Wildlife Refuge,* Conservation in Action 2, there'd been joking around the office that they should perhaps take disguises along, just in case. The Parker River assignment presented Carson with a challenge different from the one at Chincoteague. This time, in addition to capturing the natural majesty of the refuge, she had to make an argument for its existence—something that many people who lived near it didn't want to hear. Carson and Howe arrived in Newburyport near the start of duck season, unwelcome emissaries from Washington.

Carson was drawn to the kinds of places ducks and other birds visited; she felt the same pull of the sea, sand, and marsh. Not surprisingly she fell in love with Plum Island. There were cottages and larger homes on the north end of the island, but inside the refuge to the south it was wild. The ocean, rising over a level bottom, broke in long, sweeping rollers against a beach so straight that, were it not for the haze of mist and blowing sand hovering above the surf, you could see down the entire length of the island. The sea was changeable, a bluest blue under the sun, and the color of unpolished steel beneath stormy skies. Standing at the water's edge, Carson said, the loneliness of the Atlantic was palpable; there was nothing but water from there clear to Spain. Above the tide line the coarse sand rose up steeply to the dunes, which gave way to a tangle of craggy hills and deep wind-hollowed craters. In the looser sands grew bayberry and poison ivy and cranberries, and beyond this first carpet of greenery were thickets of shrubs and stunted trees that formed the spine of the island and harbored many animals, including pheasants and deer. On the inland side was the marsh. Nothing but water and grasses at high tide, it was a web of black, muddy clam flats when the water retreated.

Carson and Howe toured the island and marsh day after day, traveling with the refuge manager in a specially constructed "command car" that constantly threatened to roll over or bog down in the island's sandy mazes. Carson quizzed the refuge manager closely and took copious notes. Howe marveled at Carson's stamina, but it was taxing work and Carson confessed in a letter to Shirley Briggs that she thought she'd need to go off somewhere and hibernate when it was done. Carson said she was starved at the end of a long day in the field. They found a restaurant in Newburyport that served big steaks, and they ate there every night, sunburned and bruised and scratching at insect bites. Back at their hotel they shared whiskey from the flask Carson usually brought along for fieldwork. Howe hoped the weather, which had been dark and gloomy, would improve enough that she could try taking some color photographs to go along with the black-and-whites she had already shot. She wished for a telephoto lens, too, as the wading birds and ducks tended to stay out of range.

There were rumors in town that opponents of the refuge were planning acts of sabotage—and, in fact, Carson and Howe were shown some broken traps where ducks had been freed from a banding operation. The refuge manager assured them an animal had probably been responsible, but other members of the staff weren't so sure. Some of them warned Carson that getting shot at was a possibility. In the end, the only violence Carson and Howe experienced was in town one day when a wayward football struck the rear end of the car they were riding in.

Carson began the second Conservation in Action pamphlet with a blunt challenge to anyone who opposed the Parker River Wildlife Refuge. She wrote that it was New England's "most important contribution to the national effort to save the waterfowl of North America." Millions of Americans, she said, had a stake in this effort—two million duck hunters and many more bird lovers for starters, but also everyone who understood that wildlife was an important part of America's heritage that was threatened by the widespread loss of natural habitat to agriculture and other forms of development. The government meant to correct this situation and for that reason had now established some two hundred refuges for waterfowl across the country. Within this system of sanctuaries, none were so important as those located in the Atlantic flyway, the easternmost of the four main migratory routes connecting north and south across the United States. The reason, Carson explained vividly, was the concentration of birds that occurred along the Atlantic seaboard in places like the Parker River refuge:

> A striking fact about the Atlantic flyway—a fact which dominates the conservation problem—is the extremely limited area of its winter range compared with the vast extent of its breeding grounds. The nesting area extends from Greenland across much of northern Canada; the wintering grounds are confined to a narrow strip of coastal marshes along the east coast of the United States. A map of the flyway looks like a huge, distorted funnel with a long slender stem. Imagine that for one half of the year all the contents of the funnel have to be contained within the stem and you can understand the compression of birds within their winter range.

Parker River was the only federal refuge managed mainly for waterfowl that was within the northern part of the Atlantic flyway. Carson explained that following the breeding season some migrating waterfowl stopped there as they came south along the seacoast, while others that nested farther inland often made their arrival on the coast near Parker River. Carson—who after visiting the refuge spent a few days at the Audubon Society in Boston researching this information—said these facts had come to light through bird-banding projects, although the importance of Parker River on "one of the great highways of bird migration" had been known for generations. Among ornithologists, Parker River was considered the single most critical sanctuary location anywhere on the East Coast. When the FWS acquired the property in 1942, development of the refuge had to wait because of the war. But there were already signs that ducks were coming back. In 1944 only about two thousand waterfowl were seen in the refuge. By 1946 the number had risen to fifteen thousand.

The most common waterfowl species at Parker River was the black duck, a close relative of the mallard and much prized by sportsmen. Its strong flight makes it a challenging target, and its diet of mostly plants makes it fine table fare. But black ducks were in crisis. After they weathered the droughts of the 1930s better than other ducks, black duck numbers began falling precipitously in the mid-1940s. In 1945 the black duck flight had been considered a "complete failure." The reasons for the decline of black ducks were not completely known, Carson wrote, but among them were the drainage of wetlands by developers and a recent streak of bad weather during the nesting seasons in Canada.

Parker River and other waterfowl refuges could replace some of the ducks' lost breeding habitat. But the chief aim at Parker River was to provide a resting spot for migrating ducks. And this, Carson argued, was exactly why duck hunters should welcome the presence of the refuge. Although sportsmen could not shoot in the refuge, they could shoot near it. Having come to Newburyport in September, Carson had seen the situation for herself. Black ducks were present in the refuge throughout the year—a handful of local birds simply never went away—but it was in September and October, when the fall flight arrived from the north, that the area began to "get the feel of real black duck country."

"As you drive out from the town to Plum Island," Carson wrote, "you can see them gathering in the harbor, small black forms riding the outgoing tide, bobbing like boats at anchor. Today perhaps there are a thousand. Tomorrow morning there may be five thousand; next week as many more."

Carson had learned more than just the lay of the land and the composition of the flora and fauna at Plum Island. She also demonstrated a thorough understanding of duck hunters and of duck hunting—and of the black duck, a "dabbling" species that feeds in shallow water. She explained that because hunting was still permitted in areas adjacent to the refuge, waterfowlers could actually anticipate better shooting than ever because ducks resting in the refuge would trade in and out of the protected area in greater numbers.

To make the refuge more productive as duck habitat while at the same time avoiding the infringements on the local economy that many in the area had feared, the refuge managers were approaching their mission in two ways. One was to make improvements in the marsh. The other was to leave some things as they were. Clamming and hay cutting were allowed to continue as before. Meanwhile, the U.S. Fish and Wildlife Service, Carson wrote, was increasing the production of duck forage by constructing a system of impoundments in which water levels could be controlled. These were drained in the summer and planted with assorted grasses and pond weeds that ducks feed on. In the fall, the impoundments were flooded for arriving ducks to set down on and feast on the plants. There was also a new series of artificial islands in the marsh, built from marsh sod, that gave the ducks a place to nest that was safe from the tidal flooding that occurred during the breeding season and was preferable to the thickets on Plum Island and their resident predators. Carson, herself a bird-watcher but no bird hunter, included an inventory of birding opportunities at the refuge that made it an "irresistible attraction." It was almost possible to hear the chafe of corduroy and the clank of binoculars between the lines. There were more than three hundred bird species in the area, Carson reported, including some that were sufficiently uncommon that "the hope of surprising an ornithological rarity gives zest to often repeated visits." Having been there in the fall and not in the summer, Carson made no mention of Plum

Island's most quarrelsome inhabitant: the greenhead. An aggressive blood-feeding horsefly whose bite is excruciating, greenheads in July and August make the island hazardous to human visitors almost everywhere except on the windswept beach.

Altogether, Carson wrote four installments of the Conservation in Action series, and coauthored another that featured the Bear River Wildlife Refuge in Utah, a waterfowl sanctuary far away from Carson's beloved seashore and, at sixty-five thousand acres, many times bigger than other refuges she had visited. The fifth in the series, *Guarding Our Wildlife Resources,* was longer and different from the others: It was not about a specific refuge. It was, rather, a summary assessment of the state of wildlife conservation in the United States. Carson structured it as a serial tragedy—a story of natural wealth repeatedly squandered, differing only in the details from one class of wildlife to another. From America's earliest days, the pattern had been the same, whether it was beaver or ducks or salmon: What once seemed to be inexhaustible stocks had been depleted through overharvest, by the destruction of natural habitat, and, all too frequently, because of an ignorance of the basic biology of many game species.

The good news, Carson wrote, was that for many species—even some such as the bison and the whooping crane that had come perilously close to extinction—there was a recovery under way, thanks to an awakening among the public and in Washington. There were now three hundred National Wildlife Refuges. Three and a half million acres were devoted to reestablishing waterfowl and other migratory species, and almost fifteen million refuge acres harbored large mammals such as elk, deer, and bison, all of which were on the increase. Part of that success, Carson explained, was owed to a growing awareness that wildlife problems could not be addressed in isolation—that every species, including humans, was dependent on and embedded in the web of interactions that connects all living things.

Taking a decidedly ecological tone, Carson wrote that wildlife conservation did not serve only the interests of species in distress—or the concerns of hunters or fishermen or nature enthusiasts—but was in service to the totality of existence: "For all the people, the preservation of wildlife and of wildlife habitat means also the preservation of the basic resources of the earth, which men, as well as animals, must have in order to live. Wildlife, water, forests, grasslands—all are parts of man's essential environment; the conservation and effective use of one is impossible except as the others are also conserved."

Guarding Our Wildlife Resources was published in 1948. In the spring of that year, Aldo Leopold learned that Oxford University Press had decided to publish a book he'd been working on for seven years called "Great Possessions." The book was a collection of essays based on Leopold's seasonal observations of nature near a shack he kept as a country retreat in a wooded area on the Wisconsin River north of Madison. The Shack—everyone called it that—was a converted chicken coop. For Leopold it was a good place to be close to the earth, to think, and to write. But for a time he had trouble getting anyone committed to "Great Possessions." Four publishers had already turned it down before Oxford said yes. But Leopold died unexpectedly only a week after getting this good news. Oxford determined the book could still be published, though they didn't like Leopold's title and eventually came up with a different one. They called the book *A Sand County Almanac.*

In one of the book's essays, Leopold proposed what he called the "land ethic," a concept that, as he put it, "changes the role of *Homo sapiens* from a conqueror of the land community to plain member and citizen of it." An important principle of the land ethic was that conservation should not be undertaken for purely economic ends. Leopold wrote that of the twenty-two thousand higher plants and animals found in Wisconsin, no more than 5 percent could be "sold, fed, eaten, or otherwise put to economic use." Even so, each of these organisms was part of a "biotic community," the continuing stability of which depended upon their presence. When *A Sand County Almanac* was reissued in 1966 it was embraced by an environmental movement that had coalesced around the idea that nature was in charge of humanity and not the other way around. Leopold's explanation of the land ethic was seen as prophetic: "A thing is right," Leopold wrote, "when it tends to preserve the integrity, stability, and beauty of the biotic community. It is wrong when it tends otherwise."

And so American conservation had evolved over a half century, from the first tentative efforts at increasing wildlife populations by creating sanctuaries and establishing game laws, to a more generalized plea for the preservation of natural assets in their totality. The management of game remained central to this debate—it drove federal policy, and the economic support of sportsmen enabled Leopold and others to study resource issues. Yet Leopold and Carson now argued that conservation could not be confined to a select segment of the natural world, but was of necessity about the preservation of the myriad interspecies relationships that make up what Leopold called "the biotic community."

Leopold believed that conservation still had a long way to go because human beings tended to see the natural environment as a "commodity" that, if sufficiently restocked with animals to shoot and fish to catch, might be thought of as "conserved." This, he said, was not true. "When we see the land as a community to which we belong," Leopold wrote in *A Sand County Almanac,* "we may begin to use it with love and respect." Leopold realized that he was stepping beyond the limits of science in making this argument and that what he had written in *A Sand County Almanac* was an appreciation of the intangible features of nature: "That land is a community is the basic concept of ecology, but that land is to be loved and respected is an extension of ethics. That land yields a cultural harvest is a fact long known, but latterly often forgotten."

Carson and Leopold did not believe, as had the naturalists who had come centuries before them, that nature was the sacred and inviolate creation of God. On the contrary, it was human beings who left their marks upon the earth. But these were not necessarily permanent and need not be damaging. Humanity, they believed, is compelled to find a better way. The beauty of the conservation impulse—part of the "cultural harvest" as Leopold called it—is its optimism. If civilization overtaxed nature we have it in our power to restore it. And failing in this is to fail at protecting our own interests, since humanity is not apart from nature but of it. Essential to the idea of conservation was a belief that we could be the secular shepherds of the earth—gamekeepers for every living thing, ourselves included. In the fifth Conservation in Action booklet, Carson announced the "awakening of a vital conservation sentiment"—sentiment by its nature being among the most heartfelt and urgent of motivations.

Between the research trips to Chincoteague and Plum Island, Carson had managed to take an entire year's allotment of vacation in one four-week block. She had always wanted to see the Maine coast, and in July Carson and her mother—accompanied only by their two cats now that Marjorie and Virginia were grown—drove six hundred miles to Boothbay Harbor. They rented a cottage on the eastern shore of the steep-sided estuary of the Sheepscot River, which was less a river where it met the ocean than a long, broad saltwater bay rimmed with rocky tide pools that filled and emptied with the ebb and flow from the open sea. The cottage was hidden away in a forest of spruce and birch, and built so close to the water that Carson thought if she jumped out a window she'd fall in. There wasn't another cottage in sight and the only sounds were the cries of the birds, the tolling of a bell buoy, and the lapping of the water on the rocks. Sometimes when the wind came in from the south Carson could make out the sound of crashing surf.

Carson lost herself in bird-watching and exploring the tidal zone. She thought even the cats noticed how the water rose and fell. Enraptured, Carson wrote a letter to Shirley Briggs, telling her that if she could only figure out how to manage it she'd happily spend the rest of her life in Maine. Or the summers at least. Carson said that every night around sunset, they heard what she thought was the ethereal call of a hermit thrush. "I have never before heard the hermits," she admitted, "so am not sure, but it sounds the way one ought to sound."

Of all the places she'd visited on the Atlantic shoreline, the Maine coast was the one she wished to call home. Living by the sea and learning to read the changes that come over it as the days and months progressed through the seasons was something she'd been thinking about for a dozen years, ever since she'd discovered a remarkable book in a corner of the Pratt Library in Baltimore. The book was Henry Beston's *Outermost House*. Though not so well known or as overtly metaphysical as *Walden*—to which it is often compared—*The Outermost House* inspired in its readers an awe and longing for nature not unlike what many people felt in reading Thoreau's classic. To those who know it, *The Outermost House* is one of the great American books. Set on the outer arm of Cape Cod, the book follows the unfolding events of a single year as one might watch them from the window of a snug cottage standing on a high section of beach and looking out over the breakers upon the Atlantic Ocean—which is more or less just how it happened.

Beston was born in 1888 in Quincy, Massachusetts. Tall, sturdy, and disarmingly handsome—he looked a little like Ernest Hemingway—Beston attended Harvard and in the winter of 1915–16 served with the Section Sanitaire Américaine No. 2, an ambulance unit attached to the French army fighting World War I. Beston was nearly killed by an artillery shell at the Battle of Verdun, where more than three hundred thousand soldiers died in one of the grimmest struggles of the war. He returned to Massachusetts suffering the effects of combat fatigue and—much as Henry Williamson had done under similar circumstances—began writing.

In 1923, Beston did a magazine piece about the Coast Guard operations on Cape Cod, where nightly beach patrols were conducted alongside the crashing surf no matter the weather. Accompanying the patrols on their six-mile rounds, Beston found the experience bracing and a therapeutic distraction from the memories of war. In 1925 he bought thirty-two acres of sand dunes above the beach near the Eastham Life Saving Station, on the outer arm of Cape Cod about a third of the way up from the elbow where it bends to the north toward Provincetown. Here Beston built a two-room cottage, twenty by sixteen feet, that featured an abundance of shuttered windows, a brick fireplace, and an outdoor pump that was a surprisingly reliable source of fresh water. Beston, who envisioned the place as a weekend retreat, named it the Fo'castle. He kept a small writing desk and several comfortable chairs in the main room, where he often provided shelter and company for the beach patrol and was rumored to harbor the occasional bootlegger. One night when the surf was churning, Beston took in fifteen injured and waterlogged fishermen who had made it through the breakers after their boat caught fire and sank directly offshore from the cottage.

Beston stayed at the Fo'castle in the fall of 1925. A year later he was back for what he planned as a two-week stay. It turned into nearly four months, during which he began keeping a journal of what he saw and did. Beston continued his visits to the Fo'castle in every season through 1927, and as his manuscript grew he found that it could be assembled as if he had been there continuously over the course of a single year. It was a beautiful and vigorous life as he roamed the beach and the dunes—after walking on sand for a few months, Beston, who was over six feet tall, said he weighed 190 pounds and was "as strong as a bear." *The Outermost House* was published in the fall of 1928. Early on in the book, Beston explained his decision to live in the Fo'castle as a function of the irresistible pull of the sea in front of the cottage, the swampy lowlands behind it, and the high hills of clay and sand on which it stood:

> Outermost cliff and solitary dune, the plain of ocean and the far, bright rims of the world, meadow land and marsh and ancient moor: this is Eastham; this the outer Cape. Sun and moon rise here from the sea, the arched sky has an ocean vastness, the clouds are now of ocean, now of earth. Having known and loved this

land for many years, it came about that I found myself free to visit there, and so I built myself a house upon the beach.

Beston began his chronicle of a year on the beach as summer gave way to autumn. He followed the fading sun as it came back fainter each day and for ever-quickening hours, through quiet days and stormy ones, sometimes all but blinded by the dazzling sand and other times alone with his thoughts in the absorbing dark of night. Onward into winter and then spring and back to summer, in one vivid, tactile passage after another, Beston watched a world of air, sand, and water, finding in just these three ingredients a universe of meaning. There were spectacular shipwrecks and moments of serenity so intense that Beston felt himself lost in a cosmic panorama:

> Night is very beautiful on this great beach. It is the true other half of the day's tremendous wheel; no lights without meaning stab or trouble it; it is beauty, it is fulfillment, it is rest. Thin clouds float in these heavens, islands of obscurity in a splendour of space and stars: the Milky Way bridges earth and ocean; the beach resolves itself into a unity of form, its summer lagoons, its slopes and uplands merging; against the western sky and the falling bow of sun rise the silent and superb undulations of the dunes.

When Carson first read *The Outermost House,* the idea that such a life could be lived left an indelible impression—though any thought that she might one day retreat to the seashore must have seemed impossibly remote. In 1940, while she was working on *Under the Sea-Wind* in the library at Woods Hole, Carson and two friends had taken a day trip out to Eastham. They walked up the beach and soon enough found the Fo'castle, which Carson recognized at once from Beston's description of it. Carson was transfixed and sat for a long time on the dunes gazing out to sea. She said she was going to write a letter to Beston about the experience, but she put it off, and the moment of imagining herself inside the picture he'd created in *The Outermost House* passed.

The Conservation in Action series had given Carson a chance to write something that went outside the usual boundaries of government work, but it did not alleviate the longings she had confessed to William Beebe in 1945. She was searching for something, and the failure of *Under the Sea-Wind* still ached. As always, her thoughts turned toward the ocean.

Carson was impressed by the torrent of new sea-related scientific findings published in the years after the war. She kept files of clippings and technical papers about waves and weather and currents, and was particularly interested in what was being learned through the increased sophistication of sonar. One observation that had at first baffled researchers was the discovery of a "phantom bottom" in the ocean. Everywhere around the world, sonar soundings taken during the day indicated a depth of only around 250 fathoms, even in areas known to be many times as deep. At night, however, this "deep scattering layer," as the sonar-reflecting region was also known, vanished. Researchers eventually determined that the phantom bottom was alive and comprised a variety of fish, squid, and tiny marine creatures such as krill that make a daily migration out of the depths at nightfall to feed on plankton near the surface. Biologists already knew that marine life tended to congregate at the surface after dark, as netting operations were more successful at night. Migration remained one of Carson's favorite themes, and the global scale of this heretofore undetected mass movement of animal life was amazing, as the community of marine organisms within this movable realm would ultimately turn out to be the largest discrete biomass on earth.

By 1948, Carson had begun thinking about a new book, one that would explore our dependence on the ocean—which she believed was going to increase as the land endured the ever-greater degradations of modern civilization. She made plans to visit Woods Hole to work in the library at the end of the summer, but she delayed this trip and instead went up at the end of September for an eight-day fish-census cruise aboard the *Albatross III,* the U.S. Fish and Wildlife Service's latest incarnation of the former Bureau of Fisheries research vessel. Equipped with sonar, dredging winches, laboratories, and refrigerated fish storage rooms—and now powered by an 805-horsepower diesel engine—the 179-foot-long steel-hulled ship could cruise for 4,500 miles without refueling.

Carson began enlisting a group of experts she hoped would help her with information and might review the book for accuracy. One of these was the marine biologist Henry Bigelow, who was an expert on waves and the oceanographic curator at the Museum of Comparative Zoology at Harvard. Carson hoped Bigelow would have access to the great backlog of unpublished ocean research that had accumulated during the war. He didn't, but he did eventually agree to read and comment on a chapter about waves when Carson had it done.

Carson was not shy about asking eminent scientists to read and correct her work, or to give up their own hard-earned findings. It was a stepwise process. When someone agreed to help she often asked for an introduction to the next expert in the chain. Most of them cheerily joined the team, even though Carson was essentially an unknown writer. It helped that as she built out her network many of the people with whom she corresponded liked her writing and understood that she was someone who could translate hard science into digestible prose—although this took a few scientists outside of their comfort zones. One university professor Carson consulted about the geology of the sea floor told her he didn't comprehend flourishes such as "sense of the sea" or "dominance of the sky."

An unusual source was the Norwegian ethnographer and explorer Thor Heyerdahl, with whom Carson initiated a brief and strained correspondence. Heyerdahl believed—incorrectly—that Polynesia had been originally colonized by people who crossed the Pacific Ocean from South America. In 1947, Heyerdahl and a crew of five built a forty-five-foot-long balsa raft, the *Kon-Tiki,* and sailed it 4,300 miles from Peru to the Tuamotu Islands in an attempt to prove his theory, in the end proving only that it could be done. A no-doubt skeptical Carson wrote to Heyerdahl requesting information about South American colonization of the South Pacific. Heyerdahl wrote back, politely informing Carson that he was himself at work on a book about the *Kon-Tiki* expedition and was not in a position to share information, though he promised to keep her in mind and let her know when his book was out.

Carson—who might or might not have known Heyerdahl was writing a book that she might eventually compete with—probably couldn't decide if he was an expert or a nut. She waited more than a year and then wrote again to Heyerdahl, this time asking him about the phantom bottom. Carson had heard that at night great numbers of small squid jumped onto the *Kon-Tiki* as it drifted westward over the open ocean. Did Heyerdahl think the deep scattering layer might, in fact, be made up mainly of squid?

Heyerdahl, civil but again testy, reminded Carson that his book about the voyage—titled simply *Kon-Tiki*—was already out in six languages and was being translated into seven more. All of his important observations, he said, were in the book. In the meantime, he faced another deadline for a second book about his ethnographic theory of Polynesian settlement and was too busy to give her a detailed answer. He said, however, that he felt pretty sure that the deep scattering layer was not squid, or certainly not mainly so. It was true that shoals of squid sometimes launched themselves out of the ocean like flying fish, and had on occasion "bombarded" the raft. But this happened both at night and in the daytime. At night, they had observed a diverse assortment of marine life around *Kon-Tiki,* including luminous plankton and tiny copepods—but also larger fish. One night, they saw the phosphorescent trails of three large bodies passing below them that appeared to be longer than the raft. Heyerdahl said he didn't think of himself as an expert, but he was inclined to believe that the scattering layer was mostly plankton. In the end Carson decided to leave the exact composition of the deep scattering layer an open question.

Carson had meanwhile signed on with an agent. She talked with several before settling on Marie Rodell, an editor and mystery writer who was just launching a literary agency in New York. Carson sent Rodell a chapter about the formation of an island that she'd already written for "Return to the Sea," as she was calling the new book. Rodell sent it around to several magazine editors, hoping to sell parts of the book as Carson completed them. Rodell also shopped *Under the Sea-Wind* to book publishers for a possible reissue. But nothing happened on either front.

Undaunted, Carson sent Rodell several copies of *Under the Sea-Wind,* along with a note wondering if she should personally inscribe one for Rodell. "When you have made me rich and famous," Carson joked, "it might be nice to have."

SIX

Author Triumphant

B y February 1949, Carson had finished two more chapters of "Return to the Sea" and told Rodell she had another two "reasonably well in mind." It's hard to know if this was true—Carson tended to exaggerate her progress and underestimate the time she'd need to complete new material. But she was immersed in work on the book. A month later she told Rodell that she'd written less than she'd hoped to, though in revising one of the completed chapters she had so enlarged it that it could now be split in two.

In April, Rodell—working hard for one of her first clients—discussed the book with the editor in chief of Oxford University Press in New York, who expressed interest. By May she was in serious discussions with Oxford. Carson wanted an advance of $1,000 on signing a contract. Oxford preferred to split that into two payments of $500, one at signing and the other later. On June 3, 1949, Oxford sent Rodell the contract for "Return to the Sea," along with a request that they be allowed to read each chapter as it was finished. Carson resisted this, telling Rodell she wanted to revise the chapters with her alone and show them to Oxford only after a final polishing. Meanwhile, Carson made plans for a helmet-diving trip in Florida in July.

Shirley Briggs accompanied Carson on this adventure, which could only be described as a failure, though it would be transformed into a mythological feature of Carson's biography. Carson and Briggs arrived in Miami at the same time as a stretch of bad weather. They went out several times, only to be turned back by rough seas and murky water. Carson thought the storm clouds made the many small barrier islands look "lonely and melancholy." Between these unsuccessful excursions, Carson and Briggs amused themselves by wading in the surf and enjoying dinner at Howard Johnson's.

Carson finally got to climb into the water in a protected area of Biscayne Bay that was about eight feet deep. She was surprised by the sudden lightness of the eighty-four-pound helmet once she went under the surface. Carson descended on a ladder that nearly touched the bottom and spent a few minutes gazing out of her rapidly fogging faceplate. This surely took a large measure of courage for the swimming-challenged Carson, who said her anxiety was increased by the disconcerting whooshing sounds of the pump as it sent air down the line and into her helmet. A strong current was running and Carson had been warned not to stray from the boat. So she clung to the ladder, feet firmly planted in a bed of seaweed. She saw a few brightly colored fish and climbed back up.

Carson carefully recorded her impressions of being underwater in a small, blue Collegiate notebook. She also unself-consciously wrote to William Beebe—a man who'd walked over miles of ocean reef and ridden the bathysphere a half mile down into the abyss—with a full accounting of what she referred to as her "diving experiences." She said that the difference between having dived and not having dived was "tremendous." In fact, she said, the whole world now seemed different to her.

A couple of weeks later Carson was off again, this time with Marie Rodell to join another collecting cruise aboard the *Albatross*

III. On July 27, 1949, the two women boarded the ship at Woods Hole, bound for a two-week fish-census trip to the Georges Bank. Carson later remarked that few women had been out on such a vessel and that probably fewer still had ever visited the Georges Bank fishing grounds.

It was a hot morning. Rodell thought the *Albatross III* looked "small and uninviting" as it lay alongside the wharf. The crew warned them—in Carson's case unnecessarily, as this was her second time aboard—that the narrow ship was notorious for its heavy roll in any kind of sea. Rodell said the ship's sideways heaving through the waves was hard to describe, but it seemed they corkscrewed along in a "figure eight," with a pause midway around. On the second day the weather turned cold and windy. Rodell and Carson sat in the wheelhouse and watched the sonar tracing the ocean bottom. Carson found this thrilling, especially when the *Albatross III,* after traveling for hours above areas of level sea floor, at last passed over the sheer canyon walls that outline the Georges Bank, and the bottom fell away sharply into the abyss. The dredging hauls—a deafening clank and grind of winches and cables—were mostly disappointing, with only a few unremarkable fish coming up in the nets. The crew tagged some flounder and haddock. One day they saw a couple of sharks and a school of dolphins. They had several days of fog.

Like all writers trying to make a living, Carson was always thinking about her next project even while in the middle of the current one. Not long after returning from the *Albatross III* cruise, Carson told Rodell about a collection of Mexican bird paintings by the artist Louis Agassiz Fuertes that had been found in the U.S. Fish and Wildlife archives, and which the Fuertes family was now interested in publishing. Carson wanted to write an introduction for the book, and for a while it seemed the Fuertes family was all for it. But when Rodell brought the idea to Oxford they declined on account of the expense involved in color reproduction. Rodell then approached Paul Brooks, the editor in chief at Houghton Mifflin, with the project.

Brooks quickly read *Under the Sea-Wind* and was impressed. He agreed to consider the Fuertes book, though he actually had something else in mind.

In the summer of 1950, Brooks and Carson exchanged letters about an idea circulating at Houghton Mifflin for a guide book to the seashore. Carson, who as usual sensed possibilities in what sounded like a dull topic, expressed interest. She told Brooks that she thought what was wrong generally with guidebooks is that they too often merely cataloged "creatures" without giving the reader a complete picture of where they lived and how they might be observed. The problem of what to put in and what to leave out—the book could be only so long, after all—was secondary to how the writer approached the material. Carson thought this should involve giving the reader an idea of what life was like for the plants and animals described, and that this would entail an "unobtrusive" discussion of various seashore environments and what someone could expect to find in them. This was obviously what Brooks wanted to hear, because he took a few weeks to get everyone at Houghton Mifflin on board and then wrote back and asked Carson if she'd be willing to do it. He said he completely agreed with her that the "environmental point of view" was essential to the book. "I imagine you have plenty of demands on your time," Brooks said, "but I hope that you will consider this seriously."

Carson told Marie Rodell she was keen to do the book, and as it eventually worked out she could not settle on terms with the Fuertes family and nothing more came of that project. Had Carson, Rodell, or Brooks known what they were getting into, this discussion might have gone differently. Rachel Carson was about to become the most famous writer in America.

In the fall of 1948, Carson decided to seek financial assistance to help support the research she planned for "Return to the Sea." She applied for a grant of $2,250 from the Eugene F. Saxton Memorial Trust, run by the publishing firm of Harper and Brothers. Carson provided a detailed preliminary outline of "Return to the Sea" and an itemized list of expenses she expected to incur—the main one being a four-month leave without pay from the U.S. Fish and Wildlife Service. Carson explained that she would need the money she was applying for regardless of any offer a publisher might make for the book, as the fellowship was meant solely to defray expenses whereas a publisher's advance would be much-needed income from the project.

In July 1949, the Saxton Trust informed Carson that she had won the fellowship. To help them with the public announcement of the award, they asked Carson to submit a brief biography. Elated, Carson dashed off a four-paragraph bio and sent it in with a cover letter saying that the prospect of being able to take time off to work on the book without interruption was "incredible good fortune" and that she would be "eternally grateful to the Trustees for making it possible." Thinking the Saxton people would be happy to know how the book was coming, Carson also mentioned that her agent had recently agreed to terms with Oxford University Press. Carson got a letter back from the trust a few weeks later with the surprising news that they wanted some of their money back. Specifically, they wanted to deduct the amount of Oxford's advance from Carson's grant.

Furious, Carson pointed out that she had explained in her application that she needed the fellowship money irrespective of any publisher's advance and reminded them that their own rules provided for such "exceptional" funding of established authors. The trust disagreed. They wrote to her again, accusing Carson of taking advantage of the trust's limited resources and in effect denying funding to other deserving applicants. To make the point more firmly, they informed Carson that the people who worked for the Saxton Trust did so without compensation and, in fact, even paid the cost of the postage on the letter telling her so.

The Saxton episode turned out to be one of many such instances in Carson's life that showed how fiercely she defended her finances and her writing. Quick to anger at any perceived injustice, Carson loathed compromise. Eventually, Marie Rodell stepped in between

Carson and the Saxton Trust, working out a deal in which Carson would receive her quarterly installments of the fellowship until she turned in the manuscript to Oxford in the spring—a deal that amounted to about three-quarters of the original grant and that was better than what the trust had proposed. Carson wrote to the trust to grudgingly accept these terms, though she warned them that her publishing contract provided for an extension of the deadline and she might not deliver it on time. In that event, she said, she assumed she'd get her final installment of the grant. In the meantime, Carson concluded, would they please send her two copies of the official news release announcing her fellowship?

Carson got the second $500 installment of her advance from Oxford in the fall of 1949. She also received a courtesy copy of a new book from Oxford—Aldo Leopold's *Sand County Almanac,* which she said she looked forward to reading, though for the time being she was preoccupied with selling parts of her own book. As Carson finished more chapters of "Return to the Sea," Rodell dutifully circulated them to one magazine after another. She sent seven chapters to the *Atlantic,* which turned them down after thinking it over for three months, saying that while they liked the material, the magazine had recently acquired a multipart story with a "sea theme" and that another article in a similar vein would be too much of a good thing. This was an echo of what had happened with *Under the Sea-Wind,* which the magazine had initially expressed interest in serializing but never did, citing conflicts with other nature pieces. More rejections stacked up: *Holiday, National Geographic, Coronet, Collier's,* the *Saturday Evening Post,* and on and on. Although most of the rejections were polite, one editor at *Town & Country* complained, "I don't like Miss Carson's writing at all." In her correspondence with Rodell, Carson remained upbeat and didn't dwell on the steady refrains of no. In any event, she was still writing, and now she had something else to contemplate.

In April 1950, Carson and Rodell started talking about changing the book's title to "The Sea Around Us." Apparently, neither of them was familiar with a poem by T. S. Eliot called "Dry Salvages," though Carson would later discover it on her own. "Dry Salvages" is one of the poems in Eliot's *Four Quartets*. The Dry Salvages is a real place, a group of rocks on which a lighthouse stands off the coast of Cape Ann in Massachusetts. Part of the poem goes like this:

> *The river is within us, the sea is all about us;*
> *The sea is the land's edge also, the granite*
> *Into which it reaches, the beaches where it tosses*
> *Its hints of earlier and other creation:*
> *The starfish, the horseshoe crab, the whale's backbone;*
> *The pools where it offers to our curiosity*
> *The more delicate algae and the sea anemone.*

Eerily, the poem touched on more than just Carson's new working title. In the line that includes "hints of earlier and other creation," Eliot raises the theme on which Carson planned to open her story of the sea. Carson wanted her readers to understand that the sea was the earth's incubator and that we are all descendants of the life forms that first arose and evolved in the sea. Evolution changed but did not end our relationship with the sea, and that is why men are drawn to the ocean and fascinated by its secrets. In one of several little brown notebooks in which Carson jotted chapter outlines, sources, and even early fragmentary bits of narrative, she tried out several possible beginnings for *The Sea Around Us*. One of them was "So long ago that we do not know when it happened—and certainly we do not know how—living creatures developed in the sea. Developed and evolved until all the major groups of animals and many of the plants had arisen."

Carson didn't keep those words in the book, but she stuck with the new title, and in June 1950, Oxford said they liked it, too. June was proving to be an exhilarating month, as Rodell had gotten her first nibble. *Science Digest* offered fifty dollars for a condensed version of one chapter. Rodell was just about to say yes to this when something surprising happened. She heard from Edith Oliver, a young part-time editor at the *New Yorker* magazine. Oliver was a lively character. She'd studied acting and had appeared on several radio dramas, including *The Philip Morris Playhouse*. For four years in the late 1930s and early '40s, Oliver had written the radio quiz show *True or False?* and later wrote and produced another game program, *Take It or Leave It: The $64 Question*. She started contributing to the *New Yorker* in 1947, writing short pieces for "The Talk of the Town." She would eventually spend more than thirty years as the *New Yorker*'s influential drama critic. But in 1950 her job apparently included reading manuscripts that arrived at the magazine's offices. One that she read and fell in love with was Carson's chapter on waves from *The Sea Around Us*. Oliver told Rodell how much she liked the excerpt and asked if she could see more. Rodell abruptly told *Science Digest* to wait.

It would be hard to overstate the importance of the *New Yorker*'s interest in *The Sea Around Us*. The magazine—literate, revered, slightly snooty and widely read because it was—had the power to make an author's reputation and send book sales soaring. Carson, however, remained calm while Rodell continued her efforts at placing chapters of the book with other magazines. But the *New Yorker* kept asking to see more. By midsummer Oliver had carefully read five chapters and had gotten eight more to look at. She'd also begun sending the material, with her enthusiastic endorsement, to the magazine's editor in chief, William Shawn.

Carson thought the magazine was only trying to decide which chapter to publish and hoped they'd make up their minds on one soon. "Darn the *New Yorker*," she told Rodell. "I wish they'd get busy with waves and get it in print by September some time. It just might mean a thousand bucks, plus some nice advertising." Oliver promised Rodell they'd make a final decision on the material by the middle of August. Rodell, meanwhile, sold the *Yale Review* a chapter on the volcanic origins of Bermuda called "The Birth of an Island" for seventy-five dollars. She sold another on ocean salt to the patiently waiting

Science Digest, explaining that it had been "too technical" for the *New Yorker.* But the rejections continued as well. *Reader's Digest* turned down a chapter on the connection between ocean currents and climate, telling Rodell, "The piece isn't quite right for a large measure of popular impact," a statement that proved as ironic as it was clumsy.

Sometime around the middle of August 1950, Rodell learned that the *New Yorker* was not interested in publishing a chapter of *The Sea Around Us*—they wanted to publish ten chapters. William Shawn himself would do the editing, and while it was understood the chapters would have be condensed they would still represent a large portion of the book. Carson told Rodell she was "in a daze." A month later, Carson wrote to Rodell that she was going into the hospital for a few days.

Despite her eager participation in intramural field hockey during her college days, as an adult Carson always struck people as slight, bordering on frail. She suffered occasional illnesses, but this sounded more ominous. Carson was going to have a "small cyst or tumor" removed from her left breast. She tried to reassure Rodell—not entirely convincingly—that the surgery was minor. But the chance that it could turn out otherwise caused Carson to deliberate carefully on a surgeon:

"The operation will probably turn out to be so trivial that any dope could do it," she told Rodell, "but of course there is, in such cases, always the possibility that a much more drastic procedure will prove necessary. They tell me the present method is to section the tissue while the patient is still under anesthesia, and if there is reason to do so, they go right ahead with a much more extensive operation. Hence the need for a surgeon with some judgment. In any event, I'll be at Doctor's Hospital, where a very dear friend is a nurse, and will be in excellent hands in that respect. I'm going to try to get it over with next week."

The surgery came off uneventfully and the mass removed from Carson's breast was benign. Carson dashed off to the North Carolina shore for a short and needed vacation. The ocean was wild, as it was "blowing a gale," she told Rodell.

Carson's correspondence from this time shows a subtle change coming over her. She still signed her letters "Ray," but there was a new insistence in them. Carson was determined that her second book would not end up like the first, and despite the waves of good news enveloping *The Sea Around Us,* she continued to microman- age every phase of its prepublication life—while worrying endlessly about future projects and income. Carson was impatient with Oxford for not yet having the book in galleys so it could be considered by the Book-of-the-Month Club. Rodell reminded her that Oxford had accommodated a delay in the book's publication schedule in order to let the *New Yorker* bring out its excerpts. In addition to the Fuertes book, which was, for the time being, still on the table, Carson was planning the seashore guide for Houghton Mifflin, plus a book of essays for Oxford. She recklessly told Rodell she thought she could work on all three projects at the same time. In October 1950, Car- son—who'd gotten a $900 advance from Houghton Mifflin—applied for a $3,000 Guggenheim Fellowship to help finance the travel she'd need to undertake for the seashore book, enlisting support from her ever-widening network of expert mentors.

Carson was never shy about mentioning awards she received, and she put in for them and collected them avidly. One of the references she listed on her Guggenheim application was William Beebe. Beebe told her he couldn't understand why she needed a fellowship, given that she enjoyed so much success selling chapters of *The Sea Around Us,* but said he was flattered that she thought his name would help her chances. Then in early December 1950, Carson learned that "The Birth of an Island" in the *Yale Review* had won the AAAS–George Westinghouse award for science writing. Established in 1946 by the American Association for the Advancement of Science with funding from the Westinghouse Educational Foundation, the award carried a prize of $1,000. Riding this whirlwind of attention, Carson mentioned to Rodell that she was thinking of turning *The Sea Around Us* into a documentary film—admitting that Rodell would probably think her "utterly mad" for having such an idea.

There were strains at the FWS. Carson had been promoted to editor in chief of the Division of Information and now earned $6,400 a year. Her colleague Kay Howe had been chosen to do the illustrations for *The Sea Around Us,* but now it seemed they might be on the move. Rumors were circulating that FWS was going to be relocated. Cities on the list as potential destinations included Kansas City, Denver, and Albuquerque. Carson hated this prospect and warned Rodell that such a move could make it nearly impossible to carry on her work on the seashore book, as any of those places were far away from the ocean and from her publishers and agent. She said she'd fight to keep "her unit" in Washington so as not to risk a dislocation that would be "utterly destructive of everything worthwhile I might be doing."

March 1951 brought mixed news. Staples Press, a London publishing house, was going to bring out a British edition of *The Sea Around Us.* Carson also learned she'd received the prestigious Guggenheim Fellowship, a happy development that was partially offset when the Book-of-the-Month Club chose General Omar Bradley's *Soldier's Story* over *The Sea Around Us* as a main selection. Carson's book would be an alternate. Astonishingly, *Vogue* magazine bought the chapter on ocean currents that *Reader's Digest* had turned down.

In April, Carson got her first advance copies of *The Sea Around Us.* She and Rodell were disappointed in the binding, which was so flimsy that the books began falling apart with the slightest handling. While the first printing was under way, Oxford agreed to rebind all the copies still on hand and to use the improved binding on all copies going forward. In May, William Shawn sent Rodell a check from the *New Yorker* for $5,200, along with a note: "We are delighted about publishing this. Thank you for sending us that original chapter, on Waves, and starting us off on the whole happy venture." Rodell deducted her 10 percent and forwarded Carson the balance. The next month, Carson applied for a year's leave without pay from the FWS. By midsummer she would be contemplating never returning to government work. She told Rodell she believed *The Sea Around Us* could do well enough to carry her for a few years. "If I'm not solidly established as a full time writer by that time I ought to be shot anyway," Carson said.

The ten chapters from *The Sea Around Us* appeared in consecutive issues of the *New Yorker* on June 2, 9, and 16, 1951, under the headline "The Sea: Unforgotten World." Tantalizingly, the pieces ran as a "Profile." *New Yorker* profiles were legendary but had never before been about something other than a person. The challenge to the magazine's readers to think of the sea as a living entity matched the enticing *New Yorker* format, in which a long article began on a full page and then wended its way, never jumping to the back of the magazine but always just continuing on in long, single columns of type that ran through and alongside one captivating ad after another. The opening article came to an end midway down page 59, next to an ad for a product that you could evidently take anywhere and forever: Amelia Earhart luggage.

The response to "The Sea" was overwhelming. The *New Yorker* reported that the series generated more letters to the editor than any profile in the magazine's history and that they were, almost invariably, filled with praise for the author and for the *New Yorker*'s inspired decision to publish her. Walter Winchell, the prominent newspaper and radio gossip reporter, read the first installment and reported that the series was a "cinch for reprint in anthologies," apparently unaware that it would shortly come out as a book. Many readers wrote to the magazine wanting to know more about Carson. Form letters went out in response: "At one time aquatic biologist on the staff of the Bureau of Fisheries, Miss Carson is now Editor-in-Chief of the United States Fish and Wildlife Service. In working on the Profile of the Sea, she took part in an oceanographic expedition in the North Atlantic and engaged in diving among the Florida coral reefs." The *New Yorker* was still parked on nightstands around the country when Oxford published *The Sea Around Us* on July 2, 1951, and the buzz about Carson turned into a roar.

In the spring of 1950, Oxford had learned about a book called *The Sea and Its Mysteries,* by John S. Colman, that was being published in England. It soon developed that the book also had a U.S. publisher and would come out in America later that year, far ahead of *The Sea Around Us.* Colman was director of the Marine Biological Station at Port Erin on the Isle of Man, and Carson and Oxford were understandably concerned about this competition. But when Colman's book came out it made little impact—which led to a different worry. Was the ocean a subject of only slight interest to readers?

Carson thought *The Sea and Its Mysteries* had been dismissed as "an introduction to oceanography," possibly because that's essentially what it was. Evenly written but without the grace and awe Carson brought to the subject, *The Sea and Its Mysteries* was not at all the kind of book Carson had set out to write.

Carson's particular genius was in making science come so alive that the reader did not think of it as science. Introductions, after all, are often soon forgotten. Instead, Carson distilled ocean science as if it were the most fascinating and comprehensible thing in the world, making a challenging subject plain to everyone. It would be hard to imagine a popular book more densely packed with scientific information than *The Sea Around Us*—or one that travels so entertainingly through the facts. The ocean was always a story to Carson, and she told it like one. She began at the beginning, with a quote from Genesis—"And the earth was without form, and void; and darkness was upon the face of the deep"—perhaps seeing no contradiction between the biblical explanation of creation and the one she proceeded to offer, which was all about physics and geology and biochemistry on a roiling, evolving planet that had taken billions of years to become itself. In Chapter 1, "The Gray Beginnings," Carson explained the latest understanding of the origins of the earth, its ocean, and how life began—a majestic opening rendered in simple terms:

> Beginnings are apt to be shadowy, and so it is with the beginnings of that great mother of life, the sea. Many people have debated how and when the earth got its ocean, and it is not surprising that their explanations do not always agree. For the plain and inescapable truth is that no one was there to see, and in the absence of eyewitness accounts there is bound to be a certain amount of disagreement. So if I tell here the story of how the young planet Earth acquired an ocean, it must be a story pieced together from many sources and containing whole chapters the details of which we can only imagine. The story is founded on the testimony of the earth's most ancient rocks, which were young when the earth was young; on other evidence written on the face of the earth's satellite, the moon; and on hints contained in the history of the sun and the whole universe of star-filled space. For although no man was there to witness this cosmic birth, the stars and the moon and the rocks were there, and, indeed, had much to do with the fact that there is an ocean.

The earth, Carson wrote, was about 2.5 billion years old and had been, when it first formed, a ball of hot gases that gradually cooled and then liquefied. Somewhere after this condensation but before the earth's crust completely hardened, the sun's gravitation pulled at the still-plastic surface of the earth and caused a great, oscillating solar tide that finally rose so high that it became unstable, came loose from the planet, and fell into orbit around the earth as the moon. The earth continued to cool, its surface becoming a hard, barren sheet of rock beneath an atmosphere that filled with water vapor. Carson, acknowledging that there were competing theories, wrote that the continents had been much as they are now since early in the earth's history.

Eventually it began to rain. The rain washed minerals from the rocks and collected in the low areas of the earth's uneven crust, and in time the oceans were formed. And there, in the warm, salty sea, a handful of light elements—including carbon and nitrogen, hydrogen and oxygen, sulfur and phosphorous—combined into complex molecules of protoplasm that had the ability to reproduce themselves and initiate the continuous thread of life—though, as Carson cautioned, "no one is wise enough to be sure."

All of this represented the state of knowledge at the time, and it was mostly wrong. The earth is much older, more than 4.5 billion years, and the moon is believed to be a chunk of the earth that was blasted from the planet when it collided with another large body during an early phase of the development of the solar system. The continents are much younger than the earth. As recently as 250 million years ago they were all part of a single supercontinent now called Pangaea. And while the exact sequence of chemical events that gave rise to life remains unproven, the publication of *The Sea Around Us* came on the eve of a series of discoveries through which science would at last look deep inside the "protoplasm" that is the basis of life.

In 1951, just as *The Sea Around Us* came out, Linus Pauling of the California Institute of Technology discovered that proteins are composed of long chain molecules called polypeptides that are made from twenty different amino acids. Two years later, James Watson and Francis Crick, working at Cambridge in England, discovered the structure of DNA and explained that in addition to being self-replicating, DNA was also a template for RNA, which chemical machinery inside the cell uses to assemble polypeptide chains into protein. This one-way flow of genetic information—DNA to RNA to protein—became formally known as the Central Dogma of biology.

And yet the beauty of Carson's opening chapter was that it did not rely on perfect scientific accuracy but rather on being so graceful in the telling that if one were to correct it with just a handful of discoveries made over the ensuing half century it would still track, and not very differently from the way Carson composed it. While life evolved in the sea—a theory not in dispute then or later on—the earth's land masses were barren, and in a few sentences Carson captured the sheer brutality and emptiness of a place without life:

> Imagine a whole continent of naked rock, across which no covering mantle of green had been drawn—a continent without soil, for there were no plants to aid in its formation and bind it to the rocks with their roots. Imagine a land of stone, a silent land, except for the sound of the rains and winds that swept across it. For there was no living voice, and nothing moved over its surface except the shadows of the clouds.

There's an old saying that great writing is simple but not easy, and so it is. The search for that one plain but inobvious word that will do the work of five, the agony of untangling a complex idea that has become a mess of phrases in the writer's mind, the willingness to keep doing it over and over and over again until it is right—all of that plus some luck yields prose so clear that it seems a child could have written it. Carson said that the "backbone" of the work she did on *The Sea Around Us* was "just plain hard slogging—searching in the often dry and exceedingly technical papers of scientists for the kernels of fact to weld into my profile of the sea." Her information came from more than a thousand sources, she said, and she had been helped more than she could say by the many experts who volunteered their thoughts and insights. What she did not talk about were the many hours late at night, when she worked best, that had been devoted to making prose out of fact—though to her readers this was everything. Wind and wave and salt, the life of the darkest deep ocean, the great currents that traverse the globe and set the climate—these are magnificent things that, without care, become lifeless on the printed page. Here was Carson on what happens when humans reach an island and its ecosystem is no longer insulated from the rest of the world:

> Most of man's habitual tampering with nature's balance by introducing exotic species has been done in ignorance of the fatal

chain of events that would follow. But in modern times, at least, we might profit by history. About the year 1513, the Portuguese introduced goats on the recently discovered island of St. Helena, which had developed a magnificent forest of gumwood, ebony, and brazilwood. By 1560 or thereabouts, the goats had so multiplied that they wandered over the island by the thousand, in flocks a mile long. They trampled the young trees and ate the seedlings. By this time the colonists had begun to cut and burn the forests, so it is hard to say whether men or goats were the more responsible for the destruction. But of the result there was no doubt. By the early 1800s the forests were gone, and the naturalist Alfred Wallace later described this once beautiful, forest-clad volcanic island as a "rocky desert," in which the remnants of the original flora persisted only in the most inaccessible peaks and crater ridges.

Carson wrote that one of our "blackest records" was the destruction of ecosystems on oceanic islands, which are unusually susceptible to the effects of the invasive species that hitchhike around the world with human travelers. Birds, goats, hogs, cattle, dogs, rats, and cats—these could transform abundance into barrenness, as could saws and axes and guns. She did not mention, though she might have, the human diseases delivered upon islands where some illnesses were unknown and against which the native population had little resistance.

Carson's interest in exotic species was prescient, as were the changes she reported in the world's climate. There was, she wrote, a groundswell of evidence that the earth was getting warmer. Carson pointed to rising sea levels, melting glaciers, and shrinking areas of sea ice in the Arctic. Reports from fishermen and ornithologists indicated that fish and birds were extending their ranges northward as the sea in the higher latitudes got warmer. All of this was, Carson wrote, part of the long-term cycling of the earth's climate, over which shorter-term changes were sometimes superimposed. In other words, a shifting climate was normal and to be expected, and was most likely the result of complex interactions involving tides, changes in the earth's orbit, alterations in the great ocean currents, and perhaps varying levels of solar activity.

She did not mention, though she might have, the theory that rising levels of carbon dioxide in the atmosphere caused by human activity were amplifying the natural greenhouse effect—an idea that had been around for a half century but was still widely doubted. Carson, in fact, noted several near-term beneficial effects of a warming climate—longer growing seasons and better commercial fishing harvests in the northern ocean. Over a longer period, well, nothing is permanent on the face of the earth, and in times past the oceans have risen and fallen, changing the shape of the world:

> Where and when the ocean will halt its present advance and begin again its slow retreat into its basin, no one can say. If the rise over the continent of North America should amount to a hundred feet (and there is more than enough water now frozen in the land ice to provide such a rise) most of the Atlantic seaboard, with its cities and towns, would be submerged. The surf would break against the foothills of the Appalachians.

In 1951 the printed page was alive and omnipresent, the dominant feature of the media landscape. There were more than two thousand daily newspapers in America. Every city of any size had several, and each of them had a literary editor. The papers set aside ample spaces committed to reviews, columns, and even excerpts of popular books. And there were the glossies—*Look, Life, The Saturday Evening Post, Holiday, Collier's, Coronet,* and, of course, *The New Yorker*—that also devoted many column-inches to literature. Five decades hence, authors would sell their books in ten-minute interviews on TV, but in the early 1950s you published and then you waited for the reviews.

The Sea Around Us generated nearly universal critical acclaim. The book was reviewed so thoroughly, so favorably, and so widely that few people could have been unaware of the phenomenon named Rachel Carson. Writing in the *New York Herald Tribune,* Francesca La Monte, who was associate curator of fishes at the American Museum of Natural History in New York, said Carson had done what no one before had managed: "The story of the sea with its islands and mountains and depths and of mankind's attempts to solve its mystery and exploit its treasures has been told before and often," La Monte wrote. "But Rachel Carson has made of it one of the most beautiful books of our time."

This, it turned out, was the consensus. One review after another heaped praise on *The Sea Around Us.* Everyone noted Carson's lyrical powers, and use of the word "poetic" by reviewers bordered on unanimous—although Jonathan Norton Leonard took exception to this characterization in the *New York Times Sunday Book Review.* Leonard wrote that the errors poets make when they write about the sea "annoy scientists," whereas scientists attempting to write about the subject too often got lost in their own "bleak and technical jargon." But *The Sea Around Us* would raise objections on neither side, he said. "It is written with a precision more than sufficient for its purpose," Leonard wrote, "and its style and imagination make it a joy to read." Leonard, in fact, seemed smitten. "It's a pity," he wrote, "that the book's publishers did not print on its jacket a photograph of Miss Carson. It would be pleasant to know what a woman looks like who can write about an exacting science with such beauty and precision."

Some reviewers expressed alarm over Carson's description of a warming climate and rising seas. Nobody took issue with Carson's emphasis on evolution as a central feature of life on earth—though the reviewer for the *Indianapolis Times* felt compelled to point out that the sea is "the source of our life, speaking biologically and not theologically." The critic at *Newsweek,* in an otherwise glowing review that called *The Sea Around Us* "hypnotic," cautioned that too much of a good thing sometimes got to be too much, period. "In only one respect does [Carson's] book fall into the weakness of so much modern nature writing," *Newsweek* said. "A kind of scientific piety pervades such prose, mournful references to endless cycles and astronomical distances, which begin by being impressive and end by becoming almost magical incantations."

Carson landed on the cover of the *Saturday Review of Literature,* which ran another extremely positive review. An accompanying profile reported that she had researched the book, in part, by "diving among the Florida coral reefs," where—evidently in response to being queried about this—she told the *Review* it was hard to walk over the sea floor, but so exhilarating that one didn't mind. "We surmise she wouldn't mind anything to do with her beloved ocean," the *Review* concluded. The *Buffalo Evening News* agreed: "Part scientist, part poet, and inevitably, one assumes, part sunbather, Miss Carson has written a superb book, one half-way between the Thoreau of the 'Journal' and the Darwin of the 'Beagle.'"

Carson never objected to the exaggerated claims about her supposed helmet diving exploits, nor did she mind being described—as she was in many reviews—as a working scientist with a gift for writing, rather than the other way around. A week after its review of *The Sea Around Us,* the *New York Times Sunday Book Review* carried a short note about Carson that seemed to have been based, at least in part, on an interview with her. The piece said that Carson had taken up helmet diving at the urging of William Beebe and had made "a number of dives in the reefs" in Florida. The *Times* reported that Carson called these experiences "interesting" but said they didn't really have much to do with her book. Unwilling to amend her diving "experiences" to the singular and unable to resist a further embellishment, Carson added that she thought "the fish must have been pretty surprised to find a woman looking out at them from the helmet."

In a publicity piece written for her British publisher, Carson herself pointed to the cruises on the *Albatross III* as having been a major part of her research for *The Sea Around Us.* Candidly she conceded that she was little more than an observer on these collecting trips. She again alluded to having done "a little helmet diving on the coral reefs off the coast of southern Florida." The image of Carson as a salt-splashed scientist braving the rolling seas of the North Atlantic or submerging herself among the fish in tropical waters was, meanwhile, at odds with a publicity photo that made the rounds, in which a pretty but docile-looking Carson was captured standing on a dock with a pair of binoculars hung from her neck.

Proving that everyone seemed to have fallen in love with Rachel Carson, Oliver Deane Hormel, the book editor for the *Christian Science Monitor,* offered a physical description of the suddenly prominent author, calling her "slight of figure, modest, unassuming." Hormel said Carson had an "elfin quality about her" that contrasted with the "serenity of her serious, wide-set, intelligent eyes." Society columnist Mary Van Rensselaer Thayer, careening wider of the mark than she could have imagined, referred to Carson as Washington's "newest glamour gal."

In a short essay she wrote for the *New York Herald Tribune,* Carson tried to give her swelling legion of fans a more down-to-earth picture of herself. This time avoiding any claims for her ocean adventures, Carson explained that she was really just a dogged researcher who consumed so many technical reports and scientific articles that she sometimes questioned why she had tackled such a large and difficult subject. People are often curious about how writers work, and so Carson revealed a few things about the lonely, quiet hours that are an author's lot.

Admitting she was a slow writer who revised her work over and over, she said that she worked best late at night, and that when she'd had stretches of uninterrupted time to devote to the book she often wrote through the night nearly until dawn—and then slept during the day. It had taken her many years to learn to compose on the typewriter, and she still relied on longhand for difficult passages or when, for some reason, the words came more slowly than usual. Reading was a source of both inspiration and escape, she said, and some of her favorite sea stories included Melville's *Moby-Dick,* Beston's *Outermost House,* and a book about a voyage up the Amazon called *The Sea and the Jungle* by H. M. Tomlinson. Carson added that she always kept a copy of Thoreau's *Journal* and a volume of Richard Jefferies's nature essays by her bedside, reading a few pages from one or the other being a pleasant ritual before she went to sleep each day.

She wanted everyone to know that she was, in the end, an ordinary person: "In minor ways I am a disappointment to my friends, who expect me to be completely nautical. I swim indifferently well, am only mildly enthusiastic about seafoods, and do not keep tropical fish as pets. Speaking of pets—my very closest non-human friends have been cats."

To be fair, Rachel Carson wasn't the first writer to let the press make more of her than she was. And she also had to endure the opposite. Many reviewers expressed surprise that a woman had written a book like *The Sea Around Us*—the implication being that the rigors of science and the forbidding aspect of the ocean deeps should have made these subjects off limits to her. The *Cleveland Plain Dealer* referred to Carson as a "government girl," calling to mind a woman in makeup and heels parked behind a typewriter in Washington. The *Boston Post* described her as both bold and feminine, as if these should be mutually exclusive. Perhaps, the *Post* speculated, she was a mermaid: "Apparently there are few photographs of Miss Carson anywhere on view, but we have worked this out. Rachel is probably no lady scientist at all, but an enchantress who lives in a cave under the sea, and there the light is awfully bad for pictures of authors."

It's doubtful that many of these reviewers read the acknowledgments in *The Sea Around Us,* an extended thank-you note to the many experts and archivists who had helped her, revealing an author whose work was mostly carried out in libraries and by way of the U.S. Postal Service.

Carson also heard from friends, colleagues, and an avalanche of readers. Among Carson's fans were Alben Barkley, the vice president of the United States; Fleet Admiral Chester W. Nimitz; and one Thor Heyerdahl. Carson had been sure to see that Heyerdahl received a copy of *The Sea Around Us,* as she had managed to include what little information he'd given her in the book. Heyerdahl sent a postcard from London—there was a picture of *Kon-Tiki* on the front—telling Carson her book was wonderful. "I am in the midst of writing an ethnographic work," Heyerdahl said, "but could not drop your book when I picked it up." Carson also got a generous note from her former editor Quincy Howe, who'd left Simon and Schuster to teach at the University of Illinois. Howe said how delighted he was with the success of *The Sea Around Us* and that he was sure Hendrik van Loon, who'd died in 1944, would have felt the same. She was, Howe told Carson, their greatest discovery.

A few letter writers offered gentle corrections to a handful of mistakes in *The Sea Around Us*. Carson had gotten the term "lee shore" wrong, confusing it with a windward shore that is sheltered from the weather. A number of people—perhaps wondering just how much seagoing experience Carson really had—wrote to point this out. Carson had also been unaware of the peculiar geography of Panama by which the Pacific end of the Panama Canal actually lies *east* of the Atlantic end. Someone caught that, too. One letter that probably impressed itself on Carson's memory came from a man named R. M. Much, who informed her that salmon no longer migrated into either the Androscoggin or Kennebec rivers. Anybody dining in a restaurant on what the menu claimed to be "Kennebec salmon" was being cheated, he said. Much speculated on what might be a contributing cause of this disappearance. "May I also point out," Much wrote, "that the Androscoggin is lined with mills which pour their chemicals profusely . . . and have for almost a hundred years. Salmon cannot take that kind of diet."

Mostly, though, people wrote to say how much they enjoyed *The Sea Around Us* and how they shared Carson's affection for the ocean. Some sent her poems they'd written about the sea. Others invited her to stay with them at their beach homes. A number of them asked for her autograph and a photo. A man named Alfred Glassel of Houston, Texas, wrote to tell Carson that while fishing off of South America he'd recently caught "the first legal 1,000 lb. game fish." Apparently, he just thought she'd want to know. Glassel enclosed an eight-by-ten black-and-white photograph of the huge black marlin hung up on the dock at Cabo Blanco, Peru, as he stood alongside his catch looking jaunty.

Even Marie Rodell was suddenly the object of public affection. "Why just the other night a man called me up at my apartment and asked me if it was true that I was Miss Carson's agent," Rodell said to a reporter at one of Carson's book signings. "I said I was and he started talking about the book. He went on and on and at last I asked him exactly what he wanted. He said he just wanted me to tell Miss Carson her book was poetry. He was drunk I guess, but just the same I thought it was kind of sweet."

Carson's attention to detail survived the crush of publicity. She had insisted that Oxford abandon its proposed use of a sans-serif typeface for chapter headings, as she thought this was too textbookish. Sensing that a large readership for *The Sea Around Us* was ahead, Carson and Rodell were angry with Oxford over the more serious matter of limited first printings that had caused shortages and out-of-stock periods at many bookstores. Not so believably, Oxford pleaded that although they always knew *The Sea Around Us* would be a bestseller, they'd been so overwhelmed with orders that it was as if they were "caught in an undertow." The publisher said their main problem was just buying enough paper to meet the demand.

The thought that anyone might want to buy her book and be unable to find a copy was vexing to Carson—though she complained even more bitterly to Oxford about what she considered its minimal advertising for *The Sea Around Us*. Carson kept a close count of ads that ran in papers such as the *New York Times* and the *New York Herald Tribune*. She told Oxford if there was one thing she hated it was opening up a literary supplement and finding ads for competing books and none for her own. She also continued to harp on the binding, which even after being upgraded still tended to show wear with even light use.

The Sea Around Us made the *New York Times* bestseller list on July 22, 1951—coming in at number five. It was still at number five a week later, trailing Omar Bradley's *Soldier's Story* and Heyerdahl's *Kon-Tiki,* which was a fixture at number one. It was a good time for books. On the fiction list were Herman Wouk's *Caine Mutiny,* James Jones's *From Here to Eternity,* and a brisk, biting novel featuring a wise-cracking teenaged antihero named Holden Caulfield—J. D. Salinger's *Catcher in the Rye.* But as the summer moved on, *The Sea Around Us* began climbing. In mid-August it was at number two, right behind *Kon-Tiki,* and by early September the order was reversed. *The Sea Around Us* would remain at number one for the rest of the year and far into the next, setting new records for the most consecutive weeks atop the list.

In November 1951, as sales of *The Sea Around Us* passed one hundred thousand, Oxford told Carson it was eager to reissue *Under the Sea-Wind* as a featured book the following spring. There was some question whether this would fulfill Carson's contractual obligation concerning Oxford's option on her next book. Oxford in the end decided that, rather than enforce its option with Carson, they would simply let Carson and Rodell decide whether to offer another book to them—and would trust that they would be so disposed. In December, Rodell sold *Life* magazine rights to a condensation of *Under the Sea-Wind,* which the magazine planned to illustrate with photographs by Margaret Bourke-White.

On April 20, 1952, *The Sea Around Us* finally dropped back to number two on the *New York Times* bestseller list—and *Under the Sea-Wind,* which had gone into a second printing with Oxford even before publication, joined the list at number ten a week later. Sales of *The Sea Around Us* passed two hundred thousand. Carson now had two of the ten bestselling nonfiction books in America, and wild rumors surrounded her work. One was that more than a dozen publishing houses had turned down *The Sea Around Us* and that Oxford University Press had considered it a long shot when they took a chance on the book. Another was that the original manuscript had been a staggering two hundred thousand words long. In fact, Carson had cut only a single chapter—it was about commercial fishing—from the book. Still another claim, probably the only one that Carson might have wished were true, was that Simon and Schuster had discovered a third, previously unknown book by Carson in its warehouse. Rodell did her best to set the record straight.

No matter how well either book did, Carson was always convinced it could have been better. Both she and Rodell thought that Oxford had again skimped on advertising—Rodell complained there was little or none through the summer following publication—and that this caused *Under the Sea-Wind* to slip on the bestseller lists prematurely. Oxford's initial advertising schedule for the book had actually been generous, with buys in forty-five daily newspapers from one end of the country to the other, including full-page ads in the *New York Times,* the *New York Herald Tribune,* and the *Chicago Tribune.* That winter, the Book-of-the-Month Club picked *Under the Sea-Wind* as an alternate selection for June.

In letters to Rodell that were often whiny and interlaced with vague suspicions, Carson said she was skeptical of Oxford's sales figures—which seemed too low for books that were bestsellers. Carson and Rodell also quarreled over what Rodell described as her client's "constant refusal" to make public appearances at cocktail parties and book signings. Carson, writing back to Rodell from Maine in longhand while sitting under a hair dryer, said she understood why her publisher and her agent wanted her to do more of this but insisted it would be shortsighted, as her work could go forward only if she could maintain her life as it had been before *The Sea Around Us.*

Carson was feeling the downside of the fame that she craved and now seemingly could not avoid. Oxford received a steady influx of requests for interviews with Carson, as well as invitations for her to speak. She so routinely said no to these inquiries that the publicity department got in the habit of turning them down for her. The previous October, Carson had spent a strange afternoon in New York, as one of the speakers at a Book and Author Luncheon at the Astor

Hotel. The event was sponsored by the *New York Herald Tribune* and the American Booksellers Association. Also on the dais were James G. McDonald, former U.S. ambassador to Israel, and Jimmy Durante, who was the subject of a new biography, *Schnozzola*.

During her speech, Carson played audio recordings of shrimp and other marine life. When it was Durante's turn, after hearing talks on international diplomacy and the wonders of oceanography, he pulled his prepared speech from his pocket, tore it up, and declared: "Watsa use?" After a couple of ad-libbed reminiscences, Durante played the piano a little and then demonstrated the art of "cake walking," a prancing dance step that had origins on plantations in the American South.

Carson had been involved in every aspect of the prepublication plans for *The Sea Around Us,* sending Oxford the names of institutions and important persons who were to get advance copies, and even longer lists of review media that needed to see the book. Early in the process—in fact, just about the time she was submitting the manuscript in the summer of 1950—Carson had campaigned to have Oxford submit *The Sea Around Us* for the John Burroughs Medal, an award given annually to the best book about natural history. In April 1952, Carson found out that she'd won the Burroughs Medal.

As splendid as this news was, it came at the end of a season of accolades—the biggest of which was the National Book Award, which she learned she'd won in early January. Although she misplaced the original letter from Oxford informing her of the prize, a whirlwind of planning for the presentation took place over the next several weeks as there was a heavy schedule of interviews and receptions connected with Carson's visit to New York. The award ceremony was held at the Hotel Commodore. At the head table with Carson were the poet Marianne Moore, who'd won for *Collected Poems* and who looked tiny under an enormous tricornered hat, and James Jones, who'd won the fiction award for *From Here to Eternity.* Jones was widely rumored to have been a compromise winner after the judges could not decide between *The Caine Mutiny* and *The Catcher in the Rye.* The women wore corsages. Jones, dressed in a light-colored suit that made him appear even larger than he was, looked like he wanted to slug somebody.

In her acceptance speech, Carson said that an author's "real education" begins on publication day, when you learn how people react to what you have to say. She said she had been struck by the number of readers who were surprised by the popular success of *The Sea Around Us* even though it had a lot of science in it. This didn't seem right to her—Carson said science was not a realm unto itself, and anyway, science and literature had the same aim, which is to "discover and illuminate truth."

> We live in a scientific age, yet we assume that knowledge of science is the prerogative of only a small number of human beings, isolated and priestlike in their laboratories. This is not true. The materials of science are the materials of life itself. Science is part of the reality of living; it is the what, the how, and the why of everything in our experience. It is impossible to understand man without understanding his environment and the forces that have molded him physically and mentally.

Carson added a cautionary note that seemed apt in a world inclined to war in a nuclear age. She said that by studying the natural world and seeing it in the context of a history billions of years long, human follies came into perspective. "Perhaps if we reversed the telescope and looked at man down these long vistas," she said, "we should find less time and inclination to plan for our own destruction."

It was a good time. RKO, the movie company, began work on a documentary based on *The Sea Around Us*—an unexpected fulfillment of Carson's earlier speculation that such a film could be made. It was to be written and directed by Irwin Allen, who would one day become famous as the "Master of Disaster" for films such as *The Towering Inferno*. Carson tried to be helpful to the project, searching for existing film footage and correcting Allen's script, which she disliked enough that she threatened to remove her name from the film. When Carson saw a first cut of the movie in January 1953, she was shocked that many of the factual errors she had pointed out in the script had nonetheless ended up in the movie. Oxford complained to RKO, and Marie Rodell complained to Oxford, mentioning the possibility of a lawsuit. In February, Allen and Carson met in New York to resolve their differences and, based on changes Allen agreed to make to the film, Carson withdrew her objections.

The finished film—though wildly uneven—was a colorful and entertaining look at the marine environment. Allen got the story started off on an inept biblical note by commingling Carson's explanation of the origins of the earth with her allusion to Genesis. Much of the movie appeared to have been filmed in the big aquarium at Marineland in Florida, though there were also pretty sequences shot underwater on coral reefs and others showing the surf crashing on spectacular coastlines. Some scenes—including a "fight" between a shark and an octopus and another in which a snorkel diver slashed open the belly of a small, harmless shark—were staged and must have distressed Carson, as they suggested the ocean was a dark, menacing place. But Allen didn't have to supply any artifice for the film's most grisly segment, the bloody harpooning of a large baleen whale by a commercial whaling vessel. The movie ended scarily with scenes— some real and some fake—of icebergs calving off Arctic glaciers. The voice-over offered the disturbing thought, made to seem far more immediate than Carson had explained in the book, that the earth was warming and the seas were rising and perhaps would not stop before inundating much of human civilization.

When Oxford proposed a new printing of *The Sea Around Us* with a dust jacket adapted from the film, Carson said absolutely not, as it would "cheapen and misrepresent" the book. Allen's film went on to win the Academy Award for Best Documentary Feature, but Carson always hated it, and she likely regretted a missed opportunity to have worked with someone else. In March 1952, Marie Rodell had met with a young French marine researcher named Jacques Cousteau, who expressed interest in collaborating with Carson on a movie about the sea. Cousteau said he was about to embark on a long ocean expedition aboard his ship *Calypso*. Rodell thought this sounded interesting, and she found Cousteau charming. But she declined on Carson's behalf because she'd also heard that Cousteau's recent invention—the Aqua-Lung—was "no good."

In the spring of 1952, Carson got away to Key West to work on the seashore book and to escape the unceasing requests for her time. She told Oxford that she'd have little room for promotional work in the coming months, as she was planning a research trip to Woods Hole and a vacation in Maine. Still on leave from U.S. Fish and Wildlife, Carson had decided she would not return. On her resignation, which took effect in June, Carson gave as her reason for quitting "to devote my time to writing."

That summer, flush with success, Carson bought some land on Southport Island near Boothbay Harbor. She admitted that it felt "strange and inappropriate" to think of herself as an "owner" of a piece of the seashore. The lot was 350 feet deep, heavily wooded, and had a 140-foot frontage on Sheepscot Bay. It was near the village of West Southport, not far from the Hendricks Head lighthouse, and about a half mile south of a promontory called Dogfish Head.

Carson ordered a spacious cottage that would be ready the next summer. It was long and low, and featured a writing study with built-in varnished bookshelves and desk, plus a worktable where Carson could examine marine specimens. The main room was finished in knotty pine and had a redbrick fireplace. An enormous window overlooked the bay, filling the cottage with light. A long deck with white railings was perched between the cottage and a shrubby bluff, down which a narrow, winding, root-tangled path led to the rocks and tide pools at the shoreline.

At low tide, a large, uneven tableland of rock emerged along the shore. Directly below the cottage was a small, gravelly shallow area that could almost be called a beach. The tide pools were full of mussels, periwinkles, sponges, urchins, barnacles, and seaweeds. Although the rocks were treacherous when wet, a steady and sufficiently curious person could inch out onto them to inspect the pools, or venture to the edge and gaze at the open ocean beyond the widening funnel of the bay to the south. West across the bay were the sun-bleached rocks of Georgetown Island. Sometimes the swell of the North Atlantic swept into the bay in long, smooth columns, and the water was dotted with the brightly colored floats of countless lobster traps. Carson said that whales occasionally ventured into the bay and could be observed "blowing and rolling in all their majesty."

Back in New York, Marie Rodell moved her office from East Fifty-fourth Street to Fifth Avenue.

PART TWO

Silent Spring

SEVEN

Dorothy

Southport Island belongs to a network of rocky peninsulas and islands that project into the ocean from Boothbay Harbor, Maine, bordering the estuaries of the Damariscotta and Sheepscot rivers. The island lies close to the mainland, to which it is connected by a bridge. It is about three miles long from north to south, a little less than half that wide across at its broadest point, and is shaped like a shark's tooth. Heavily wooded, the island's forest is dominated by spruce and fir, with maples, birches, and other hardwoods mixed in. The shoreline is steep almost everywhere. In 1953, Southport Island had 250 permanent residents and another 368 families owned summer properties there. When Rachel Carson built her cottage she became Southport Island's second most famous part-time citizen, the first being the actress Margaret Hamilton, who lived in a house on an islet just off the island's southern tip and who was said by everyone to be much nicer than her most memorable character, the Wicked Witch of the West in the 1939 movie *The Wizard of Oz*.

In the 1880s a Massachusetts Civil War veteran named Constant Whitney began visiting Southport Island with his family on summer vacations. In 1887 he bought a parcel of land on the shore of Sheepscot Bay, not far from the village of West Southport, near a steamer landing at the rocky point of Dogfish Head. At first the family camped there in a tent, then for several summers more they inhabited a rough single-room house that had a loft above. They dug a well that provided water for them and for several nearby cottages, and that also served as the community refrigerator, with milk and other perishables kept cool in buckets lowered to just above the water.

One summer a shipload of lumber washed ashore directly in front of the cottage. Family legend has it that Constant Whitney declared that as the Lord had seen fit to provide him with the materials for a house it was his duty to build one. He did so, moving a little closer to the water. Whitney and his heirs gradually expanded the new cottage in the ensuing years, adding a kitchen, bedroom, and bathroom, plus an expansive porch on the front that looked out grandly over the bay. The cottage was passed down through the family, one generation to the next, until it belonged to Constant's granddaughter, Dorothy Freeman, and her husband, Stanley.

In 1939, Stan and Dorothy bought a sloop and moored it in the cove near the cottage. Sixteen and a half feet long, with a white lapstrake hull and a green canvas deck, she was a "Town Class" design, which originated in Marblehead, Massachusetts, and at the time was the official racing class of the Southport Yacht Club. Her sail number was 158. This matched the first number chosen in the Selective Service lottery just before the war, and the Freemans named her *Draftee*. Stan and Dorothy loved cruising on the bay, and Stan and their son, Stanley, Jr., raced *Draftee* every Saturday and Sunday in July and August.

On Stan Freeman's birthday, July 15, 1951, his son and daughter-in-law gave him a copy of *The Sea Around Us,* telling him to be sure to bring it to Maine so they could read it, too. The Freemans took turns reading aloud from Carson's book on *Draftee* as they cruised on Sheepscot Bay that summer. A year later Dorothy was surprised to read in the local paper that Rachel Carson had purchased property in, of all places, West Southport—and was going to build a summer home there. Just before Christmas she decided to send Carson a note welcoming her to the island, mailing it to the famous author by way of her publisher in New York and having no idea what, if any, response to expect. Carson surely received hundreds of letters every month.

But Carson did respond. She sent Dorothy a note thanking her for the "thoughtful and charming" greeting from her new neighbors. Carson said she'd been in love with the Boothbay Harbor area for a long time and now looked forward to having a summer writing retreat. She said she hoped to be in her cottage by June—and asked the Freemans to please stop by to get better acquainted. Dorothy could scarcely believe it.

A half year later, on June 2, 1953, the Freemans got up early at their home in West Bridgewater, Massachusetts, to watch the coronation of Queen Elizabeth II in London on their new television. Film of the twenty-seven-year-old monarch's installation had been flown to North America for broadcast on TV within hours of the actual ceremony. This would have been the most interesting event of the summer had they not gone up to Southport Island and called on Rachel Carson at her new cottage after suppertime on July 12. In the evening light of midsummer Stan and Dorothy walked down the short, rocky path to Carson's back door and into a different life.

Carson liked the Freemans right away. Although they were older than she was, Carson felt the three of them—but especially she and Dorothy—were much alike in their feelings for the Maine coast and for nature in general. Dorothy was pretty and vigorous. She had a New England accent, so that her new friend's name came out as *Rachul Cahsin*. Stan was tall and handsome, with a high forehead and thinning hair. He was an accomplished amateur photographer who won over Carson when she learned he liked to take pictures of the many kinds of wildlife that visited Sheepscot Bay. Carson insisted they come back in a few weeks to inspect the shoreline below her cottage. The tides would not be so extreme as they were in the spring or later in the fall—when shore explorations were best—but there would still be wonderful things to find among the rocks. Carson advised them to wear sneakers and pants they could roll up, but promised that if anyone had to go in over their knees she'd do it, as she would have a change of clothing close at hand. The Freemans, starstruck yet also surprisingly at ease with Carson, were eager for another visit.

The collecting expedition came off one Sunday in early September. It was a happy affair. Marie Rodell was up from New York for the weekend and everyone, including Carson's mother, Maria, got on well. Carson had advised Stan and Dorothy to come in the late afternoon in time to catch the falling tide. Dorothy was startled by the wealth of sea life that, unbeknownst to her previously, dwelled in the tide pools and crevices of the shoreline at West Southport. Carson—demonstrating an unsuspected agility—showed them how to climb along the slippery rocks and where to stop and peer beneath an overhang or reach into the water to retrieve a specimen. Dorothy watched as Carson all but stood on her head to peer into the recesses of a small cave at the sea anemones clinging to the stone.

Anemones, small, tentacled predators that come in a wild and colorful assortment of species, were one of Carson's favorite marine animals. She heaved away at mats of seaweed and collected bits of muck and algae in the small specimen bottles she carried with her, filling them as she went. She also had a bucket for larger captives. Dorothy never realized that sponges lived in the waters around Southport Island, and she especially enjoyed finding some. There was a good swell running that day, and a few waves crashed heavily enough on the rocks to soak everyone. Afterward, they warmed up with tea by the fireplace and then visited Carson's study, where they looked through the microscope at what Dorothy called a "new world" that was "wonderful, beautiful, and unbelievable." Dorothy could not get over seeing the pincerlike spines of a starfish under magnification, though she said it was only "one of a hundred eye-openers" that day. Dorothy also studied Carson more closely.

The author of *The Sea Around Us* wasn't what she'd expected.

Carson had become so famous that after a photograph of her with her cat appeared in a newspaper the cat started getting fan mail. So it was surprising to Dorothy that Carson seemed "tiny" and often wore a wistful expression. It was hard to believe that so much knowledge resided in such an unimposing person. Dorothy sensed something sad in Carson, who seemed overwhelmed by her sudden prominence. Still, she was humble and kind, and always ended a day like this one by taking all of the specimens she'd collected back down to the water to release them.

Carson was similarly impressed with her visitors. Stan had given Carson a picture he'd taken of some seagulls and she thought it looked nice on her end table. The Freemans had also commiserated with Carson over the recent death of a beloved cat, which Carson said had been heartbreaking and all but impossible to get over. Carson was only sorry they wouldn't have more time to get better acquainted that summer, as the Freemans had to return to West Bridgewater. She sent Dorothy a farewell note, beginning it once again with "Dear Mrs. Freeman" and closing with a suggestion that they drop such formalities and call each other by their first names. She reminded Dorothy how happy she was that Dorothy had written to her the year before and said she was glad to have started "this very pleasant friendship."

From the start, Dorothy worried that Carson would misread her intentions and think she was being friendly on account of Carson being a famous writer. Dorothy—who would soon enough prove a capable correspondent herself—respected the demands of the writing process and worried that in making friends with Carson she might interfere with her work. Carson had no such reservations. She wanted to get to know the Freemans, Dorothy in particular. The seasons at West Southport were regrettably short—the municipal water system utilized aboveground pipes and had to be shut down in the fall and did not reopen until spring. There was no possibility of staying on or even visiting through winter. Carson said she was sorry they hadn't spent more time together over the summer, but agreed with Dorothy that this meant they could look forward to the following season in

Maine. Evidently, Dorothy wrote several letters to Carson while Carson was still at West Southport—but urged Carson not to take time from her writing to respond.

Even so, in late September—perhaps experiencing the "wistfulness" Dorothy perceived in her—Carson sent off a long letter telling Dorothy everything that had been happening on Sheepscot Bay. Instinctively, Carson seemed to sense that Dorothy was eager to keep track of what she was doing. She enclosed a snapshot she'd taken down at the water's edge during a spell of unusually high surf—the kind that almost never broke with such violence so far up in the bay. And she gave Dorothy a close accounting of various species of marine life she'd recently examined, including, she said merrily, an "exquisitely beautiful worm" that she had discovered living among a colony of diverse creatures hidden under the pink crust of corallines that covered the rocks in many places. Carson told Dorothy not to laugh—it was the "most beautiful worm in the world."

Carson said the tides since Dorothy left had been magnificent and that for a while she felt she should divide her explorations among various locales. One of her favorite places nearby was Ocean Point, a sprawling, boulder-strewn headland east of Boothbay Harbor. In the end, though, Carson said she felt she owed it to herself to get better acquainted with her own shoreline and so had stayed close to home. Now it was going to be difficult to say farewell. She also wanted Dorothy to know that her writing was an often trying enterprise, no matter who was around to keep her company.

Carson said she was happy to know that Dorothy and Stan had reread *Under the Sea-Wind* and *The Sea Around Us* and had liked them just as much after having met the author. She told Dorothy she had to make herself bring her letter to an end or else it would start to feel like another book. Tentatively, almost as a person might lightly touch the hand of another in whom they were interested, Carson closed by saying "My best to all the Freemans, and to you my affectionate regard."

A week later, Carson wrote again. This time she urged Dorothy to keep writing and forget her concerns that in doing so she would cause Carson to neglect her work. She was behind on the book for reasons that had nothing to do with Dorothy, she said. A big one was that she'd decided to completely rewrite a long section. Almost as an afterthought, Carson mentioned that she was going to be in Boston at the end of December for a scientific meeting and wondered if Dorothy might come into the city and meet her for lunch. This time Carson signed off "Affectionately yours, Rachel."

Carson went off to Myrtle Beach, South Carolina, for more research on the seashore book, and she hunkered down long enough during a gale to write a couple of long, chatty letters to Dorothy. Carson was accompanied by her mother and the two nieces, Virginia and Marjorie. Also along was Marjorie's twenty-month-old son—Carson's grandnephew—Roger. Carson told Dorothy she was delighted by Roger's enthusiasm for the beach. She took him out after dark to hunt by flashlight for ghost crabs and laughed when he picked up a strange shell and called it a "winkie," as he did the periwinkles he'd collected at Southport Island. Carson reiterated how wonderful Dorothy's letters were and how every one was filled with things they absolutely had to talk about at length the next summer.

As for their proposed meeting in Boston at the end of the year—Carson wanted to make a definite plan. She admitted to being nervous about the conference she was attending, a meeting of the American Association for the Advancement of Science at which she was going to deliver a formal paper on the effects of climate change on sea life along the coast. A capable but reluctant public speaker, Carson was more anxious than usual about making a presentation before such an august group of scientists—a prospect she told Dorothy that was "unnerving." Carson wanted to make sure that she and Dorothy would meet the day after the AAAS talk, as she would then be at ease and better able to give Dorothy her full attention.

Carson told Dorothy she was glad Dorothy liked a book she had recommended—*Conversation with the Earth* by the German geologist

Hans Cloos. Meanwhile, the storm in South Carolina had caused a number of interesting reef creatures normally found offshore to fetch up onto the beach. Carson told Dorothy how much fun she'd had examining brightly colored sponges, sea squirts, crabs, starfish, urchins, and even a "fair-sized octopus" that reminded her annoyingly of Irwin Allen's documentary based on *The Sea Around Us,* in which an octopus had been made out as a "monster of the deep."

Carson continued to make passing references to the seashore book, which was still not going well—though she was always careful to explain that this was her fault and in no way Dorothy's. She confessed the progress she'd made over the summer had been disappointing. Although Paul Brooks at Houghton Mifflin was being patient, Carson almost wished he wasn't so understanding, as she felt the end of the project was still so far off that it made her feel "desperate." Miserable, Carson told Dorothy that life was too short to spend so much time on one book. She wondered if getting started on a new chapter might be easier if she typed the words "Dear Dorothy" on the first page.

Silver Spring, Maryland, had been Carson's home since 1938, except for the time she spent in Chicago during the war, and for a couple of years immediately after that when Carson and her mother lived in nearby Takoma Park, Maryland. Back in Silver Spring in the fall of 1953, Carson was beginning to think of herself as having several homes—the one in Maryland, of course, but now also the summer place at West Southport and, figuratively at least, in a charming cottage of the mind and heart that had come to life on the pages of the letters that had begun to flow between her and Dorothy.

Dorothy liked small, pastel-colored stationery—sometimes it had a flower or some other decorative design in the upper left corner—and she wrote her letters in a neat, up-and-down longhand that marched precisely across the page, leaving small margins at either end of every perfectly level line. Sometimes she made drafts in pencil before committing them to ink. Carson, who occasionally typed her letters, tended to write them on whatever was at hand. Sometimes that was pretty stationery like Dorothy's, but it could also be a note card or plain typing paper.

In mid-November, Dorothy proposed that, rather than just meet for lunch after Carson's speech in Boston, Carson should come down to West Bridgewater where she could spend a whole afternoon and evening with Dorothy and Stan before catching a late train back to Maryland. Carson said this would be fine, though she could not disguise her disappointment at the prospect of not having time alone with Dorothy in Boston. She told Dorothy she liked to imagine arriving in Boston and coming off the train "into your arms" even though she knew that wasn't possible. Carson said that between the crush of preparations for her speech and the impending Christmas holidays she was "going mad."

For Carson, one of Dorothy's most endearing traits was her love of literature. Carson was eager to share the work of her favorite writers with Dorothy, and one of the first she brought up was Richard Jefferies. Carson admitted that Jefferies was an "uneven" writer and said that because he was also prolific it would be easy to go astray by picking up the "wrong" volume of his work. She said she had always loved the essay collection *Jefferies' England* and suggested Dorothy try to find it at the library. If it wasn't there, Dorothy could borrow her copy.

Carson wanted Dorothy to like Jefferies because she considered him her "literary grandfather," and she outlined for Dorothy his place on the family tree of her work. "I am sure that my own style and thought were deeply influenced, in certain critical years, by Henry Williamson, whose *Tarka the Otter* and *Salar the Salmon* are, I'm convinced, nature writing of the highest order. And Williamson has said that he owes the same sort of debt to Jefferies."

Cryptically, Carson added that Dorothy could expect another letter soon, as there was something Carson just had to tell her.

By their own estimate, Carson and Dorothy had been in each other's company for a little over six hours that first summer at Southport Island. Now, after exchanging letters for a few months, the two women felt themselves in the grip of a mutual attraction that was thrilling and utterly surprising. In early December, Carson wrote to iron out the details of the Boston trip and to tell Dorothy how wonderful her latest letter had been. Carson had mentioned that she sometimes wrote to Dorothy long after midnight, and this had made Dorothy again feel she was imposing. Carson told her not to worry, as she was a "nocturnal creature" by nature. Dorothy had also wondered in her letter how different their lives might be had they not met as they did the preceding summer. Carson airily dismissed this question—it only reminded her that they *did* meet. She said she felt sure they would have done so one way or another, no matter what. And then she told Dorothy something that she had never told anybody else:

> And, as you must know in your heart, there is such a simple answer for all the "whys" that are sprinkled through your letters: As why do I keep your letters? Why did I come to the Head that last night? Why? Because I love you! Now I could go on and tell you some of the reasons why I do, but that would take quite a while, and I think the simple fact covers everything.

Carson's AAAS talk, at the grand old Mechanics Hall in Boston, went well. Having received a couple of honorary degrees after *The Sea Around Us,* Carson was listed on the program as "Dr. Rachel L. Carson." To meet her audience on its own terms, Carson made a presentation that was more technical, more grounded in emerging science than in her popular writing. She discussed changes in the biotic populations of the seashore environment that were caused by a warm shift in the climate and perhaps subtler alterations in oceanic plant communities and the chemical composition of seawater. And she alluded to a novel concept that would gain traction in the coming years—the idea that life on earth is a continuing biological experiment in which we are both observers and participants:

The edge of the sea is a laboratory in which Nature itself is conducting experiments in the evolution of life and in the delicate balancing of the living creature within a complex system of forces, living and non-living. We have come a long way from the early days of the biology of the shore, when it was enough to find, to describe, and to name the plants and animals found there. We have progressed, also, beyond the next period, the dawn age of the science of ecology, when it was realized that certain kinds of animals are typical of certain kinds of habitats. Now our minds are occupied with tantalizing questions. "Why does an animal live where it does?" "What is the nature of the ties that bind it to its world?"

As Carson was leaving the hall after she finished, she was startled to find Dorothy waiting for her. Carson impulsively kissed her and whispered, "We didn't plan it this way did we?" They went back to Carson's room at the Sheraton Hotel and sat on the bed for a languorous hour smiling at each other, unsure what came next. On the way south from the city they stopped to watch some ducks swimming on a pond. As they sat in the car both women had the urge to say something that neither could bring herself to say. They did not know what was happening, but they did not resist. When Dorothy later took Carson upstairs for a short rest at their home in West Bridgewater, Carson called after her "Hurry back."

Carson slept fitfully on the train later that night. She told Dorothy in a letter written on New Year's Day 1954 that every time she had woken up on the way home she could feel the "sweet tenderness" of Dorothy's presence. She said she felt sure Dorothy had sensed the same thing about her after she was gone. The two women would later remember this time together as the Thirteen Hours, when a "little oasis of peace" entered both their hearts. Carson said it had been "truly perfect." So often, she said, reality was a disappointment when expectations were high—but it had not turned out to be so for the two of them. Carson told Dorothy there was not a single thing she

would change about her, even if she could. She thought these lines
from Keats—dear to so many romantics—described the way she felt:

A thing of beauty is a joy forever:
Its loveliness increases; it will never
Pass into nothingness; but still will keep
A bower quiet for us, and a sleep
Full of sweet dreams.

Now everything between Carson and Dorothy was understood. Although Carson would always address her envelopes to "Mrs. Stanley
Freeman," they began to call each other "Darling," and professions
of love filled their letters. Carson was already imagining their time
together at West Southport come summer—and was unhappy whenever she remembered that Dorothy would have less time there than
she would. Both women soon realized that the things they said to
each other in their letters might meet disapproval from Stan or Carson's mother, Maria—the "craziness" between them was something
other people could only misunderstand. Given the endless stream of
mail going back and forth, Carson thought it was going to be difficult
to hide their correspondence or to somehow manage to occasionally
share only a paragraph or two from a much longer letter. Carson said
the subject didn't require any further elaboration—she was sure that
Dorothy knew what she meant.

Carson proposed that they start writing letters in two parts, one
that was general and newsy and could be shared with family and
friends, and a private one that would be for them alone. Eventually
they began referring to these private inclusions—they usually came
folded inside the general letter—as "apples." Whenever there might
be any doubt as to whether something should be kept between just
the two of them, they indicated that it should be "put in the strong-
box." Onward went the correspondence, which became even more
frequent and at greater length to accommodate their letter-within-
a-letter strategy. Sometimes they would stop off and resume writing

later the same day or even the next, so that the letters often became a diarylike compendium of events and reflections. They also began to telephone each other from time to time, thrilled at the sound of each other's voices. Just when it was hard to imagine their feelings could deepen, Carson sent Dorothy a long, revelatory "apple" that was unlike any she had sent before or ever would again. Dorothy had proposed that they stop writing to each other—the letters now came and went daily—until Carson was done with the seashore book. Carson would not consider it.

She told Dorothy that she wanted to forever banish any doubts Dorothy might have about her love, and confessed that she'd been in love with Dorothy even before she and Stan had left West Southport the previous summer. Dorothy, she said, had a "particular combination of qualities" that were hers alone, and that Carson needed to have in her life. Their love reminded her of the parable in which a man said that if he had only two pennies he would spend one on bread and the other to buy a "white hyacinth for his soul." Without Dorothy, nothing else Carson could do—no book she could write—would be worthwhile. Dorothy was her "white hyacinth," words that soon came to mean much more than a passing allusion. The two women would forever after remember Carson's momentous declaration as the "Hyacinth Letter," and the flower itself became a permanent symbol of their devotion to each other. Eventually, they would think of February 6, 1954, the date of the white hyacinth letter, as a momentous anniversary.

From the beginning, however, there was a third party in their relationship: Carson's work. As she wrote to Dorothy:

> I don't suppose anyone really knows how a creative writer works (he or she least of all, perhaps!) or what sort of nourishment his spirit must have. All I am certain of is this; that it is quite necessary for me to know that there is someone who is deeply devoted to me as a person, and who also has the capacity and the depth of understanding to share, vicariously, the sometimes crushing

burden of creative effort, recognizing the heartache, the great weariness of mind and body, the occasional black despair it may involve—someone who cherishes me and what I am trying to create.

Carson probably didn't intend to confess as much self-involvement as came across in this letter—though there was no getting around how much the success of *The Sea Around Us* had changed her. Or at least had brought to the surface an ego that had been waiting years to appear. Even now—after all the awards and the bestseller lists, the mountains of fan mail and the approving audiences—there still lived inside Carson the young girl from Springdale who thought there could never be a higher, more exalted calling than to be a writer. And yet in Dorothy Carson had found someone who loved her *even though* she also understood what it meant to be Rachel Carson. As for Carson, she said she had no idea what she could offer Dorothy in return, but was willing to accept without question that she "filled some need" in Dorothy's life.

The seashore book for Houghton Mifflin had outgrown Paul Brooks's original idea and was taking Carson much longer to complete than anyone had imagined when the project was first discussed back in 1950. Brooks envisioned something practical that would capitalize on Carson's writing ability without depending entirely on it. He thought the book would be a pocket-size field guide with a concise text and perhaps fifty pages of illustrations. When Carson asked how soon it was needed, Brooks said he didn't have any "special deadline" in mind, but hoped to have a completed manuscript in hand by late in the summer of 1951—shortly after the publication of *The Sea Around Us*—as this would give Houghton Mifflin enough time to bring it out the following spring.

Carson, unwilling to be rushed, asked Marie Rodell to tell Brooks she could turn in a manuscript sometime in the spring of 1952. Carson and Brooks decided on an illustrator for the book, a former colleague of Carson's at U.S. Fish and Wildlife named Bob Hines, who went to work making drawings of marine life. Everyone liked Hines, who was young and handsome and made lovely pictures. Carson, not oblivious to the promised delivery date but suddenly swamped by everything that happened following the publication of *The Sea Around Us,* traveled up and down the East Coast, sometimes accompanied by Hines. She made notes and wondered how she'd ever get the book done. Paul Brooks, well aware of his tremendous luck in having landed Carson before the world knew who she was, realized he would now have to give her as much time as it took. He told Carson her reports about new demands on her time were a "masterpiece of understatement," as he knew what was required of a bestselling author. Besides, he said, all of this attention would be a "long-range gain for the seashore book."

But still.

As Carson's proposed delivery time for the book came and went in the spring of 1952 it became clear the book was evolving and she had begun to think of it less as a "field guide" than as something different and still undefined that was going to be longer and more labor intensive than they had planned. Lovell Thompson, Houghton Mifflin's publisher, pressed for Carson to send them a "dummy," a mock-up layout of the book into which text and illustrations could be inserted as they arrived. Carson had herself proposed doing this earlier in the project—she thought Bob Hines could design the book around his drawings. But now she refused, reminding Brooks that they had agreed she was to be "free to develop the book in what seems to be my own peculiar style." Having got started, Carson insisted that her "taste and judgment" alone should dictate what she wrote about and in what detail. A predetermined format would, she said, "put me in a straightjacket [*sic*]." Summing up the situation in a way that must have made Brooks a little queasy, Carson said that she and Hines had completed their field work and made enough "preliminary" progress on the text and illustrations that they could now really get started.

This set off alarms at Houghton Mifflin, as Brooks hurried to reassure Lovell Thompson that all was well and that Carson was only taking advantage of the latitude he had given her. Brooks said he had encouraged Carson "all along" to let the book develop as she saw fit. It was now obvious that whatever that meant, the result was going to be "more important" and also "more literary" than the original concept. Brooks acknowledged that working with a writer and an illustrator could be complicated, but he told Thompson that Carson and Hines knew each other so well that he felt they could be trusted to work everything out as if they were a single author. He said he thought it would be a mistake to make them conform to the usual conventions of a guidebook. Stating what was by then obvious to everyone involved, Brooks said he also doubted that "Seashore Guide" was going to be an adequate title. Thompson, not entirely satisfied, told Brooks he was worried that Hines might be "illustrating one kind of book while Rachel is writing another."

Around Christmas 1952, Carson visited the west coast of Florida and its shell-covered barrier islands. At New Year's, she got off a portion of manuscript to Brooks, warning him that it was still rough and would need much further revision. She also proposed a title for the book: "The Edge of the Sea." Brooks was pleased with the copy and with the new title—he told Carson that some of the writing was equal to her best work and that she should put aside worries that this book would be a weak follow-up to *The Sea Around Us*. Carson and Rodell, who had begun discussing how best to spread out Carson's income across different years for tax purposes, now sensed a potential windfall and took steps to deal with another bestseller. Rodell asked Houghton Mifflin to change Carson's contract to ensure that she would not receive income in excess of $7,500 in any one year, with earnings above that amount to be deferred until later.

But all was not well. In March, Carson and Brooks privately discussed options for dealing with Bob Hines, who had fallen far behind on the drawings. Carson admitted that she had little room to complain, being woefully late herself with the text, but she thought things were really getting so far out of hand that they might have to give Hines an ultimatum that he finish or leave the project. Carson said she understood that Hines, who still worked at Fish and Wildlife, had other freelance work and needed the income it produced. But she thought maybe they'd made a mistake in paying him up front for the illustrations for *The Edge of the Sea*. Perhaps, she suggested, Brooks could dangle an additional advance payment to Hines that would be paid on receipt of all the completed drawings as an inducement for him to finish by the middle of the summer.

As for the writing—Carson still labored. She said she was "suffering tortures" over the manuscript, though she added hopefully that this seemed normal for her. Brooks, hoping to ease Carson's worries and maybe motivate her in the process, immediately offered to double Hines's $1,000 advance, with the additional amount to be paid in installments as the drawings were finished. Relieved, Carson thanked Brooks for stepping in and gave him an enthusiastic update on the material she was working on from her visit to the Florida Keys. Although the heat was oppressive—Carson said she could never live in such a climate—she thought the geology of this southern archipelago and all its islands and reefs and mangrove bays was fascinating, though she admitted that it was easy to talk about it and "agony to put on paper."

Not long after the Hines discussions, Marie Rodell wrote to Brooks claiming that Carson had come "unstuck" in her writing and that it was now proceeding more easily. Carson may have communicated something like this to Rodell, but it wasn't true. Only a few days later, Carson told Brooks that she was heading down to Myrtle Beach to get away from the book, on which she had been "overconcentrating" so much that she was now in a state of nervous exhaustion. She said she was heeding "medical advice" that she take a vacation—and that she thought this would in the long run actually speed up final delivery of the book.

Brooks, diplomatically changing the subject, alerted Carson that Houghton Mifflin was having second thoughts about using color in any of the illustrations, as this could become "brutally expensive" and they were determined to keep the cover price of the book from getting too high. He said the plan for now was to wait until the finished manuscript and illustrations were in hand and then make a precise cost estimate on which a final decision could be made. Carson responded that this seemed only reasonable.

Carson was ill in May 1953 with a respiratory infection. Then her mother suffered a bout of elevated blood pressure that required attention before they could travel to Maine and the new cottage. In late June—only days before she went to West Southport to meet the Freemans for the first time—she was still in Silver Spring, still struggling with the manuscript. She told Brooks that as she worked on the section about the Florida Keys and their varied habitats, something clicked. For the first time, she said she had a clear idea of how the whole book should be written. The problem, she said, had been thinking about each chapter as a freestanding "biography" of one group of marine organisms—and the book as simply a series of such smaller pieces. Now it was clear to her that a greater unity was needed, an overarching narrative that would make the book more like a companion to *The Sea Around Us.* Naturally, this would mean rewriting much of what she'd already done. Carson did not speculate on how long that might take.

Carson, it seemed, was the sort of writer who would sooner put herself through hell several times over than take the path of least resistance. The more dissatisfied she was with *The Edge of the Sea,* the less she tried to fix it by tinkering. Now, determined to more or less start over, Carson found that the "freedom" to do nothing but write that she had so coveted for so long was, in reality, a prison. How was it, she wondered, that she'd written *The Sea Around Us* in her spare hours late at night while still holding down a full-time government job—but now, with nothing to interfere with her travel or her thoughts, no claim on her time and concentration other than whatever she decided to do, she had gotten so lost? Carson's brave assertion to Brooks that she had finally figured out how to do the book was meant to settle her own thoughts as much as to reassure him.

In July, Bob Hines was finishing up the illustrations for *The Edge of the Sea*—late, but still far ahead of Carson, who promised to deliver a "substantial chunk" of manuscript in September. She told Brooks that she was "really terribly upset over being so far behind." She also provided her unlisted number at the cottage in Maine and gave him the news that because it was so well concealed it had "defied the efforts of the curious" to discover her whereabouts.

But September also found Carson more honestly confessing to Dorothy that she really hadn't gotten anywhere on the book that summer. Brooks, as usual, remained calm. He even visited Carson at the cottage for a couple of days. In October, Carson told him she now believed the final text for *The Edge of the Sea* was likely to run to about ninety-five thousand words—or nearly double what Brooks had proposed at the outset. She said the revisions she was now making were a great improvement, but that it remained slow going. Carson and Brooks agreed to set the end of March 1954 as the new deadline for delivery of the finished manuscript—a date that would have made the book two years late had Carson met this objective, which she did not.

March came. Carson wrote to Brooks to say that, although she had tried mightily, there was no way the book would be done that month. She said she thought it was "realistic" to think she'd instead finish by the end of May. "The book and the writer being what they are," Carson said, "the 'real thing' doesn't simply flow on schedule so many words per day—as I know you understand."

Carson probably did believe she'd be done in May, because she told Dorothy she absolutely had to finish before June so she could arrive in Maine free from book worries—and she asked Dorothy to make sure she didn't weaken in her resolve. One day she spoke to Dorothy on the phone, and when she got down to work afterward the words came to her in a flood. She told Dorothy that it was fun to pretend, whether it was true or not, that the sound of her voice was an inspiration. "When things go reasonably well, as they did then," Carson said, "I feel hopeful that maybe it *can* be finished, and maybe it is not too bad." But just two weeks after telling Brooks to look for the manuscript at the end of May she wrote to him again and said it was hopeless and that Houghton Mifflin should give up on its planned fall publication. She didn't make a new promise of delivery by a certain date—saying only that she'd continue "working right along."

This time, Brooks pushed back. In April he had a long heart-to-heart with Carson and reported to Lovell Thompson that he believed a fall publication would be possible after all—Carson's protest notwithstanding. He also told Thompson that they had decided not to use any color illustrations, except on the cover, and that Bob Hines had done such fine work that they should probably offer him another $250 advance. Brooks said it could even be $500, as he was sure they would sell more than enough books to cover it, but that he'd wait to see if Hines asked for more money. Brooks then wrote to Carson telling her how well he thought the book was coming along. "But the main thing is you have written a text which is meant to be read, not just consulted," he said. "It leaves one with a vivid mental picture and a sense of the relationship between these infinitely various forms of life. Among your wealthier readers it should start a run on microscopes. Before next fall I think I shall buy stock in an optical company."

Not everyone at Houghton Mifflin was so sanguine. One editor told Brooks that the manuscript wasn't on a level with *The Sea Around Us* and, in fact, "reeked of a guide," which was not surprising as that is what it started off to be. Brooks took this criticism to heart and started editing the manuscript in a way he hoped Carson would agree brought cohesion to the factual and literary sides of the story— and avoided any mention of its guidelike qualities. To Brooks's relief, Carson was appreciative of his suggestions—accepting many of the changes and ignoring others. She started making yet another round of revisions she thought would take the book in the direction Brooks wanted it to go, but she also reminded him that she wasn't writing the book in order, and that when he read the opening chapters many of the questions he was raising now would answer themselves. Of course, she also told him she would need more time.

When Brooks got Carson's latest changes it was as if a fog had lifted. He told her she'd managed a "miracle of creative revision," and everyone at Houghton Mifflin was "immensely pleased." This was an understatement. Memos went around the Houghton Mifflin office calling Carson's latest efforts "wonderful" and packed with "atmosphere and poetry." The editor who had initially complained to Brooks now marveled at the "dexterity and grace" with which she had taken their editing suggestions and improved on them, and said that the manuscript was now much better than it would have been had Carson merely said yes to all of their ideas. Carson was happy to hear this, but she urged Brooks to hold back on doing more of this detailed editing as the material he had in hand still needed further revising, and it would be a wasted effort to fine-tune it at this point. With things seemingly getting on track, everyone involved was overjoyed when Marie Rodell learned that the *New Yorker* wanted to serialize *The Edge of the Sea*.

In August 1954, Brooks again visited Carson at West Southport. She took him exploring in the tide pools below the cottage and showed him some new manuscript pages, which he said he liked. But back in Maryland in November she wrote to say her writing schedule for the fall in Maine had been ruined by too many visitors to the cottage, by her mother's weeklong hospitalization for bursitis, and by not one but two hurricanes that had come through. At one point the wind roaring across the bay had been so strong that they had packed up the book manuscript and made ready to leave in case the cottage was blown apart. More pleasant news was that Carson had sighted a whale and found moose tracks near the cottage, though they never caught a glimpse of the moose. She admitted that none of this was what Brooks really cared about. She said she was determined to finish the manuscript by the end of January, and that this time she believed she could do it. Any earlier, Carson said, was not realistic. She also asked Brooks to indulge her decision not to send him any more installments of the manuscript until the whole thing was done. Brooks wrote back to say that the end of January would be okay with him—but that anything later than that would be "bad." Carson, perhaps hoping to ease the annoyance with her at Houghton Mifflin, ordered two copies of a book by Lovell Thompson to give out as Christmas presents.

But in early January—it was now 1955—Carson told Brooks she hoped to have a "fairly complete" manuscript to him "around the first of the month"—meaning February. This would of course depend, she said, on many things, including her mental and physical condition. At the end of January she told Brooks she might take a couple of weeks longer. A month later she said it would be a few more days. Then, on March 15, it was done—three years behind schedule.

Brooks wrote to tell Carson what a "wonderful woman" she was. "This is indeed a momentous occasion and a happy day for us as well as for you," he said. "As I read this once again, I am convinced that it contains some of the best writing you have ever done and that there are passages here that are superior to anything in *The Sea Around Us*."

Nowhere in Carson's long, difficult correspondence with Paul Brooks on the progress of *The Edge of the Sea* had she mentioned her friends Stan and Dorothy Freeman. Possibly he met them on one of his visits to West Southport, though there is nothing to suggest he understood how important they had become in Carson's life—and certainly no evidence that anyone other than Carson and Dorothy knew the full extent of their intimate relationship.

In February 1954 the two women continued to explore the depths of their feelings for each other—which Dorothy described as "The Revelation." Carson's only regret was having taken so long to put into words what she felt for Dorothy. Dorothy said they were caught up in an "overpowering emotional experience." Carson said it was a process of "discovery" in which each progressive stage of getting to know each other led to still more urgent feelings. She constantly fought a desire to stop working and visit Dorothy, but she knew she could not give in to this as she wanted to "earn" their time together when it came. "But, oh darling, I want to be with you so terribly that it hurts!" Carson told Dorothy. Sometimes they were surprised by uncanny parallels between the lives they lived away from each other—a thought or experience that occurred to them both at the same time even when they were apart. They called these coincidental connections "stardust."

In late March 1954, Carson caught an Eastern Airlines flight to Boston. She told Dorothy how much she liked flying, although she thought that might be because she was always "very lucky about the weather." Carson met with Paul Brooks and spent three days with the Freemans down in West Bridgewater. Dorothy had promised to bring Carson breakfast in bed, which Carson coyly wrote would depend on a "consideration" that she didn't specify. The visit was wonderful, Carson said, though it was clear that much of the upcoming season in Maine would be spent working on *The Edge of the Sea*. This would make the summer "less peaceful" than she hoped, with fewer hours to spend with Dorothy. But, Carson told Dorothy, the book was near enough to being finished that most of what she'd have to do over the summer would be routine, as the "creative" work would be done by then. It's hard to say what this meant or whether, against all odds, Carson actually believed it was true. She also admitted to Dorothy that the book was like a "dragon" that held her in its clutches.

In April, Carson delivered two speeches, one at the Cranbrook Institute of Science in Detroit and the other before an audience nearly a thousand strong sponsored by the Theta Sigma Phi association of women in communications in Columbus, Ohio. A few weeks later, Carson went to New York to accept an award from the Limited Editions Club, as one of ten American writers who had produced books likely to be regarded as classics. Carson thought it odd that Pearl

Buck, who'd won the Nobel Prize for literature, was not among the honorees. The ceremony was at the Pierre Hotel and began with champagne at seven thirty followed by a dinner and several wine courses. Carson told Dorothy she didn't like champagne, proof that she wasn't "meant for literary life"—an odd remark, as Carson relished the many aspects of literary life that didn't involve lavish dinners and speechmaking. She also downplayed the award itself, telling Dorothy that it was merely the fleeting "judgment of a committee of my contemporaries," adding grandiosely that only posterity could decide if *The Sea Around Us* was a classic.

Then, for five days in May 1954, Carson put away all thoughts of work. Stan Freeman was traveling on business, and Carson and Dorothy went up to West Southport together from Boston. They'd planned this for months, and when it came it was hard to believe they had the world to themselves. They stayed mostly at Carson's cottage, where they fell out of time for a while, dining late and then staying up by the fire far into each night—one time straight through to dawn—talking and talking and talking, lost in their feelings, watching the full moon shining through the trees, never wanting to sleep, not wanting a moment less of each other's company.

They had lazy, laughter-filled breakfasts and tramped the woods, reading aloud to one another from E. B. White and H. M. Tomlinson. Carson, who was happy that Dorothy liked Tomlinson seemingly as much as she did, thought his writing was "magical" and said it affected her in a "peculiar way" that she couldn't "quite define." One day they heard the hermit thrushes singing gloriously. Another time Dorothy surprised Carson when she used a term—"rote"—that Carson claimed never to have heard and doubted was a proper English word. She was later amused to discover that it was, but insisted that it was unlikely either of them would ever see it in print. Dorothy said their visit had been like a symphony. Carson called it "the Hundred Hours." Later on, both would refer to this as their "Maytime."

Carson briefly returned to Silver Spring, where she started making a list of books to take back up to Maine, including Edwin Way Teale's *Circle of the Seasons,* Roger Tory Peterson's *Field Guide to Birds,* and Darwin's journal from the *Beagle* voyage. She told Dorothy there were so many more books she wanted them to share that there would never be enough time to read them all. The summer, she said, already felt short and crowded. To hurry herself back to Maine—and giving in to the means now at her disposal—Carson bought a "terribly sporty looking" Oldsmobile. It was light green, with a white top, wide white sidewall tires, and "automatic and power" everything. Carson said the car was so advanced that all she had to do to drive it was "sit there."

Carson and Dorothy marked their time together, event by event, moment to moment. Like beads on a string, one by one the thoughts and feelings and times they wished never to let go of tethered them to each other in shared memory. There were momentous occasions between them—like the Thirteen Hours or Maytime—but also many small gestures and impressions that were the foundation of their affection, and to which they referred again and again. Carson told Dorothy she loved simply being at West Southport with "the rocks and the bay, the sunset and the clouds." Nothing made her happier, she said, than that unmatched perfume of the Maine coast in summer, an intoxicating blend emanating from the exposed rockweed along the water's edge and the sun-drenched spruces of the forest.

Dorothy enjoyed exploring the shoreline with Carson, then sitting with her at the microscope to see what they had found. One time Carson took Dorothy to a special place, a hole in the rock at Ocean Point that, beneath a low ceiling only inches above its floor, held a translucent pool of water. Carson called it her "Fairy Cave." It was only accessible during the lowest tides of the year, and even then could be glimpsed but for short periods, as the ocean surge sometimes swept up and over the mossy rock from which the cave could be observed. In this hidden liminal world, Carson discovered a glittery, living universe:

Under water that was clear as glass the pool was carpeted with green sponge. Gray patches of sea squirts glistened on the ceiling and colonies of soft coral were a pale apricot color. In the moment when I looked into the cave a little elfin starfish hung down, suspended by the merest thread, perhaps by only a single tube foot. It reached down to touch its own reflection, so perfectly delineated that there might have been, not one starfish, but two. The beauty of the reflected images and of the limpid pool itself was the poignant beauty of things that are ephemeral, existing only until the sea should return to fill the little cave.

Dorothy seemed to remember everything—a day when the tide was high just at noon, another when Carson came to her with cakes and blueberries. Or a night when they sat on Dorothy's porch watching the moonlit waters on the bay. On a nice day in July 1954, Stan and Dorothy took Carson sailing aboard *Draftee,* an outing Carson probably had not looked forward to. Months earlier the woman who in the minds of millions was an intrepid sailor and reef diver alerted Dorothy that she was a hopeless landlubber who knew nothing about boats. Carson confessed a reluctance to embrace the "amphibious life" at West Southport. Then, on the day of their cruise, Stan accidentally steered too near the shore in front of Carson's cottage and the boat lurched as it scraped over some rocks. Carson told Dorothy she'd later had a good laugh about this and added—not all that convincingly— that she hoped they'd take her out again. Dorothy remembered this adventure more pleasantly, telling Carson that it had given her a good excuse to "hold your hand."

Carson and Dorothy agreed to think of Carson's public persona as "the other woman." Carson claimed that she could never fully believe that the famous Rachel Carson was actually her. More practically, Carson wanted Dorothy to know that while many people might idolize her, she understood that Dorothy was not among them and instead loved her for who she truly was.

Nothing was off-limits between Carson and Dorothy—their certainty that they could tell each other anything was as durable as the rocks at Southport Island. In a candid, almost elegiac letter to Carson, Dorothy once tried to explain the importance of her marriage. If at times it seemed there must be two Dorothys—one for Stan and one for Carson—in truth there was only a single Dorothy, one whose remarkable fortune was to be loved by two people at once. Dorothy knew Carson would understand.

It was a rainy late afternoon. Dusk had settled early and Dorothy was in a melancholy mood. She told Carson that she felt suspended in time. Earlier in the day she'd been cross with Stan, and although she apologized at once and hugged him, she knew he'd been hurt by what she'd said. Now he was having a nap and Dorothy retreated to an upstairs bedroom, telling Carson she found herself "in the corner that belongs in my heart only to you—you know where and why." Dorothy turned on the radio—a Mahler symphony was playing—and began reading Laurens Van der Post's *Venture to the Interior*, a gripping, sometimes harrowing account of a British exploratory expedition into an uncharted region of southern Africa. Dorothy was unable to explain how, but the final chapters of the book had been moving "beyond reason" to her:

> Suddenly, at one of the most dramatic moments in the book before its climax—the music overpowered me so that I had to stop reading. Floods of tears just streamed from my eyes. The music had been subdued and at times a rich human voice had become part of it. At the time it reached me it was carrying an exquisite melody in the high strings with dark shadings in the lower strings. It seemed to complement the book completely. Then I began to think of Stan asleep in the other room and suddenly underneath the lovely melody was a pattern of discord in the brasses, incongruous and intruding—almost a warning to me it seemed. And then I knew that I've got to tell Stan how wonderful has

been my life with him, how good he has been to me, how rich our life together has been. He's made me so happy—given me so much. I feel I have in no way repaid him for his years of devotion.

One time, as Carson and Dorothy lounged on the rocks above the tide pools, Carson had gotten into a confessional mood that she later regretted, but Dorothy assured her that such confidences were precious to her. When they were apart, Carson and Dorothy often wrote to tell each other of things they'd seen or done that would have been more meaningful had they been together. Nature and music could make either of them cry, and it was hard to tell whether such experiences were more intense when shared or when they arrived in a letter. Dorothy told Carson she missed her more when a flight of geese passed overhead or there was intense phosphorescence on Sheepscot Bay. Dorothy said Carson had reawakened her love of the natural world—Stan's, too—but that above all it had been finding someone who understood her so perfectly that had transformed her life when nothing of the kind had been expected.

"Darling," she wrote to Carson, "you and I on our Island are looking at a light so bright—invisible to others—a glorious, miraculous light that has brought to me and I hope and believe to you, untold happiness."

Carson had finally written a letter introducing herself to Henry Beston, admitting to him that she'd meant to do so some twenty years earlier, after she'd found his cottage from *The Outermost House* on that trip from Woods Hole to the outer Cape. Beston had long since settled at a country place he called Chimney Farm in Nobleboro, Maine—close enough to visit. Carson told Beston he'd been recommended to her as someone who would know where she could go to hear veeries, their song being in her estimation "one of the most deeply moving of bird voices." She was also eager to thank Beston for having written a penetrating review of *Under the Sea-Wind* after its reissue by Oxford. Beston invited her to come over, and she went with Dorothy, and again later that summer with her mother—whom Beston and his wife, Elizabeth, found delightful.

At the end of the season, Carson sent Dorothy a first edition of *The Sea Around Us,* telling her there were not many such in existence and that it would sadden her if Dorothy did not have one. She said they both understood the book's significance in each of their lives, and she also told Dorothy about the lines from Tennyson's "Locksley Hall" that had convinced her that her destiny was entwined with the sea:

And so, as you know, it has been. When I finally became its biographer, the sea brought me recognition and what the world calls success.

It brought me to Southport.

It brought me to you.

So now the sea means something to me that it never meant before. And even the title of the book has a new and personal significance—the sea around Us.

Carson and Dorothy were both passionate about the Christmas holidays, and for them it would always be a time for recounting things they'd done together in the last year and for looking ahead to what was to come. But in the weeks leading up to the holiday season in 1954, their letters became more expectant than usual—they were going to escape together to New York just after New Year's, and the logistics of this meeting mixed confusingly with worries that it might appear to be an assignation. Carson had recently discovered Eliot's "The Dry Salvages," and had been struck by the several lines in it that seemed full of meaning for them, especially the phrase "time not our time." She wondered if Dorothy was counting the days until their arrival in New York as she was.

They debated over which hotel was best. Carson thought either

the St. Moritz or the Barbizon-Plaza would be fine. She said she really
didn't care, as long as wherever they went was "out of range." They
also debated whether Carson should register under her "usual" name.
Carson decided that using an alias would make her feel silly. Besides,
she told Dorothy, "the hotel management doesn't matter." A more
important consideration, in Carson's mind at least, was the possibility
that, given their train schedules, they would arrive at the hotel at the
same time. Could they, Carson wondered, hide their emotions and
restrain themselves long enough to get up to their room? Or would
they give themselves away right there in the lobby? Dorothy thought
they could affect a nonchalant air. She told Carson that when they
were alone at last she wanted to spend an hour just being close to her
without speaking a word. Carson said she liked Dorothy's suggestion
for that first hour—and afterward they would see what happened.

Carson and Dorothy spent two nights at the Barbizon-Plaza. Apparently there had been some discussion about the advisability of Carson's spending a second night there, as Dorothy later thanked Carson
for staying over with her for what would otherwise have been a "desolate" night alone. Dorothy told Carson their room had been filled
with a "rosy glow" that vanished the moment Carson departed, leaving just an empty room. She said how nice it would be for them to be
able to remember the hours they'd had together. "Thus far I have no
regrets," Dorothy added. "How wonderful also."

A day later Dorothy again wrote to Carson to say how happy
their time together had been. She said it was "queer to see the moon
above the skyscrapers" but that seeing it with Carson was all that mattered: "Darling, again let me tell you how sweet every moment of our
being together was for me. Another lovely memory to be added to so
many others. Of course, I believe the setting for our type of happiness
is at its best in the natural world but if we can't always have that we
can create our own 'quiet bower' in a man-made environment, can't
we? It wasn't too bad, was it dear?"

Carson and Dorothy were together in New York for about forty-
four hours—long enough, somehow, for Dorothy to feel the need to,

say at the end that she had no regrets about any of it *thus far.* Carson, meanwhile, was uncharacteristically circumspect in the days following their meeting—saying little more than it had made her happy and that she could now return to *The Edge of the Sea* with renewed energy. She said they'd had a "lovely interlude."

Dorothy's caution—did she fear that regret would come with time?—was as unusual as Carson's reticence. Had they been intimate in a way they were now reluctant to acknowledge? Sex seems not to have been part of their relationship, or at least not an essential feature of it. Their surviving correspondence describes a transcendent, romantic friendship that existed in a realm above ordinary physical love and desire. Nowhere in their many hundreds of letters to each other are there the declarations of mutual attraction so common among sexually intimate couples. Their longing for each other was intense, an "overpowering emotional experience" that swept them up like an inrushing tide. They remarked often on the impossibility of anyone else understanding their feelings for each other. Rarely together in the same place for long—a few days here and there, sometimes a week or longer at West Southport—their relationship existed mainly on paper and in their own hearts and minds.

Their differences were complementary. Carson was famous and ambitious and had never given a thought to living any life other than a writer's life. She knew a lot about the world, but nothing of love. Dorothy was private and shared a rich, loving marriage with Stan. Together they had a son, and now a daughter-in-law and a grandchild named Martha whose company was a delight. Dorothy could cook and take care of things; Carson, despite years at the head of a sprawling family, was indifferent to domestic matters.

What they shared was an intensity of feeling for nature and books and music—a love for the beautiful things in life that are associated with the highest category of Platonic love. Platonic Eros is a hierarchy, with carnal desires at the bottom rung of what the classicist Allan Bloom called Plato's "ladder of love." At the top is "beauty itself," and it was on this highest rung that Carson and Dorothy began their affair of the heart. From the beginning, they related to each other mainly through their shared appreciation of "beautiful things" that were larger and more perfect than themselves.

A few weeks after their rendezvous in New York, Dorothy wrote to tell Carson that the night before, feeling anxious and having had too much coffee, she'd lain awake for a long time. At last her thoughts settled on their time together in Maine the previous spring, their "Maytime":

> Oh, darling, live over those days together sometime. Such happiness as those days brought to me. I remember the morning I got up before you did, to stand at the window for a long while looking down on your own special world. Darling, the tears came that morning—the whole situation was so lovely—so far lovelier than anything my wildest imagination could conjure up. Do you remember?

Alone with this memory in the small hours of the morning, Dorothy said she'd gone to get the letters Carson had sent the previous winter confessing the fullness of her love. Dorothy wondered how many hours Carson had spent writing them—they were so perfect and so finely composed—and she thought how the world would have valued that time had Carson instead devoted those same hours to writing things meant for everyone. Dorothy was amazed at how much they had discovered about each other over the past year and at the way there always seemed to be still another level of deeper understanding that could be achieved.

Although they never doubted one another, their letters sometimes betrayed the inherent fragility of what was a mostly long-distance relationship. They frequently worried that their words might be misconstrued. In letter after letter, one or the other of them finds herself apologizing for some slip of the pen—only to hear back at once that there was no misunderstanding for which to be sorry. For a while,

Dorothy had asked herself how long this incomparable thing could last. But no more:

> Darling, I'm sure now that with me it will last as long as I shall live—the year has not dulled my love and devotion to you by one little neutron—in fact my love is as infinite as that beautiful morning star which is my first ritual of each day—to look out at it and speak to you, to reach you in your subconscious for I always hope you are asleep. This morning I thought what a lovely experience it would be if we could watch that star rise together.

Despite the uncanny synchronicity between Carson and Dorothy—the conviction that their thoughts and feelings about life were identical—their relationship surely meant different things to each of them. For Carson, Dorothy was the one great love of her life. To Dorothy, Carson was the person who'd opened a world for them to share, one in which the birds would always sing, the rhythm of the sea would never cease, and the words for everything would endure. When Carson finished *The Edge of the Sea,* she decided to dedicate it to "Dorothy and Stanley Freeman—who have gone down with me into the low-tide world and have felt its beauty and its mystery." Overwhelmed, Dorothy and Stan asked her to consider this carefully. Carson answered that her only concern was whether *The Edge of the Sea* was a good enough book for the purpose. "I thought of waiting for another," Carson said, "but who knows what else will be written, or how that will turn out."

EIGHT

The Enduring Sea

C arson was determined to make *The Edge of the Sea* different
from the guidebooks that commonly grouped organisms
together by taxonomy—whether that was finches with
finches or crabs with crabs. Instead, she planned to organize her marine subjects according to the communities they shared and the
habitats in which they could be found. This ecological approach not
only reflected emerging scientific principles—much as she explained
them in her lecture to the AAAS in Boston—but would also make it
easier for readers who actually wanted to go down to the ocean and
know what kinds of plants and animals they were seeing.

Practical utility remained an essential part of the idea in spite
of Carson's conviction that it could be made as readable as *The Sea
Around Us*. As Carson drafted and revised early versions of the manuscript, its evolution to the longer and less discursive book it would
become moved closer to what she had in mind. A few other books
had taken similar approaches, notably Douglas Wilson's *Life of the
Shore and Shallow Sea*.

Published in 1935, *Life of the Shore and Shallow Sea* was really a book about the near-shore marine environments, and how they are influenced by tides, waves, light, temperature, and the like. The inhabitants of these regions, rather than simply being cataloged, were considered according to specific characteristics or life stages. So the chapter "Locomotory Movements," for example, looked at animals that swim, others that drift or walk or burrow their way into the sand, and some—like the cuttlefish or the octopus—that travel by means of water-jet propulsion. Wilson's cast of characters necessarily grew big and varied, from urchins to marine mammals such as seals and whales. Offering an observation that was well ahead of its time, Wilson also speculated on the daily movement of plankton and small marine animals from deep water to near the surface after dark that would soon take center stage in the debate over the "phantom bottom."

. But *Life of the Shore and Shallow Sea,* although nicely illustrated with photographs, was a challenge for amateur beachcombers to use. Plus, Wilson was British and so were his shoreline and its denizens. A better model, Carson thought, was a handsome book—already regarded as a classic—called *Between Pacific Tides* by Edward F. Ricketts and Jack Calvin. In the spring of 1951, as Carson was again marshaling a group of expert correspondents to help her with information and fact checking, she had written to Dr. T. A. Stephenson at University College in Aberystwyth, Wales. Stephenson had recently published a paper on the Florida Keys that Carson admired, and she wondered when he might do something similar on northern Florida and the Carolina coast. Carson was interested in this research, she said, as it related directly to her current project:

> I am at work on a popular guide to the seashore life of the Atlantic coast, in which I am departing from the traditional method of organization and am grouping the animals and plants as they are found on the shore. The basic idea is somewhat like that used in Ricketts and Calvin's *Between Pacific Tides* (although mine will be a less ambitious book) but we do not now have an Atlantic coast guide based on an ecological treatment.

Had she written to Stephenson a few months later—this was just before *The Sea Around Us* came out—Carson might have been less deferential toward *Between Pacific Tides*. As it was, she had already told Brooks in a less guarded moment that if the guide to the Atlantic coast turned out well they could proceed to do one on the Pacific shore. Whether Carson would have taken herself to the other side of the continent to work for months on coastlines she did not know is doubtful; she never did. But she had a few things in common with Ed Ricketts, who was the primary author of *Between Pacific Tides*. Ricketts was a kindred spirit in his passion for low tides and surf-pounded shores, and like Carson he knew what it was like to publish something at the wrong time. Beyond that, they could not have been more different.

Ricketts was originally from Chicago. He was ten years older than Carson and not so well educated, having departed abruptly from Illinois Normal State University after a messy encounter with a married woman. He traveled some, held various jobs, did a stint in the army, and ended up at the University of Chicago where—with another interruption following another dicey sexual escapade—he fell under the influence of a professor named W. C. Allee.

Allee didn't invent ecology, but he was on his way to becoming a towering figure in its emergence as a way of understanding the natural world. Like other scientific disciplines, ecology developed slowly and unevenly from early origins, particularly in Greek philosophy. It began to have recognizable principles in the nineteenth century and finally started to flourish in the twentieth. By the 1930s ecology was a robust science, and it owed a lot to the work of Allee, whose studies focused on animals not as individual organisms, but as *groups*. Allee had worked on marine ecology at Woods Hole early in the century, and in 1931 his book *Animal Aggregations* would establish itself as one of the foundations of ecological science.

In this same period, the studies of plants and animals were becoming more integrated, and researchers began talking about "biomes," large-scale segments of the total environment that could be understood only by learning how the life forms occupying them interacted and how such interactions were subject to environmental influences. The ocean is a biome, and within it are multiple zones that have unique characteristics—among them the intertidal zone over which the sea regularly advances and retreats, and where the life forms are adapted to the dramatic change in conditions that takes place several times each day.

Ricketts had gotten married and moved to the Monterey area in California, near the Hopkins Marine Station, which was the West Coast version of the Marine Biological Laboratory at Woods Hole. Monterey Bay, sheltered from the high Pacific surf in places and deep in the middle—the Monterey Canyon, as it's called, is more than eleven thousand feet deep—is home to an abundance of marine life. Ricketts loved exploring the tidal pools and mudflats around the area. He opened a biological supply company called Pacific Biological Laboratories, shipping specimens around the country and managing to eke out a living despite the Depression. The catalog started out with a few items—sponges, jellyfishes, corals, and such—but as the business expanded it came to include many other marine organisms, as well as rats, cats, and snakes. Ricketts operated out of a dilapidated house on a section of the waterfront called Cannery Row, across the street from one of the area's most popular brothels.

Part scientist and part salesman, Ricketts was also a proto-bohemian. He believed there was another dimension of knowledge that resided outside of everyday experience—a place where the truth behind everything could be perceived as whole and perfect—and he liked to talk about "breaking through" to that place in small ways, always hoping for more. Free in his thoughts, free in his behavior, Ricketts hated the idea of social restraint in all its forms. He sometimes wore a beard and regarded his marriage vows more as suggestions than rules whenever it suited him to do so.

The lab on Cannery Row became a hangout for an assortment of pretty girls, writers, artists, and other colorful types who loved Ricketts and appreciated his willingness to keep the place well stocked with phonograph records and cold beer. One member of this informal association was a young writer named John Steinbeck, who had a success in 1935 with a book of stories called *Tortilla Flat* that was soon followed by three memorable novels about the downtrodden and the dispossessed: *In Dubious Battle, Of Mice and Men,* and finally *The Grapes of Wrath,* which would come out in 1939, the same year as *Between Pacific Tides.* In 1945, Steinbeck published a raucous novel called *Cannery Row,* about a ragtag Depression-era group of friends whose lives in a crummy waterfront community center on their spiritual leader and benefactor—a marine biologist named Doc, whom Steinbeck based on Ed Ricketts.

In May 1948, at the end of a long day in the lab, Ricketts got in his car and went to buy a steak for dinner. He failed to stop as he approached the tracks of the Southern Pacific Railway and was hit by the Del Monte Express coming from San Francisco. Ricketts died three days later from injuries sustained in the crash, shocking everyone on Cannery Row, some of whom probably suspected he was not mortal. Ricketts was fifty-one when he died, but people who knew him said he looked ten years younger.

Steinbeck had studied biology and was captivated by Ricketts and by Ricketts's love of the intertidal seashore. For several years they contemplated the idea of coauthoring a guidebook to Pacific coastal marine life. In the spring of 1940, Ricketts and Steinbeck came up with a slightly different plan. They chartered a seventy-six-foot fishing vessel, the *Western Flyer,* and with its captain and crew of four, embarked on a four-thousand-mile collecting trip into the Sea of Cortez—more commonly known as the Gulf of California—which lies between the Baja peninsula and Mexico proper. Moving from one anchorage to the next, they went ashore at each stop to observe and collect and catalog marine organisms. They also pondered what such life forms might teach us about ourselves in order to—as Ricketts would put it—break though to a more far-reaching view of life:

We have looked into the tide pools and seen the little animals feeding and reproducing and killing for food. We name them and describe them and, out of long watching, arrive at some conclusion about their habits so that we say, "This species typically does thus and so," but we do not objectively observe our own species as a species, although we know the individuals fairly well. When it seems that men may be kinder to men, that wars may not come again, we completely ignore the record of our own species. If we used the same smug observation on ourselves that we do on hermit crabs we would be forced to say, with the information at hand, "It is one diagnostic trait of *Homo sapiens* that groups of individuals are periodically infected with a feverish nervousness which causes the individual to turn on and destroy, not only his own kind, but the works of his own kind."

Given the unusual collaboration between Ricketts and Steinbeck, it was not surprising that the book that resulted from this forty-day odyssey was big and wonderful and strange. *Sea of Cortez* was almost six hundred pages long and divided into two parts—a narrative of the trip and a descriptive inventory of the species collected. Ricketts handled the scientific section; both men worked on the narrative, which was based on journals kept by the captain of the *Western Flyer* and by Ricketts, as well as Steinbeck's own idiosyncratic impressions. The narrative tracked their journey as they visited different kinds of coastal environments—rocky headlands, tidal flats, beaches, coral reefs, and muddy, stinking thickets of mangrove. There's a salty, ironic flavor to the travelogue portion of the narrative, which is interrupted at one point for a lengthy and nearly impenetrable excursion into Ricketts's metaphysics of "non-teleological thinking." This was his idea—now a generally accepted principle—that biology does not operate as preferential striving toward some ultimate objective. If, for example, one regards evolution as a teleological process, then one sees the product and *purpose* of evolution as a better or "higher" organism. But the reality is that evolution only results in organisms better suited to prevailing conditions. Simply put, nature does not have a plan—it just happens.

Sea of Cortez was published on December 5, 1941, two days before the attack at Pearl Harbor, and it suffered the same fate as Carson's *Under the Sea-Wind,* collecting a handful of nice reviews before being swallowed up and lost in the turbulence of war. Carson presumably read *Sea of Cortez*—she read everything about the ocean and sea life—and she might have felt an affinity for the narrative portion of the book, as it was more like her own writing than was the unadorned, factual text of Ricketts's *Between Pacific Tides.*

What drew her strongly to *Between Pacific Tides* was not the narrative—there was hardly any—but its approach. Ricketts organized the book around the different kinds of shoreline encountered on the Pacific coast. These were further subdivided according to the marine life that was present within discrete zones that were differentially governed by the tides and surf. So a "rocky shore" on the open coastline, for example, could be divided into four zones, segmenting it from a few feet above the high-tide line, where organisms could be classified as "marine life" only by virtue of intermittent wetting from the spray coming up from the surf, down through the high-tide and mid-tide reaches, all the way to the levels of the lowest tides. This was useful, as any reasonably alert person could find his or her way to these places-within-places and identify what was living there from Ricketts's plainspoken descriptions. In some cases, Ricketts supplemented the straightforward catalog of species with more entertaining information:

Many years ago, when the Pismo clam was as common on exposed beaches in southern California as are sand dollars on bay and estuary beaches, teams of horses drew plows through the sand, turning up the clams by the wagon load. Now adults of the species are almost unobtainable in the intertidal zone. Experienced diggers with rakes or forks work at low tide, wading out waist deep or even shoulder deep, where the surf frequently breaks over them. It is hazardous work, for the diggers must feel their way along bars that are separated from the shore by deeper channels, and now and then the surf claims a victim.

For most species, Ricketts provided a careful description and sometimes a longer natural history, explaining peculiarities such as hermaphroditism in oysters or the curious habits of nemertean worms, which when disturbed break into pieces that undergo a subsequent regeneration and become complete worms again. The only thing missing in *Between Pacific Tides* was the voice of someone standing above this elemental environment and feeling within it the slow pulse of geologic time and the mighty force of evolution that lies inside and beyond the surging waters—a voice that belonged more naturally to Rachel Carson than to Ed Ricketts. And it came to her again as she turned her attention to the ocean's border. *The Edge of the Sea* would be the only book Carson wrote in the first person singular.

Carson explored many places along the Atlantic seaboard, from Maine to Key West, as she researched *The Edge of the Sea*. At every place she stopped, she took time to record the look of the shore and the sea, how the wind felt and what the surf sounded like, and how the sky and sand appeared. These descriptions were accompanied by detailed lists of plants and animals observed, many of which would later be drawn by Bob Hines. Carson was a master assembler, putting down bits of observation and narrative in related blocks of notes that were later joined together—though she again often used the same notebooks to keep track of expenses and other matters. Mixed in with notes on a section of rocky coast were plans and specifications for the cottage she would soon build at West Southport.

Carson revisited familiar places, some more than once, including Beaufort and Woods Hole. But she also made new discoveries, her favorite being St. Simons Island, Georgia, where the gradual slope of the sea bottom caused a vast tidal flat to emerge at low tide, creating a beach that periodically extended far into the ocean, as if the sea had not merely retreated but had rather moved itself nearer the horizon. Carson confided to her notebook the intense pleasure she took in exploring this expanse of sand, where she estimated as much as a half mile of shallow sea floor was exposed at low tide, and where you could walk out a long way over the firm sand and barely get your feet wet. At the outermost edge, where the sand mixed with clay, there were the same standing ridges that Carson had seen at Beaufort many years before, like shadows of the waves that would soon creep back toward land and inundate the ground on which she stood.

And yet nothing compared to Carson's own shoreline in Maine and its otherworldly menagerie of marine treasures and oddities. Carson wrote to an old college friend that her good fortune there was boundless:

The tides following the recent full moon have fallen to really spectacular lows and have proved to me that I'm living on a very exciting shore. I don't see how I could have picked a much better place for collecting purposes. I must try some color photographs, for I've never seen such a range of color in starfish—and they are simply lying about all over the place, in water and out of it, as inlanders would probably expect them to be, but as they practically never are in real life. The beautiful little red one, Henricia, is very common, and the northern star, Asterias vulgaris, comes in every conceivable color. We found a ten-inch one yesterday. Just below low water, the bottom is just paved with that beautiful calcareous alga in a rich rose color, and there are literally hundreds of green urchins lying about over it. And I've never seen so many anemones—big ones—and clusters of the soft coral, Alcyonium—and funny, fat little sea cucumbers down under layers of horse mussels, which themselves are hidden under a thick mat of Irish moss and brittle stars. Last night I went down after dark to return a big starfish I'd borrowed on the previous low tide, and it was quite eerie, with the big crabs, that hide during the day, slithering around over the rocks; and the anemones hanging down from the roof of their cave, seen by flashlight, looked like something Charles Addams dreamed up.

The Edge of the Sea was Carson's most personal book—the only one derived extensively from her own fieldwork—and her voice made it come alive. She still haunted the library, still read journals and technical papers, still consulted with experts. But in an important way she finally freed herself to enter a story, to take her readers in hand as together they explored the seashore. Utterly at home in the intertidal world—like Ricketts, she segregated it into different types, such as rocky shores and sandy beaches—Carson made *The Edge of the Sea* less a description of that realm and more of a lively guided tour. Writing of the sand dollars that lie just under the sand at St. Simons Island, Carson noted the subtle pattern on their backs, like a five-petaled flower that repeated the "meaning and the symbolism of the number five," which she called the "sign" of the echinoderms, a family that includes the five-legged starfish. Beneath the sand was a strange kingdom of burrowers, of which she was constantly aware:

> Walking back across the flats of that Georgia beach, I was always aware that I was treading on the thin rooftops of an underground city. Of the inhabitants themselves little or nothing was visible. There were the chimneys and stacks and ventilating pipes of underground dwellings, and various passages and runways leading down into darkness. There were little heaps of refuse that had been brought up to the surface as though in an attempt at some sort of civic sanitation. But the inhabitants remained hidden, dwelling silently in their dark, incomprehensible world.

Carson called the edge of the sea an "elusive and indefinable boundary," one that changes daily with the tides and thus has a "dual nature . . . belonging now to the land, now to the sea." And the shore is also altered over the course of many eons, as the climate shifts and the level of the ocean by turns rises and then subsides. As always, Carson regarded the sea with the greatest affinity, but also with awe, for it is the source of all life and the wellspring of history, a place where each day of the world bears allegiance to all the ages of the world, and to which we are inexorably drawn. In a draft of *The Edge of the Sea,* Carson composed an epilogue. Eventually she turned it into a short, haunting chapter called "The Enduring Sea" that comes at the conclusion of the book. In it, Carson describes a foggy night at Southport Island. As she listens from the window of her study, she is surrounded by the "sea sounds" of a rising tide. She thinks how this same tide is "pressing also against other shores" she has known and loved:

> Then in my thoughts these shores, so different in their nature and in the inhabitants they support, are made one by the unifying touch of the sea. For the differences I sense in this particular instant of time that is mine are but the differences of a moment, determined by our place in the stream of time and in the long rhythms of the sea. Once this rocky coast beneath me was a plain of sand; then the sea rose and found a new shore line. And again in some shadowy future the surf will have ground these rocks to sand and will have returned the coast to its earlier state. And so in my mind's eye these coastal forms merge and blend in a shifting, kaleidoscopic pattern in which there is no finality, no ultimate and fixed reality—earth becoming fluid as the sea itself.

In May 1955, Carson complained to Paul Brooks about the biographical profile of her that Houghton Mifflin had drafted for the jacket of *The Edge of the Sea.* She thought it came off as an unseemly attempt to "build up" the book's author, when, in fact, she was already well established. Carson had a point—*The Sea Around Us* had sold more than a million copies and had been translated into eighteen languages. Carson disingenuously said the mere thought of writing her own bio was too unpleasant to even think about. But she managed, eventually submitting an exhaustive biography that gave a detailed accounting of every award and distinction she'd won for *The Sea Around Us*. Brooks said it was great but that he'd have to shorten it a little.

About a month later Carson was at West Southport, busily corresponding with an editor at the *New Yorker* named Sanderson Vanderbilt on the excerpts of *The Edge of the Sea* that were being readied to appear in the magazine in two installments. Just before the Fourth of July, she told Vanderbilt she needed a ten-day break in order to prepare and deliver an important speech. In truth, Carson was indulging her habit of doing things for the least likely of people.

Although she was often overwhelmed with fan mail and requests for information, Carson routinely took time to compose long, thoughtful letters in response to inquiries from students or teachers. She thought nothing of saying no to speaking engagements—the more important and high profile they were the less likely she was to accept. But she had a soft place in her heart for struggling organizations. The speech she mentioned to Vanderbilt was to be given at a fund-raiser for the fledgling Lincoln County Cultural and Historical Association in Maine. Carson spoke at the Wiscasset High School auditorium—not far from Boothbay Harbor—and accompanied her talk with color slides Stan Freeman had taken near her cottage and out at Ocean Point the previous summer.

Carson was unhappy when she learned that Houghton Mifflin had set November 9, 1955, as the publication date for *The Edge of the Sea*. Ignoring the fact that she had delivered the often-delayed manuscript years after it was due, she complained that Houghton Mifflin was now jeopardizing the book's prospects with its "late publication" schedule. Carson took her case over the heads of Paul Brooks and Lovell Thompson, writing instead to Houghton Mifflin president Henry Laughlin to urge an earlier release for the book. She said a big reason *The Sea Around Us* had done so well was that it came out almost immediately after its serialization in the *New Yorker*. With *The Edge of the Sea* set to appear in the *New Yorker* in late August, Carson thought whatever momentum it got from the magazine would evaporate by mid-November. She also claimed that many people had told her they finished their Christmas shopping by November 1 and were already disappointed that they wouldn't be able to give *The Edge of the Sea* as a holiday gift.

Laughlin was out of the country, then abruptly back home to see his terminally ill mother through her final hours. In his stead, Lovell Thompson—who must have found Carson's insistence on an earlier publication pretty rich—patiently explained that every book has its own life and that what had been important to the success of *The Sea Around Us* would be much less so with *The Edge of the Sea*. Thompson assured Carson that she was now a famous bestselling author whose name alone would carry *The Edge of the Sea* and that booksellers and readers would eagerly snap it up whenever it came out. Besides, he said, reproducing Bob Hines's drawings made the book's production schedule challenging and hard to modify. But he said they'd think it over.

A week later he wrote to Carson again, saying he thought they could issue the book on either October 31 or November 1. When Henry Laughlin got back to the office a few days after this message, he at once wrote to Carson, telling her deferentially that *The Edge of the Sea* was to be Houghton Mifflin's "big book of the season" and that they would do everything possible to ensure its success. Laughlin said they would try for publication in the third or fourth week of October.

"The Rim of Sand" appeared in the August 20, 1955, issue of the *New Yorker*. It was followed in the next issue by "The Rocky Shores." Alerted to another book coming from Rachel Carson, an eager readership awaited *The Edge of the Sea* when it was published on October 26. Few were disappointed.

Reviewing *The Edge of the Sea* in the *New York Times,* Charles Poore caught the joyous mood that would prevail in most of the notices. The "main news," Poore wrote, was that Carson had "done it again." He said her new book was as "wise and wonderful" as *The Sea Around Us* and that she had a remarkable knack for making the reader care about "all sorts of spiny and slime-wreathed creatures that you've hitherto regarded with hearty loathing when you wanted to go in swimming and the tide was low." Poore was struck by how Carson avoided being overly technical and by the way the breadth and variety of her enthusiasms became contagious in her prose:

> Apparently Miss Carson can do no wrong. Even when she gets off that bit about how a thousand years are but a moment in the life of nature that the cosmic wallahs favor, we find ourselves nodding fatuously and saying to ourselves, "How true," for all the world as if Miss Carson were to exercise a patent on the notion. Matter of fact, though, as she shows, life whizzes by rather briskly for many members of her cast. And if they are under-privileged in comparison with modern man in the sense that they can't wallow in fretfulness over hydrogen bombs and such, they do take, like little men, the ceaseless surge and thunder of the sea.

Earl Banner, writing in the *Boston Globe,* said the book was even better than *The Sea Around Us.* Exercising a Bostonian's innate distaste for all things Manhattan, Banner assured his readers they needn't worry that the earlier magazine serialization would diminish the impact of the book. "Since so many *New Yorkers* end up in the trash barrel . . . this should have no important affect [*sic*] upon book sales," he wrote. Freely mixing its metaphors in a brief, unsigned notice, *Time* magazine likened the natural world portrayed in *The Edge of the Sea* to an "underwater ballet," explaining that "Author Carson has shown her remarkable talent for catching the life breath of science on the still glass of poetry."

There were a few dissenters. Writing for the *New Republic,* Jacquetta Hawkes said it felt to her as if Carson had "exhausted the heart of her subject" in *The Sea Around Us* and was now working around its margins in a way that was "a little sad." And Farley Mowat wrote in the *Toronto Telegram* that Carson had tried to repeat the lyric qualities she'd achieved in *The Sea Around Us,* but that she had overdone it this time and succumbed to a "mazy sentimentality." This, Mowat, said, was something that often happened to writers—himself among them—who tried to "deal with a factual subject in too markedly a literary manner."

Perhaps the most perceptive review came a few months after publication, in a British journal called *Books and Bookmen,* in which John Langdon claimed that people who obsessed over the beauty of Carson's prose risked losing sight of what her books were about. Good writing, Langdon said, "is not a mere matter of style." If it were, he concluded, then "we should be as blind in reading books as when we scan the seashore, seeing alike the leaping adjective and the tumbling wave." Langdon likened writing to painting, in which the point is not the cleverness of the brushstroke but how recognizable is the reality it shows. He said he was not surprised that so skilled a naturalist as Carson would find a way of explaining what she knew:

> It is not an accident of history that Gilbert White and Charles Darwin described flora and fauna with genius, nor that the great mariners and voyagers in distant lands can re-create their experience as part of our own. They wrote as they saw and their honest, questing eye, their care for detail is raised to the power of art by a deep felt love of nature, a respect for all things that live and move and have their being.

Four weeks after its release, *The Edge of the Sea* joined the *New York Times* bestseller list at number eight. Solidly atop the list at number one was Anne Morrow Lindbergh's acclaimed memoir *Gift from the Sea,* the story of a famous woman's attempt to find meaning in her life during a beachcombing sojourn on Captiva Island in Florida. In mid-December, with *The Edge of the Sea* at number four and *Gift from the Sea* still at number one, the two First Ladies of the sea were joined on the bestseller list by Walter Lord, whose account of the sinking of the RMS *Titanic* in *A Night to Remember* came in at number twelve, reminding everyone that the sea could be treacherous as well as beautiful.

Carson, exhausted and anxious—though as always protective of her interests—closely monitored the reception of *The Edge of the Sea*. She told Dorothy Freeman that the thrill of unexpected success that had come with *The Sea Around Us* could never happen to her again, but that this was all right as it had been replaced by Dorothy's devotion. Dorothy's support was a "rare flower" Carson would treasure, no matter what. Because *The Edge of the Sea* was so firmly anchored in scenes from the Atlantic seaboard, Carson doubted that it would sell well enough in other parts of the country to equal her earlier effort. She would have to make do, she said, with being satisfied if the book could at least be judged on its own merits, though she was braced against the probability that it wouldn't be.

"I know that, even if this book achieves acceptance, acclaim, and sales that by any reasonable standards amount to 'success'—still by comparison with *The Sea* it will fail," she said. When *The Edge of the Sea* did make it onto the bestseller lists—not just in New York but also in Chicago—Carson said she was content and would be even if it never went to the top. "I'll be happy that it is Mrs. Lindbergh's book and not something sensational or trashy that holds that position." Carson told Dorothy that she had never met Anne Lindbergh but that she would like to, preferably "on a beach."

As it became clear that she had another success, Carson insisted that the flood of good reviews for *The Edge of the Sea* was a shock and frankly hard to believe. She told Dorothy she was too aware of the "many flaws" in the book to read the critics without serious reservations. The best thing, she said, would be to think of the reviews as something she could maybe live up to in the future. Not surprisingly, Dorothy felt differently and suggested that when they could be together again they could read the reviews out loud and relish them line by line.

Carson had recently been approached by the Ford Foundation to write a script for the CBS-TV cultural series *Omnibus*—an idea that intrigued her even though she had doubts about the medium. She told Marie Rodell that she was "indifferent" to television, but realized that it now reached a large audience and so could not be ignored. Plus, Carson thought the program's subject—clouds—would present an interesting challenge. But as she got further into discussions with the people from *Omnibus*—whom she described to Dorothy as "difficult"—Carson had second thoughts. Over the course of several months, Carson tried to understand exactly what was wanted of her, while Marie Rodell attempted to finalize the contract with *Omnibus*. Carson felt herself in the unpleasant position of being tentatively committed to something that she might not want to go on with. Dorothy, hoping to calm Carson's worries—and aware that Carson paid little attention to television—told her she liked the *Omnibus* series and thought the program generally well done. Dubious, Carson wrote back to say that if that were true, then it must be by way of "some miracle I can't explain."

But Carson went to work on the script in her usual way—creating files about clouds, making lists of things to include, jotting down ideas and drafting fragments of script on random pieces of paper and in her ever-present spiral notebooks. She decided that television people were simply different and that the *Omnibus* staff was working in a way that was completely normal—"for them." The subject, though, seemed uncannily familiar.

Carson saw the atmosphere as an "ocean of air," with humanity standing on the bottom and watching the clouds floating above us. "In relation to the air-ocean," she wrote, "we are exactly like deep-sea fishes, with all the weight of tons of air pressing down upon our bodies." Carson and *Omnibus* eventually came to terms, and the program aired on a Sunday afternoon in early March 1956. Afterward, one of Carson's neighbors in Silver Spring stopped over to say that he'd have known she'd written it even if her name hadn't appeared in the credits at the end. In a letter to one of the production assistants at *Omnibus,* Carson fibbed that her initial foray into television writing had been "fun."

Another phase of Carson's life was coming to an end. Ever since the publication of *The Sea Around Us,* Carson had been besieged with requests from magazines wanting to write profiles of her. She always said no, frustrating Marie Rodell no end. In August 1955, Rodell discussed an idea with J. Robert Moskin, the articles editor at *Woman's Home Companion,* that she thought might overcome Carson's reluctance to embrace the role of public figure. Moskin said that rather than interview Carson, he wanted her to write an article for the magazine telling parents how they could instill an appreciation of nature in their children. The tentative title was "Teach Your Child to Wonder," and Rodell and Moskin calculated that it would appeal to Carson because of her special relationship with her grandnephew, Marjorie's now four-year-old son Roger. It did.

"Help Your Child to Wonder," as the piece was finally called, ran in the July 1956 issue of *Woman's Home Companion,* under a tempting subheadline announcing it as "her first magazine article since the publication of her bestselling books *The Sea Around Us* and *The Edge of the Sea.*" In writing about her experiences with Roger by the ocean's edge or up among the spruces on the hillside behind the cottage in Maine, Carson revealed something of herself and her own feelings about nature, just as Rodell had hoped she might. The whole point, Carson argued, is not to try to "teach" a child about the natural world, but rather to simply share with him or her the act of looking at and listening to the world around us all.

Carson believed that adults lose a natural curiosity about nature that they have as children, but that it takes only a willingness to visit a beach or a forest to rediscover a human fascination with the environment and to transmit it to even the youngest of children. How could a child not be enchanted by the sight of a ghost crab scurrying away over a nighttime beach before the searching cone of light from a flashlight—or by the discovery of a tiny evergreen taking root in the forest if he or she is told it must be a Christmas tree for squirrels? All that is required to make this happen is for adults to pay attention to nature as if it were something never seen before that might never be seen again. To make the point, Carson detoured into a personal reflection, freely disclosing her innermost feelings and mentioning— though not by name—Dorothy:

> I remember a summer night when such a thought came to me strongly. It was a clear night without a moon. With a friend, I went out on a flat headland that is almost a tiny island, being all but surrounded by the waters of the bay. There the horizons are remote and distant rims on the edge of space. We lay and looked up at the sky and the millions of stars that blazed in the darkness. The night was so still that we could hear the buoy on the ledges out beyond the mouth of the bay. Once or twice a word spoken by someone on the far shore was carried across on the clear air. A few lights burned in cottages. Otherwise there was no reminder of other human life; my companion and I were alone with the stars. I have never seen them more beautiful: the misty river of the Milky Way flowing across the sky, the patterns of the constellations standing out bright and clear, a blazing planet low on the horizon. Once or twice a meteor burned its way into the earth's atmosphere.
>
> It occurred to me that if this were a sight that could only be seen once in a century or even once in a human generation, this little headland would be thronged with spectators.

When Dorothy read a draft of the piece it made her cry. Carson said she thought the article revealed a different side of her that would to some extent satisfy the public's curiosity about Rachel Carson. That year at Christmas, Carson bought herself an expensive Fisher phonograph that featured an AM/FM radio. The music from it played like a stirring soundtrack behind plans for a future that had long seemed impossible but that now whirled in Carson's imagination like a raging fever. For years, Carson and Dorothy had wanted to acquire a section of land behind Carson's cottage at West Southport and convert it into a nature sanctuary they planned to call the Lost Woods, a name taken from an essay by H. M. Tomlinson. The question was always one of money. But now Oxford University Press had agreed to generous royalty terms on a junior edition of *The Sea Around Us,* which was to be issued by Golden Press. There was enough money in this project to take care of Marjorie, who was in poor health with arthritis and diabetes, and Roger for the foreseeable future. Meanwhile, Simon and Schuster wanted to renew its association with Carson on an anthology called "The World of Nature." If it did as well as Carson believed it could—the book was to be part of a series that was already selling strongly—the royalties could be as much as $150,000, an astonishing sum and more than enough to proceed with the Lost Woods.

Dorothy, who for a long time had worried about the financial burden Carson bore in caring for her family, was overcome with joy. To think that it had begun long ago, in their "Maytime," and might finally become a reality was almost too much to believe—even though it seemed that Carson had met one obligation only to take on another. "And now this Dream—I know its accomplishment will have its satisfaction for you, but beyond that, the joys and rewards are going to be shared by so many others that even in this you are losing yourself," Dorothy wrote. "Do you wonder I worship you?"

A month later, after a hospitalization from which she never fully recovered, Marjorie died. Shocked by her niece's sudden passing and painfully aware of the fact that she would soon turn fifty, Carson began making arrangements to adopt Roger.

NINE

Earth on Fire

On the morning of January 22, 1954, a ninety-three-foot wood-hulled tuna boat named the *Lucky Dragon* departed Yaizu harbor on the southeastern coast of Honshu Island, Japan. At the helm was Hisakichi Tsutsui, a replacement for the ship's regular captain, who was ill. Tsutsui, although licensed as a fishing boat captain, was one of the youngest members of the twenty-three-man crew. Most of the men regarded the fishing master Yoshio Misaki as their leader. The *Lucky Dragon* was heavy and slow, powered by a 250-horsepower engine that was assisted, when the wind was right, by sails carried on two short masts.

It was cold, and two days out they struck bad weather that lasted four days. After the storm subsided, Misaki gathered the crew together and told them they were not going south to the calm fishing grounds near the Solomon Islands—as everyone had been told—but were instead making for Midway Island, which was far to the east and known for treacherous seas that grew steep on their long fetch across the open Pacific Ocean. Nobody wanted to go that way, but in the end they agreed with Misaki that the fishing was likely to be better in that direction. The men weren't paid a straight wage, but instead shared in the proceeds from the catch, so the more fish they brought home the more they would earn.

The *Lucky Dragon* was a "long line" tuna boat that put out a single line, as much as fifty miles long, to which hundreds of shorter, baited lines were attached at intervals. At two forty-five in the morning of February 7, 1954, the ship was south of Midway Island when Misaki ordered the crew to start fishing. The line stayed out for four hours as the *Lucky Dragon* drifted lazily nearby. It took another thirteen hours to haul the line back in. The catch was poor—only fifteen fish. The radio carried reports of better fishing beyond Midway, closer to Hawaii. But the *Lucky Dragon* was already near the limit of its range. For a few days the crew struggled with broken fishing lines, bad weather, and a balky engine that needed constant attention. Misaki wanted to go north, which would shorten the return voyage to Japan and likely produce more fish. The crew agreed that the fishing might be better in that direction, but the seas would be much more dangerous. Instead, they implored Misaki to head southwest. Reluctantly, he agreed.

For the next several weeks, the *Lucky Dragon* made its way toward the Marshall Islands, first going south and then west. The fishing remained poor. By the end of February, they had brought in only 156 fish and some of the crew now regretted not listening to Misaki. A couple of hours before dawn on March 1, 1954, the long line was put over once again. The *Lucky Dragon* cut its engine and drifted silently on a calm sea beneath the stars and a few wandering clouds.

A crewman named Shinzo Suzuki woke up when the engine stopped and, unable to go back to sleep, went out onto the fantail of the ship. The morning air was warm and heavy. Scanning the dark horizon, Suzuki spotted the blinking light from a float on the long line. He was looking to the west when all at once a blinding wall of light burst into the sky and lit up the surface of the ocean. In seconds it went from searing white to yellow before changing again into a mix of yellow and orange and red, a monster light that Suzuki could not stop looking at even as he began yelling to the crew that the sun had suddenly risen in the west. Sleepy and confused, the crew came on deck and stared gaping at the terrifying light, which grew dimmer but continued to spread and rise into the sky. Minutes went by. Then the *Lucky Dragon,* all ninety-nine tons of her, shivered and lurched as if the great weight of the thousands of feet of ocean beneath her keel had reached up and tapped the hull. In the same instant a roar like the end of the world passed over the ship, followed by two deep, concussive shock waves. Terrified, the crew flattened themselves on the deck. Nobody knew what was happening.

Misaki considered ordering the *Lucky Dragon* ahead at full speed in a direction away from the light. But he couldn't bring himself to abandon the long line that was still in the water, even though he knew it hadn't been out long enough for any kind of catch. While the crew began hauling in the line, the radio operator, a man named Kuboyama, made a hasty calculation. Guessing that the loud sound wave had hit the ship about seven minutes after they'd first seen the light in the sky, Kuboyama estimated that the *Lucky Dragon* was roughly eighty-seven miles from whatever had happened. As he looked at their position on a chart with Misaki, Kuboyama saw that there was nothing in that direction but a vast stretch of ocean and a few small piles of sand called Bikini atoll, which was eighty-five miles away.

Dawn came as the crew worked at retrieving the long line, but the sky was pale and strange. After a few hours what at first looked like a gentle snow began to come down, though the men quickly realized it wasn't snow but something more like sand or maybe ash. It was gray and it coated everything. Some of the men thought it might be salt and a few of them picked up a pinch and tasted it. Misaki thought maybe it was volcanic dust and he again checked his charts to see if there was a volcanic island nearby that could have erupted or even exploded like Krakatoa. But he couldn't find anything.

Whatever the gritty stuff falling out of the sky was, it continued to rain down on the ship, turning everything it touched a milky, sickly shade of gray. The *Lucky Dragon* started to look like an apparition.

The men tried to wash down the main deck and some of the fishing gear and found that the dust, which seemed heavier and stickier than either sand or salt, was hard to clean away. Some of the men complained of aching eyes, and later on others noticed that they weren't hungry at mealtime. A couple felt nauseated. Just before midnight, Shinzo Suzuki, who'd been the first to see the frightening light, got out of his bunk to stand watch and promptly threw up.

The *Lucky Dragon* set its course for home. One by one, the crew fell ill. Their eyes hurt and were clogged with grit and an oozing, yellowish discharge. Suzuki could not get out of bed. The men felt their skin begin to itch and burn, especially the palms of their hands where they'd handled fishing lines covered with ash. Sores appeared on their skin, and they noticed that everyone looked as if they'd gotten a sunburn. Misaki thought there was something about the ash that wasn't right, and he collected some—it was still all over the ship—and stored it in a bowl by his bunk so that somebody could investigate it when they got back to port. The radioman Kuboyama thought the same thing and put a sample of the ash wrapped in paper under his pillow. But nobody tried to get rid of the dust, which wasn't just on the decks and the gear, but was now on everyone's clothing and in their hair and in the galley where they ate.

As the *Lucky Dragon* neared Japan some of the crew found that their hair was falling out. Kuboyama, who everyone agreed was the best-educated man among the crew, regarded this latest symptom with alarm. He recalled that hair loss was one of the after-effects of exposure to radiation that had occurred in the bombings at Hiroshima and Nagasaki. He met with Misaki and the two of them agreed that the whole crew should visit the hospital as soon as the *Lucky Dragon* made port. By the time they reached Yaizu harbor on March 14, 1954, the men looked terrible. Their "sunburns" had deepened to the point where their faces and hands looked blackened. Everybody was convinced the *Lucky Dragon* had wandered into the Pacific Proving Grounds, an area in the Marshall Islands that was restricted because of ongoing nuclear testing by the United States.

This was puzzling, as the restricted area was centered on Eniwetok atoll, which had been the site for all of the U.S. nuclear tests in the Pacific since two atomic bombs had been detonated at Bikini atoll in 1946. Eniwetok was three hundred miles west of the *Lucky Dragon*'s position on the morning of March 1, 1954. Somehow, nobody aboard the ship had gotten word that the restricted area had recently been extended far to the east in anticipation of a new series of tests at Bikini. Gradually it sunk in that what crew had seen that morning and what was now making them all sick could only have been one thing: an atomic bomb.

It turned out to be worse than that.

The *Lucky Dragon* never did enter the restricted area of the Pacific Proving Grounds, coming only within twenty miles of its eastern boundary—a position that should have been safe. What the ship ran into was not a line on a chart but rather the unintended consequences of a fierce arms race between the United States and the Soviet Union, combined with a horrific scientific miscalculation.

Experiments in nuclear fission, a chain reaction in which energy is produced by splitting the nuclei of heavy elements such as uranium or plutonium, had first been conducted in laboratories in 1939. It seemed likely that when the Manhattan Project was launched during World War II, the known principles of fission could be applied to building an atomic bomb. The certainty that Nazi Germany was working toward the same objective made development of a bomb all the more imperative. But as early as 1922, scientists had also speculated that the release of energy through a thermonuclear fusion reaction with hydrogen as a fuel—essentially the same thing that happens inside the sun—could be used in an explosive device. There were uncertainties, the most serious of which was the possibility that such an explosion might set off a chain reaction involving the light elements in the earth's crust and atmosphere, instantaneously extinguishing all life and converting the planet into a star in an apocalyptic flash of light and heat. Subsequent calculations suggested that such a catastrophic event was unlikely—though the matter needed further consideration as different kinds of fuels were contemplated. The eventual "good news" was that a self-propagating, earth-destroying chain reaction could not be initiated by a bomb because so much of the explosive energy would dissipate as radiation.

During World War II, the scientists with the Manhattan Project worked simultaneously on the development of both the atomic and the hydrogen bombs. Although the latter was still largely theoretical, some of the researchers argued it should be the main objective, with fission devices needed only as triggers for hydrogen bombs. But the atomic bomb won out. On August 6, 1945, an atomic bomb called "Little Boy" destroyed the city of Hiroshima, Japan. Three days later, "Fat Man" was dropped on Nagasaki. Tens of thousands died in both cities—most of them civilians who were incinerated or pulverized in the explosions—and many thousands more were sickened by radiation. Japan surrendered six days after the second bomb, and with the war at an end further development of a hydrogen bomb slowed.

But in August 1949, the Soviet Union, a onetime ally that had evolved into a potential enemy, successfully tested its own atomic weapon. The United States—fearing a hydrogen device might be next for the Russians—urgently renewed work on a thermonuclear bomb. The early prototypes were not practical weapons, as they used large amounts of supercooled liquid fuels and were the size of buildings. The first explosive hydrogen device—it was far too big to be called a bomb—was detonated in a test called "Ivy Mike" on the tiny island of Elugelab, part of the Eniwetok atoll, on November 1, 1952. The initial fireball was more than three miles wide. It slowly transformed into a mushroom cloud twenty miles high and one hundred miles wide. An observation plane flying at 40,000 feet fifteen miles away detected a heat pulse on its wings of more than ninety degrees Fahrenheit. Elugelab was erased; in its place was a water-filled crater more than 160 feet deep and over a mile in diameter. When scientists examined debris from the blast they discovered that the periodic table would have to be enlarged, as two new heavy elements—later named "einsteinium" and "fermium"—had been created in the nuclear inferno.

As impressive and frightening as Ivy Mike was, the Air Force demanded faster development of an "emergency capability" weapon, meaning one that could be produced efficiently and at a size small enough for delivery from a bomber. A practical bomb also had to be light enough that its descent could be slowed by a parachute after it was released in order to give the plane enough time to escape the ensuing blast. A year and a half later, as the *Lucky Dragon* rode at ease on the dark Pacific swell east of the Marshall Islands, a new and compact "dry" device using isotopes of hydrogen and lithium as fuel sat waiting on a small patch of reef in the Bikini atoll. The test was named "Castle Bravo" and the device itself was called "Shrimp."

The firing center for the Castle Bravo test was in a heavily reinforced bunker about 30 miles away, across the atoll's central lagoon, on the island of Enyu. When the controller touched the trigger the sky itself seemed to explode in a hellish fireball that was visible more than 250 miles away. Moments after the blast, but before the sound from it reached Enyu, the bunker started to move. It took the men in the bunker a few seconds to realize that they were feeling the ground shock wave, which travels faster than sound travels through the air, but which nobody had ever experienced before because it was normally absorbed by the earth over a short distance. This was an indication that everything had not gone as planned—which was confirmed as the mushroom cloud above Bikini atoll shot through the troposphere and into the mid-stratosphere some 114,000 feet above the ground, taking with it many tons of hot, irradiated coral reef and sand. A number of other islands in the atoll were leveled and a change in the wind from southerly to westerly sent the immense cloud of radioactive "fallout" careening through the upper atmosphere to the east, where some of it would come back to earth on top of the *Lucky Dragon* and its crew. Within days it was determined that a large section of the northern portion of the Marshall Islands—an archipelago of atolls and individual islands scattered over a thousand miles of ocean from east to west—was contaminated with radiation. Native inhabitants from several islands downwind of the test had to be evacuated.

Data collected during the test eventually showed that one of the Shrimp's lithium isotopes that was expected to be inert instead amplified the fusion reaction, increasing the power of the device beyond what had been predicted. Castle Bravo was supposed to produce an explosion equal to six million tons of TNT. But Shrimp exploded with the power of fifteen million tons of TNT—two and a half times what had been expected and the equivalent of one thousand bombs the size of the one dropped on Hiroshima.

On its return to port, the *Lucky Dragon* and its unlucky crew became the object of intense curiosity and concern. The men were so dark they frightened people on the waterfront, and those with families were met with shock and disbelief at home. When the ship was inspected it was found to be contaminated with varying amounts of radioactivity—the highest levels being topside and on exposed gear. The *Lucky Dragon* was moved to quarantine on the opposite side of the harbor so it could be examined further before being burned at sea. Officials hastily tracked down the ship's catch—which had already been auctioned off, mostly to fish markets in Osaka and Tokyo. They found the fish were also radioactive and had to be confiscated and buried.

Meanwhile, the crew, treated first by local doctors, then at more sophisticated facilities in Tokyo, grew more uneasy about their fate. The condition of the men puzzled medical authorities—who had plenty of experience with radiation sickness and who had the assistance of the American-run Atomic Bomb Casualty Commission in Hiroshima. The ABCC wasn't a treatment facility, but a research organization that had been studying the aftereffects of the atomic attacks nearly a decade before. Yet no one who examined the men of the *Lucky Dragon* had seen symptoms like theirs.

Most of the crew seemed in good if less than robust health. Only Shinzo Suzuki had been too ill to work his watches on the return voyage, and although a number of crew members complained of poor appetites, it seemed unlikely that any of them had received lethal doses of radiation, as they would have been much sicker by then if they had. But the doctors were perplexed by the crew's darkened skin and suppurating lesions. They were even more alarmed by the fact that the men were radioactive. Routine bathing and washing hadn't completely removed the residue of the ash that had fallen from the sky onto the *Lucky Dragon*. Men who still had their hair—where by far the most radioactivity was detected—were shaved bald and scrubbed and rescrubbed until all the ash was removed. As the men's dermatological symptoms improved, the doctors waited to see if they would become more ill before they got better, as this was typical in radiation exposure. And with one exception they did.

The crew of the *Lucky Dragon* would end up confined to the University of Tokyo Hospital for more than a year. Initially they suffered from fatigue and loss of appetite. Later it was bleeding gums, then falling white blood cell counts and compromised bone marrow. Treatments included frequent blood transfusions and the regular administration of antibiotics to fight infections. Some of the men developed liver problems and jaundice that turned their once-blackened skin deep yellow. After only a couple of months their sperm counts had fallen to zero.

But then everyone began to improve—including the radio operator Kuboyama, who in August spoke with reporters on behalf of the crew. Kuboyama said the men hoped they would receive compensation from the United States for their hospitalization and lost income. He said he was feeling much better. But a month later, as the rest of the crew continued to recover, Kuboyama took a turn for the worse and died of liver failure. Japanese and U.S. authorities disagreed over whether the cause was radiation sickness or a hepatitis infection Kuboyama might have contracted from one of his many blood transfusions. Either way, Kuboyama's death was the direct result of his proximity to the Castle Bravo test and thus became a tragic emblem of what was by then a serious international incident. Japanese fishing boats at sea all across the Pacific radioed condolences. The American ambassador to Japan offered his sympathy to Kuboyama's family and sent the widow a check for a million yen on behalf of the "American government and people."

The story of the *Lucky Dragon* had, of course, made headlines in the United States—where officials were initially vague as to what kind of test had taken place at Bikini atoll on March 1, 1954. At first, the contaminated fish seemed to be the main concern. The *New York Times* reported that the catch of mainly tuna and shark from the *Lucky Dragon* was sufficiently radioactive as to pose a threat to human life, and frightened Japanese housewives were avoiding the normally bustling fish markets. Then, not quite two weeks after the *Lucky Dragon* came home shrouded in radioactive dust, two more Japanese fishing boats returned to port with dangerous levels of radioactive contamination after fishing in areas east of the Marshall Islands. None of the crew on either ship had fallen ill, but people were shocked to learn that one of the boats, the *Bright God* out of Shiogama, a port city northeast of Tokyo, had been exposed to the same "shower of radioactive ash" that had burned the crew of the *Lucky Dragon* despite being some 780 miles away from the Castle Bravo test site. The Japanese government, while conceding it had been informed the previous fall about upcoming atomic testing in the Pacific Proving Grounds, insisted that the *Lucky Dragon* never got any specific warning about the Castle Bravo test and never entered the restricted area.

On March 24, 1954, during a news conference, President Eisenhower acknowledged that the Castle Bravo test had produced an explosive force "never experienced before" that had "surprised and astonished the scientists," who were now rethinking precautions for future testing. One immediate step the United States took was to enlarge the restricted area to encompass four hundred thousand square miles—about eight times the size of the original restricted zone. Then on March 28, three weeks after the test, the *New York Times* in an editorial abandoned the official description of Castle Bravo as a test of an "atomic device" and instead called it what everyone by then knew it was—a hydrogen bomb.

The *Times* said that the development of a hydrogen bomb was a cause for great concern under any circumstances, but that given what had happened to the *Lucky Dragon* even more caution was now needed to protect human and marine life in the mid-Pacific. Anticipating the concept of "mutual assured destruction" that was to become the central premise of a controlled Cold War, the *Times* took the occasion to hint that the U.S. victory in the race to build a hydrogen bomb meant that there was "still hope, though at present a faint hope, that the recent event in the Pacific may lead to some effective agreement with the Russians for the international control of atomic energy, no matter for what purpose it may be used."

Public concerns did not slow the pace of testing in the Pacific Proving Grounds. Another hydrogen bomb was exploded at Bikini atoll on March 27, 1954, followed by another on April 7, then by three more detonations—one "boosted fission" device and two hydrogen bombs.

In early April, the Japanese government asked the United States to halt future testing in the Pacific Proving Grounds during tuna fishing season, which ran from November to March, and to ensure that the Japanese commercial fleet received advance notice of all upcoming tests. U.S. officials started negotiating financial compensation for the crew of the *Lucky Dragon,* while at the same time striving to reassure the public that there was no general radioactive contamination of fish in the Pacific Ocean. Japanese officials were dubious.

In July 1954, a team of Japanese scientists visited Bikini atoll, where they found fish and other marine life "seriously affected" by the H-bomb testing. This was the same conclusion reached in 1947, a year after the previous testing at Bikini, when it had been reported that "everything that grows on Bikini or swims in the water is radioactive." Even so, the scientists seven years later endeavored to calm fears about seafood back in Japan by eating some raw fish caught in the waters near Bikini atoll, apparently without ill effect. Their report said that although fish in the area were "radioactive about the gills and internal organs," it seemed to be safe to eat their flesh. Three months later, a large catch of tuna arrived at Yokohama in which one of every ten fish was found to be radioactive. They'd been caught one thousand miles east-northeast of the Marshall Islands.

The fleeting, cataclysmic chain reaction at the center of a nuclear explosion has been likened to a small manmade star that appears for an instant and annihilates everything nearby. In July 1945, scientists working on the Manhattan Project wondered exactly what would happen when they exploded the Trinity device in the first-ever nuclear test in New Mexico that month. Most were confident—though not certain—that earlier calculations suggesting the bomb might set the atmosphere on fire were wrong.

The intended consequences of such a weapon in battle—death and destruction on a massive scale—had also been predicted. Devastation would be caused only partly by the heat and radiation that would vaporize everything close to the blast. The main destructive effects would come from the shock wave traveling outward and extending over a much larger area. Because the earth would absorb and also reflect much of the energy from a blast at ground level, a bomb would have to be detonated in the air above its target to achieve maximum results. Little consideration was given to the secondary contamination of remote locations from radioactive debris transported high into the atmosphere. But such fallout was to become the great fear of the nuclear age.

The mushroom cloud is not a unique signature of a nuclear bomb. A big explosion of any kind can create one, blowing a hole in the air and filling it with hot gases that rise rapidly, creating a powerful updraft of fire and smoke and vapor that vacuums in the storm of dust and debris caused by the blast and carries it all, elevator-like, straight up. A nuclear explosion, being so much bigger and hotter than any conventional explosion, creates a huge mushroom cloud that not only picks up a great volume of debris but also makes it radioactive. And because it can rise far above the altitude of the jet stream, the radioactive debris in the mushroom cloud from a nuclear bomb does not fall straight back to earth, but instead becomes entrained in upper-level wind currents, merging with the weather itself as it sweeps over oceans and continents, eventually raining back to earth where it will.

News of the hydrogen bomb test at Bikini atoll and the subsequent plight of the crew of the *Lucky Dragon* reached an American public largely unconcerned that what had happened on the other side of the world, in the middle of a vast ocean, was also happening here, over American farms and suburbs and cities. Between 1951 and 1955, the United States conducted *forty-nine* aboveground tests of nuclear devices at the Nevada Test Site, sixty-three miles north of Las Vegas. None involved hydrogen bombs, and some were small "safety" tests that produced little radiation and no fallout. In some tests the bombs were dropped from airplanes; in others they were exploded on towers.

The power of these devices varied considerably—from a small fraction of what was delivered when Little Boy went off 1,900 feet above Hiroshima, to some that were two or even three times as powerful as Little Boy. The resultant mushroom clouds carried hundreds of different fission products into the atmosphere, including at least twenty kinds of radionuclides—atoms with unstable nuclei that emit radiation—that were the most dangerous components of fallout. This continuing conveyance of radioactive debris into the atmosphere contributed to a perpetual global cloud of radioactive contamination also coming from nuclear testing by the Soviet Union and the United Kingdom. All of this debris sooner or later returned to earth.

People could experience "ambient" exposure to radioactive fallout simply by getting close to it or touching it on the ground. Or they could inhale or ingest it. One effective route of delivery turned out to be cows pastured on ground that received fallout. Cows that ate contaminated grass gave milk that contained concentrated radionuclides—milk that was, in turn, consumed by humans, mainly children.

Nuclear testing in Nevada was widely reported, of course, but the public paid little attention to fallout other than as a product of nuclear war, should one occur. Radioactive fallout had been discovered with the first atomic explosion—the test of the Trinity device. In his top-secret report on the test to President Truman, General Leslie Groves, who was the military head of the Manhattan Project, said that Trinity proved not only that the atomic bomb was powerful—it produced what were described as "tremendous blast effects"—but that it also sent skyward a lingering mushroom cloud that was more massive than anticipated and that rose to an altitude that surprised everyone.

The Manhattan Project scientists were convinced that a temperature boundary in the atmosphere at about seventeen thousand feet would be an impenetrable barrier to any cloud from the explosion that might reach that high. But the mushroom cloud from Trinity "surged and billowed upward with tremendous power" and in the space of five minutes had shot past seventeen thousand feet and reached an altitude of forty-one thousand feet. It was understood that the blast cloud would contain "huge concentrations of highly radioactive materials," and Groves felt it necessary to explain how worrisome this new symbol of total warfare was:

> The cloud traveled to a great height first in the form of a ball, then mushroomed, then changed into a long trailing chimney-shaped column and finally was sent in several directions by the variable winds at different elevations. It deposited its dust and radioactive materials over a wide area. It was followed and monitored by medical doctors and scientists to check its radioactive effects. While here and there the activity on the ground was fairly high, at no place did it reach a concentration which required evacuation of the population. Radioactive material in small quantities was located as much as 120 miles away. The measurements are being

continued in order to have adequate data with which to protect the Government's interests in case of future claims. For a few hours I was none too comfortable about the situation.

General Groves also informed the president that he had managed to keep local press coverage mostly confined to what the government's official release said about the test, though some enterprising reporters had talked with a number of eyewitnesses who described the explosion. One of these, Groves said, was "a blind woman who saw the light."

The extent of the fallout from Trinity had far more distant boundaries than General Groves realized. A few months after the Trinity test, the Eastman Kodak Company in Rochester, New York, started seeing blips and streaks on unexposed film it manufactured for industrial X-ray equipment. After some investigation, Kodak determined that the film was being contaminated by radiation emanating from the cardboard containers into which it was packaged. The cardboard had come from a couple of different suppliers in Iowa and Indiana—paper mills that drew their water from rivers flowing out of midwestern watersheds that were downwind of the Trinity test, albeit many hundreds of miles downwind.

The far-reaching effects of fallout were more dramatically observed in late January and early February 1951, following a series of Nevada nuclear tests that took place in the space of just over one week. The first bomb in the series, called "Ranger Able," was a small one—less than one-half of one-tenth the size of Little Boy. But when it went off one thousand feet over the desert after being dropped from a plane it sent radioactive debris up in a mushroom cloud that reached seventeen thousand feet. Even though this was well beneath the jet stream, tracking planes followed the cloud all the way across the country. It arrived in New England after only two days. Along the way it became entangled with a storm, and radioactive snow fell on upstate New York. Ranger Able was followed one day later by "Ranger Baker," a bomb sixteen times as powerful. This time the mushroom cloud rose to thirty-five thousand feet and again headed for the East Coast, where three days after the test radioactive snow fell in Central Park in New York City.

Subsequent tests in the Ranger series broke windows in Las Vegas and entertained people by lighting up the sky before dawn every couple of days. When "Baker Fox," the final bomb in the series and a behemoth almost twice as big as Little Boy, was detonated on February 6, 1951, crowds of gawkers parked their cars in the early morning darkness along the highways outside the bombing range to watch the display. The blast again smashed windows many miles away, and the searing light from the explosion, first white then dark red, startled passengers on an airliner passing over Durango, Colorado, six hundred miles to the east. The mushroom cloud rose above forty thousand feet, caught the wind, and headed straight south over Las Vegas en route to Phoenix, Arizona; Brownsville, Texas; and on out over the Gulf of Mexico.

On went the tests, in Nevada and in the Pacific, always with the same fearful urgency that had become part of the national psyche in America and in the Soviet Union as the two countries built out arsenals capable of destroying the planet many times over. H. G. Wells had predicted as much, back in 1914 in a book titled *The World Set Free,* in which he imagined warfare in the 1950s involving "atomic bombs." The arms race had, in fact, begun in 1939—the same year that Paul Müller discovered the lethal properties of DDT in his lab in Switzerland—when Albert Einstein sent a letter to President Roosevelt telling him about recent experiments in physics that might lead to a new kind of weapon unlike anything before.

Dr. Einstein explained that scientists in several countries—including Germany—were working on nuclear fission. If fission could be induced in a sufficiently large quantity of uranium, Einstein said, it might lead to a chain reaction that would release "vast amounts of power and large quantities of new radium-like elements." The likelihood of achieving this in the near future was all but certain. Fission, Einstein told the president, could be used for energy production or for building bombs. Einstein thought such bombs would be too big to be carried on airplanes, but one could perhaps be put on a boat and exploded near an enemy port, where it "might very well destroy the whole port together with some of the surrounding territory."

An important consideration for America would be to secure a source of uranium, as there were poor stocks of the ore in the United States. Einstein pointed out that Czechoslovakia had good uranium mines, but that Germany had recently halted sales of the ore when it took control of Czechoslovakia. As this seemed to mean only one thing, Einstein urged that the United States—even though it was not yet at war with Germany—speed up its experimental work on nuclear fission at once.

After the war, the American fear of a competing nuclear state was transferred to a new enemy, the Soviet Union—whose 1949 test of an atomic bomb had been ahead of the timeline predicted by U.S. intelligence. It was followed by a hydrogen bomb in 1955. The Soviet program was believed to have been aided by an American husband-and-wife espionage team, Julius and Ethel Rosenberg, who supposedly handed over diagrams of atomic weapons and other documents that enabled Soviets to accelerate their development efforts.

It was actually unclear if the Rosenbergs gave up anything of real value to the Russians—or whether Ethel was even directly involved—but they were caught up in a new kind of public hysteria. The Rosenbergs were convicted of spying and were put to death in the electric chair at Sing Sing prison in 1953. Ethel's execution was unusually brutal, as two applications of the current failed to kill her, and the third, which finally ended her life, set her on fire.

President Truman all but shut down America's civil defense efforts at the close of World War II, but after the Soviet atomic test in 1949 and the outbreak of war in Korea a year later—seen by some as a distraction initiated as a prelude to a Soviet move in Europe—Truman launched a new agency called the Federal Civil Defense Administration in early 1951. Not surprisingly—given its ludicrous mission of protecting the United States in the event of nuclear war—the agency was widely distrusted, chronically underfunded, and in constant dispute with states and cities as to who was responsible for what.

The agency's mission was to develop plans for the evacuation and sheltering of the entire U.S. population in the event of nuclear war. In practice, the agency mainly distributed pamphlets and short films— many aimed at schoolchildren—with advice on how best to survive a nuclear attack. It also plastered public buildings with the civil defense logo to indicate which ones were suitable as bomb shelters in the event of an air raid. But as the decade progressed, the concept of civil defense grew increasingly tenuous. Just one month after the Castle Bravo test at Bikini atoll, civil defense officials in New York said they had to completely rethink how best to respond to a nuclear attack in which a single hydrogen bomb could level the city. The only solution seemed to be a complete evacuation of eight million people—an improbable undertaking given the Air Force estimate that it could provide an advance warning of about one hour in the case of a Soviet attack with long-range bombers. A year later, citizens in Washington, D.C., were mortified to learn that Congress had allocated $115,000 for civil defense in the nation's capital—compared with the $650,000 annual budget for the national zoo.

In the early 1950s, the civil defense advice dispensed to the public emphasized the likelihood that most people would survive a nuclear war. Anyone unfortunate enough to be close to ground zero of an atomic bomb explosion—from a weapon comparable to the bombs used against Japan or possibly a little larger—would, of course, be killed outright, as would many others within a radius of a couple of miles. But the effects of heat and blast and initial radiation that were the main threats diminished the farther away you were.

Civil defense officials also insisted that there was little to fear from the "radioactive clouds" sent high into the atmosphere in an atomic explosion, as the debris within them emitted much less radiation than was given off in the initial blast and would be "carried off harmlessly" and dispersed over a large area. This had been the case in bombings of Hiroshima and Nagasaki, where all of the radiation sickness had been attributable to exposure to "explosive radiation" and not to lingering radioactivity that precipitated out of the sky.

It was also assumed that atomic bombs would be routinely set to detonate high over their targets—which would maximize the blast effects and also reduce the volume of radioactive debris sent skyward. People were told that it would be safe to leave cover "after a few min-utes" following an atomic attack in order to assist the injured and help fight fires that were likely to have started. The notion that an atomic detonation would render a large area uninhabitable for a long time was dismissed as a "myth." The U.S. Department of Defense said that for fallout to become a significant danger over a longer period would require the simultaneous explosion of "thousands" of atomic bombs.

Of course, as Castle Bravo demonstrated, a single hydrogen bomb could easily be a thousand times as powerful as an atomic bomb, and as the U.S. and Soviet nuclear arsenals shifted to hydrogen weapons, everyone had to rethink the meaning and nature of nuclear warfare. An aerial burst of a hydrogen bomb could be expected—depending on the size of the weapon—to cause massive damage as much as twenty miles away from ground zero and would fill the sky with tons of deadly radioactive debris. By the end of the decade fallout was seen as the *major* threat in a nuclear exchange that would kill millions of people initially and pose a continuing danger to tens of millions in its aftermath. This meant that, in theory at least, everyone in the United States needed access to a fallout shelter with supplies of food, water, medicines, and other necessities that could last at least two weeks. In 1955, the Civil Defense Administration spent $8.3 million trying to develop "survival plans" for communities across the country—a grim undertaking that in the end seemed pointless.

The folly of civil defense planning grew in direct proportion to the increasing danger inherent in a nuclear exchange with the Soviet

Union. In fall of 1957, the Russians launched *Sputnik,* the first man-made earth satellite—gaining a shocking advantage over the U.S. space program and signaling that the Soviet Union would soon be capable of attacking the United States with rockets armed with nuclear warheads. This would cut any advance warning of an attack from an hour or two to something like fifteen minutes—rendering meaningless the concept of mass evacuations from targeted areas.

The Americans and the Soviets had both been working on missile systems since World War II, and in the late 1950s and early '60s, the nuclear arsenal was rapidly deployed among growing fleets of long-range, land-based rockets and missiles that could be launched from submarines anywhere in the world. Armageddon, which had been coming into view since Trinity, could now be envisioned as two great shadows rising from the earth simultaneously and passing each other in opposite directions above the atmosphere, curving toward the end of all things in a white-hot hell of thermonuclear doom.

It was understood, of course, that not every American city would be targeted. But the lesson from Castle Bravo and the tests that followed was that living through a nuclear attack was only the first step in surviving whatever would come after that, as radioactive fallout would prove similarly deadly over a much greater area. Nuclear warfare was a two-headed demon that killed whatever was close to the fire and poisoned everything else.

In 1958, a high-ranking civil defense official declared that the "saving grace" in a nuclear attack was that anyone who wasn't vaporized in the initial blast would have some time to reach shelter before the fallout began to come down. But the original plan to build a nationwide system of fallout shelters never happened. Civil defense officials had imagined an elaborate complex of underground community shelters, protected areas in schools and other public buildings, and subsidized private shelters for individual property owners. But the cost of such a system—estimated at a then unimaginable $300 billion—was prohibitive. In 1957, President Eisenhower rejected a more modest proposal for a $40 billion national shelter system, on the novel theory that total nuclear war was an unacceptable proposition. "You can't have this kind of war," Eisenhower said. "There just aren't enough bulldozers to scrape the bodies off the streets." By the 1960s, the question some civil defense planners had begun to ask was whether in the event of nuclear war "the survivors would envy the dead."

Anxiety over the prospects of nuclear confrontation—mixed with a growing awareness of the mushroom clouds rising regularly over the American desert—were reflected in what became a science fiction subgenre unto itself, the "radioactive mutant" film. The prototype—a giant lizard called *Godzilla*—came from Japan in 1954 and gave rise to a string of B-movies produced in America, all formulated on the idea that exposure to radioactivity could change the nature and appearance of someone or something, and always for the worse. One favorite was a 1957 film called *The Amazing Colossal Man*, about an army officer injured in a nuclear test who suddenly grows to a height of sixty feet—a size at which insufficient blood supply to his brain sends him rampaging. Another was *Them!*, a surprisingly well cast and ingeniously written shocker that came out the same year as *Godzilla*. It was about an outbreak of radioactively enhanced killer ants that had morphed to the size of Studebakers and developed a paralyzing scream. These silly but nervous entertainments came after a more sober and cautionary issuance from Hollywood, the 1951 classic *The Day the Earth Stood Still*, in which an alien arrives on earth accompanied by a robot with immense powers. Their mission is to inform the planet's inhabitants that if they continue the development of nuclear weapons an interplanetary police force would have no choice but to destroy the earth.

This was, of course, an indictment of the so-called Cold War between the United States and the Soviet Union—though the term seemed an antiseptic way of describing the grim images of nuclear holocaust that every American carried at all times, a mournful fear that one day—no one could say when or for sure—the sky might light up as if from a thousand suns and that would be it. None of this was lost on America's children, who drilled regularly for the end of the world. If a teacher suddenly yelled "Flash!" every kid over the age of five knew that meant to "duck and cover" by whirling to the floor and crouching beneath his or her desk, arms wrapped tightly around heads to wait patiently for the shock wave to arrive. There were also panic-inducing policies concerning who was to go where in the event there was a warning of an imminent attack. For many kids, this meant that if you lived close enough to school to run home in less than fifteen minutes you could do so—and presumably then at least die with Mom and Dad. Those who lived farther away were to stay put and let death visit them at school.

These same children, having learned this lesson well, came of age in the 1960s having no problem believing that the world could end and that human technology could end it by means both seen and unseen.

Even after the attacks on Japan, atomic warfare—though a fearsome possibility—remained an abstraction for most people. Nuclear weapons were built in the belief that having them meant they would never be used. But this was not true of the other new weapon of the modern age. DDT had been invented to fight a war without end. The insecticide helped eradicate dwindling populations of malaria-carrying mosquitoes in the United States and in Europe, where the disease was already on the way out, and was then almost immediately commercialized for use in agriculture and many food service industries, in forestry, and for residential insect control. Nobody understood exactly how DDT worked, though it was clearly some kind of nerve poison. It was also relatively inexpensive to manufacture and its lethal effects persisted long after it was applied, notably when it was sprayed on the inside walls of buildings. As synthesized, DDT is a whitish powder. It doesn't dissolve in water but can be formulated into dusts, oil-based sprays, and aerosol "bombs" used for fumigating entire rooms. People sprayed their beds with DDT to control bedbugs, delighted that a

A sober-looking Carson, standing second from right, with her Pennsylvania College for Women field hockey team. She played goalie. © RACHEL CARSON COLLECTION/CHATHAM UNIVERSITY ARCHIVES (ALL PHOTOS ON THIS PAGE)

Carson's senior portrait at PCW, 1928.

Biology professor and Carson mentor, the glamorous PCW student favorite Mary Scott Skinker.

Pioneering deep-sea explorer William Beebe inside the bathysphere, in which he rode with Barton a half mile into the abyss.
© WILDLIFE CONSERVATION SOCIETY

Above: The brooding nature lover Richard Jefferies, whose writing Carson adored.
© RICHARD JEFFERIES SOCIETY

Above: Henry Williamson, Carson's main literary influence. She loved his books and ignored his fascist politics.
© HENRY WILLIAMSON LITERARY ESTATE

Right: Ed Ricketts, the prince of Pacific tides and Steinbeck's model for "Doc" in *Cannery Row.*
© ED RICKETTS JR.

Carson's 1944 employee photo
at the Fish and Wildlife Service.
UNITED STATES FISH AND WILDLIFE SERVICE

Odd company: Carson with Marianne Moore and James
Jones at the National Book Award ceremony, January 195?
© QUEENS LIBRARY/ARCHIVES/NY HERALD-TRIBUNE PHOTO MORGUE

Left to right: Captain Sorrell, Carson, *New York Times* books editor Francis Brown,
New York Herald-Tribune books editor Irita Van Doren, and Carson's agent, Marie Rodell,
at the 1951 publication party for *The Sea Around Us* on board the RMS *Mauretania*
in New York.

Above: Carson at Woods Hole, 1951.
© LINDA LEAR CENTER FOR SPECIAL COLLECTIONS
AND ARCHIVES, CONNECTICUT COLLEGE
(BOTH PHOTOS ON THIS PAGE)

Left: Paul Brooks.

Above: With the publication of *Silent Spring,* Carson's name was everywhere, including in the comics. © PEANUTS WORLDWIDE LLC; DIST. BY UNIVERSAL UCLICK. REPRINTED BY PERMISSION. ALL RIGHTS RESERVED.

Opposite, above: A DDT truck takes the war against insects to Jones Beach, New York, in 1945. © BETTMANN/CORBIS

Opposite, below: Carson testifying before a U.S. Senate committee in the spring of 1963. COURTESY LIBRARY OF CONGRESS

Left: President Kennedy at his August 29, 1962, news conference. Asked whether the federal government would investigate the safety of pesticides, Kennedy said that because of "Miss Carson's book," it already was. JOHN F. KENNEDY PRESIDENTIAL LIBRARY

Carson with Roger at Southport Island, 1960.
© ERICH HARTMANN/MAGNUM PHOTOS

Dorothy Freeman.
FREEMAN FAMILY COLLECTION

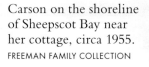

Carson on the shoreline
of Sheepscot Bay near
her cottage, circa 1955.
FREEMAN FAMILY COLLECTION

single application worked "for months." DDT went wherever people lived or ate or grew their food.

As the first in a wave of synthetic insecticides that came into use after World War II, DDT steadily replaced natural pesticides such as pyrethrum, which is derived from chrysanthemum flowers, and an assortment of arsenic-based compounds that were heavily used on crops such as cotton and tobacco—a poisonous additive that made cigarettes even more toxic than they inherently were. Nobody kept close records of how much DDT was used, or where—especially early on. But the speed with which it entered into widespread use was breathtaking.

In 1943, a sample of just six pounds of DDT arrived in America and was promptly subjected to testing by the U.S. Public Health Service, the U.S. Department of Agriculture, and the Kettering Laboratory at the University of Cincinnati College of Medicine. The results suggested it would be safe and effective in battlefield situations. It was mass-produced during the war to fight typhus, malaria, yellow fever, and encephalitis, and its use against those insect-borne diseases continued after the war.

In 1950, about 12 percent of the DDT made in the United States was shipped overseas for malaria control. Meanwhile, production for agricultural, commercial, and home uses soared. Domestic DDT use peaked in 1959, when Americans used eighty million pounds of it, and over the course of the nearly three decades during which it was available in the United States, an estimated 1.35 billion pounds were used. A number of companies produced DDT and other synthetic insecticides: DuPont, Dow Chemical Company, Union Carbide Chemicals, Velsicol Chemical Corporation, Monsanto, Thompson Chemicals Corporation, American Cyanamid, and Shell Chemical Company.

DDT is an "organochlorine" compound, that is, a molecule built on a backbone of carbon atoms to which atoms of hydrogen and chlorine are attached. It is sometimes referred to as a "chlorinated hydrocarbon." The success of DDT—coupled with the fact that researchers almost immediately discovered that insects sometimes developed a resistance to it—touched off a feverish effort to develop related chlorinated hydrocarbon compounds that also worked as insecticides. DDT was soon joined by a host of toxic cousins. These included lindane, chlordane, heptachlor, toxaphene, dieldrin, aldrin, and the apocalyptically named endrin, which had a toxicity many times that of DDT. It was a thriving international business, as the United States continued to produce quantities of all these chemicals that far exceeded domestic demand. In 1952, the combined production of aldrin, dieldrin, endrin, heptachlor, chlordane, and toxaphene was forty-nine million pounds. By the end of the decade it was double that.

Some of these compounds were more dangerous to use than DDT—chlordane and dieldrin, for example, are readily absorbed through the skin—and some cases of severe reactions to DDT were actually reactions to the "carrier" solvent in which it was sprayed. Although the public was warned not to spray DDT on animals, many people did anyway, dousing their cats and dogs with DDT. The sometimes serious skin reactions that occurred in pets were caused not by the DDT, but by the kerosene in which it was dissolved. Organochlorine compounds, whether they are absorbed, inhaled, or ingested, are highly lipophilic, meaning they are readily stored in fatty tissue and can accumulate over time with chronic exposure. They also tend to stick on surfaces and to remain active in soils.

Chemists at the same time discovered that compounds called organophosphates also had insecticidal properties. Organophosphates are not inherently poisonous, and they comprise a diverse group of biologically important molecules—DNA is an organophosphate. But certain manmade organophosphates were developed that are potent disruptors of nerve impulses—the deadly nerve poison sarin is an organophosphate, as is the nerve agent VX. Both are chemical warfare compounds designated as weapons of mass destruction by the United Nations. Insecticides based on organophosphate compounds include parathion and malathion. Organophosphate insecticides are more toxic than those based on organochlorines, though they are less persistent in the environment. Organophosphates are more easily metabolized and tend not to be stored in fat—but they can do extensive damage to the nervous system during acute exposures, especially in a developing fetus.

The "safety" of a pesticide is a relative question, as the toxicity of any substance depends on the dose and the route of exposure. Calling a compound an "insecticide" identifies its purpose and suggests that its effects are specific to the targeted pests. But, in fact, scientists had determined only that insects could be killed with doses of DDT that didn't seem harmful to people, and, for all anybody knew, enough DDT would kill a person in the same way it killed a bug. Because all life on earth evolved from common ancestors, all living things share certain biological features. The most obvious is DNA, which is present in all living organisms—other than some viruses—and which performs the same function in all of them. A specific sequence of DNA—a gene—makes RNA, which makes the same protein whether it's in a mouse or a whale. And the more alike two organisms are, the more their respective genomes resemble each other. A human and a chimpanzee have genomes that are 96 percent identical. Above the molecular level, many biological processes are also "conserved" among different species.

One such feature is the transmission of electrical signals along nerve cells, or neurons. These impulses, powered by the rapid movement of ions across the cell membrane, carry sensory information and control muscle movements. In certain types of neurons these messages must cross gaps—as happens at the juncture between a neuron and a muscle—and this is accomplished by chemical chaperones called neurotransmitters. Once the impulse has been delivered across such a juncture, specialized enzymes neutralize the neurotransmitter and restore the chemical balance in the gap.

During the early development of the organochlorine and organophosphate insecticides, such cellular processes were incompletely understood. But because these poisons caused twitching and rigidity and convulsions it was thought that they must in some way interfere with nerve impulses, possibly by disrupting the actions of neurotransmitters or by interfering with the flow of ions across the neuron's cell membrane. Either could lead to the repeated firing and intermittent paralysis of muscle cells. Which is exactly what was observed in the case of insects poisoned by DDT or other insecticides. The ultimate cause of death following such "general uncoordinated activity" was believed to be "metabolic exhaustion."

After their initial studies, researchers started to wonder whether pesticides, especially the fat-soluble organochlorines, could build up in the body of someone repeatedly exposed to them—and if such a bioaccumulation did occur, what would be the effects of the increasing body burdens of pesticides? But it would be years before scientists would learn that special proteins, embedded in the membranes of cells or deep within their nuclei, act as hormone receptors—and that these receptors can make mistakes, binding to pesticides or their by-products as if they were hormones and thereby initiating willy-nilly, out-of-control cellular responses that can lead to disease and reproductive issues.

Putting aside the long-term health hazards arising from pesticide exposure—cancer and birth defects, for example—fatal or serious human "intoxications" by organochlorine insecticides were thought to be rare, usually the result of careless application by agricultural workers, suicide attempts, or accidental ingestion by children. Whether pesticides were environmentally safe—that is, whether their continued use over long periods posed a risk to ecosystems generally—was a different question, one the FWS had continued to ask, ever since its preliminary investigations on DDT in 1945.

The first tests were inconclusive. DDT from aerial spraying across forestlands killed insects and was powerfully lethal to fish and shellfish in waters that received overspray. The absence of obvious harm to birds, mammals, and amphibians in the field trials was contradicted by lab experiments showing that DDT was toxic to every kind of animal tested. Outside the lab, repeated field testing over the same areas showed that as DDT concentrations increased, more species were harmed. The same was true in laboratory experiments, where every species tested—mice, rabbits, bobwhite quail, frogs—got sick or died from DDT exposure. One intriguing finding was that birds seemed to tolerate being sprayed with DDT, but fell ill or died when they were fed DDT.

As expected, these interweaving lines of inquiry, in the field and in the lab, consistently showed that the higher the dose, the more lethal the effect. This preliminary research led to guidelines intended to limit the concentrations of DDT used in spraying projects. As the scientists at Patuxent saw it, using DDT to treat buildings for mosquitoes or even soldiers in delousing programs presented a limited threat to the environment. Using it on croplands, forests, and residential neighborhoods upped the ante. "As soon as DDT was taken outdoors," they reported in 1947, "the dangers were instantly multiplied."

These early investigations did not keep pace with the rapidly expanding use of DDT almost everywhere and all at once—especially in the growing use of airplanes in aerial spraying operations. In a summary report at the close of 1947, the Patuxent group said unknowns about DDT still outweighed the evidence of its safety in general use, particularly with respect to collateral damage that might befall "beneficial" species in ways that could profoundly alter ecosystems:

> The nature of complications that might be expected following the wide scale use of DDT out-of-doors are many and varied. Entomologists have contemplated the possible complications that might arise with the elimination of natural control agents along with the pest species. Horticulturists, plant pathologists, and others, have been concerned over possible direct toxic effects to the plants themselves, and to indirect consequences that might develop with the accumulations of the toxicant in the soils. Ver-

tebrate biologists have watched the growing popularity of DDT and its increased use in wildlife habitats, and speculated on what the end result would be for valuable game and non-game species.

The investigators struggled to reconcile effects seen in the lab—which could be controlled but might not predict what would happen in the environment—with findings from the field, where the supposedly controlled "dosing" of an area with DDT was an imprecise endeavor, complicated by weather and forest cover and local topography. Birds and animals sometimes simply fled areas being sprayed with DDT, leaving researchers to wonder whether they had safely moved out or became sick somewhere else. The investigators presumed that killing much of the insect population in a spraying operation would starve certain other species that eat insects. How could anyone determine, in such an open and complex environment, whether birds and animals that disappeared were poisoned or simply departed for some other reason?

Some effects of DDT spraying were surprising. Trout in northern Idaho whose diets usually consisted of ants, worms, and water-hatching insects suddenly turned up with bellies full of crayfish that had been paralyzed by DDT, whereas trout in nearby streams that hadn't been sprayed seemed not to eat crayfish at all. But like all of the results from this study—which involved aerial spraying over an area of four hundred thousand acres—this finding was of limited value because of the problems inherent in conducting well-controlled experiments in such a vast environment. The sprayers were careless about where they dropped DDT, and they didn't stick to a reliable schedule. In the end, the investigators were never sure whether they were checking a treated area or an untreated one or, for that matter, whether any given finding was a "before" or "after" observation.

It was also apparent, as the Patuxent group investigated private spraying operations, that DDT was commonly being applied in concentrations far above FWS recommendations, which were two pounds per acre—and only one-fifth pound per acre in areas with aquatic habitats. In one orchard in Allegany County, Maryland, a grower trying to control codling moths treated his trees multiple times over the course of the summer with DDT at concentrations of between fifteen and twenty-two and a half pounds per acre—for an estimated season's total approaching *seventy* pounds an acre. The researchers said a "cursory" survey found only about a third as many birds on the property as there were in surrounding areas that hadn't been sprayed.

In response to the burgeoning market for synthetic pesticides, Congress in 1947 passed the Federal Insecticide, Fungicide, and Rodenticide Act—which, though often modified, would live on in perpetuity as the primary legal authority for the regulation of these and related products. In its initial incarnation, FIFRA stipulated how pesticides in interstate commerce were to be formally registered and labeled, but the law in no way limited the sale or use of pesticides. It was this anything-goes environment—which was sure to play out over the course of many seasons in many years—that most worried the Patuxent group. Based on their own studies, it appeared by 1949 that DDT could be applied at a rate of two pounds per acre as many as four times a year without causing harm to nesting birds. Mammals appeared to be even less susceptible to DDT than birds were, but care and lower concentrations had to be used near water. Nobody knew what a higher dose—between two and four pounds an acre—would do. At five pounds per acre there were grave consequences.

In one study of a spraying program for gypsy moths, 83 percent of the bird population was wiped out within two weeks. A year later bird numbers in the area were still around 15 percent below normal. In other areas, where similar spray concentrations appeared to be less lethal to birds, the explanation was often that the birds had completed their nesting periods and simply flew away when the spraying began. None of these findings addressed the question of what happened when spray concentrations were ten or fifteen or even thirty times the recommended levels. Most important, they shed no light on how spraying the same places over a long period might multiply, over and over, year after year, the amount of DDT in the environment.

In their 1949 assessment, the Patuxent researchers said this was their biggest concern: "Although the immediate advantages of DDT as a control agent have been demonstrated on a wide scale, the possible hazards, particularly those resulting from repeated and long-time use of the insecticide, are not so well known."

A year later, the Patuxent researchers began backing away from the proposition that applications of DDT at low concentrations could be considered "safe." Even at low rates of application—like the ounce or two per acre needed to control mosquitoes—DDT disturbed food chains and caused a variety of species to desert treated areas. And there were some invertebrate species, including mites and aphids, that were resistant to DDT and whose populations exploded when competing species were exterminated with insecticides—an effect by which one group of pests was simply exchanged for another.

The researchers acknowledged a growing concern for preserving the "balance of nature," but said this was a difficult issue to assess. Insecticides were typically used in settings—on croplands and in buildings and on residential areas—that were far from pristine, and where nature was already unbalanced through human intervention. In remote, undisturbed ecosystems, a balance of floral and faunal species could be maintained for long periods—but this meant only that the "balance of nature" was more of an abstraction than a realistic endpoint in areas of human activity. The scientists also warned that this division of the world into discrete segments—the treated landscape where pests were "controlled" and the pristine regions thought to be beyond the reach of synthetic pesticides—could dissolve if the use of chemical controls became so heavy that the patchwork of areas being treated blurred and melded to the point that the total environment became contaminated:

> Many types of control projects are routinely utilizing amounts of DDT which are hazardous not only to insect populations generally, but to many species of vertebrate life. In careful appraisals of experimental five pound per acre applications, it has been estab-

lished that local extermination is a real threat for many invertebrate species. The direct kill of many vertebrates was also found
to be appreciable at this dosage level. Single or total seasonal application rates for some types of control may involve 5 to 15 times
this amount. Such a pollution of lands and waters, if extended
to large continuous blocks, would undoubtedly have most dire
effects.

By 1951, the Patuxent pesticides project had determined that the
cumulative effect of spraying DDT at a supposedly "safe" concentration over the same area year after year ultimately led to sharp declines
in bird populations. Over the course of four years following the first
field testing there, bird numbers in the treated areas had fallen by 26
percent, and for a handful of species the decline approached half of
the original population.

Meanwhile, an ever-widening uncontrolled experiment was taking place across the country. In 1947, the city of Princeton, New
Jersey, launched an effort to eradicate Dutch elm disease by spraying
elm trees with DDT. Dutch elm disease is a devastating fungal infection that is transmitted from tree to tree by bark beetles specific to
elms and which is almost always lethal. Arriving in North America in
1928, the disease had swept through cities and villages in the eastern
United States, where elms were a principal shade tree, and continued
its march westward across the continent. Local officials everywhere
were desperate for a way to preserve their stately elms. In the first
year of the Princeton spraying program, nearly every elm tree in the
city was treated with a 1 percent DDT emulsion. For each tree, this
worked out to about one and a half pounds of DDT—three-fourths of
what the Patuxent group believed was safe for an entire *acre* of forest.
The city doubled the DDT concentration the following year, so that
every tree in the city got about three pounds of DDT.

The 1948 spraying produced immediate complaints from residents
about dead birds or the sudden disappearance of birds, and a number
of landowners declined further treatment for their elms. A group of

researchers, including scientists from U.S. Fish and Wildlife and the Bureau of Entomology and Plant Quarantine in the U.S. Department of Agriculture, investigated the Princeton situation in 1949, when the city's trees were again doused with three pounds of DDT each. It was a challenging environment. Because the whole city was involved it was hard to find a nearby tract of unsprayed elm trees that could serve as a control site. Within the town there were so many elms that it was hard to imagine that birds would not be repeatedly exposed to DDT even as they moved around from tree to tree to avoid the spraying teams—making it hard to assess their total level of exposure.

Only a handful of dead or dying birds—twenty-six in all—were found in Princeton after the spraying. All of the birds recovered alive that later died showed the usual symptoms of DDT poisoning: tremors and the loss of the ability to fly, followed by the inability to stand. Subsequent necropsies showed DDT residues in all of the dead birds, although this wasn't proof that they had died of DDT poisoning, as similar residues might well have been present in the birds that lived—none of which were captured and examined. The researchers also monitored nests and found that only 44 percent of the nestling birds in the sprayed area survived, whereas 71 percent of nestlings in the untreated tract lived to fledge by midsummer. More noticeable than the direct mortality from the spraying was a general decline in bird numbers. For species that were found in both the sprayed and unsprayed areas, DDT appeared to cause a 22 percent decline in the overall population. Where they went and what happened to them was unknown. But bird numbers in the unsprayed area increased by 6 percent.

Experiments on birds at the Patuxent Research Refuge produced more definitive results—but only slightly. In one test, hatchlings from nesting birds in areas aerially sprayed with DDT suffered "considerable mortality," with only 28 percent surviving, versus 86 percent that made it to fledging in the unsprayed area. DDT residues were found in the tissues of the dead birds, but in wildly varying amounts. This experiment also showed that birds from the *unsprayed* area had

DDT residues in their tissues—a finding that was hard to understand and that confounded the effort to draw conclusions from the experiment. Since nobody knew what constituted a lethal dose of DDT for hatchling birds—or how tissue levels of DDT corresponded to the amount of DDT ingested—it was hard to say in even a general way what these results meant. Compounding the uncertainty was the fact that the spraying had killed 94 percent of the insects in the test area, so the hatchlings might simply have died of starvation.

By the mid-1950s, however, researchers had designed more precise testing regimens and there was no longer any doubt that DDT was extremely toxic to birds. Experiments at Patuxent found that when adult quail were fed a diet composed of just .025 parts DDT they all died. For some reason, young quail were less susceptible to such small amounts of DDT, though when they were fed a diet that was .05 percent DDT they all died, too. Pheasants were similarly vulnerable to DDT; starlings less so. The researchers were intrigued to find that while all the birds showed DDT concentrations in their body tissues, the amount was unrelated to the dose or to their total consumption of DDT—but instead appeared to correlate directly with the severity of the symptoms of poisoning. These included weight loss followed by tremors and muscular incapacity a day or two before the birds died.

These findings, however, had little effect on the widespread use of synthetic pesticides. Nor was the pesticide business slowed by the growing evidence that DDT posed hazards beyond its acute toxicity. DDT that was captured in fatty tissues accumulated over time and could reexpose a bird or animal to its own body burden of poison when fat reserves were utilized—as during a period of food scarcity, for example—and the biological effects of remobilizing stored DDT were unknown. Another "subtle" effect of DDT that had been observed was intergenerational: Birds that consumed as little as three *ten-thousandths* of an ounce of DDT on a daily basis for two months would show no symptoms but suffered significant reductions in fertility and in the survival of their young. On went the chemical tide anyway. By 1956 there were two hundred registered chemical pesticides—

not only insecticides like DDT, but also fungicides, rodent killers, and herbicides—and there were more than six thousand commercial products based on these active ingredients. Annual pesticide production was by then 700 percent of its pre–World War II level, with annual sales estimated at nearly a quarter of a billion dollars.

By 1959, the Patuxent group had cut its best guess at a "safe" concentration for the aerial spraying of DDT in half—down to one pound per acre. At two pounds per acre the collateral damage commenced, as most vertebrate species—birds, mammals, reptiles, amphibians—were affected at that level. Five pounds an acre resulted in "serious mortality among most species." Aquatic species of fish and shellfish, which had been known to be the most vulnerable to DDT from the start, were of special concern. The recommendations now called for no more than 0.2 pounds per acre over wetlands—and 0.1 pounds or less if there was more than one application.

The threat to aquatic species was demonstrated in a series of spectacular fish kills. In 1954, a half-pound-per-acre DDT spraying program over the Miramichi River drainage in New Brunswick, Canada, was undertaken against an outbreak of spruce budworm. It killed 91 percent of the river's young Atlantic salmon—good old *Salmo salar*—and some of the adults. The area was sprayed again in 1956 and the same thing happened once more. Nobody was sure whether the fish succumbed to DDT or starved to death following the massive die-off of stream insects that were killed along with the budworms. In 1955, another DDT campaign against the spruce budworm produced similar results along a one-hundred-mile stretch of the Yellowstone River in Montana. Three months after the area was sprayed with DDT at a rate of one pound per acre, young trout and several other fish species died off en masse. Officials in this case were sure the cause was starvation after the stream invertebrates in the river were destroyed in the spraying.

A campaign to eradicate gypsy moths in the forests of the eastern United States was begun in 1957. The gypsy moth was an import from Europe that was injurious to hardwood trees, as gypsy moth larvae have a voracious appetite for foliage and are present when trees are leafing out in the spring. Again, fish and shellfish kills were reported from wetlands within or near the sprayed areas—the most notable being a substantial die-off of crabs in a salt marsh on Long Island, New York. But worries increased when a discovery by the Patuxent group indicated there might be previously unimagined long-term effects from exposure to DDT:

> Immediate mortality of individuals is not the only cause for concern. Effects that are long-delayed may be serious. During the past year, an important indirect effect was reported: species feeding upon earthworms died from pesticide poisoning a year after the area was treated. The earthworms, known to be resistant to DDT and capable of storing it in their tissues, continued to live while containing reservoirs of DDT sufficient to cause secondary poisoning of their predators. Studies in progress give indication that other pesticides also can be stored by resistant organisms. Few studies have been made to determine what effect this phenomenon has upon wild populations, but field reports from several localities in the Midwestern United States suggest that this may be the reason why the numbers of certain birds are being reduced in local areas.

While the pesticide studies from Patuxent and elsewhere were sometimes inconclusive, one firm rule held up year after year: The more scientists learned about the effects of DDT and other pesticides on wildlife, the greater the collateral damage they observed. And there was another important consideration: The U.S. Fish and Wildlife Service concerned itself only with fish and wildlife. Human beings were someone else's problem.

In 1950, the American Medical Association's Council on Pharmacy and Chemistry set up a Committee on Pesticides. The AMA said the need for more information about problems associated with the use of "economic poisons" had been apparent for some time already. Within months the committee produced its first report. The subject was organophosphate insecticides, parathion in particular. The committee said that organophosphate insecticides were "among the most toxic materials commonly used for pest control and are capable of producing severe systemic effects and death unless directions for handling and use are strictly observed."

Human exposure to organophosphate insecticides was a constant danger because they could be inhaled, ingested, or directly absorbed through the skin or eyes. Symptoms of organophosphate poisoning included unsteadiness, twitching, nausea, cramps, involuntary urination and defecation, blurred vision, giddiness, anxiety, sensations of floating, mental confusion, drowsiness, loss of coordination, generalized weakness, slurred speech, repetition of the final syllables of words, loss of reflexes, coma, convulsions, and death.

Organophosphate poisoning occurred most often among farmworkers who applied them. Symptoms could appear after a single exposure, and they were more severe after repeated exposures or by exposure to two or more different organophosphate insecticides. The committee cited a number of cases. One was a thirty-eight-year-old farmer who could not read and who sprayed his tobacco crop with parathion evidently unaware that the chemical was dangerous. The victim smoked while he sprayed and stood so near the sprayer that he became soaked from head to toe. He died within fifteen hours. Another was a thirty-one-year-old university entomologist who had worked with parathion and other insecticides for months before deciding one day to forgo a mask and protective clothing. Late in the day he complained of nausea and went home—where he died before medical help could arrive.

Yet another was a twenty-six-year-old member of a spraying crew using parathion in a citrus grove, whose job was to keep the tanks filled. After two weeks on the job he got sick and was hospitalized.

Following a recuperation that lasted a month he returned to work. On his first day back he reached into the solution in one tank up to his elbows. He also neglected to wear a protective mask, as he complained that they made him uncomfortable and prevented him from smoking while he worked. The next morning he felt ill and was rushed to the hospital, where he died six hours later. There were also cases involving workers in pesticide production plants, including one foreman who, along with a coworker, was splashed with highly purified parathion. He sent the coworker to the showers, but declined to clean himself up and died twenty-one hours later. Then there was a ten-year-old child who found a whiskey bottle in the crook of a tree and decided to drink some of its contents, which were later determined to be tetraethyl pyrophosphate, or TEPP, an insecticide closely related to parathion. The child foamed at the mouth and died within fifteen minutes.

The AMA was worried not only about such acute poisonings, but also about the long-term effects of pesticide accumulations in body fat. Scientists at the time had only a limited understanding of the hormonal and enzyme activities in fat tissue, but they knew that the deposition or mobilization of fat also involved the liver. It thus seemed a "reasonable assumption" that a buildup of chlorinated hydrocarbon poisons could disrupt important metabolic processes.

Studies already completed on DDT showed that fat tissue was a "biologic magnifier" of the insecticide. Rats that were fed tiny amounts of DDT over periods of time gradually built up body burdens of the poison, resulting in slowing heart rates and liver damage. And while researchers still lacked assays to detect the storage of other chlorinated hydrocarbon insecticides in fat tissue, everything pointed in that direction. Chlordane was known to have a "high order of chronic toxicity," and dieldrin and aldrin appeared to be as bad or worse. Researchers had to assume that chlorinated hydrocarbons would not be stored only in fatty tissues, but in any tissue or organ where fats were present. These included the membranes of every cell in the body—which are composed of a double layer of lipid molecules—as well as embryonic fat cells that help regulate fetal development.

By the spring of 1951, the AMA was advising physicians on how to treat patients poisoned by dieldrin and aldrin, particularly in the southern United States, where these new insecticides were coming into wide use on cotton and tobacco crops. Both appeared to be as toxic as parathion if absorbed through the skin and were believed to be somewhere between three and six times as toxic as DDT.

Like the Patuxent researchers—who complained of being unable to thoroughly test insecticides as fast as they were being developed—the AMA struggled to assess the effects of increasing insecticide use in residential and commercial settings. In 1952, the Committee on Pesticides began looking at electric and thermal vaporizing devices that had been newly invented to fumigate houses, schools, restaurants, industrial plants, and hospitals. Some vaporizers worked continuously, sending out a steady invisible fog of insecticide. Nobody knew whether such "atmospheric dispersal" was safe, or even how effective it was. The committee found that "technologic improvements in chemicals and in methods of dispersal" came faster than did knowledge of "the physiologic actions of the insecticidal ingredients, particularly with respect to their chronic toxicity and inhalation hazards." These devices discharged insecticides—usually DDT or lindane—as vapors or fumes that were airborne for a time before recrystallizing on floors, walls, and ceilings, where they remained a potent contact poison for long periods. At least that was the idea.

Testing showed that insecticides dispersed unevenly from vaporizers and tended to concentrate at potentially unsafe levels in the air and on the surfaces closest to the machines. DDT sometimes accumulated so heavily on the walls and ceilings near the vaporizers that crystals of the insecticide flaked off and fell to the floor, coating it with toxic dust. Lindane, the committee said, looked to be safer than DDT in vaporizers—although this wasn't certain, and the main factor driving an increasing use of lindane wasn't safety but rather the growing resistance some insects had to DDT.

Although cases of allergy-like reactions were being reported among people in homes or businesses where insecticide vaporizers had been installed, the AMA found that the government had limited authority under FIFRA to regulate either the devices or the insecticides they dispersed. This was especially problematic because the AMA also found that few people used the devices properly. The supposed safety and miraculous effectiveness of synthetic pesticides were so widely believed that people often tampered with vaporizers to increase their output. The AMA put part of the blame on the manufacturers of vaporizers, whom they accused of promoting the devices for use in homes, hospitals, nurseries, or anywhere food was handled—even though the evidence suggested such uses were risky.

By 1954, the AMA categorically opposed the use of insecticide vaporizers in homes. Lindane had largely replaced DDT as the poison of choice in such machines. Two years earlier the AMA had reported that the toxicity of lindane was comparable to DDT in some situations, different in others, and in general difficult to assess. It was known that lindane didn't accumulate in fat tissues as readily as DDT did, which led to the promotion of lindane as an insecticide that was safer than DDT for use in devices that dispersed insecticides continuously. But more research now indicated that lindane was "stored in significant amounts" in the brain and liver. Researchers also suspected that acute toxicity results obtained in testing on lab animals did not translate to humans.

The AMA was troubled by accounts of poisonings involving children who accidentally ingested lindane, which was usually formulated as pellets or in a white granular form for use in home vaporizers. In one case an eighteen-month-old toddler who ate one and a half pellets of lindane while her mother was putting a new vaporizer together was rushed to the hospital where she spent the better part of seven hours convulsing and vomiting. She lived. So did several slightly older children who threw up and went into convulsions after drinking a homemade soft drink their mother had inadvertently "sweetened" with lindane crystals she mistook for sugar. Alongside such reports came stories about representatives of vaporizer makers who insisted that any child who ingested lindane would suffer nothing worse than a tummy ache.

Of course, children can accidentally ingest and be poisoned by any number of chemical products common in most homes. The difference with insecticides is that they *are* poisons and when they are used as intended people are exposed to them on purpose. For the AMA, the use of insecticides in vaporizers was crazy: "Insecticidal poisons that are effective because of deliberate continuous pollution of the atmosphere have questionable safety. Their use in this manner is contrary to hygienic standards for safe atmospheric and working conditions."

By the spring of 1957, the questions surrounding synthetic insecticides were serious enough that one major manufacturer suddenly announced it would stop making them. The Thompson Chemicals Corporation, which was based in Los Angeles, said it was halting its production, distribution, and research on "presently known" insecticides, saying that after twelve years of study the company was convinced the "wide-scale" use of insecticides on agricultural crops offered only temporary benefits in pest control and were "at best palliative, and will perhaps prove dangerous and uneconomic in the long run." The people at Thompson were also worried that the "ingestion of presently employed insecticides" might be hazardous to "humans and other warm-blooded animals," a possibility they said was "of a highly serious nature."

These sentiments were not unanimous. In 1954, Dr. Wayland J. Hayes, Jr., chief of the Toxicology Section of the U.S. Public Health Service, delivered a paper to a meeting of the American Public Health Association in which he pooh-poohed concerns about chronic DDT poisoning in humans, as no case of it had ever been confirmed. Hayes argued that humans—like animals—stored DDT in fat tissue, but only up to a threshold level, beyond which no increased storage occurred regardless of continued exposure to DDT. In theory, then, since chronic DDT poisoning had never been observed, it must be all but impossible, as evidently a person could not store enough in his or her fat tissues to get sick.

This was true, Hayes insisted, even though a recent study of meals served in restaurants had found widespread DDT contamination of food. Although some foods did not contain detectable amounts of DDT, many did—especially fatty items or foods that were fried in fats—and a "balanced meal" in an American restaurant was almost certain to include a serving of DDT. Hayes did not say whether the DDT came from some treatment in the restaurants or if it arrived on the food fresh from the farm. But the amounts, Hayes pointed out, were smaller than the doses that incarcerated volunteers had taken without ill effect. Hayes published his report the next year in the *American Journal of Public Health,* which touted the article as an antidote to the "baseless rumors of the hidden dangers of DDT."

The safety of DDT was also official policy at the U.S. Department of Agriculture, which in 1957 authorized an aerial spraying campaign against the gypsy moth over three million acres of New York, New Jersey, and Pennsylvania. The department said the public had become "unduly alarmed" over the alleged hazards of DDT spraying to both human health and wildlife. DDT, said the officials, was deemed safe in small doses by the U.S. Public Health Service and had been in widespread use in the United States and around the world for more than a decade. They said there was no evidence that a single spraying of DDT at a rate of one pound per acre would harm mammals or birds and would kill only a few fish.

One age was passing into the next. For a half century, the idea of preserving the natural world had been seen as our obligation to the earth's bounty—which was meant for our use but which required our care. The enactment of game and fish laws, the intelligent management of resources, the establishment of wildlife refuges, and the preservation of pristine wilderness—each instance an example of self-imposed restraint—all belonged to the larger cause of conservation. Conservation was a hopeful, noble, and inherently nonpartisan cause, a quest for the betterment of the world. Its foundation was the conviction that we could protect and enjoy what nature had provided—in perpetuity. From generation to generation, a well-tended earth would endure.

But in 1939, the means for undoing nature itself had been discovered in laboratories in Europe and the United States. DDT and nuclear fission were to become the twin agents of a great change of heart and will. In virtual lockstep, the two technologies, deadly and yet beguiling, were perfected in war and then loosed on a world living uneasily at peace. In the 1950s, their residues—unseen and unbidden—turned up everywhere, a feast of radionuclides and chlorinated hydrocarbons. Fearful of radioactive fallout and largely oblivious to the dangers of pesticides, everyone fed themselves both poisons. This was the new age, a time when nature—that part of existence outside of humanity—would no longer be the main object of concern. Now it was to be the total environment, ourselves included. In the age of conservation, the species that had needed our protection were the animals and birds and fish. In the new age of environmentalism the species that most needed our help would be us.

One age was ended, another begun. The world was ready to know this. All it would take was someone who recognized what was happening and who was willing to say it out loud.

In the summer of 1957, Rachel Carson—along with her mother and Roger—moved into a new house, a spacious brick rambler with large windows that Carson had had built among the trees on a large corner lot in a wooded section of Silver Spring called Quaint Acres. Carson was tired. Roger was an energetic boy who needed more supervision than she could have imagined. The months following the publication of *The Edge of the Sea* were otherwise unproductive. In 1956, Carson served on the Conservation Committee of the National

Volunteers for Stevenson. Attentive as always to the smallest publishing considerations, Carson earlier that year expressed her unhappiness with the sales of *The Edge of the Sea,* which had begun sliding down on the *New York Times* bestseller list after reaching number four. She told Paul Brooks she was disappointed in Houghton Mifflin's advertising, which she thought relied too much on occasional large ads rather than a constant stream of smaller ones. The latter, she thought, would help the book more. She said once the book dropped off the bestseller list it would be "hard to get it back on." Carson was also annoyed that some bookstores had removed *The Edge of the Sea* from their window displays—though she admitted there probably wasn't anything Houghton Mifflin could do about that.

Polite but understandably defensive, Brooks wrote back telling Carson they had already spent $20,000 on advertising for *The Edge of the Sea* and sending her a long list of newspapers and magazines in which ads had been placed—calling it "one of the strongest such lists that has ever come across my desk." He also reminded her that the book had already sold seventy thousand copies—a strong showing and especially so given the Atlantic coast orientation that they always knew would limit its appeal in the western part of the country. Brooks said he felt sure the book would continue to sell steadily for years to come, bestseller or not.

Meanwhile, Carson's work stalled. *Life* magazine invited her to write an article on the jet stream and how it affects weather—offering the tempting sum of $5,000. But the project bogged down in a disagreement between what Carson thought the story was and what the editors at *Life* wanted. When the whole idea was finally scrapped, Carson told Marie Rodell that she was henceforth "allergic to Life." One idea that never went anywhere at all came from Dow Chemical, which was putting up a new plant on the Texas gulf coast and asked if Carson would write about twenty-five words to go on a plaque for the building's state-of-the-art aquarium. Rodell told the company it was "extremely unlikely" that Carson would agree to such a thing—whereupon Dow made it clear that they were prepared to pay whatever it took to get Carson's participation. Carson declined to name a price.

Carson's vague idea for a book called "Remembrance of the Earth," about the origins of life, would not itself come to life and slowly faded from her thoughts. She made no progress on "The World of Nature" for Simon and Schuster and confessed to Dorothy Freeman that she felt "terribly alone" with her problems. She said she was sometimes overcome with panic that she would not see Roger through to adulthood and was haunted by thoughts of what would become of him if something happened to her. Carson was also bitter about the dramatic change in her personal circumstances. Caring for Roger would surely complicate her writing just when her career was taking off. "Sometimes I think I *can't* go on," she told Dorothy. "At other times it seems possible. But always I know I must. Life is such a queer business—great visions, great opportunities opened up, and then a door slammed. I don't understand it; I never will."

Carson's mood remained bleak. It was looking as if the "Lost Woods" project was not going to happen, as the landowners of the Southport Island property wanted an exorbitant price. Carson told Dorothy it had been a year since she had actually believed she'd ever write again. But now she at least had a magazine assignment, a piece called "Our Ever-Changing Shore" that she'd been asked to write for *Holiday*. Carson's plan was to write it from personal recollections of some of her favorite places—the high dunes near Provincetown on Cape Cod, Plum Island in Massachusetts, St. Simons Island in Georgia. Her biggest challenge, she told Marie Rodell in a contemplative letter, would be trying to explain the pristine beauty of the shore when development was devouring untouched sections of it seemingly everywhere:

> The undisturbed shore is one of the best places to see Nature at work: in the geologic cycles by which the relation of sea and land is undergoing constant change, and in the flow of life by which species come and go, new forms are evolved, and only those that

can adjust to a difficult environment can survive. Yet when man takes over all this is changed. Within the long cycles of the earth what we do probably makes little difference; yet within the restricted cycle that is completed within one person's life the shore can never again be itself once man has "developed" it.

The dismal truth is that shores such as we are proposing to describe are fast disappearing, and may well do so completely within the life of some of us.

Early in 1956, Carson got into a running feud with the Musical Masterpiece Society, which offered monthly recordings to members much as the Book-of-the-Month Club sent out a book selection each month. Carson subscribed—but then decided the recordings were inferior and canceled her membership. When another shipment arrived the month after she'd quit, Carson paid for it anyway. She then started getting notices that her account was delinquent. Furious, she wrote the company a scalding letter, reviewing the facts that showed her blameless and her account not in arrears. Leveraging her notoriety, Carson went on acidly:

> In case my name is not familiar to you, I suggest you consult the membership records of the Authors' Guild, the P.E.N. club, and the National Institute of Arts and Letters. You might also look in Who's Who. After this research, you might conclude that I am a reasonably responsible person, quite able to pay the small sum involved, and not at all likely to endanger my credit by neglecting it if I owed it.

The amount Carson supposedly failed to pay was $3.80.

Carson didn't like change, which sometimes challenged even her belief in science. Exhilarated by the technologies that had allowed men such as William Beebe and Jacques Cousteau to probe the depths of the ocean and that were enabling biologists to begin exploring the inner workings of the human cell, Carson was at the same time dismayed by the onslaught of chemical poisons that had contributed to what would soon be called the "green revolution" in agriculture—a period of explosive growth in crop production made possible by improved seed stocks, new plant hybrids, and the massive application of chemical fertilizers and pesticides. Much of this was happening in underdeveloped countries where food scarcity was a long-standing problem. But the use of pesticides on such a massive scale was progress that came at too great a cost, Carson thought.

There were also questions that Carson seemed to prefer not be asked, problems that should not be solved, places that ought to remain unvisited. When the Soviet Union launched *Sputnik* in October 1957—which was followed into orbit a month later by a second Russian satellite—Carson was appalled. She thought everyone now faced a "strange future" and confided to Dorothy that it made her feel ill. This was only partly a concern about the inevitable uses of rocketry in warfare. Fascinated by the sea, so much of which is dark and cold, Carson was terrified at the thought of humanity extending its reach into the infinitely darker and colder and more mysterious realm that was outer space. Human beings had an affinity for the sea—the cradle of life—and it was only natural that they would venture there. But to visit space would be to part company with the earth and become disconnected from the biological and geological cycles from which all life and all human intelligence had arisen. Where then after that? It was all, Carson thought, "deeply disturbing."

Earlier that year Carson had turned fifty. No longer young, not yet old, she seemed not to belong entirely to the time in which she was living. She paid little attention to a changing culture that was leaving behind such relics as Richard Jefferies and H. M. Tomlinson, or to the new tastes of a younger generation that no longer knew or cared about the classical music she loved. Carson enjoyed listening to concerts and classical recordings, but never mentioned coming across any other kind of music, even though it would have been hard not to. In July 1954, while the crew of the *Lucky Dragon* was confined to Tokyo University Hospital, a young Memphis truck driver named Elvis Presley recorded a song called "That's All Right," and popular music hadn't been the same since.

If Carson was aware of the extent to which nuclear fears had penetrated middle-brow entertainment she didn't seem to consider it important—though she would have enjoyed at least one of Hollywood's less-cheesy endeavors, a 1957 film called *The Incredible Shrinking Man*. Based on a clever and disturbing novella titled *The Shrinking Man* by Richard Matheson, it's the story of a man named Scott Carey who begins to grow smaller after his boat drifts though a strange mist during an otherwise placid day at sea. At first Carey notices he's losing weight. Then one day he finds he's looking directly into his wife's eyes—even though he'd always been four inches taller. Carey continues to shrink. His distraught wife begins to see him as a child. Their sex life gets weird and then stops. He's harassed and beaten by a group of young boys. Eventually he ends up living a desperate existence in his basement, where he is terrorized by a spider and by his own cat. And he keeps getting smaller.

Matheson, unspooling the story in a series of flashbacks while Carey tries to stay alive as he approaches microscopic proportions, reveals what's happening midway though, when the doctors who have been studying Carey's condition tell him they've found a "toxin" in his body. And they have an idea what may have produced it:

> Tell us something, they said. Were you ever exposed to any kind of germ spray? No, not bacterial warfare. Have you, for instance, ever been accidentally sprayed with a great deal of insecticide?
>
> No remembrance at first; just a fluttering amorphous terror. Then sudden recollection. Los Angeles, a Saturday afternoon in July. He had come out of the house, heading for the store. He had walked through a tree-lined alley, between rows of houses. A city

truck had turned in suddenly, spraying the trees. The spray misted over him, burning on his skin, stinging his eyes, blinding him momentarily. He yelled at the driver.

Could *that* possibly be the cause of all this?

No, not that. They told him so. That was only the beginning of it. Something happened to that spray, something fantastic and unheard of; something that converted a mildly virulent insecticide into a deadly growth-destroying poison.

And so they searched for that something, asking endless questions, constantly probing into his past.

Until, in a second, it came. He remembered the afternoon on the boat, the mist washing over him, the acid sting on his body.

A spray impregnated with radiation.

And that was it; the search was over at last. An insect spray hideously altered by radiation. A one-in-a-million chance. Just that amount of insecticide coupled with just that amount of radiation, received by his system in just that sequence and with just that timing; the radiation dissipating quickly, becoming unnoticeable.

Only the poison left.

Strictly speaking, a "toxin" is a biologically produced poison—snake venom, for example. But technicalities aside, Matheson's story—which was told all the way through in that same rattling machine-gun style—neatly combined the twin fears of the modern age. Toxicologists actually have a name for the thing Matheson imagined, the synergistic combination of two poisons that results in a single more powerful one. It's called "potentiation." The symbolism would not have been lost on Carson.

The threat of radioactive fallout was more realistically explored in Nevil Shute's bleak, postapocalyptic 1957 novel, *On the Beach*. Set in the not-too-distant future of 1963, the book tells the story of humanity's last days on earth in the aftermath of a "short, bewildering" war in which nuclear exchanges involving a handful of small countries equipped with primitive atomic bombs spin out of control into an all-out thermonuclear conflagration among the superpowers. Military officials in the United States, Russia, and China—their civilian leadership all killed in the initial bombings—exhaust their nuclear arsenals. Now everyone in the Northern Hemisphere is dead, either blown to bits or fatally sickened by a vast cloud of radiation that is moving inexorably southward, steadily blotting out what remains of civilization. In Australia, where most of the action takes place, the survivors know they have only months to live.

What makes Shute's nightmarish story even more disturbing is the pluckiness of the survivors, who carry on with their lives almost—but not quite—as if nothing terrible has happened. It's a shocking contrast to the barbarism and chaos that would seem more likely under such circumstances. Although they are low on fuel and essential supplies, people continue on in their jobs as best they can. They attend their swank private clubs for port and cigars, go out dancing, take fishing vacations, hold neighborhood cocktail parties, and make plans for their children as if they had a future. The attempt at normalcy in the face of doom is heartbreaking—and a potent indictment of the policies and technologies that would make such a thing imaginable.

Carson thought most of what was on television was terrible, though she sometimes found musical events that suited her or science programs that she deemed superior to TV's usual fare, which she described as "puppets vs. cosmic rays." One time she stumbled upon an interview with the architect Frank Lloyd Wright in which Wright explained that he had had to choose whether to conduct himself with "honest arrogance" or "hypocritical humility." Wright said he'd picked honest arrogance. Carson thought this was not surprising but shocking all the same. "It somehow crystallized my belief," she wrote to Dorothy, "that a large share of what's wrong with the world is mankind's towering arrogance—in a universe that surely ought to impose humility, and reverence."

Carson thought a fine example of human arrogance was playing out in the news from several parts of the country that year. The USDA's spraying campaign against the gypsy moth was under way in the Northeast, while in nine southern states an "all-out" effort to eradicate fire ants had begun. The nonnative pest—they were often called "imported fire ants"—arrived in Alabama sometime before 1920, spreading across the southeast in the decades afterward. While they caused little direct damage to crops or forestlands, fire ants built large mounds that interfered with farm machinery, and their painful stings were a nuisance to agricultural workers and to children who encountered them while playing outside. There was so little evidence that fire ants caused economic losses to crops or to livestock that it was debated whether they were anything more than a minor nuisance. But under provisions of the Federal Plant Pest Act of 1957, the U.S. government was providing matching funds to assist state agencies and private groups in a plan to treat more than twenty-two million acres with heptachlor or dieldrin by the end of the decade in an attempt to rid the region of fire ants forever.

By 1958, reports from the field indicated sharp wildlife declines in areas being treated for fire ants. On a single ten-acre tract in Alabama, nine species of birds, plus an assortment of small mammals, fish, and frogs, turned up dead or dying one week after an application of heptachlor. The same story was repeated across the south. In Louisiana every single red-winged blackbird and meadowlark vanished from an area treated with heptachlor, and several species of birds and mammals found dead in the area had residues of heptachlor in their bodies. Earthworms, a food source for many species of ground-feeding birds, also contained heptachlor—five months after the treatment. If birds weren't poisoned by eating contaminated worms they alternatively faced starvation, as only about 20 percent of the earthworms survived exposure to the chemical. On a ranch in Texas, heptachlor killed more than 90 percent of the birds found along the edges of dirt roads. On other parts of the property it killed more birds, plus mammals, snakes and lizards, frogs, and fish. In Florida, cats, dogs, and chickens reportedly succumbed. Ranchers in Georgia claimed more than one hundred head of cattle had been killed. Officials in a town in Alabama said they had to haul fifty dead dogs to the city dump.

A report from the Alabama Division of Game and Fish, taking note of the seemingly catastrophic collateral damage to wildlife, said the hasty decision to use insecticides believed to be many times more potent than DDT was ill advised and had overwhelmed wildlife agencies. Meanwhile, new research on the toxicity of heptachlor with respect to *human* health was under way, and the findings were sufficiently alarming that in the fall of 1959 the FDA banned the use of heptachlor on food crops. In 1954, Congress had authorized the FDA to begin setting tolerances for pesticide residues in food. The guidelines essentially required that any pesticide found in food had to be either proven completely safe or present in amounts small enough to be deemed safe.

It had been discovered that heptachlor oxidized after it was applied, forming a compound called heptachlor epoxide that coated the foliage of plants. This had gone unnoticed because standard assays for heptachlor alone did not detect heptachlor epoxide. Better detection methods now showed that heptachlor epoxide residues ended up not only in food crops but also in meat and milk from livestock that consumed forage treated with heptachlor. Preliminary testing indicated that such residual contamination magnified the risks of using the insecticide, as heptachlor epoxide had an acute toxicity greater than heptachlor alone. In January 1958, the *New York Times* published an editorial opposing the fire ant eradication program and blasting the government for being reckless:

> It is rank folly for the government to embark on an insect-control program of this scope without knowing precisely what damage the pesticide itself will do to both human and animal life, especially over a long period. No one yet knows the answer to this question or to many other related questions of insect control—yet

the department plunges blithely ahead. But enough is known to raise the gravest concern on the part of many scientists and conservationists.

Similar questions had been raised about the DDT spraying campaign against the gypsy moth in the Northeast, which had been carried out as planned in the spring of 1957.

Later that year, three Harvard biologists—including the young Edward O. Wilson, an expert on ants who would become one of the world's best-known biologists and environmentalists—wrote to Agriculture Secretary Ezra Taft Benson asking him to stop the fire ant program. They said they endorsed the position already taken by the National Wildlife Federation and agreed with the federation that using heptachlor and dieldrin was likely to cause damage to the environment that would exceed anything the ant might do. But they also had deeper concerns:

> Broadcast application of insecticides will affect not only wildlife, but the native insect fauna, and could produce deep-set disturbances of the prevailing ecological system of checks and balances. The final result might well be further decline of wildlife, now deprived of part of its food source, or the emergence of new insect pests, once they have been freed from the natural enemies that held them in check.

The scientists added that Wilson himself was studying fire ants and that there were promising alternative techniques for controlling them by means that would not affect other species. They accused the USDA of failing to consider such alternatives and said the department's research on chemical control methods had been "entirely inadequate."

Meanwhile, in the fall of 1957, a group of fourteen residents on Long Island had filed a suit seeking a permanent injunction against the federal government to prevent further spraying there. The group was headed by Robert Cushman Murphy, a prominent naturalist and former curator of birds for the American Museum of Natural History. At a hearing in federal court in early December, an attorney for the plaintiffs said nobody had demonstrated that the gypsy moth was causing problems on Long Island and that the only people defending the spraying campaign were government workers afraid to contradict the official position on the supposed safety of DDT. An assistant U.S. attorney responded that there was no issue to decide, as the government had no plans to spray the area again the following summer. Siding with the residents, the judge ordered a speedy trial.

Carson, who routinely clipped newspaper accounts of pesticide issues and kept track of the latest studies, had an already swelling set of files on the subject as the Long Island case went to trial in early February 1958—just days after Carson had heard from one of the plaintiffs, a woman named Marjorie Spock. Spock had been contacted by Marie Rodell, who told her that Rachel Carson was watching the court proceedings with interest. Spock immediately wrote to Carson to say it was "wonderful news" hearing that the acclaimed author was concerned about pesticides.

Carson thought the trial demanded coverage by someone who could explore the larger concerns about the increasing use of chemical poisons. But a courtroom is not a seashore, and Carson gave no thought to visiting the trial herself. Instead, she took the occasion to introduce herself to another writer she hoped might accept the assignment: the New Yorker's E. B. White.

She told White about the lawsuit, imploring him to write about it in the New Yorker. She said she had been convinced for years that chemical pesticides were a "threat to the entire balance of nature and even more immediately to the welfare of the human population." She offered to send White "scores" of studies and reports that would convince him this was so. The Long Island lawsuit was an attempt to gain legal traction in a cause that had already been taken up by organizations including the National Audubon Society and the National Wildlife Federation, which were demanding the government halt large-scale spraying operations until their effects on nontargeted species were better understood. Carson knew that the Audubon Society was particularly worried about the rapid expansion of spraying programs, which it believed had already begun the "secondary poisoning" of wildlife and human populations that would soon become "catastrophic." The society had argued that the hazards from insecticide use "may well rank in seriousness of adverse effects with the dangers of radioactive fallout."

To personalize the problem, Carson told White—who, like her, had a place in Maine, albeit one where he lived year-round—that next summer's gypsy moth program was rumored to include parts of Maine. More definite were plans to continue the fire ant spraying in the south, where the coming season was to see greater use of dieldrin, which she said was about twenty times as toxic as DDT. If it were applied at the proposed rate of two pounds per acre, Carson said, it would be like spraying DDT at forty pounds per acre. And the known effects of dieldrin on men and animals, she added, were "alarming."

White wrote back at once. He agreed that the pesticide issue was "of the utmost interest and concern to everybody." It disturbed him that in discussions about their use some special group or interest was always being considered and "never the earth itself." But he said he was too busy to take on the job of reporting the Long Island trial. Instead, he told Carson he'd forwarded her letter to William Shawn at the *New Yorker* to see if he might find somebody to do it. What White really thought, however, was that Carson should do it herself. He said he didn't make assignments for the magazine, but that he was sure Shawn would be receptive.

TEN

Collateral Damage

By the time Carson received E. B. White's letter suggesting she write about pesticides herself Carson had already decided as much. She wrote to Paul Brooks and William Shawn saying she felt compelled to look into the subject but was having trouble deciding how to proceed. She said she had a number of writing projects that were unstarted because of her "difficult personal situation." She seemed to be thinking of collaborating with another writer or writers, as she mentioned the possibility of doing a magazine article that could serve as a chapter in a book for which she might also write an introduction and do "some general editorial work." She said it was hard to think of taking on anything more than that, but that she wanted to discuss the idea further.

Carson's hesitance wasn't due entirely to the new demands of her life as an adoptive mother—though her circumstances were now dramatically altered. At six, Roger was no longer the cooing toddler she could amuse for an hour or two at the beach before turning him back over to Marjorie. He could be distractingly energetic—Carson once said he was as "lively as seventeen crickets"; at times she was the only person who could "hold him down." He was also prone to infections and respiratory problems. Roger was fond of Stan Freeman—he sometimes called him "Uncle Stan"—which delighted Carson, who thought Roger benefited from the occasional presence of a father figure. But her overwhelming feeling about Roger was one of obligation. When Dorothy had offered to have Roger visit her and Stan in West Bridgewater not long after Marjorie's death, Carson said it was impossible to even think of sending the boy off alone. Better to keep him close, part of a household that now included one aging mother, one active child, and a beleaguered author who felt blocked and entangled in domestic commitments beyond her control.

Carson had also come to believe that one reason she was having trouble doing any real work was her uneasiness with the fact that human beings had acquired the means to reshape the world. It had made her miserable in ways she was only just coming to terms with. She told Dorothy that it was troubling to think about and harder still to put into words, as she felt that her most cherished beliefs were crumbling:

> But I have been mentally blocked for a long time, first because I didn't know just what it was I wanted to say about Life, and also for a reason more difficult to explain. Of course everyone knows by this time that the whole world of science has been revolutionized by events of the past decade or so. I suppose my thinking began to be affected soon after atomic science was firmly established. Some of the thoughts that came were so unattractive to me that I rejected them completely, for the old ideas die hard, especially when they are emotionally as well as intellectually dear to one. It was pleasant to believe, for example, that much of Nature was forever beyond the tampering reach of man.

Carson said that when humans cleared a forest or dammed a river the world went on. She had always believed that the environment molded life, not the other way around. And yet so it had come to be. This was disorienting. Carson confessed that she had "shut her mind" to what was happening for a long time, but now she had opened her eyes again and realized it was pointless to ignore the changing world and "worse than useless" to resort to "eternal verities" that had turned out to be not so eternal after all. She said maybe it was time for somebody to write a book in light of a new reality and that it might be "the book I am to write."

Carson said that however one wanted to understand the "space age universe," the most important thing was to do so with humility rather than arrogance. Arrogance had created DDT and the hydrogen bomb, and arrogance was, in her mind, as much the problem as what it had begotten.

On April Fools' Day 1958, Carson had several long telephone conversations about a book on the pesticide problem. One was with Paul Brooks, who was already committed to publishing it at Houghton Mifflin. Another was with the science editor at *Newsweek* magazine, a man named Edwin Diamond. Diamond had been proposed as a collaborator on the project. A third call, one that excited Carson most of all, came from William Shawn at the *New Yorker,* who told her he would like to run a long, two-part piece from her on pesticides.

The *New Yorker* had been among the first to criticize chemical pesticides. In the spring of 1945, the magazine's "The Talk of the Town" section had run an item about DDT, reporting on its value to American forces fighting in the South Pacific—where islands were being routinely sprayed prior to Allied invasions—but also raising questions about its safety. The lethality of DDT to insects was well proven, the magazine said, but so also were its toxic effects on wildlife. As for how safe it was for people—nobody could say. Even if it turned out to be relatively harmless to humans, American naturalists, the *New Yorker* said, were worried about what would happen when DDT went into general use in the United States, and insects of every kind—the good and the bad, the creepy and the beautiful—began to disappear.

Carson realized the impact the *New Yorker* would have on the book's visibility, not to mention the handsome check she would get from the magazine. Adding to this good news was Shawn's suggestion that Carson start thinking about yet another topic he thought she could do for the *New Yorker*. The subject, said Shawn—who apparently had decided that Carson could do anything—was "the universe."

For the time being, though, pesticides would be Carson's world. In April she agreed, without much enthusiasm, to Brooks's suggested working title for the book, "The Control of Nature." Privately, Carson had been thinking of it as "the poison book." She at this point saw it as a relatively short book, on the order of six chapters comprising fifty thousand words. Carson was to write the first and last, Diamond the middle four. The two authors would share a byline, but the copyright was to be Carson's exclusively. It was also understood that Diamond—who was to earn a $1,500 advance for the book—would have no financial interest in the *New Yorker* serialization, but would be expected to help Carson with the research on it. Everyone agreed to a tentative deadline for delivery of a manuscript by the end of June 1958.

Diamond signed a letter accepting these terms on May 3 and sent it back to Marie Rodell. But two days later the collaboration collapsed. Rodell informed Diamond that Carson viewed her partnership with him as unworkable. Diamond had not delivered the research materials he had promised and was apparently busier at *Newsweek* than anybody had understood. He had also irritated Carson by not staying in regular communication with her. Rodell told Diamond that collaboration required a close working relationship, but this had "proved impossible on your end." Diamond evidently asked them to reconsider, but a few days later was again told that it was over. In mid-May, Paul Brooks stepped in and told Diamond that any thought he had of resurrecting a coauthorship with Carson was "out of the question." Brooks asked Diamond to either return the money he'd already been paid—he'd gotten half of his advance at the outset—or hand over his research materials.

A few weeks later, Carson told Brooks she'd gotten a transcript of the Long Island trial on her own and was in contact with all of the principal witnesses. She said if Diamond sent him anything he should send it right back. Diamond, meanwhile, ignored Brooks for several weeks before finally sending him some material from the trial near the end of June. Insensitive to the extent to which he had alienated everyone, Diamond told Brooks he was withholding a cache of additional information he'd gathered through interviews during the trial, but that he'd be willing to share everything if "we can work something out" that would allow him back into the project. Brooks, who was on vacation when Diamond's materials arrived at Houghton Mifflin, returned the package when he got back to the office, telling Diamond coldly that he was sure Carson already had all of it in her files.

The scope of the book grew quickly, as Carson began researching and corresponding with experts, and the ridiculously ambitious goal of completing a manuscript by midsummer was scrapped. The plan had been to publish the book in January 1959, but Brooks once again accepted a delay from a writer he knew could not be rushed. In June, Carson met with William Shawn in New York. Shawn now said he'd like to have as many as fifty thousand words for the *New Yorker,* which Carson thought might turn into three articles and probably make up almost the whole book. Better still, Shawn told Carson the story needed to be told from her point of view. She told Dorothy that meant she would be "pulling no punches."

By the fall, Carson sounded like a writer with a terrific but daunting story that was going to be hard to contain. She told Dorothy that she was "actually happy and excited" about it. The subject, though unpleasant, was intellectually challenging, and she was corresponding with many brilliant people who stimulated her thinking as the work went along. She said she continued to worry about having enough time uninterrupted by family obligations to throw herself completely into writing, but that her general feeling about it was good.

Within weeks of this optimistic moment, Carson's mother, Maria, who was now eighty-nine and in poor health, began to fade. On November 22, 1958, she suffered a minor stroke and subsequently developed pneumonia. By the end of the day on November 30, she was unconscious inside an oxygen tent in her bedroom at the house in Silver Spring. Carson sat up next to her mother's bed through the night. Around five thirty the next morning Carson walked out into her darkened living room and peered at the sky from the picture window. Orion was up and the Milky Way shone brightly, much as it had on a snowy night of sledding back at PCW so many years before. She went back to her mother's room, and Maria died a few moments later with her daughter at her side, holding her hand. They had come this far together, not knowing that it was the beginning of the last chapter of Carson's own life.

Brooks waited a couple of months while Carson grieved and adjusted to the terms of her life once more before he asked her for a progress report. As he must have expected, the book was going to be longer and more complex than anyone had thought—certainly more than fifty thousand words—and rigorously documented. She told Brooks that the book they'd all had in mind the preceding summer would have been "half-baked at best." In the months since then, Carson said it had become increasingly clear to her that the threat to human health from synthetic pesticides—which she had always wanted to emphasize—really was the center of the story. She thought it was striking that, as a matter of policy, the American Medical Association and the U.S. Public Health Service maintained the idea that pesticides could be used safely—while routinely publishing findings that argued the opposite. She said the main problem with respect to human health wasn't acute poisoning—which usually resulted from either accidents or negligence and ignorance of the dangers of handling such compounds. Rather it was the still unknown long-term effects of lifelong exposures to pesticides, which linger in the environment, become embedded in food chains, build up in the tissues of the population at large, and, perhaps most frighteningly of all, were transmitted from mothers to their offspring.

But Carson was not immune to the kinds of scientific temptations that were behind assurances that DDT was safe and had earned its creator a Nobel Prize. She told Brooks she was intrigued by newly created manmade insect diseases that might be used as pesticides—a kind of "biological control" she believed could be formulated so as to target a single species and have the added advantage of leaving no residues in the environment. Another interesting idea—further off in the future but no less tantalizing—involved neutralizing specific hormones necessary for insect metamorphosis. This would effectively prevent a targeted species from reaching sexual maturity and thus interrupt its reproductive cycle—an outcome that, if achieved, would be a kind of "Utopia," Carson said, though it was still an open question whether the effects of such a hormone-based pesticide could ever be limited to just one species of insect. A hormone that killed off fire ants or gypsy moths wouldn't be much of an improvement over DDT if it also killed honeybees and butterflies.

As usual, the science of extermination proceeded faster than anyone's ability to anticipate unintended consequences. One ironic new technology being developed for controlling certain insects was the deployment of radioactively sterilized males of the species into the environment. Decades later, such biological controls would be found to have unexpected limitations and dangers—including the same collateral damage problems that plagued poisons such as DDT. But for now it was important to Carson that there be plausible alternatives to the use of synthetic pesticides.

Carson said she hoped this update would give Brooks a clearer picture of the shape of the book. She said she felt she was at last on the right track, but added without apology that she would "not be so rash as to predict when you will have the manuscript." Carson sent an almost identical letter to William Shawn at the *New Yorker.* Brooks wrote back to say that he was horrified by the pesticide situation but heartened by the direction the book was taking.

In the summer of 1958, Marjorie Spock had forwarded to Carson a large file of materials relating to the Long Island lawsuit—which the plaintiffs had lost that spring and were now planning to appeal. Over the course of the sixteen-day trial the residents had failed to convince a federal judge—it wasn't a jury trial—that the spraying campaign had done any real harm other than to a few fish and crabs. The plaintiffs argued that the DDT had contaminated milk in dairy herds and that it also posed a potential—if unspecific—threat to their own health. They testified that spray planes dropping the DDT-and-fuel-oil mixture sometimes made multiple passes over the same area—making it certain that the application rate in some places was higher than intended.

A surprise witness who appeared on behalf of the residents was Dr. Malcolm Hargraves, from the Mayo Clinic in Minnesota. Hargraves, who specialized in blood diseases, told the court he was convinced that DDT and other chlorinated hydrocarbon pesticides played a role in the development of leukemia and lymphoma, and that while the Mayo Clinic did not formally endorse this position most of the doctors there believed it was true. Hargraves—in testimony Carson could not have failed to notice—also said that the more that was learned about the effects of DDT on human health, the more dangerous it looked, a situation that paralleled what was being learned about human exposure to atomic radiation.

The key witness for the government turned out to be Dr. Wayland J. Hayes—the same Dr. Wayland J. Hayes who four years earlier had dismissed concerns about DDT in the *American Journal of Public Health,* even though it then contaminated almost everything Americans ate when they went to a restaurant. Hayes pointed to two studies. In one, employees at a plant that manufactured DDT had shown no ill effects despite continuous exposure to the pesticide over long periods. In another, a group of prisoners volunteered to swallow large doses of DDT for eighteen months. Again, Hayes said, nobody got sick. Hayes thought these results put the Long Island residents' puny exposure to DDT into perspective. "The amount of DDT which was absorbed by humans as a result of the gypsy moth spray program was so small as to not be measurable," Hayes testified.

Before the judge could issue his decision, however, the State of New York said it was canceling the spraying program for 1958—the same thing it had said the preceding fall, but about which there had been conflicting reports since. New York officials said that while the program had been effective against the gypsy moth, the state wanted to find different pesticides that would be less persistent in the environment. The state also said it wanted improved flight programming, so that spray planes did not make repeated applications to the same areas, and that it would stop paying pilots by the gallon of pesticide applied—an obvious temptation to overdo it.

In June the court issued a broad ruling that said not only had the government acted legally in its spraying campaign, but that the evidence was "overwhelming" that the spraying had, in fact, succeeded in eradicating the gypsy moth from the area in the process—a key finding in that it tipped the balance between the public purpose of controlling the moth and the unproven private concerns that the residents had been put at risk. In a twenty-four-page decision, the judge, Walter Bruchhausen of the federal district court in Brooklyn, chastised the plaintiffs as whiners whose only real complaint was their annoyance with spray planes flying over their properties:

Although the plaintiffs contend that the chemical is deleterious to health and likely to cause future ailments, they presented no evidence that they or anyone else was made ill by the spraying of DDT in the Long Island area.

I hold that the mass spraying has a reasonable relation to the public object of combating the evil of the gypsy moth and thus is within the proper exercise of the police power of the designated officials.

Whether an imported leaf-devouring pest such as the gypsy moth could rationally be called "evil" was debatable. The moth was brought into the country in the 1860s for use in a scientific experiment from which it escaped and then spread—a story so plain and predictable that a biologist would have seen it as routinely opportunistic on the moth's part. The judge's allusion to a "police" power for federal and state agriculture officials must have galled the residents on Long Island who believed their community didn't need such protection. But Carson was less interested in the outcome of the lawsuit—which the plaintiffs would lose again on appeal—than she was in Marjorie Spock's reports on some of the latest and most damning research on DDT. One set of findings stood out—research by an ornithologist named George J. Wallace at Michigan State University. As it happened, the campus of Michigan State in East Lansing had been undergoing annual spring DDT spraying operations against Dutch elm disease since 1954. Wallace and his graduate students had studied the effects of the treatments on local bird populations—especially robins. Every year Wallace and his team recovered dozens of dead or dying birds after spraying operations. The birds captured while still alive routinely showed the classic symptoms of chlorinated hydrocarbon poisoning.

More recently, Wallace had begun conducting a careful bird census on one part of the campus in order to determine the overall effect of DDT use on annual bird numbers. His findings were startling. Spraying operations were causing a *total* elimination of robins in the treated areas. As in past studies at Patuxent, Wallace could not be sure that some birds didn't simply fly out of the area to avoid the sprayers. But he discovered something that put any such exodus into perspective: The number of dead or dying robins they recovered exceeded the number of robins that had been present in the area in the early spring, before the spraying operations began. This could only mean that robins living outside the sprayed areas converged there after the treatments and had been poisoned by DDT residues present in the environment.

Tissue analysis of the dead birds showed high levels of DDT. This included brain tissue, where DDT was found at levels comparable to those in experimental lethal poisonings. Wallace would eventually find DDT residues in some forty species of birds in the treated areas. Aerial feeders such as swallows and nighthawks appeared to be free of DDT contamination. So were transient species that passed through the treated areas in the fall. As might have been expected, Wallace also observed a long-term general decline in the population of robins on campus. He suspected reproductive issues, and sure enough, annual inspections of nests showed that some robins built nests but did not lay eggs in them. In other cases, the birds laid eggs that did not hatch. Tissue analysis showed DDT loads in the birds' testes and ovaries.

Wallace and other researchers pieced together a story that showed the insidiousness of DDT's entrapment in the food chain and the role it played in the demise of the robins. Heavy spraying of the elms with an emulsion of DDT killed the bark beetles that transmitted Dutch elm disease from tree to tree—along with all the other insects present, both the "good" ones and the pests—and left the foliage coated with the persistent poison. The leaves fell to the ground in the fall, where they were consumed by earthworms that feed on leaf litter. This, of course, killed some of the worms, while the ones who survived picked up a heavy body burden of DDT, which they stored through the winter. In the spring the robins returned, ate the toxic worms, and succumbed to the poison used in the *previous year's* spray program. Tests on worm tissues indicated that as few as eleven earthworms could provide a lethal dose of DDT to a robin—about as many as the bird consumes every minute while it is feeding.

Carson thought this toxic cycle through the food web over time demonstrated the unusually sinister nature of DDT contamination. Unlike a poison whose toxicity could be measured by a single dose, DDT lingered in the environment, where it became concentrated in the reproductive organs and the food sources of wildlife that were never its intended targets. Deadly and enduring, a little DDT went a long way.

Wallace had been studying the effects of DDT on birds as the U.S. Department of Agriculture continued to urge citizens to participate in a campaign against Dutch elm disease. Locating and dealing with infected trees was the responsibility of landowners, who in some states—New York was a model example—were assisted by "scouts" from state agencies who were on the lookout for trees in need of spraying. The Agriculture Department recommended spraying three or four gallons of a 12 percent DDT emulsion on every infected elm—and on the deadfall from trees that had already been killed by the disease.

Carson was intrigued with her new letter-writing friend Marjorie Spock. An unusual woman and younger sister of Dr. Benjamin Spock—the famed pediatrician and later antiwar activist—Spock held an advanced degree from Columbia and had worked as an educator and school administrator in New York before moving to Long Island to take up "biodynamic gardening," one of several disciplines belonging to a cultish philosophy called "anthroposophy." As a young woman, Spock had studied with the founder of anthroposophy, Rudolf Steiner. Steiner believed that true knowledge resided in a spiritual dimension that was accessible by way of inner thought processes disconnected from the literal world.

Anthroposophy was the underlying principle of a form of dance Spock also practiced called "eurythmy," an all but unfathomable art form in which the performers—though visible in ordinary time and space to the audience—supposedly entered an "etheric" or "supersensory" realm outside of conventional reality. The movements were cryptically linked to tones, time signatures, the alphabet, and the signs of the zodiac. Anthroposophy also figured in the interdisciplinary educational doctrines employed in the popular Waldorf private schools. Biodynamic gardening, another of Steiner's spin-off movements, was essentially a variation of organic gardening that emphasized the proper fermentation of compost heaps, supposedly achieved by interlayering special medicinal herbs with manure and other organic matter. Spock devoted herself to Steiner's methods, which she shared with her live-in partner, a woman named Mary Richards who went by the nickname Polly.

It's unclear how much Carson knew about Spock's unusual beliefs—but Spock was a cheery and engaging correspondent who was excited at becoming acquainted with Carson and whose letters made more sense than did her private ideas. Spock was delighted when she learned that Carson's interest in the Long Island case had grown into a book project. The two women got better acquainted by mail, and early in the summer of 1958 they spoke at length on the telephone. Spock wrote to Carson immediately afterward to say what a pleasure it had been to talk with her and that it would never have happened if not for the DDT spraying case. "I have to reflect very often on the silver linings to the clouds in this suit," Spock said. The trial, she confessed, had been a "terrible ordeal," even though her own time on the witness stand hadn't been as bad as she'd anticipated.

Spock—who also had a summer retreat in Maine—stopped in to meet Carson face-to-face in West Southport in the summer of 1958. They were by then a mutual fan club, and not long after their meeting Carson insisted they address each other by their first names. Spock later told Carson that no matter how the Long Island lawsuit turned out, Carson's book would almost certainly be more important. "I can hardly wait until your book is done & published," Spock wrote to Carson, "as I believe it's going to make the biggest difference anything could possibly make in the spraying picture."

Carson gave Spock periodic updates on her research. She mentioned an interview she'd done with an official from the FDA who was plainly "exultant" over the judge's ruling in the Long Island case. She also confided to Spock her belief that although science had gotten the pesticide question wrong with chlorinated hydrocarbons and organophosphates, science could ultimately solve the problem it had created.

In October 1958, *Life* magazine ran a story about the prospect of controlling insect pests with "juvenile hormones" that would inhibit sexual maturation. Carson was already corresponding with several experts on this idea—including Edward O. Wilson at Harvard and Howard Schneiderman at Cornell, who would one day pioneer the development of genetically modified crops as head of research for the Monsanto Company. Encouraged about the prospects of developing pesticides based on hormones, the scientists believed these could theoretically be formulated to affect only targeted species—but they also urged caution.

Schneiderman said it was still unknown how "higher animals" would respond if exposed to hormones that seemed to have no obvious function outside the insect world. And getting an answer to that question would take time. Schneiderman thought it might take five or ten years to develop a safe hormone-based pesticide. Carson told Spock she thought the article in *Life* made some exaggerated claims, but that it was "one straw that shows that the wind is beginning to veer away from chemicals as now used." Carson also said she was amused to learn that the USDA was starting to look into such biological controls, and she wondered whether Secretary of Agriculture Ezra Taft Benson's "right hand knows what his left hand is doing." Benson had been named as a defendant in the Long Island lawsuit.

It would be hard to overstate Carson's labors in her effort to get a handle on the "spraying picture," as Marjorie Spock called it. Her usual method—library research and a protracted back-and-forth shuttle of letters between herself and a long list of experts—produced a sea of paper. Carson sometimes employed a secretary to help her with the correspondence, but even so the threads of the story went in so many directions that it was dizzying. Carson filled file folders with scientific studies and reports, and kept card catalogs indexing hundreds of the latest findings.

The contamination of food and the environment by pesticides suggested similarities with the issues surrounding radioactive fallout and the explosive development of chemical products and medicines—

which, like pesticides, were promoted as safe, effective, economical, and the latest in scientific ingenuity. The marketing slogan "Better Living Through Chemistry"—widely appropriated from the DuPont Corporation's long-standing catchphrase "Better Things for Better Living . . . Through Chemistry"—seemed to be everywhere. One common compound that had found its way into surprising corners of the environment was penicillin—the antibiotic whose curative powers had caused a great boom in its use.

Penicillin was first used in the United States in 1942, when some twenty-nine pounds of the drug were produced here. By 1956, the annual U.S. production of penicillin approached five hundred thousand tons. Like DDT, penicillin had multiple uses. It had wide clinical applications in the treatment of human illnesses and infections. It could be formulated in different ways—as ointments, powders, sprays, tablets, and injectable liquids—and saved tens of thousands of lives and cured millions of nonlife-threatening conditions. But there were problems. About 10 percent of the population turned out to be allergic to penicillin—either on first contact with the drug or in the course of repeated dosings. And while it wasn't fully realized at the time, bacteria develop resistance to antibiotics, and the more widely they were used the less effective they became. But new applications were being found for penicillin and other antibiotics in the control of livestock and plant diseases, and as an after-processing preservative for meats, poultry, and fish. This provided another route of human exposure to penicillin through food. A 1957 report from the U.S. Food and Drug Administration minimized the risk from antibiotic contaminants in the food supply—though it did so in a way that was not comforting:

It should be emphasized that the problem of contamination with antibiotics in our foods and particularly in milk is a small one compared to our other current food safety problems which have arisen in large part as a result of technologic progress in food production, processing, and distribution. In the processing of food, preservatives, antioxidants, colors, bleaches, flavors, coatings, drying agents, moistening agents, thickening agents, sequestering agents, "aging" agents, stabilizers, emulsifiers, neutralizers, acidifiers, and sweeteners are used.

The FDA left out DDT and other pesticide residues—but these were, of course, known food contaminants as well. *Time* magazine reported that although food contamination was supposedly regulated, there were growing amounts of "subtle new pollutants" in the American food supply that posed a danger to human health. *Time* said the food supply contained "illegal quantities" of DDT, penicillin, and hormones "either by accident or by design." The story cited the example of milk—which was supposed to be thrown out for three days following the administration of penicillin or other antibiotics to a dairy herd. And yet penicillin turned up in milk with worrisome frequency anyway.

Early in 1958, Carson learned that *Reader's Digest* had a story in the works that was going to be friendly to pesticides. Carson wrote a long letter to the editor warning him of mounting scientific consensus that synthetic pesticides were unsafe. She said she felt sure that "a publication with the *Digest*'s enormous power to influence public thinking all over the country would not wish to put its seal of approval on something so potentially hazardous to public welfare." Having been turned down by *Reader's Digest* on numerous story proposals—including her 1945 idea for a piece on DDT—Carson was probably less interested in protecting the magazine than she was in projecting her own views on pesticides.

It worked. Carson got an immediate answer from *Reader's Digest*—where there had to be chagrin at being second-guessed by the esteemed Rachel Carson on an unpublished story—thanking her for her insight and assuring her that the magazine would "weigh all the facts" as it proceeded. Evidently the facts brought the piece around to Carson's point of view, as the story when it finally appeared in June 1959 was titled "Backfire in the War Against Insects," and Carson thought it well done. She wrote to the author, Robert Strother, saying as much and informing him that she was at work on a book about pesticides. Carson asked Strother—who had been flooded with letters from people with stories to tell about bad experiences with pesticides—if he might share some of the responses with her, which he graciously agreed to do.

In the spring of 1959, the U.S. Department of Defense and the Atomic Energy Commission admitted that they had overestimated how long radionuclides from nuclear weapons testing would remain aloft in the atmosphere. Their original calculation predicted that such radioactive debris would stay high in the stratosphere for as long as seven years, during which time it would decay and disperse and gradually come back to earth as minimally radioactive fallout distributed uniformly across the globe. Now the officials couldn't agree on how much shorter this cycle really was—but said it might be as little as two years. This meant that nuclear testing debris not only came down sooner and radioactively hotter as fallout, but it also fell over a more concentrated area. In fact, with respect to at least one radionuclide of special concern—strontium 90—the most contaminated area on earth was the United States. Given the steady pace of testing in the western part of the country, and the normal patterns of weather movement from west to east, a reasonable person could have wondered if a lot of radioactive debris stayed in the air for more than a few days, let alone a few years.

Strontium 90, which has chemical properties similar to calcium, is absorbed into bone tissue and had been linked to leukemia. Government officials were getting worried that even though the immediate risks to humans from nuclear testing appeared slight, there might be long-term consequences. And there were a number of radionuclides of concern, including iodine 131, which, like ordinary iodine, is readily stored in the thyroid gland. All of these substances had entered the human food supply—mostly in milk. Wherever these isotopes ended up in the body, they bombarded the surrounding tissue with radiation.

Some were longer lived than others. Iodine 131 has a half-life of just eight days—that is, the amount of radioactivity it emits is reduced by 50 percent every eight days, continuously. But its supply was also being replenished every time another bomb sent a radioactive cloud into the sky. Strontium 90 has a half-life of more than twenty-eight years and so it came down in fallout with nearly the same level of radioactivity as it acquired in the explosion and stayed that way for a long time. Scientists believed exposure to such continuous low-level radiation would lead to an increased incidence of cancer—and that over much longer periods, subtle genetic mutations induced by radiation would cause a steady increase in birth defects.

In 1958, a group called the Greater St. Louis Citizens Committee for Nuclear Information committed itself to a project that would measure the effects of exposure to radiation—by collecting baby teeth. Like calcium, strontium 90 also concentrates in teeth, and the plan was to compile data on strontium 90 levels in the baby teeth of children growing up during the period of atmospheric testing so it could be correlated with health issues many years after. A half century later, in 2010, a preliminary study of men who died of cancer in middle age showed that their baby teeth had contained more than twice the amount of strontium 90 as had been measured in men from the same area who were still alive.

The government took the position that radiation in fallout was far below the normal background level of radiation from natural sources—cosmic radiation and radioactive elements in the earth's crust—and that it was difficult to demonstrate any direct effects from such scant exposure. Still, the government admitted that the available evidence suggested that *any amount* of radiation might be harmful and that it was "virtually certain that genetic effects can be produced by even the lowest doses. These effects in the children of exposed parents and all future generations may be of many kinds, ranging from minor defects too small to be noticed to severe disease and death."

In 1958, California Institute of Technology chemistry professor Linus Pauling, who had won the Nobel Prize in chemistry in 1954 for his work on the chemical bond and the nature of complex biological structures—and who would win the Nobel Peace Prize in 1962 for his campaign against nuclear warfare—presented the United Nations with a petition signed by more than eleven thousand scientists from forty-nine countries asking for an end to nuclear weapons testing. The scientists pointed out that radiation from natural sources regularly *does* cause genetic mutations in human beings, some of which lead to birth defects. Adding even a small amount of extra radioactive exposure could only compound this.

One radionuclide that especially worried Pauling was carbon 14, which has a half-life of eight thousand years and would therefore work its slow changes on the human genome over the course of many millennia. Pauling and the cosigners of the petition told the United Nations that only an immediate halt to nuclear testing could minimize whatever damage had already been done: "Each nuclear bomb test spreads an added burden of radioactive elements over every part of the world. Each added amount of radiation causes damage to the health of human beings all over the world and causes damage to the pool of human germ plasm such as to lead to an increase in the number of seriously defective children that will be born in future generations."

In March 1958, the Soviet Union declared a halt to further atmospheric testing of nuclear weapons—on the condition that the Western nuclear powers do the same. A few months later, President Eisenhower announced that the United States would impose its own one-year moratorium. A year after that, the United States extended its moratorium for another twelve months. As the second moratorium period came to a conclusion, Eisenhower told the Soviets that the United States would again feel free to resume testing at its discretion—but would not do so without advance notice. There the matter rested.

Carson had been friends with the popular and prolific nature writer Edwin Way Teale for many years. Teale and his wife had visited Carson at her cottage on Southport Island—Teale said he would never forget seeing the perfect reflection of the Milky Way on the glassy waters of Sheepscot Bay at midnight. The Teales also shared Carson's love of cats, and the two writers often compared notes on both their pets and the writing business. Carson urged Teale to find a way to serialize his work in magazines. In May 1958, just as Carson had begun work on "The Control of Nature," Teale wrote to encourage her to examine the parallels between pesticides and radioactive fallout. He told her about a friend who'd recently set off an alarm meant to intercept smugglers of radioactive materials at Idlewild Airport some six months after he'd visited Las Vegas:

> I don't care about Las Vegas. It couldn't happen to a better town— but it indicates what the future holds as this dangerous material is not discarded and continues on and on piling up.
>
> If the world isn't populated by a race of monsters it won't be the fault of those who are barging ahead.

Paul Brooks shared this view. In his internal memo outlining "The Control of Nature" for other executives at Houghton Mifflin, Brooks explained that while the subject of pesticide use might seem "rather specialized," plenty of readers were already concerned about the increasing use of chemical poisons and that their ubiquitous and invisible presence in the environment offered "a clear parallel to the problem of nuclear fallout." In both cases—radiation and pesticides— Brooks said the risks were cumulative and involved potential interference with the genetic regulation of life, including human life.

From her earliest thinking about the book, Carson had been careful to make an important distinction between radioactive fallout and the use of pesticides. The former was a by-product of warfare and, as such, arguably something humanity would prefer to forgo—if only theoretically. There was no rational argument for exploding nuclear weapons in the atmosphere, apart from the tortured idea that doing so would prevent the same thing from happening in anger and on a massive scale. But Carson felt that she could not take an absolute stand against the use of pesticides—which she felt were sometimes useful and advisable if applied sparingly and with care. This was an important point, as she would later be accused of calling for the total elimination of chemical poisons—as part of a concerted campaign to discredit her, even though she had repeatedly said something different. When Paul Brooks asked Carson about a mosquito spraying program in his own neighborhood outside of Boston, she offered careful advice. Brooks said the town was using helicopters to "spot spray" areas where mosquitoes bred. Carson agreed with him that this was preferable to more widespread spraying that had gone on in the past.

"I hate to advise you on your helicopter problem," Carson wrote. "Of course it is better than airplane spraying, and I know it is not realistic to take a flat position against any spraying at all. I am afraid there have to be compromises, much as I hate any part of it."

Sometime in early 1959, "The Control of Nature" acquired a broader and even less graceful new working title—"Man Against the Earth." Carson again felt only lukewarm about the new title, which she perhaps unconsciously realized still said exactly the wrong thing. Both titles suggested a separation between human beings and nature that was contrary to one of the book's premises—that we are part of nature, and that what is poisonous to one organism is likely to be poisonous to another. The idea of balancing human interests against those of the natural world was scientifically nonsensical. In May, Brooks told Carson he wanted to list "Man Against the Earth" in Houghton Mifflin's publishing schedule as a February 1960 release. This assumed not only that she was almost done, but that they could also get the *New Yorker* serialization ready in time for the articles to run just before the book came out. Brooks said he needed Carson to be honest with him about whether she could meet such a deadline. Carson wrote back to assure him she would finish soon, that a February publication date would work, and that the new title was growing on her.

When the Houghton Mifflin list came out in June, Carson and Marie Rodell were alarmed by a flurry of press reports hinting that the author of several pleasant books about the ocean would soon publish a depressing book on pesticides. Carson wrote to the publicity department at Houghton Mifflin warning that future press releases about the book would need to be carefully worded to avoid any tinge of sensationalism, as the subject was already enmeshed in "violent controversies." She said she wanted to make sure she had a say in anything further that came out ahead of the book. In the meantime, she promised to send the publicity department a description of the book that would better prepare them to explain what it was about when the time came. Carson admitted that it was a hard book to characterize. "Even I find it so," she said.

Filed away alongside Carson's voluminous scientific research, however, was a page of notes—mostly handwritten—in which she had outlined the "basic themes" of the book, which were several. Carson thought that pesticide spraying was an example of applied entomology that amounted to "Stone Age science" in its clumsy disregard for unintended damage to the environment but which had at its disposal a formidable arsenal of chemical weapons "possessing all the deadliness of the Atomic Age." Working against nature, rather than with it, Carson wrote, made the whole concept of spraying a "negative force." She believed the economic case for pesticide use was unsound, and that the claims for the safety of chemical poisons was not only a "big lie" but assumed a level of public gullibility she found offensive. Carson also thought—as she had for some time—that science itself had gone astray, and that chemical pesticides were only one example of technology that had been developed and deployed without proper consideration of the consequences. Engineers, she said, were "practical technicians" who could find a way to do almost anything but never stopped to ask whether something *should* be done. Finally—and standing apart from the other ideas—was her desire to show how pesticides and radiation were two halves of the same problem.

Carson did not make the kind of progress on the book over the summer of 1959 that she had imagined she would when she told Paul Brooks to announce it as a February 1960 release. Both Carson and Roger were laid low by illnesses while they were at Southport Island—Roger was actually hospitalized for a week with a respiratory infection. Carson did make time to let Houghton Mifflin know of her displeasure at finding *The Edge of the Sea* out of stock at the bookstore in Boothbay Harbor. Months of frustration were capped off in September when, as Carson and Roger were driving from Maine back to Silver Spring, their car was hit by a truck near Baltimore. Nobody was hurt, but settling the insurance and arranging for repairs were another distraction from work.

In December 1959, Carson wrote a long, plaintive letter to Brooks—it was part apology, part promise of better things to come. She told him how grateful she was for his patience—and that she knew how sorely she tried it. She said that what kept her going even though she'd failed in her promise to deliver the manuscript—most recently by the end of the year—was her certainty that the work she was doing was necessary, that it would give the book an "unshakable foundation." Carson felt that people who criticized pesticide use without fully understanding the science did more harm than good and ended up as "targets" of those whose interests involved the continued use of chemical poisons. She assured Brooks that while she might be attacked for what she was writing, she would have the weight of evidence on her side. She said she knew that he understood all this, but that in the end she alone could comprehend the immensity of the task she had set for herself. That it took so long was almost unbearably frustrating. On a positive note, Carson told Brooks that she'd recently hired a wonderfully competent new assistant—her name was

Jeanne Davis—who had a college degree, was married to a doctor, had worked at several medical schools, and had experience reading the kinds of scientific literature that was piled high in Carson's study.

Carson also apologized for the piecemeal approach she was taking—working on chapters or sometimes just parts of chapters in a seemingly random order. She really couldn't explain why, but that it was the only way she could handle the material and it wasn't going to change. She promised to send him another almost completed chapter soon. While Brooks took a genuine interest in all of this, she knew that what he really needed to know was when she might finish the book. Carson admitted that she didn't know, but if things went "reasonably well," she might be done by February—a hopeful thought so lacking in conviction that Brooks probably discounted it out of hand. Carson said she and Roger had both been feeling better lately, though she had developed some sort of thyroid condition that caused brutal headaches and sometimes cost her hours or even an entire day of work.

Brooks wrote back just before the holidays to wish Carson—not unselfishly, he said—a happy and creative New Year.

Carson was aware that other writers were looking into the issue of pesticides—and that there had been a general concern about contamination of the food supply for some time, even before the development of synthetic pesticides. All the way back in 1933, Arthur Kallet and F. J. Schlink had published a book called *100,000,000 Guinea Pigs* arguing that Americans were the unwitting participants in a vast, uncontrolled experiment involving the adulteration of food, drugs, and cosmetics with a growing assortment of chemical additives. Kallet and Schlink accused the FDA of complicity in what amounted to mass poisoning. They placed a special emphasis on the use of lead arsenate as an insecticide on fruit and vegetable crops.

Lead arsenate, they explained, leaves a toxic residue on produce that can easily be removed by the grower with a mild solution of hydrochloric acid—but which cannot be washed off with a simple rinse under a faucet in someone's kitchen. The consumption of lead arsenate subjects a person to not one but two poisons—lead and arsenic. The government had set a low tolerance limit for arsenic residues in food—and prohibited *any* residual lead—but Kallet and Schlink claimed the FDA made no serious attempt to police the situation. Farmers, not knowing better or not caring—or both—overused lead arsenate and rarely succeeded in removing it from their crops before delivering them to market. Kallet and Schlink said that lead arsenate was probably more poisonous than anyone realized, as the investigation of arsenic toxicity at low concentrations had only recently come under study. Lead, meanwhile, presented a different concern:

> Lead, the other metallic residue of lead arsenate spray, is certainly far more dangerous. But here we find a curious situation. Lead is a cumulative poison. Part of the lead taken into the body is stored and may become dangerous to the point of disaster when enough of the metal has collected. The amount necessary to cause noticeable symptoms depends on the health, ruggedness, or personal peculiarities, of the individual concerned. The Food and Drug Administration admits this hazard and states that no residue of lead whatever is permitted on fruits and vegetables coming to market. Despite this, there is not the slightest evidence that any effort is being made to enforce this drastic dictum.

This, of course, was an argument familiar to Carson—as were many of the assertions in a more recent and still more alarming book, William Longgood's *Poisons in Your Food,* which her former publisher, Simon and Schuster, brought out in the early spring of 1960. Like Kallet and Schlink, Longgood concerned himself not only with chemical pesticides, but with the whole toxic smorgasbord of synthetic additives and adulterants present in the food supply, especially in the dairy case, where the "milk you give your children to make them grow and have strong bones" was laden with strontium

90 from fallout, plus an assortment of other poisons, antibiotics, and insecticides. Longgood, whose prose was blunt and ungraceful, was particularly attentive to toxicity testing that was either insufficient or that suggested the seriousness of a particular residue ending up eaten or drunk by an unsuspecting consumer. One especially ghoulish test involved Carson's bête noire:

> One factor that makes DDT so effective as an insecticide also makes it so treacherous for man—its amazing persistence. In an extraordinary feeding demonstration, researchers applied DDT to hay growing in the field, fed the hay to beef animals, slaughtered the cows and fed their flesh to pigs, which in turn were slaughtered and analyzed; after these two complete digestions the DDT was found to remain intact.

Longgood—an experienced newspaper reporter who'd previously covered international affairs and written a book about the Suez Canal—got roughed up in the press over *The Poisons in Your Food,* which many found over the top. John Osmundsen, reviewing Longgood's book for the *New York Times,* caught the flavor of the criticism. Osmundsen accused Longgood of ignoring the demands of modern agriculture, which was dependent upon fertilizers and pesticides, and of overlooking research indicating that many food additives had been found safe at low concentrations. Worse, Osmundsen wrote, was an absence of balance and perspective that should have come naturally to a seasoned journalist. Osmundsen said the book was a "selectively documented, sometimes inaccurate, frequently hysterical tract against the use of any chemicals in foods." He thought the book "scientifically indefensible," but conceded that Longgood might have made a few good points worthy of further consideration, including concerns about the use of pesticides on crops and livestock—a seemingly central issue Osmundsen chose to mention as almost an afterthought.

Carson was aware of the controversy around *The Poisons in Your Food,* which she'd made a conscious decision not to read lest it influence her own book. Although she'd once referred to her book as a "crusade" in a letter to Dorothy Freeman, Carson was worried that what had happened to Longgood could happen to her. Her main hope, she told Marjorie Spock, lay in the careful consideration of the science that would not just support her case but make the argument without any interpretation on her part. This was a daunting task, one that caused her doubts and anxiety and seemed so unlike anything she had done before. She wrote:

> It is a great problem to know how to penetrate the barrier of pub-
> lic indifference and unwillingness to look at unpleasant facts that
> might have to be dealt with if one recognized their existence. I
> have no idea whether I shall be able to do so or not, but knowing
> what I do, I have no choice but to set it down to be read by those
> who will. I guess my own principal reliance is in marshalling all
> the facts and letting them largely speak for themselves.

It's not clear why Carson believed the public was indifferent to the hazards of pesticide use—and, in fact, the recent "cranberry scare" offered evidence to the contrary. In early November 1959, cranberries grown in Washington and Oregon were found to be contaminated with a weed killer called aminotriazole—which was known to cause thyroid cancer in laboratory rats. Although the risk to humans remained unknown and the cranberry crops in the major producing states of Wisconsin, Massachusetts, and New Jersey were thought to be uncontaminated, the government advised consumers not to buy or consume cranberries unless they knew where they had been grown. Panic ensued. Grocers across the country pulled cranberries off their shelves, restaurants stopped selling menu items containing cranberries, and millions of families started getting ready for a Thanksgiving feast without one of its essential ingredients. Angry cranberry growers feared their record $50 million crop was likely to turn into a substantial loss and called for the resignation of Arthur Fleming, the secretary of health, education, and welfare, who had made the original announcement of the contamination. The general manager of Ocean Spray Cranberries, Inc.—a cooperative that marketed about three-fourths of the U.S. cranberry crop—accused the government of overzealousness and said the public should instead be told that there was "not a shred of evidence" that any person had ever suffered ill effects by eating contaminated cranberries.

Aminotriazole had initially been tried as a weed control in cranberry bogs in 1957—prior to its approval by the U.S. Department of Agriculture. About three million pounds of cranberries from that experiment were later destroyed, and the following year the government decided to permit the use of aminotriazole on cranberry bogs only after the harvest was in. But in early 1959, one of the principal manufacturers of aminotriazole submitted its safety testing on the pesticide, which included its connection with cancer in rats. The company insisted these findings could not be used to interpret human risk, but the FDA banned the use of aminotriazole on food crops anyway.

Efforts mounted to reassure the public about the safety of cranberries. In Massachusetts, a crowd of nearly ten thousand people drank a thousand gallons of cranberry juice in a stunt organized by a local radio station. Cranberries figured in the developing presidential campaign, too. In Wisconsin, Senator John F. Kennedy drank a cranberry juice toast in the town of Marshfield. A few days later and just thirty miles away in Wisconsin Rapids, Vice President Richard Nixon ate four helpings of cranberries—despite the advice of Arthur Fleming, who told him not to. Two days after that, the Chicago Board of Health seized a shipment of cranberries from Wisconsin after tests showed it was contaminated with aminotriazole. Cranberry sales were halted in Chicago. The ban spread across communities in every part of the country. The growers continued to argue that the government's position was a hysterical response to a nonthreat.

In 1959—as now—the regulation of pesticides and other potentially dangerous chemical products defied common sense in an important way: Safety testing is performed not by the regulatory authority, but by the chemical manufacturers. The government specifies which tests are required and how they are to be conducted, then carefully reviews the findings that the companies submit. The party with a vested financial interest in the data is the same entity that supplies the data—a fact that would likely unnerve the public if many people understood that this is how things are done.

Not surprisingly, agricultural chemicals companies reacted heatedly to what came to be known as the "cranberry scare." One senior chemical executive complained that it could take as many as five years and perhaps $2 million to bring a new product to market. All pesticides then being sold had been rigorously investigated and could be reliably considered safe, he said, and any further restrictions would make the development of new products prohibitively expensive. The value of this industry—about $278 million in sales in 1959—was not lost on anyone, including politicians eager to choke down tainted produce. In late November the *New York Times* reported that the cranberry scare was only one problem facing the agricultural chemicals industry. The panic had come at the same time as criticism from "wildlife and conservation groups and from pure food enthusiasts who believe that chemical residues on agricultural products pose a threat to health," although the *Times* did not pursue such concerns beyond this brief mention.

For Carson, the cranberry scare was a preview of coming attractions—a glimpse of how a battle would be waged over this evolving general concern for the total environment. Conservationists had long run into trouble with corporations and other vested interests, usually over the allocation of resources and land. But this was different. Any challenge to the safety of a pesticide was a direct threat to somebody's bottom line. An entire industry—with all its associated business entanglements, shareholders, scientific departments, and political allies—depended on the ever-expanding sale and use of chemical poisons. The suggestion that a company would put expediency and profits ahead of public safety was accusatory on its face, which only inflamed passions on both sides of the issue.

But a fight over pesticides would be not only about safety versus economics, but also about patriotism. "Wildlife and conservation groups and pure food enthusiasts" could easily be characterized as "nature lovers and organic faddists," and from there it was easy to believe that they must be in league with political extremists—people who were likely to be, on some fundamental level, slightly un-American.

February 1960 came and went. Carson's progress slowed at least in part because of her pursuit of the complicated link between pesticides and cancer—a topic she once planned as only a small section of one chapter but now intended to devote two whole chapters to. And she was again experiencing a string of health issues. Early in the year she had developed a duodenal ulcer. She told Marie Rodell she'd have to subsist on baby foods for a while. While she was still being treated for it, she came down with a bad case of the flu that progressed to pneumonia. This was followed by another sinus infection—Carson was terribly prone to these.

In March she wrote to Brooks, telling him about all of this and saying that while she continued to make headway on the book she had to ration how much time she spent on it, as only rest would ensure the complete healing of her ulcer. She tried to make light of her health issues, telling Brooks that it would be easy to assume the topic of her book had given her the ulcer, but that that was not the case at all. She said she found the whole subject of pesticides—though of utmost concern—completely fascinating. Carson did sourly allow that any fair-minded ulcer should have waited to strike until she was done with the book. Still, as unsatisfying as her current pace was, she said she truly felt as if the hardest parts of the book were now done.

But there was something else Carson did not tell Brooks—either because she didn't want to worry him further or because it would be a few days before she discovered it herself—but two masses had developed in her left breast. Within a week of her letter to Brooks, Carson had scheduled surgery to find out what they were. Carson wrote again to Brooks—who had expressed sympathy over her health issues and told her not to worry about the slow progress she was making on the book—and this time she hinted she might be seriously ill. She said she was going to have surgery that she hoped would not be "too complicated," but admitted that she couldn't count on it. Enclosed with this disturbing news were Carson's drafts of the two chapters on cancer for "Man Against the Earth."

Paul Brooks had begun to sense the extent of the material Carson was trying to manage as she researched the book. He told her that, unlike a historian who could let a story unfold over the course of multiple volumes, she had the harder job of culling and compressing everything into just one book with a "larger and larger background behind it." He said "Man Against the Earth" would be like an iceberg, and when it was published Houghton Mifflin would do everything it could to let readers know how much of it lay beneath the surface. Carson wrote back to say that she liked this metaphor and that it reminded her of something she wanted to take up with him.

She had been thinking about how best to list the many sources she had relied on and felt sure that nobody wanted to see the book "sprinkled with footnotes." Instead, she said she wanted to include an appendix listing her principal sources for each chapter—something she thought would be useful to anyone interested in pursuing the subject in more detail, and would also refute any suggestion that the book was composed of "ill founded" personal views. She thought—probably correctly—that most readers don't care about these things and would simply ignore the bibliography.

Carson also told Brooks of her unhappiness with their latest working title—and said Marie Rodell in particular hated it. Rodell thought the title was misleading. Carson said she understood that using the word "earth" not in the usual sense—meaning dirt—but rather to encompass the totality of an interdependent global ecosystem, was problematic and that "non-ecologically minded people" would likely be baffled by it. She thought the word "against" was almost as wrong—it suggested the "horrid concept" of humanity as a kind of overlord, which was, of course, the sort of problematic thinking that the book was meant to point out. She didn't yet have a better title but thought the best thing would be for everyone to keep an open mind and "pray for inspiration." She had been thinking about how the problems with pesticides and radiation were similar, and said perhaps this would lead to an answer:

> In my flounderings I keep asking myself what I would call it if my theme concerned radiation, having some illogical feeling that that would be easier. As you will have seen in the cancer chapters, I keep hammering away at the parallel. Whether radiation or chemicals are involved, the basic issue is the contamination of the environment. "Poisoning" is of course an accurate term, but a word I think we should avoid as tinging with melodrama a theme that is basically a somber tragedy.

Carson said she also wanted to consider including drawings or photographs—maybe both—to help illustrate some of the more technical concepts in the book. She ended this letter with a gloomy note about her impending surgery, telling Brooks her trip to the hospital was now set for the following Sunday. She said that "with luck" she would be home by Wednesday, but added ominously "otherwise at the end of the week."

The operation had been delayed a week while Carson's sinus infection cleared up. In a letter she wrote to Marjorie Spock on April 1, 1960, Carson mentioned that she would shortly be entering the hospital "for a few days." A couple of weeks later Carson wrote again, telling Spock that her "hospital adventure" had turned into a "setback of some magnitude" that had dashed her hopes of sticking to a "tight work schedule" that spring. Carson explained that two tumors had been found in her left breast, one that was benign and the other "suspicious enough" that a radical mastectomy had been performed.

Carson, worried about Roger, "talked her way out" of the hospital after only a week and went home to recuperate. Her surgeon had given her the impression that the mastectomy had been precautionary and told her no additional treatment was warranted at the time. In her letter to Marjorie Spock, Carson made it clear that she believed she had been cured. Thankfully the cancer had been caught early and there "need be no apprehension for the future."

Carson's usual desire for privacy was now heightened. She could imagine what a cancer diagnosis might suggest to critics about her motivation in writing a book that would implicate pesticides as cancer-causing agents. She told Spock she planned to provide details about her illness to only a few special friends like her—though she admitted it might be hard to prevent the world from learning of it. "I suppose it's a futile effort to keep one's private affairs private," Carson said. "Somehow I have no wish to read of my ailments in literary gossip columns. Too much comfort to the chemical companies!"

Spock, desperate to help and captivated by alternative ideas, urged Carson to see a "Dr. Pfeiffer," who according to Spock had discovered an unusual treatment using mistletoe to counteract a "gravitational drag" that he believed caused cancer. Carson tactfully avoided a direct response and later suggested that Pfeiffer might do some assays on pesticides for her, but nothing came of it and Carson let the matter drop.

Paul Brooks, who apparently did not know the exact nature of Carson's surgery or its result, wrote to say that he liked the cancer chapters. He added that the similarities between radiation and pesticides deserved the emphasis she had given them, and that current events were in their favor on this matter. "In a sense, all this publicity about fallout gives you a head start in awakening people to the dangers of chemicals," he said. He agreed they should keep thinking about the title, and hoped Carson's hospital stay had been brief.

Weak and in pain, Carson had gone up to Southport Island with Roger in June 1960. She hoped to make headway on the book while Roger was occupied at a day camp. But it was hard going. She and Brooks arranged for him to visit her in Maine toward the end of August, and as the time for their meeting approached it was clear that Carson considered it more of an editorial consultation than a casual visit. She sent Brooks more pages through the summer—along with her overall outline for the book so he could see how everything fit together—but admitted more than once to needing his help.

She had decided to combine the two chapters on cancer into one and had finished what she called the "bird chapter" on the effects of pesticide spraying observed by George Wallace at Michigan State and other researchers. This was progress, but Carson seemed to be in a kind of fog. In September she offered a surprisingly clumsy suggestion for a new title: "Dissent in Favor of Man." Carson said it was inspired by a magazine account of Justice William O. Douglas's dissent in the Supreme Court's decision not to hear an appeal of the Long Island spraying case. Brooks wrote back and told Carson he could see what she was getting at, but that he didn't think "Dissent in Favor of Man" was right. Almost as an afterthought, Brooks mentioned an idea he had for a title for the bird chapter, which he thought might be called "Silent Spring." Carson said it was an excellent suggestion. When Marie Rodell heard about it, she said *Silent Spring* would make a good title for the book itself.

Carson considered the effects of pesticides on birds one of the most arresting aspects of the use of chemical poisons, and this had registered strongly with Justice Douglas in his dissenting opinion—in which he quoted from an article Carson had written for the *Washington Post* in the spring of 1959. Douglas's opinion—it never once mentioned a constitutional issue—emphasized that the risks of the spraying program to wildlife and to human health raised by the plaintiffs at trial hadn't been adequately evaluated by the original judge.

Douglas wrote that, while he himself did not take any position as to the merits of these arguments, he thought the questions about the wide use of chemical pesticides warranted review by the Supreme Court. In a long footnote, Douglas cited Carson's *Post* article, in which Paul Brooks might have discovered that Carson herself was on the track of the right title for the book:

> During the past 15 years, the use of highly poisonous hydrocarbons and of organic phosphates allied to the nerve gasses of chemical warfare has built up from small beginnings to what a noted British ecologist recently called "an amazing rain of death upon the surface of the earth." Most of these chemicals leave long-persisting residues on vegetation, in soils, and even in the bodies of earthworms and other organisms on which birds depend for food. . . .
>
> To many of us this sudden silencing of the song of birds, this obliteration of the color and beauty and interest of bird life, is sufficient cause for sharp regret. To those who have never known such rewarding enjoyment of nature, there should yet remain a nagging and insistent question: If this "rain of death" has produced so disastrous an effect on birds, what of other lives, including our own?

The "sudden silencing" of the birds was to become the central motif of Carson's book—but getting close to a title when the book was no closer to completion frustrated everyone. By the middle of November, Brooks seemed—for him—impatient with Carson. Based on her latest guidance, he said he was not going to announce a publication date for the book in the first half of 1961. But he said he could still change that decision if she could assure him it was almost finished. He wanted a progress report and said he would be eager to see and work on additional chapters as she completed them. He offered to meet her in New York or Washington if it would help. Carson said she would come up to New York, and they planned to talk over the book at Marie Rodell's apartment, which Carson said would make the trip easier to manage. But at the last minute she canceled, telling Brooks that she had been sick again.

Carson had found a swelling near her sternum. After taking X-rays, her doctors decided the best thing would be to start a course of radiation therapy, to which Carson agreed. She told Dorothy Freeman there was some comfort in knowing her situation more clearly and that she had decided to believe the radiation treatments would work. But she admitted it was hard to face all of this after being so sure the previous spring that her surgery had fixed everything. Now it seemed she couldn't count on ever being completely well again. Carson said it was bitterly disappointing to be laid up again when she was so pressed for time with the book, but that there was nothing to be done about it.

She hinted to Paul Brooks that she was, in fact, more angry about her care than she'd let on to Dorothy. She told him that the description of her primary tumor as "suspicious" simply hadn't been true. It was malignant and there was evidence it had metastasized. Carson had been allowed to believe otherwise "even though I asked directly," she told Brooks.

Carson was short of her fifty-third birthday when she had her mastectomy—young enough, certainly, to have a fighting chance against cancer if that's what it was. Had she been fully informed of the pathology of her disease she almost certainly would have embarked on an immediate course of follow-up treatments—radiation or chemotherapy—and might well have had a different outcome. What must have particularly distressed Carson was that she was more than capable of understanding her diagnosis and treatment options—yet was denied the chance to be fully engaged in her own case.

Once she guessed the truth, Carson consulted with Dr. George "Barney" Crile, Jr., a cancer expert at the Cleveland Clinic with whom she was already acquainted. Carson saw Crile in Cleveland in December. She wrote a letter to Dorothy while on the plane to Cleveland, feigning a casual tone and telling her a long, funny story about the difficulties she had getting to the airport that morning. At the clinic, Crile confirmed that Carson had cancer, and he designed a program of radiation treatments for her to follow back in Silver Spring. Carson relayed this news to Dorothy, who was overwhelmed but chose to adopt Carson's stoicism. Stan Freeman had had health issues for several years now—chest pains and a frightening episode of internal bleeding—and Dorothy found herself the primary moral support for both Stan and Carson. She told Carson it would be so easy to give in, to think only of the "dark side of all of this," but that if Carson wouldn't go there then neither would she.

In January 1961, the radiation treatments caused Carson's ulcer to flare up again—a not uncommon side effect, she told Dorothy. The mass in her chest seemed to be shrinking, which was good news. Carson's illness stirred Dorothy's memories of their time together over the past seven years. On a cold late afternoon at the end of January, while Stan was writing in his study, Dorothy sat on the bed where Carson had napped on her first visit to West Bridgewater and wrote her a long letter, rehearsing their relationship from the beginning. Dorothy said she remembered her initial feelings of awe at becoming friendly with a famous author. She said it had taken her a long time to "destroy the pedestal." That had come, Dorothy said, in learning that Carson shared the same cares and heartaches as anyone—and the amazing thing was that once she had brought Carson down to eye level she found herself worshipping her even more. Dorothy said she had read the "Hyacinth Letter" every night for months after receiving it, and was still inspired by it whenever she read it again. She told Carson they were "kindred spirits" in too many ways to count, and that above all, Carson had enriched her appreciation of literature and music and nature more than she could ever say. Dorothy said Carson's love was like an embrace that was always there, soothing her in good times and bad.

Dorothy's loving summary of their experiences marked the beginning of a long goodbye, without, of course, acknowledging as much. From this time forward, Carson's declining health would move between the foreground and the background of the thoughts she and Dorothy shared with each other—but it would always be there, a deepening shadow.

As Dorothy composed this long letter, Carson had again fallen seriously ill with something new. In mid-January 1961, Carson developed a staph infection that progressed to septic arthritis, settling in her knees and ankles. By the end of the month she was unable to walk and could barely stand. She told Brooks she would again enter the hospital to see what could be done. Carson said she had never been sicker in her life—which must have worried Brooks immensely given her history. She kept up a brave mood when she was hospitalized in February—she joked with Dorothy about substandard "bed-pan service"—but admitted she had been devastated seeing Roger slumped and sobbing as she was put into an ambulance for the trip.

Her exact diagnosis wasn't certain. There was a chance she was in the early stages of generalized rheumatoid arthritis. But only time would tell. When she came home a few days later, Carson could walk a short distance, but still needed a walker or a wheelchair most of the time. Gradually Carson got better—even though she had also started a second round of intensive radiation therapy. She told Paul Brooks she hated burdening him with news of her ailments, but that it seemed only fair to explain to him fully why work on the book had come to a standstill. Toward the end of March she reported she had started—ever so tentatively—writing again. Carson thought the only good that might come out of her many health complaints was a new perspective she'd gained on the book during the time she'd taken off. Now, she told Brooks, it seemed important to tighten and simplify everything—to free the story from the excessive detail she'd been trying to force into it.

In May 1961, Marie Rodell visited Carson in Silver Spring and got a shock—Carson, though she now walked with a pronounced limp, could get around the house on her own and had resumed work on the book, albeit in the random, scattered way only she could understand. Parts of the manuscript were like a collage—cut apart and rearranged, and then stapled together again. As usual, Carson seemed to use whatever was handy to write on—she alternated between long-hand and typing—sometimes resorting to ruled yellow legal paper. Unscrambling and making sense of all this was Carson's special talent, and it slowed her down and forced her to think over many times what she was trying to say—a laborious process of searching within her own writing for the right words. Carson now planned a total of nine chapters. Three were done and several more were partly so. Rodell told Brooks that with luck and "no more catastrophes," it was likely Carson would finish by the end of summer. Brooks, elated at this news, made plans to visit Carson himself. Carson said she was eager to meet with him, as they had much to discuss. She said she knew most of what she'd written was going to need revision, but that for the time being she was happier working on new material.

In June 1961, after he had seen Carson, Brooks told his boss, Lovell Thompson, that it really did look as if she would finish in an-other couple of months. Brooks must have felt a new confidence in this, because he took the occasion to ask Thompson about hiring an illustrator for the book to help convey some of the more complex ideas Carson was dealing with. Louis and Lois Darling, a Connecticut-based husband-and-wife team who created illustrations, sometimes for their own books, were well thought of at Houghton Mifflin, and in July the publisher sent a sample of their work to Carson at her cottage on Southport Island. Louis Darling, perhaps best known for illustrating the Henry Huggins series of children's books by Beverly Cleary, had also done line drawings for Roderick Haig-Brown's clas-sic fishing book, *A River Never Sleeps,* which in mood and scenery was not unlike parts of Henry Williamson's *Salar the Salmon*—the well-spring of all of Carson's work. But Carson was unsure. She thought the Darlings' drawings were "beautiful and meticulous," but said she wasn't convinced those were the precise qualities needed for a book that was still being called "Man Against Nature." Both Brooks and Lovell Thompson thought Carson was wrong about this—they were confident the Darlings would be perfect for Carson's book, and neither of them could understand her mystifying objection on the grounds of overmeticulousness.

Except for times when she was too sick to work, Carson kept up a heroic correspondence with the many experts she called on to help with technical issues, somehow managing waves of incoming and outgoing letters that would have staggered someone in far better health than she was—and that revealed the wide range of her concerns about pesticides and wildlife. Almost without exception, Carson made friends as she went.

Carson had long and involved exchanges with several people on the use of herbicides. Olaus Murie, a prominent naturalist, author, and wildlife biologist who had worked for the U.S. Biological Survey before joining the Wilderness Society as one of its directors, reviewed Carson's chapter on herbicides and helped her to understand the impact of their use in the West, where sagebrush was being converted to grasslands for cattle grazing by means of aerial spraying. The collateral damage—it could not be avoided—was the destruction of a naturally balanced ecosystem and the inevitable decline of species such as the sage grouse, pronghorn antelope, and mule deer.

Another prolific correspondent whose contributions filled Carson's swelling files was an herbicide expert named Frank Egler. An unusual sort—Carson seemed to attract them—Egler wrote long, intermittently neurotic letters about the ecological hazards of herbicide use, mainly in the control of roadside brush. Egler had been dismissed from the American Museum of Natural History in 1955 for making controversial public statements about roadside spraying and had retreated to manage a private forest reserve in Connecticut, where he got by on family money and an argumentative disposition.

Carson initially thought they were of similar minds. But in the fall of 1961, she wrote him a pointed letter disagreeing with his contention—recently published in a pamphlet called *Sixty Questions and Answers* about roadside vegetation control—that herbicides were not toxic to humans or animals. She informed Egler that one widely used herbicide "belongs in the dangerous company of chemicals that imitate radiation, duplicating many of the effects of X-rays on cell division." She told him the FWS had new, as-yet-unpublished data showing reproductive effects that might well be a "manifestation" of this attribute.

Chastened, Egler wrote back saying this was news to him and complaining, not unreasonably, that he couldn't very well have an opinion on research that had not been made public. "Am I *supposed* to know?" he asked. Still, Carson had enough confidence in Egler's judgment that near the end of her research she sent him the herbicides chapter to review, begging him to do so as quickly as he could. Eight days later Carson was floored when Egler sent her back a lengthy line-by-line critique that reflected a careful reading beyond anything she could have expected. She told Egler she would make many of the changes and additions he suggested.

In a long-running exchange that eventually took a personal turn, Carson wrote regularly to Malcolm Hargraves—the Mayo Clinic cancer expert from the Long Island lawsuit—who maintained his belief that he routinely saw patients with leukemia and lymphoma that were the result of exposure to pesticides. Hargraves conceded that he hadn't done the rigorous research needed to verify this—and in the book's discussion of pesticides and cancer Carson took care not to overstate Hargraves's anecdotal evidence. This may have been partly due to a warning she'd gotten from her own doctor at the Cleveland Clinic, Barney Crile. After reading drafts of several chapters, Crile cautioned Carson against making too firm an argument that pesticides were carcinogenic. Although he thought she offered an "impressive thesis," Crile thought her reading of the evidence was selective. He said anyone could as easily mine the scientific literature and reach the opposite conclusion.

In the spring of 1961, Carson broke her vow of silence about her own condition and asked Hargraves about a course of treatment involving gold injections that had been suggested to treat her arthritis. Carson thought gold therapy, which helped only some patients and often produced unpleasant side effects, would be dangerous to try while she was undergoing radiation therapy and prone to anemia because of its effects on her bone marrow—an astute conclusion by a patient who seemed to know more than her doctors. Hargraves concurred with Carson's assessment, telling her that gold injections were always chancy and would surely be more so in her case.

In October, Carson wrote to Brooks wondering when she would be given other illustrators' work to look at. Brooks patiently asked her to reconsider the Darlings and sent her still more examples of their drawings. The supposed delivery date for the manuscript had again passed without the book being finished, but Marie Rodell's assurances that Carson would soon wrap it up were evidently enough to keep Houghton Mifflin satisfied. In late October, Rodell told Brooks he could expect to have everything but the final chapter by Thanksgiving. A few days later, Brooks and Carson agreed to ask the Darlings to do the illustrations—to which they eagerly said yes. Brooks privately told Rodell how relieved he was that "the end is in sight."

In early January 1962, Carson was still hard at work on the book. With only one chapter to go and the rest of the manuscript already submitted to Paul Brooks and to the *New Yorker,* she pressed on as fast as she could. One evening toward the end of the month Carson's phone rang. When she answered, the soft voice on the other end of the line said, "This is William Shawn."

ELEVEN

High Tides and Low

S hawn told Carson she had turned the issue of pesticide use into "literature." It was, he said, a "brilliant achievement" that was both beautiful and profound. Carson, who told Dorothy Freeman that she valued Shawn's opinion above all others, listened quietly. For the first time, Carson allowed herself to believe that she'd gotten her message across, that she'd done what she could as well as she could, and that now the story would soon be on its own. After she finished talking with Shawn she got Roger tucked in for the night and then went into her study, where she put on a Beethoven violin concerto and had a long, happy cry.

Carson and Brooks had agreed at last on a title—*Silent Spring*. But Carson had come down with iritis, a painful eye inflammation that again limited her to a few hours of work a day. Carson told Brooks this felt almost unbearably cruel, to be so near the end and now have the added worry about whether her eyesight would hold up during the editing process. She said that when ill health impeded her progress—as it had at almost every step of the way on this book—it was like being caught in one of those dreams in which you try to run but cannot. Carson continued working and reworking on the manuscript through February and March 1962. On April 3, Brooks wrote her a letter that read simply: "Good girl!"

Everyone involved now started thinking about what would happen when—after years of work—*Silent Spring* finally came out. Brooks thought it would take heavy promotion to get people to read something that was so different from and far more pessimistic than anything Carson had written before—and which contained off-putting technical material. He had heavily edited Carson's chapter on the properties of synthetic pesticides, which included chemical diagrams, to make it more accessible, cutting it nearly in half.

Carson, meanwhile, inquired whether Houghton Mifflin's attorneys were going to review the book prior to publication in anticipation of potential lawsuits from the pesticide industry. Marie Rodell asked Brooks flatly whether Carson could get libel insurance. Everybody agreed that advance copies should be distributed to well-placed readers and critics who were likely to be friendly to the book—though how far to take this was a tricky question. One person they wondered about was Carson's former collaborator Edwin Diamond, who was the science editor at *Newsweek*. In a rare moment of cluelessness, Brooks told the publicity department there was no reason not to send Diamond an advance copy, as he didn't recall anybody having hard feelings over Diamond's exit from the project.

In early April, Carson outlined for Brooks some of the concerns she had about what was sure to be a storm of protest over the book—especially from pesticide makers, but also from the U.S. Department of Agriculture. She wondered if the USDA might even sue her, as there were many things in the book that were sure to make people in the agency "distinctly unhappy." Among these were Carson's indictment of the fire ant program, in which she argued that the fire ant became a pest in need of eradication only once government officials had chemical pesticides with "broad lethal powers" at their disposal.

With serialization of the book in the *New Yorker* set for June 1962, Carson and Marie Rodell continued their back-and-forth with the

Houghton Mifflin publicity department on how best to get out the advance word on *Silent Spring*. It was clear that everyone expected the book would force readers to take sides. Houghton Mifflin was nervous about sending out large numbers of advance copies and about a proposal—which they ultimately abandoned—to hold a luncheon for prominent people who shared Carson's commitment to the "cause." Their concern was that it might be unwise to risk stirring up a negative reaction to the book before it was even serialized in the *New Yorker*. If Carson was perceived as launching a crusade at odds with the interests of pesticide manufacturers and the policy makers who supported them, *Silent Spring* would face strong headwinds before the public even had a chance to read it. Marie Rodell pooh-poohed these worries—whatever storm was coming would come sooner or later, and it really didn't matter when. Plus, Rodell thought that the many influential people who already knew about *Silent Spring* and were likely to be supportive—people such as Supreme Court Justice William O. Douglas—might feel slighted if they didn't get to read it before it came out in the *New Yorker*.

But as the spring progressed, this internal debate seemed less relevant, as word about a controversial new book from Rachel Carson began to spread. As Marie Rodell reminded the publicity department at Houghton Mifflin when they were updating Carson's biographical profile, *The Sea Around Us* had sold nearly two million copies. Whatever Carson did next was not likely to go unnoticed in the run up to publication day. In late April 1962, Paul Brooks asked around the office if anybody had ever heard of a man named Fred Friendly, who was evidently a producer for the CBS television network. Friendly had phoned Brooks to express an interest in doing some kind of news program about *Silent Spring,* and Brooks had sent over galley proofs to CBS.

As *Silent Spring* headed into production, Carson relaxed her usual close attention to every detail surrounding the preparation and publication of her work. She was still undergoing radiation treatments. Carson thought these might end soon, but she told Dorothy that she couldn't count on it and had no choice but to continue subjecting herself to a therapy intended to kill her cancer but that posed a hazard to her general health as well. She said she could still work on most mornings, but on treatment days a heavy nausea overtook her by midday and made it impossible to go on with the revisions to *Silent Spring*. Carson admitted she wished she could go back to the previous April when she'd been operated on. "How differently I would handle it now," she told Dorothy. Carson said she was appalled at how little thought she'd given to choosing her doctors and at how easily she'd taken their word that no further treatment was needed after the mastectomy. She knew there was no use in thinking like this. But she did anyway.

In mid-April, Carson became concerned about pain and what felt like a new mass in her armpit, near the border of her original surgery but outside the area that had been receiving radiation. An examination left Carson feeling her future lay somewhere between her worst fears and her fragile hopes of recovery. The pain near her armpit was, in fact, from the spread of her cancer. But other discomfort she'd recently experienced in her neck appeared to be a side effect of the radiation treatment—not more cancer—while pain she'd felt in her back was probably due to ordinary age-related arthritis, as X-rays did not show any malignancy in her spine. Carson told Dorothy the real torture that cancer inflicts on its victims is the loss of security in one's own body. "The trouble with this business," Carson wrote, "is that every perfectly ordinary little ailment looks like a hobgoblin, and one lives in a little private hell until the thing is examined and found to be nothing much."

In May 1962, Carson had a rare evening out that left her grappling with contradictory feelings. She'd been invited to a dinner for the trustees of the National Parks Association. Among the attendees was Justice Douglas, who cornered Carson to tell her *Silent Spring* was "tremendous" and that he'd been busily "selling it" wherever he went. During a speech he gave later that night, Douglas strayed from his written remarks to tell everyone to read Rachel Carson's forth-coming book, as it gave a clear-eyed and alarming look at what the "chemical engineers are doing to our world." Carson wrote about the evening to Dorothy, telling her what an odd feeling it was to hear people discussing her "fourth brainchild."

Carson was, of course, pleased by Douglas's enthusiastic support. But something else she'd heard at the dinner distressed her. A number of people had been gossiping about Senator Maurine Neuberger of Oregon, who'd recently undergone cancer surgery and looked frail. Carson overheard someone saying "she can't last." Carson found the idea of people talking about her in the same way more upsetting than she could bear. She told Dorothy that was the reason she'd been so careful not to discuss her health with anybody she didn't have to.

Carson said she knew it would have been natural for Dorothy to have mentioned something about her writer friend being sick—but that she shouldn't say any more about it going forward. If anybody asked about her, Dorothy should say only that she had had a bout of iritis that had cleared up completely and that Carson had lately never looked better. Carson said she knew that Dorothy already understood all this—but that she probably hadn't realized how strongly Carson felt about keeping her illness private, or the depth of her fears about what would happen if word of it got out. "Whispers about a private individual might not go far," Carson wrote. "About an author-in-the-news they go like wildfire. So let people think I am as well as I look."

How well Carson looked was debatable. Never the picture of health or vigor, she aged dramatically during her cancer treatment. Carson was fifty-five when *Silent Spring* was published at the end of September 1962—but appeared to be about twenty years older.

Three long excerpts from *Silent Spring* ran in consecutive weekly issues of the *New Yorker* beginning on June 16, 1962. Although abridged, Carson's story began in the magazine almost word for word as it would in the book—with the short, foreboding fable that would become one of the great set pieces in American literature. In it, Carson imagined a nameless town "in the heart of America where all life seemed to live in harmony with its surroundings." This idyllic place, flanked in every direction by lush farm fields and cold, clear-running trout streams, was home to an abundance of wildlife—foxes and deer and especially birds, an aviary so rich during the migrations of spring and fall that people traveled great distances just to see it. So it had been, Carson wrote, since "the days many years ago when the first settlers raised their houses, sank their wells, and built their barns."

But then a "strange blight" invaded the area. It was like an "evil spell" that brought with it unexplainable sickness and death to livestock. Chickens laid eggs that did not hatch, cattle and sheep turned up dead, pigs gave birth to stunted litters that lived only days. The fish in the rivers died and the trout anglers stayed away. People, too, fell ill. Some died, leaving their families grieving and their doctors perplexed. The roadsides, formerly lush with bushes and wildflowers, were now brown and withered, "as though swept by fire." Here and there, a mysterious white powder clung to the rooftops and lay in the gutters of the houses in the town, deadly traces of something that had "fallen like snow" from the skies only weeks before. And everywhere there was an ominous quiet, a silence that closed off the town and its surroundings from the living world as if the area had become entombed:

> There was a strange stillness. The birds, for example—where had they gone? Many people spoke of them, puzzled and disturbed. The feeding stations in the backyards were deserted. The few birds seen anywhere were moribund; they trembled violently and could not fly. It was a spring without voices. On the mornings that had once throbbed with the dawn chorus of robins, catbirds, doves, jays, wrens, and scores of other bird voices there was now no sound; only silence lay over the fields and woods and marsh.

In the space of just ten paragraphs—the *New Yorker* combined them into three—Carson had written the story of the end of the world. What reader in 1962 could fail to see in this description all the bleak possibilities of the modern age? Carson's subject was pesticides, but she began in a way that just as surely evoked the images of nuclear devastation and all its ensuing sickness and pallor, right down to the residue of poison from the sky.

This was a familiar tableau, as the Cold War had offered a running preview of such scenes of annihilation in the picture many Americans already had of the colorless, lifeless void that resided behind the "iron curtain," where an oppressive society was understood to be functionally dead but at the same time a deadly threat. In September 1961, the Soviet Union had resumed atmospheric testing and by early December had detonated *thirty-one* nuclear devices, including one more than 3,300 times the size of "Little Boy," the bomb that destroyed Hiroshima. Though not a practical bomb, this gargantuan device produced the largest nuclear explosion in history. The United States immediately embarked on a crash program to restart its own testing in the South Pacific—and did so in April 1962, just as Carson was finishing *Silent Spring.* The testing continued at a furious pace through the spring and into the summer and then fall. In the month of June alone, as readers were learning of the dark promise of pesticides from Rachel Carson in the *New Yorker,* the United States exploded ten nuclear devices in the atmosphere. That year a nuclear device exploded somewhere in the world every few days.

President Kennedy had been reluctant to start testing again but felt the Soviet resumption left him no option. Such was the morbid dance of mutually assured destruction. Humanity's only hope was thought to be in the maintenance of equivalent nuclear arsenals by the Soviets and the Americans. When Dr. Albert Schweitzer wrote to the president imploring him to stop the tests, an obviously conflicted Kennedy wrote back that he, too, hated the testing—which he called a "tragic choice," but one that had to be made, as the only thing worse would have been the alternative: allowing the Soviet Union to gain a nuclear advantage that would destabilize the balance of power in the world. This, Kennedy insisted, might result in "fateful consequences for all our hopes for peace and freedom."

The resumption of atmospheric testing—even though the American tests were on the far side of the world—brought on a renewed anxiety about exposure to radioactive fallout. People had reason to be concerned: The latest round of tests had, in the space of only months, doubled the amount of fallout dispersed around the planet. The U.S. tests in the South Pacific contributed only slightly to this new rain of radioactivity in the densely populated Northern Hemisphere. But fallout from Soviet testing drifted eastward over North America, where three cities—Minneapolis, Des Moines, and Kansas City—were rapidly approaching the federally established "safe" limits for radiation, as established by the government's Radiation Protection Guides. Of special concern was the radionuclide iodine 131. Despite its short half-life of just eight days, iodine 131 was being detected in milk supplies at levels that might soon require restrictions on dairy operations in the affected areas. Government officials felt trapped by their own prior conservatism, as the radiation guides outlining safe levels had been set low based on what was expected from routine industrial operations during peacetime. The authorities felt sure that the guidelines were therefore well below what would constitute a risk of health effects—though in truth, nobody knew that to be the case.

The Federal Radiation Council, overlooking concerns such as those raised by Linus Pauling about the cumulative damage from even small health effects when they occur in large populations over long periods of time, tried to put a calming spin on the government's lack of certainty over its own policies: "We cannot say with certainty what health hazards are caused by fallout from nuclear testing. We expect there will be some genetic effects; other effects such as leukemia and cancer are more speculative and may not occur at all."

Although thyroid cancer had been induced in laboratory animals with radioactive iodine, no case of human thyroid cancer had ever been traced to such exposure. Officials in the U.S. Public Health

Service agreed with everyone else in the government that the health risk from iodine 131 in fallout was probably nil—but they insisted that steps be taken to shut down dairy suppliers whose milk contamination exceeded the guidelines. President Kennedy's science adviser, Jerome Wiesner, told the president that was only one option. Another would be to raise the threshold level of concern for iodine 131—that is, to simply rewrite the guidelines.

Meanwhile, the administration requested a nearly $2 million supplemental budget for fallout monitoring by the Public Health Service, which also planned to investigate better "countermeasures" to use in areas of excessive contamination. Wiesner recommended that the USDA be given a seat on the Federal Radiation Council, a move that was likely to restrain the council in its tendency to set fallout safety guidelines so low as to threaten farm interests—as they already did. In mid-July 1962, Secretary of Agriculture Orville Freeman—who was from Minnesota, one of the places most contaminated with fallout—ordered his staff to make plans in the event milk production had to be halted anywhere.

A month later, having been appointed to the Federal Radiation Council, Freeman warned the president that if contamination levels rose above the federal safety guides things could get politically messy. In Minnesota, milk prices had already been raised, and cows were being "dry fed" off-pasture to reduce iodine 131 contamination in milk. Freeman wasn't happy about this, and he told Kennedy that nobody on the Federal Radiation Council thought the Minnesota initiative necessary or prudent—that it was likely to make things worse while putting federal officials in a difficult position. Freeman said one possible federal response would be to announce that the Minnesota program was a strictly local, "experimental" effort while at the same time supplying Minnesota dairy operators with dry feed at reduced cost under federal disaster assistance authority. But Freeman equivocated, as launching such a program risked setting a precedent that might spin out of control. If fallout radiation levels went up in other regions, Freeman said, the federal government could find itself with a "vast and expensive" new program on its hands—words that might just as well have described the nuclear testing that caused all the trouble in the first place.

What to do? Freeman said he was working closely with Jerome Wiesner to find a balanced approach that took into account the "political, emotional, and other factors" that made the whole subject of radioactive fallout so "touchy." Freeman thought the administration's options were narrow. Downplay the potential health consequences of fallout and they risked "a lot of demagoguery" from political opponents. But too aggressive a response could also undermine public confidence in the administration by "contributing needlessly to widespread concern and alarm" that would end up producing "all kinds of bad results."

While the president mulled over the secretary's ambiguous advice, Freeman explored the possibility that the milk-price increases in Minnesota—which had been undertaken simultaneously by several dairy cooperatives—might amount to price fixing and therefore be a violation of federal antitrust statutes. Freeman was briefed on this angle by Minnesota attorney general Walter Mondale—who had been appointed to the job by Freeman himself when he was governor of the state. Mondale reported that public worries over fallout-contaminated milk in Minnesota were being used as a "cover" for the price increase by milk suppliers.

By November 1962, the government had decided to retroactively redefine its own radiation guidelines so as to remove the idea that they had anything to do with public safety. The Federal Radiation Council now torturously maintained that there was no conceivable health risk to people from fallout even at radiation levels many times greater than the guides' recommendations. In fact, people were advised to henceforth consider the guides not as "a dividing line between safety and danger in actual radiation situations." Nor did exceeding the guides necessarily mean that protective action was required. Instead, the guides were to be used only as indicators for when "detailed evaluation" of radiation exposure was warranted. The Federal Radia-

tion Council declared itself ready and willing *when requested* to provide "consultation and technical assistance" in the apparently unlikely
event that there was concern about radioactive fallout "in any part
of the country"—an astonishing claim given that there was concern
about radioactive fallout everywhere in the country.

The growing and pervasive threat from radioactive fallout—and the
government's dodgy response to it—so closely mirrored what was
happening with pesticides that Carson decided to make the connection explicit early in *Silent Spring*. People couldn't see radiation.
Sometimes they couldn't even see the fallout that carried it across
the sky and eventually back to earth. But they could understand the
dangers of an invisible poison that was everywhere, and whose effects
could last for years or even generations. If one considered the whole
long history of life on earth, Carson wrote, it was a story in which all
living things responded to and were a product of their environment.
Evolution was the steady maintenance of a biosphere in harmony with
prevailing conditions. Only recently—within the "moment of time
represented by the present century"—had one species managed to
turn this agreeable relationship around and begun to effect change in
the other direction. Carson thought it a bitter irony that the evolution
of life on earth, which had unfolded over eons, could be so shattered
as to make its continuation uncertain:

> The most alarming of all man's assaults upon the environment is
> the contamination of air, earth, rivers, and sea with dangerous
> and even lethal materials. This pollution is for the most part ir
> recoverable; the chain of evil it initiates not only in the world that
> must support life but in living tissues is for the most part irrevers
> ible. In this now universal contamination of the environment,
> chemicals are the sinister and little-recognized partners of radia
> tion in changing the very nature of the world—the very nature
> of its life. Strontium 90, released through nuclear explosions into

the air, comes to earth in rain or drifts down as fallout, lodges in soil, enters into the grass or corn or wheat grown there, and in time takes up its abode in the bones of a human being, there to remain until his death. Similarly, chemicals sprayed on croplands or forests or gardens lie long in the soil, entering into living organisms, passing from one to another in a chain of poisoning and death.

Just as it had done with *The Sea Around Us* and *The Edge of the Sea,* the *New Yorker*'s serialization of *Silent Spring* generated a tremendous response, and anticipation of the book's publication in September soared. This time, however, a noticeable portion of the reaction was negative. The Michigan Department of Agriculture took strong exception to Carson's characterization of its spraying efforts against the Japanese beetle with the insecticide aldrin. The campaign had been carried out over some twenty-seven thousand acres, including the suburbs of Detroit, in 1959. Aldrin was dropped from low-flying airplanes, and within days citizens reported finding alarming numbers of dead and dying birds.

Carson had written that the beetle wasn't a problem in need of such a heavy-handed response and that aldrin, among the most toxic of insecticides, had been chosen mainly because it was cheap. She relied on official information the U.S. Department of Agriculture had put out on the spraying program, and on the firsthand account of a prominent Michigan naturalist named Walter Nickell. In a sarcastic letter to the *New Yorker,* an official with the Michigan Department of Agriculture said that neither Carson nor Nickell knew what they were talking about—though that was to be expected, as most articles taking a stand against pesticides were crammed with "scientific errors, half truths, oblique and irrelevant references, and in some cases outright falsehoods." The writer did not offer any proof that Carson was guilty on any of those counts.

The *New Yorker* got an earful from executives at a number of chemical companies—all complaining of one-sidedness and Carson's failure to consider the economic benefits of pesticide use, especially in food production. One salty citizen in San Francisco thought *Silent Spring* reflected Carson's obvious "Communist sympathies," which were shared by so many writers "these days." He said anyone could live "without birds and animals," but not without business. The whole thing, he thought, must be some kind of sick attempt at humor. Inexplicably, he thought Carson was interested in destroying insects:

> As for insects, isn't it just like a woman to be scared to death of a few little bugs! As long as we have the H-bomb everything will be OK. I suppose Miss Carson is one of those "peace nuts" too!
>
> I wish you would print more jokes in your magazine and not so much uninteresting and critical stuff. After all, the *New Yorker* is supposed to be funny and make us laugh.

Another angry letter writer wondered when the *New Yorker* was going to run a comparable three-part series by someone competent to "refute the farrage [*sic*] of half-truths, mis-emphases and out and out misstatements" found in the *Silent Spring* articles—though he had no illusion that such a follow-up would set the record straight, as "corrections never catch up with the original untruth." The writer's specific objection was that Carson had treated pesticide users as soulless technicians with no regard for the preservation of wildlife or the protection of human health.

This seemingly reasonable complaint—that the spray men were people, too—ignored the abundant evidence that technicians were already enlisted in humanity's global nuclear suicide pact and were practicing their dark arts regularly in the American desert, on the frozen wastes of eastern Asia, and over the tropical lagoons of remote islands in the far Pacific. Living on the verge of annihilation, Carson wrote, was not living. Quoting the ecologist Paul Shepard, Carson wondered, "Who would want to live in a world which is just not quite fatal?"

"Yet such a world is pressed upon us," Carson continued in her own words. "The crusade to create a chemically sterile, insect-free world seems to have engendered a fanatic zeal on the part of many specialists and most of the so-called control agencies. On every hand there is evidence that those engaged in spraying operations exercise ruthless power."

From the start, most of Carson's critics also chose to ignore her insistence that what was needed was not an end to the use of pesticides, but rather an end to their heedless overuse—a distinction that was lost on people whose economic interests were entwined with chemical controls. But Carson made it clear. "It is not my contention that chemical insecticides must never be used," she wrote. "I do contend that we have put poisonous and biologically potent chemicals indiscriminately into the hands of persons largely or wholly ignorant of their potentials for harm."

If Carson thought that leaving the door open for the judicious use of pesticides was enough to insulate her from accusations of overreaching, she soon learned otherwise. Even before the second installment of *Silent Spring* appeared in the *New Yorker,* Carson was under attack for attempting to undermine a global initiative that had been supported for years by the U.S. Congress and by the Eisenhower and Kennedy administrations.

Since the mid-1950s, the World Health Organization, an arm of the United Nations, had made the eradication of malaria a worldwide priority. Malaria is an ancient plague. Caused by a mosquito-transmitted parasite that is known to have infected humans in Africa for five hundred thousand years, the disease kills hundreds of thousands of people every year and sickens many millions more. In 1958, Congress passed legislation authored by Senators John F. Kennedy and Hubert Humphrey allocating a contribution of $100 million to the WHO malaria project. The campaign relied almost entirely on using DDT against the mosquitoes that carried the disease. The goal was to have houses and huts in regions with malaria treated twice a year.

It was known that some mosquitoes were resistant to DDT and

that others would become so—perhaps adapting into a "super race" that not only wasn't killed by the pesticide but wasn't even discouraged from inhabiting places where it had been sprayed. And it was also understood that spray teams would never find and treat every domicile in some places with malaria, as there were often no roads, or the people were nomadic. But it was assumed that malaria would disappear from remote, isolated pockets on its own if it could be snuffed out across most of its range—the expectation being that the parasite would follow a classic pattern of decline, then rarity, then extinction, in this case by human design.

The early years of the WHO's malaria eradication program produced encouraging results. By 1960, malaria had been erased in eleven countries and sharply curtailed in a dozen more. In India, where historically as many as seventy-five million people contracted malaria every year, that number fell below one hundred thousand. As deaths from malaria went down, life expectancies went up in some countries, and so did crop production and land values. But DDT had a side effect that even Rachel Carson hadn't anticipated: As malaria started to disappear, so did the scientists who studied the disease. What had been a multidisciplinary effort to understand and control a difficult epidemic turned into the one-dimensional chore of spraying DDT wherever the disease was present.

One irate reader wrote to the *New Yorker* to protest Carson's indictment of DDT, echoing the accusation that she had made many errors—none more egregious than her claim that the insecticide had had only "limited success" against malaria and in the long run might make things worse as mosquitoes acquired resistance to DDT and the disease flared up again in areas where it was being used. Not so, the letter writer insisted. Malaria could be eradicated in seven to ten years. But this effort took money, he said, which would now be more difficult to raise thanks to Carson's "mischief." He suggested the *New Yorker*'s famous standards for absolute accuracy were in decline, as it would have otherwise learned from any number of experts that

Carson was mistaken on this point. Apparently unaware of the distinction between people who study wildlife biology and people who practice nudism, he referred to Carson as a "naturist."

The writer might have waited for publication of the book to get a fuller sense of Carson's stand on DDT and malaria. It is true that *Silent Spring* is a sustained polemic against the use of synthetic pesticides; it is impossible to find so much as a phrase endorsing their general use. Carson never did find anything good to say about pesticides. But she left room for the possibility that they might be a wise choice in situations involving public welfare.

Carson acknowledged that DDT had been essential to the successful suppression of a typhus outbreak in Italy during the Second World War. And she also pointed to its use against malaria-carrying mosquitoes immediately after the war. The problem, she said, was that insects became resistant to DDT, and there was often a rebound of insect-borne diseases in areas where it was used. This, Carson wrote, had to be carefully weighed in fighting diseases and their insect carriers—such as "typhus and body lice, plague and rat fleas, African sleeping sickness and tsetse flies, various fevers and ticks." But she conceded that these were "important problems that must be met."

By the time *Silent Spring* came out, world health officials were arguing with one another over the increasing resistance of mosquitoes to DDT and whether this might defeat the goal of eradicating malaria. It was a question that Carson could have explored but did not in *Silent Spring*. Had she chosen to, the later claim that she had single-handedly brought about millions of deaths from malaria might not have gained the widespread currency it did. Carson's intense focus on the downside of pesticide use—like the tunnel vision that permitted her an idiosyncratic reading of "Locksley Hall" and to ignore Henry Williamson's Nazi sympathies—wasn't balanced against any upside, even though she conceded there might occasionally be one.

But her decision against exploring the malaria issue more thoroughly could not have been an easy one. In 1962, the U.S. Postal Service issued a commemorative stamp in support of the malaria program, and President Kennedy reaffirmed American commitment to the eradication of the disease. The president said the program was an international effort that proved the people of the world could work together on common objectives—as he had called upon them to do in his inaugural address when he'd said, "Together let us explore the stars, conquer the deserts, eradicate disease." As it turned out, however, Carson read the zeitgeist better than Kennedy did. In 1963, faced with questions about the declining effectiveness of DDT and about its safety, the United States halted funding for the malaria eradication program. Six years later—and three years ahead of a ban on DDT use in the United States that was widely attributed to Carson's campaign against pesticides—the World Health Organization scrapped the malaria program entirely.

Decades after the publication of *Silent Spring,* Rachel Carson would still be pilloried by detractors over her supposed contribution to the continued presence of malaria in the world. It's a hollow charge and an odd legacy, as she nowhere in *Silent Spring* argued against the use of DDT to fight the disease and, in fact, allowed that the use of pesticides might well be necessary in the protection of human health. But that did nothing to blunt the hostile reaction to *Silent Spring,* which also held within it the outlines of a partisan divide over environmental matters that has since hardened into a permanent wall of bitterness and mistrust.

With the publication of *Silent Spring,* public sentiment turned to the question of the environment and our role in its protection. A half century of growing enthusiasm for conservation had faded in the Cold War, and the new fear was that we now seemed as likely to destroy the earth as to preserve it. To people conditioned to the pessimism of the nuclear age, Carson made a dire appeal: Reverse course or continue at our peril. The twin demons of radiation and pesticides, interlinked so artfully in the pages of *Silent Spring,* made tangible the idea of a "total environment" that we could choose to protect or not. The fault line between conservation and environmentalism had been crossed.

There is no objective reason why environmentalism should be the exclusive province of any one political party or ideology—other than the history of the environmental movement beginning with *Silent Spring*. The labels for Carson rained down on her like fallout: subversive, antibusiness, Communist sympathizer, health nut, pacifist, and, of course, the coded insult "spinster." The attack on *Silent Spring* came from the chemical companies, agricultural interests, and the allies of both in government—the self-protective enclaves within what President Eisenhower had called the "military-industrial complex." Their fierce opposition to *Silent Spring* put Rachel Carson and everything she believed about the environment firmly on the left end of the political spectrum. And so two things—environmentalism and its adherents—were defined once and forever.

A few days before the first installment of *Silent Spring* came out in the *New Yorker,* Carson flew to California to deliver a commencement speech at Scripps College in Claremont. She told Dorothy Freeman she was *so glad* to be away from the phone. Carson said she was desperately tired but that the cross-country flight by jetliner—her first—was thrilling. She said she never stopped gazing out the window as the continent passed under her far below.

Carson's speech was eagerly anticipated at Scripps, where the administration had been after her to visit the campus for years. But it was important to her, too. Whether she meant it mainly to offer a context for *Silent Spring* or as an unusually ambitious charge to the graduates, Carson's speech amounted to a summing up of everything she had learned and come to believe about the human place in nature. She titled it "Of Man and the Stream of Time," and it sounded, intentionally or not, like a farewell.

Carson began by telling the students that the more she had lived and thought about things, the more it seemed to her that of all the difficulties that "crowd in upon us today" the most perilous was our changed relationship with nature. She said the concept of nature was itself a tricky construct, but that she liked the simple definition that identified nature as "the part of the world that man did not make." Humanity was part of the natural order—but by tradition and through an insistent arrogance, we had long assumed that nature was under our dominion, and that we were the masters of nature and everything that inhabited the natural world. Carson said she was often mystified by the reaction when she showed people the many forms of life flourishing in a tidal pool. Were these living entities edible? Could they be made into some kind of useful product? Carson said she could scarcely understand these questions when it was impossible to "assign a value" to creatures so exquisite that their mere existence should be cause for contentment with the peerless universe.

Carson said that before the attack on Hiroshima, she had doubted that nature could ever need protection from man. The world changed—slowly, of course—but certain of its features seemed immutable: the advance and retreat of the great oceans over eons, the daily ebbing and flooding of the tides, the uncountable mass migrations of the birds and fish. These things and many more seemed beyond the reach of human influence. Until they weren't. The earth, Carson said, was nothing if not a water world that was now growing parched:

> The once beneficent rains are now an instrument to bring down from the atmosphere the deadly products of nuclear explosions. Water, perhaps our most precious natural resource, is used and misused at a reckless rate. Our streams are fouled with an incredible assortment of wastes—domestic, chemical, radioactive, so that our planet, though dominated by seas that envelop three-fourths of its surface, is rapidly becoming a thirsty world.

Life being what it is—adaptable and tenacious—nature might survive even the insults of the modern age if they did not come so quickly, Carson said. Evolution is a response to both friendly and hostile conditions, but time is its essential ingredient and time was running out:

> The radiation to which we must now adjust if we are to survive is no longer simply the background radiation of rocks and sunlight, it is the result of our tampering with the atom. In the same way, wholly new chemicals are emerging from the laboratories—an astounding, bewildering array of them. All of these things are being introduced into our environment at a rapid rate. There simply is no time for living protoplasm to adjust to them.

Carson said that measured against the "backdrop of geologic time," human beings had inhabited the world for only a moment—but a portentous one in which we had to consider our impact not only on the earth but perhaps on worlds beyond it. It had taken only a few short centuries to move from a time when we gazed out at the ocean and wondered what was over the horizon. Now, she said, "our whole earth has become only another shore from which we look out across the dark ocean of space, uncertain what we shall find when we sail out among the stars." Based on the experience of her own generation—which had brought the world to such a dangerous crossroads—Carson said it was now time for the inheritors of the earth and its many difficulties to finally prove human mastery not of nature, but of itself. "Your generation," she said, "must come to terms with the environment."

Carson thought the speech went well. Relaxing the next day, she got word that *Silent Spring* would be a Book-of-the-Month Club selection for October, with Justice Douglas, one of Carson's most ardent admirers, to write the copy for the catalog. Glad but underwhelmed, Carson wrote to Dorothy that the good thing was that now the book would find its way "to farms and hamlets all over the country that don't know what a bookstore looks like—much less the *New Yorker*." Sounding more than a little jaded, Carson said, "It is perhaps not shameless to say that after three best-sellers one does not get wildly excited about such news, which is perhaps too bad, but the deep satisfaction is there."

Carson and Roger left Silver Spring for Maine at the end of June 1962, as the early reactions to the *Silent Spring* articles were taking hold. Among the first to weigh in was the *New York Times,* which on July 2 ran an editorial endorsing Carson's message on chemical pesticides and the "generally unsuccessful effort to eliminate insect pests and the extent to which we are, in the process, subjecting ourselves to the hazard of slow poisoning through the pollution of our environment." Anticipating the storm of criticism to come, the *Times* predicted that Carson would be accused of being an alarmist who reported only the arguments against the use of pesticides while ignoring their benefits. But the *Times* carefully pointed out that Carson had made it clear in *Silent Spring* that there was room for the intelligent application of pesticides in some situations. "Miss Carson does not argue that chemical pesticides must never be used, but she warns of the dangers of misuse and overuse by a public that has become mesmerized by the notion that chemists are the possessors of divine wisdom and that nothing but benefit can emerge from their test tubes."

It's not certain that President Kennedy read the *Silent Spring* excerpts as they appeared over three weeks in June. But the president was alerted to the articles in early July by a local judge in Plattsburgh, New York, named Irving Goldman. Goldman had attended law school at Yale, and he wrote to the president as a fellow "Ivy Leaguer," imploring Kennedy to involve the federal government in stricter oversight of pesticide use. Goldman said his concern was for protecting public health now and in future generations, as pesticides were so dangerous as to make the effects of radiation "seem minor by comparison." Goldman sent copies of the letter to the USDA, the FDA, both of his U.S. senators, and his representative in the House.

The White House gave the letter careful attention. It was routed to the president with Goldman's specific recommendation underlined: "Some action should be taken forthwith to regulate the manufacture and distribution of these chemicals," and the secretary of health, education, and welfare was asked to comment on Goldman's letter. Of course pesticides were already subject to regulation by the U.S. Department of Agriculture under the authority of FIFRA and other federal statutes—but it was clear that Goldman believed far too little was being done.

Within days, Kennedy's special assistant, T. J. Reardon, Jr., had obtained a cautious draft response to Goldman from Secretary of Agriculture Orville Freeman's office. The letter took a more sanguine tone than the president himself used in his press conference a few weeks later when he would tell the country he was ordering a broad review of pesticide use in response to Carson's articles. Reardon told Goldman that the government had been regulating pesticides for nearly a century. He said that the rapid development and commercialization of newer pesticides that so concerned Miss Carson had already led to tighter controls to "insure the protection of the public." Reardon mentioned the recently created Federal Pest Control Review Board—an analogue of the toothless Federal Radiation Council—as an example of the government's diligence, and added vaguely that "all aspects of manufacture, sale, and use" of pesticides were under "constant review." He concluded on a sharper, dismissive note, informing Goldman that chemical pesticides provided "great benefits" to the country "without any grave or undue hazard to the public." Furthermore, Reardon said, "Your Government is making every effort to insure that these important aids to our abundance continue to be controlled in the best interests of the entire Nation."

Put another way, at midsummer the Kennedy administration's official position was that Rachel Carson had made much out of nothing.

Over at the USDA, where the chronically ambivalent Orville Freeman was already under siege over the radiation problems with milk, everyone seemed to understand that the concerns raised by

Judge Goldman were going to be shared by a large portion of the public—and that a firestorm was imminent. Shirley Briggs warned Carson that the Department of Agriculture was rumored to be combing over the *New Yorker* articles in search of a cause of action for libel—or even just a mistake—so far without success. Freeman told his senior staff he didn't know yet whether it was going to be official policy to "fight" with Carson but that he wanted everyone to start coming up with ideas for attacking her while at the same time working out less confrontational responses—including simply saying that pesticides were useful and carefully regulated. Freeman suggested that whichever of these approaches seemed most workable could eventually become the official policy.

Freeman did not mention—probably because he didn't have to—that farm interests, his primary constituency, were going to take exception to *Silent Spring* when it was published and were already on edge over press coverage of the articles in the *New Yorker*. He assumed more articles would come as the controversy deepened around Carson's still-unpublished book, though it's unlikely he imagined anything like the five-part series that began appearing in the Long Island daily *Newsday* on August 20, 1962.

The stories were written by a gifted young investigative reporter named Robert A. Caro—who would gain fame for *The Power Broker*, a biography of New York City planner Robert Moses, and for his ambitious multivolume biography of Lyndon Johnson. Any hope Orville Freeman or anyone else in the administration had of fashioning a calm response to *Silent Spring* went out the door with Caro's opening paragraph:

> The lid is about to blow off a behind-the-scenes controversy over swelling scientific evidence that chemical pesticides, enthusiastically promoted by the United States Agriculture Department despite 16 years of warnings, have decimated species of wildlife and now threaten man with cancer, leukemia and abnormal gene development.

Caro reported that President Kennedy—reversing field after the cool response to Judge Goldman—was now personally engaged in the pesticides issue and had ordered science adviser Jerome Wiesner to launch an investigation. He described the problem as a growing body of evidence suggesting a connection between the widespread use of chemical pesticides and rising incidences of disease in both wildlife and human populations. Caro likened the scientists' fears about pesticides to those over the horrific birth defects in Britain caused by the morning-sickness drug thalidomide—except that the dangers from pesticides were, if anything, worse because their possible effects on genes could play out over the course of many generations. He didn't draw a literal parallel between pesticides and radiation, although his concern for the impact of pesticides on future generations was identical to that raised by Linus Pauling and other scientists over fallout.

The truth about pesticides, Caro reported, was being obscured by a massive public relations campaign to promote their safety and effectiveness—orchestrated by their manufacturers, who represented an $800 million a year industry. The pesticide makers were aided in this effort by the U.S. Department of Agriculture, which "leaped aboard the pesticides bandwagon as soon as DDT was introduced" and was now running "vast" spraying campaigns of its own while encouraging the general use of pesticides by farmers. Caro said that internal reports critical of these policies were routinely suppressed and that people working in pesticide programs rarely complained about them for fear of being fired.

Caro took note of the benefits of pesticide use—rising farm productivity and sharp declines of insect-borne diseases in many parts of the world. But he reported that many scientists had been quietly warning of side effects. Now those whispers had become a scream thanks to "famed biologist and author Rachel Carson." Caro said the New Yorker series had drawn one of the heaviest mail responses in the magazine's history—and a matching flood of angry letters had arrived at the USDA, where Caro scored a coup by getting the first interview with Orville Freeman on the subject. Freeman told Caro that pesticides were "on balance" of greater benefit than harm and that there was no cause for "panic and hysteria." But Caro reported that department officials involved in pesticide programs had recently been ordered to stop blanket denials of any problems with pesticide use.

In subsequent installments over the next four days, Caro kept up an attack on official policy—or the lack of one—regarding pesticide use and portrayed the scientific community as divided on the issue. Caro saw the USDA and the pesticides industry as partners in what had become a massive, self-propagating enterprise, with neither willing to consider the collateral damage pesticides might do to wildlife or human health. He explored the possible link between pesticides and cancer, and skillfully explained how DDT and other organochlorine pesticides are stored in fatty tissues and how body burdens of stored pesticides can be magnified upward through food chains.

Caro had less success in getting Orville Freeman to give a coherent answer to the seemingly simple question of whether the USDA had oversold pesticides. It was clear that by the time Caro got to Freeman the secretary had decided against any public vilification of Carson and *Silent Spring*. Ridiculously, he told Caro that his department regarded Carson as an "ally" in bringing the pesticide issue to the attention of the American people—an odd claim given the department's long history of insisting pesticide dangers were a nonissue.

Freeman told Caro he wasn't satisfied with what his department knew about the effects of pesticide use on wildlife or on human health—which was next to nothing—and that going forward they were going to give the matter "strong concerted attention." When Caro asked Freeman if that meant they would suspend large-scale spraying operations until their effects were better understood, Freeman ducked the question, saying he thought he'd already covered that. More comfortable on the shifting middle ground, Freeman reminded Caro that a scientific consensus on pesticide safety did not exist.

Caro's *Newsday* series wrapped up just five days before President Kennedy was asked about pesticides at his news conference. The president's claim that several agencies were looking into the matter as a direct result of "Miss Carson's book" may have been technically correct—if hand-wringing and confusion could be described as looking into something. Presidential science adviser Wiesner got more direct orders to investigate the situation the day after Kennedy met with the press.

Wiesner began assembling a panel to report to the president on the pesticide problem by the following spring. At about the same time, an agency the president neglected to mention was more aggressively looking into the controversy around *Silent Spring*. The FBI had launched an investigation of Carson—though at whose request and for what reason is unknown. Apparently the agency made inquiries with the U.S. Immigration and Naturalization Service and looked into who Carson had been talking to on the phone recently—all of which suggests the FBI was curious about whether Carson was having questionable contact with foreign nationals, which, of course, she wasn't. Not surprisingly, nothing came of the investigation. The FBI's report on Carson, completed in mid-December, ran to only two pages. It was marked "Confidential," filed, forgotten, and eventually destroyed.

Carson had reason to think that one agency inside the federal government, the U.S. Department of the Interior—her former home—was going to back the position she'd taken in *Silent Spring*. Even before the excerpts started appearing in the *New Yorker*, Carson had heard from a man named Paul Knight, who was an assistant to Interior Secretary Stewart Udall. Udall, a staunch conservationist, was himself at work on a book about environmental problems, called *The Quiet Crisis*, that was to come out the following year.

Knight told Carson he was interested in the problems of communicating scientific ideas to the public and said America was in for "a lot of discussion" about pesticides and their effects on wildlife and human health. In July 1962, after the *New Yorker* series had run, Knight wrote to Carson again commending her for putting the pesticide problem on the national agenda and telling her he'd already had conversations with at least one member of Congress about how the government should respond. He told her he was speaking "off the record," but hinted that she had started something that was going to play out in a dramatic and public way. "These comments are personal and unofficial," Knight said, "although I expect that we will be directly involved before it is over."

In October, *Newsday*'s Robert Caro reported that the Wiesner committee had already learned that many of Rachel Carson's claims in *Silent Spring* were true, and the panel expected to recommend sweeping changes in federal research on pesticides and would propose legislation to curb their indiscriminate use. As for Carson's book, Caro reported that it had sold its entire first printing of one hundred thousand copies during the two weeks it had been out.

From the beginning, Carson, Paul Brooks, and everyone at Houghton Mifflin had been concerned that the downbeat, frightening nature of *Silent Spring* would discourage a wide readership. Carson had shrewdly seen that the way around this was to focus on showing "the futility and the basic wrongness of the present chemical program—even better than ranting against it, though doubtless I shall rant a little, too." This was smart, but it also underscored Carson's mature confidence in herself and her work—a conviction that she could take on a difficult subject and argue against the interests of powerful forces. Carson was comfortable in her new skin as a great woman of American letters.

The response from pesticide makers came swiftly, directly on the heels of the *New Yorker* serialization. In July 1962 the DuPont Corporation requested advance copies of *Silent Spring*, touching off a debate inside Houghton Mifflin and involving Carson and Marie Rodell over how to respond. The collective suspicion was that DuPont was contemplating a lawsuit. Houghton Mifflin publisher Lovell Thompson argued that they should comply with the request. If a lawsuit was coming, he said, it would be better to know it sooner rather than later.

Plus, if DuPont, after getting the advance copies, then dragged its feet and launched a suit later on, Houghton Mifflin could answer that the company had been given ample time to inspect the book prior to publication. Thompson's only reservation was the possibility—which he considered remote—that DuPont might succeed in getting a court to issue an injunction that would prevent publication of the book. That, he said, would be "ruinous."

DuPont did not sue. Neither did the Velsicol Chemical Corporation, a pesticide maker based in Chicago—though it threatened mightily to do so. In early August, Velsicol's general counsel wrote to Houghton Mifflin demanding it halt publication of *Silent Spring,* or at least remove any negative reference to its products, which included aldrin, chlordane, dieldrin, heptachlor, and endrin—a murderers' row of organochlorines from which only DDT was absent. Velsicol objected to Carson's characterization of all these patented products as dangerous. But the company made a specific claim for two of them— chlordane and heptachlor. Velsicol was the only company that made chlordane and heptachlor. "You are no doubt familiar with the fact," the company reminded Houghton Mifflin, "that disparagement of products manufactured solely by one company creates actionable rights in the sole manufacturer."

This same letter also darkly hinted—in a clumsily worded passage— that complaints against pesticides were part of an international Communist conspiracy, a longtime bogeyman in the Cold War:

> Unfortunately, in addition to the sincere expression of opinions by natural food faddists, Audubon groups, and others, members of the chemical industry in this country and in western Europe must deal with sinister influences, whose attacks on the chemical industry have two purposes: 1) to create the false impression that all business is grasping and immoral, and 2) to reduce the use of agricultural chemicals in this country and in the countries of western Europe, so that our food supply will be reduced to east-

curtain parity. Many innocent groups are financed and led into attacks on the chemical industry by these sinister parties.

This blend of Cold War fear-mongering—the words "east-curtain" referred to the Soviet Union and its Eastern European satellites—with the undemonstrated claim that Carson had falsely maligned Velsicol's products was the first salvo in the war pitting business interests against environmental concerns that has raged ever since. As portrayed by industry, on one side are decent, hardworking corporate citizens and the products they make for the betterment of the world and the enrichment of their shareholders. On the other side are the flakes and nature lovers who are either Communists or the hapless pawns of Communist influences. As seen from the point of view of the pesticide makers, Carson's embryonic new idea—environmentalism—was, by definition, un-American.

Houghton Mifflin forwarded Velsicol's letter to Carson in Maine. Carson sent a note back to Paul Brooks expressing confidence in her facts—and in the legal department at Houghton Mifflin. She also listed her sources for several of the assertions Velsicol had complained about. This was exactly the sort of thing Carson had expected and the reason she had worked so hard to document everything she'd written in *Silent Spring*. But Carson argued against engaging Velsicol in a back-and-forth over the accuracy of her book, and instead suggested Houghton Mifflin offer only a "routine acknowledgment" of the company's letter—which they did.

This didn't satisfy Velsicol, which wrote again to Houghton Mifflin offering "proof" for the safety of its products and demanding a meeting with the publishing company to resolve their objections to Carson's book. Houghton Mifflin declined, and this time Velsicol did not pursue the matter further—though the matter pursued them some months later. In June 1963, twenty people in Memphis, Tennessee, were sickened by what they believed were vapors coming off a creek near a pesticide plant operated by Velsicol. A few days later, a couple of dozen workmen were hospitalized after inhaling what was thought to be chlorine gas emanating from the Velsicol facility. Velsicol was hit with a slew of lawsuits.

Then, in April 1964, officials from the USDA and the Public Health Service investigated a large fish kill on the lower Mississippi River. They determined the fish had been poisoned by endrin—the most potent of the organochlorine insecticides—which along with several other powerful pesticides was being discharged into the river by the Velsicol plant at Memphis. Velsicol refused entry to its plant for the investigators, but they found endrin in the river anyway—and in the creek where the first cases of illnesses had occurred the year before. In fact, they found endrin in the Mississippi all the way to New Orleans, which used the river as a public water supply. Tests of tap water in the city showed that routine purification did not remove endrin, which was now present in the city's drinking water. Public health officials said the residues in drinking water were small, but that no level was considered safe. In early 1965, the Public Health Service made an even more alarming discovery: a four-ton, three-foot-thick deposit of endrin in a Memphis sewer that emptied into the Mississippi. City officials hurriedly closed off the sewer line, while endrin production at the Velsicol plant went ahead as usual.

Theoretically, such a reckless contamination of a large area with pesticides was impossible—or so the federal government claimed as it braced for the imminent publication of *Silent Spring*. In September 1962, the Department of Health, Education, and Welfare issued a long statement defending the government's oversight of pesticide use, on which that agency alone would spend $2.7 million in 1962. The department insisted that it recognized that pesticides involved "perils" as well as benefits, and that this was the reason the government closely regulated the industry:

The fact that they [pesticides] are poisons, potentially dangerous to man and wildlife, is a cause for serious concern. Because of this concern, the Federal Government has established protective regulations concerning the manufacture, transportation, and use of these chemicals and has led to continuing programs of research into their immediate and long-term effects on man and his environment.

The agency said it also monitored interstate shipments of various crops to ensure they complied with a law adopted in 1954 setting limits on pesticide residues in produce. A 1958 law extended this regulatory authority to processed foods. More broadly, the agency said its Public Health Service was engaged in "nationwide surveillance" of "pollutants and contaminants in the environment." And the agency said the government monitored itself—through the Federal Pest Control Review Board, which evaluated pesticide use in federally run programs "to insure that these do not present undue hazards to the public generally or to wildlife."

But just over a month later Jerome Wiesner reported to the president that a Citizens Advisory Committee had just blasted the FDA—another agency within Health, Education, and Welfare—on the issue of pesticide regulation, pointing out that the FDA could not possibly keep pace with the pesticide industry in setting tolerances for residues in food when the number of different pesticide products had swollen to some forty-five thousand. One reason the FDA was struggling, the committee reported, was that few of its field agents knew anything about organic chemistry. The committee said the FDA also needed to improve and expand its independent research on the effects of pesticides.

Copies of *Silent Spring* started circulating days ahead of its official publication date on September 27, 1962. At a meeting of the American Chemical Society in Atlantic City, New Jersey, Carson's book—which the *New York Times* reported had already caused "consternation" inside the chemicals industry—was a hot topic and the subject of sharp criticism. Industry insiders complained to the *Times* that *Silent Spring* could impede investment in new pesticides and turn the public against the use of existing ones—with calamitous results. An official from the USDA—so at home at a chemicals in-dustry trade meeting that he chaired one of its sessions—called Car-son's book "one-sided," as nowhere in it did she explain the extent to which the nation's food supply depended on the use of chemical pesticides. Nor did she acknowledge what the government was doing to regulate the use of pesticides. The *Times* reporter found a number of industry representatives who were willing to concede the overall factual accuracy of *Silent Spring* but none who agreed with Carson's conclusion that pesticide use, like exposure to radiation, was a threat to human existence.

The *New Yorker* serialization had covered only about one-third of *Silent Spring,* and with publication of the book tens of thousands of readers—including most reviewers, columnists, and editorial writers—were soon convinced that pesticides did indeed threaten human well-being. Many liked the handsome pen-and-ink illustra-tions by the Darlings—though they were eerily stark and haunting in context. Apart from the opening fable, *Silent Spring* was a sober, methodical book, put together like a high wall, each phrase a brick helping to support all the rest. At its heart was a single proposition: Because all life on earth shares a common biochemical evolutionary history, the idea than a synthetic poison can target a single class of or-ganisms and do no other harm is folly. The claim that a chemical was a "pesticide" denied the shared biology of all living things:

> These sprays, dusts, and aerosols are now applied almost univer-
> sally to farms, gardens, forests, and homes—nonselective chemi-
> cals that have the power to kill every insect, the "good" and the
> "bad," to still the song of birds and the leaping of fish in the
> streams, to coat the leaves with a deadly film, to linger on in
> soil—all this though the intended target may be only a few weeds
> or insects. Can anyone believe it is possible to lay down such a
> barrage of poisons on the surface of the earth without making
> it unfit for all life? They should not be called "insecticides" but
> "biocides."

Much of the criticism directed at *Silent Spring* ignored a key word in that passage—*barrage*. For Carson the main problem with pesticides was the heedlessness with which they were applied—and the literal overkill that came with their use. In the pages of the book, and in her many public comments about pesticides, Carson reiterated that the careful, limited use of chemical poisons was sometimes justifiable and, in certain circumstances involving the protection of human health, morally responsible. There were, she acknowledged early on in *Silent Spring*, insect problems that required control—so long as that control was "geared to realities" and was not so belligerent as to "destroy us along with the insects." Carson thought common sense should determine when chemical insect control was warranted, especially with respect to insect-borne diseases. These diseases, she wrote, were most problematic in places where human populations were overcrowded or "in time of natural disaster or war or in situations of extreme poverty and deprivation. Then control of some sort becomes necessary."

Carson was not reluctant to challenge her readers. An early chapter—the one that had given Paul Brooks fits as he worked to condense it—was called "Elixirs of Death." In it, Carson explained the toxic chemistry of the organochlorine and organophosphate insecticides. She knew it would be heavy going but justified it by arguing that "every human being is now subjected to contact with dangerous chemicals, from the moment of conception until death." This, Carson said, was unprecedented. Pesticides were now so ubiquitous in the environment and in all living things that they could reasonably be said to be "everywhere." Given that, Carson thought it incomprehensible that anyone would not want to know what these substances were and what harm they might cause: "If we are going to live so intimately with these chemicals—eating and drinking them, taking them into the very marrow of our bones—we had better know something about their nature and their power."

Most of the chapters in *Silent Spring* were just as bleak but were less technical. Carson explored the unintended consequences of using chemical pesticides when control was either unnecessary or not worth the risk to other species and to the environment generally—so the book was not so much one-sided as it was about one thing. Carson explained how pesticides contaminate soil and water, how they accumulate in the tissues of animals and people directly exposed to only slight amounts of chemical poisons, how their residues find their way into cow's milk and human mother's milk, and how they sometimes cause explosive growth in insect populations that become resistant.

Carson's exploration of the link between pesticides and human cancer—which Barney Crile had earlier warned her went too far—was scary and speculative, relying as it did on a then-primitive understanding of cell biology and on the anecdotal observations of doctors such as Malcolm Hargraves of the Mayo Clinic, whose testimony about the connection between pesticide use and leukemia during the Long Island case had so impressed Carson.

She also based part of her cancer argument on a theory advanced by a prominent German biochemist named Otto Heinrich Warburg from the Max Planck Institute of Cell Physiology. Warburg had won a Nobel Prize in 1931 and was engrossed in the study of cell respiration—the process by which food is converted to chemical energy. He was convinced that both radiation and chemical carcinogens cause cancer by disrupting normal cell respiration and producing clusters of rogue cells that form tumors. Carson was closer to the truth when she considered an alternative idea in which carcinogens directly damage chromosomes, causing gene mutations and interfering with normal cell division—effects that cascade from one generation of cells to the next, a multiplication of abnormalities that eventually produces cancerous cells. As imperfect as her analysis was, Carson reached an important conclusion: In a world in which we are surrounded by potentially carcinogenic agents, focusing exclusively on ways of curing the disease misses the chance to prevent it by reducing or eliminating its causes.

Carson wrote that the effects of exposure to DDT and other

pesticides—like exposure to radiation—was of particular concern for children. Many readers in 1962 already knew they were giving their children milk laced with radionuclides from fallout. Now Carson added DDT to the unwholesome cocktail from the dairy case. Nowhere in *Silent Spring* does Carson let go of the parallel between pesticides and radiation, and in one of the cancer chapters she found an example of pesticide poisoning that mirrored the most infamous radiation poisoning case ever reported. It was the story of a Swedish farmer who dusted sixty acres of land with a mixture of DDT and benzene hexachloride. There was a breeze that day, and as the man worked clouds of the pesticidal dust swirled around him. Later that evening the farmer felt ill, and about a week later he entered the hospital with a high fever and abnormal blood counts. Two and a half months later he died.

This was, Carson wrote, eerily reminiscent of what had happened to the radioman aboard the *Lucky Dragon*, Aikichi Kuboyama: "Like Kuboyama, the farmer had been a healthy man, gleaning his living from the land as Kuboyama had taken his from the sea. For each man a poison drifting out of the sky carried a death sentence. For one it was radiation-poisoned ash; for the other, chemical dust."

Carson rejected the idea that technology inevitably led us to abuse our environment through a desire to regulate it in our own interest. She held out hope for sophisticated biological controls that could actually target pest species in a way chemical poisons could not. She contended that pesticides, far from being a scientifically sophisticated means of pest control, were, in fact, a step backward in human progress:

> As crude a weapon as the cave man's club, the chemical barrage has been hurled against the fabric of life—a fabric on the one hand delicate and destructible, on the other miraculously tough and resilient, and capable of striking back in unexpected ways. These extraordinary capacities of life have been ignored by the

practitioners of chemical control who have brought to their task no "high-minded orientation," no humility before the vast forces with which they tamper.

Carson's closing thought was that the phrase "control of nature" represented an abhorrent idea that was "conceived in arrogance, born of the Neanderthal age of biology and philosophy, when it was supposed that nature exists for the convenience of man." Now, Carson said, we faced the "alarming misfortune" that so primitive a science had "armed itself with the most modern and terrible weapons."

On September 25, 1962, two days before publication, Houghton Mifflin held a party for Carson at the Carlton House on Madison Avenue in New York. Then a few days after *Silent Spring* came out, *Life* magazine phoned Carson to say they were moving up the schedule to run their story about her right away. Carson, who'd decided not to worry about the magazine getting into "silly personal details," told Dorothy Freeman she'd have to endure reading about the "new me."

When the article appeared in the October 12 issue, *Life* reported that Carson was "unmarried but not a feminist"—evidently an important consideration—and went on to describe her as a "shy, soft-spoken woman miscast in the role of crusader" before characterizing her as exactly that: "Like all good indignant crusaders, Rachel Carson presents a one-sided case. The world she describes so vividly in *Silent Spring* is a dream world or, more accurately, a nightmare world."

The article included several striking photos of Carson—though in one showing her at home with her microscope she looked pallid and unwell. The story itself was muddled with contradictions that suggested the magazine's editors were hedging their bets so as not to end up on the wrong side of a controversial issue. *Life* said the book was "amply buttressed by research" and featured "Miss Carson's usual literary grace," but added that in making this "undeniable case against the pesticides" Carson had "overstated her case." *Life* suggested to its readers that there must be some happier common ground where "chemistry, biology, wildlife, and mankind can achieve a peaceful coexistence."

Silent Spring was reviewed everywhere. More than seventy newspapers also ran editorials on it, and many published excerpts. The press was overwhelmingly favorable. This was not the case with articles and pamphlets put out by the chemicals industry—which matched the flood of press coverage and were sharply critical of Carson and her methods.

Writing in the *New York Times* two weeks before the book came out, Brooks Atkinson noted approvingly that the book came with fifty-five pages of source citations and references. He called Carson a "realist as well as a biologist and writer" who understood that chemical pesticides were a fact of modern life that could not be made to go away entirely, and that her plea instead was for their intelligent use with the knowledge of their potential for "deadly peripheral damage" to the balance of nature. Atkinson paid particular attention to Carson's assertion that chemical pest control was an act of arrogance in which we deceived ourselves over our place in the web of life: "The basic fallacy—or perhaps the original sin—is the assumption that man can control nature," Atkinson wrote. "Nature returns with a massive assault from an unexpected quarter. For nature has devoted millions of years to creating an order of life in which parasites and predators control one another."

Atkinson said that Carson had a sober way of stating "alarming facts" that made them the more believable. Her case for ecology was actually a case for humanity. Atkinson's preview was followed days later by two full reviews of *Silent Spring*—one on the cover of the *Sunday Book Review* that was glowing and another, by science reporter and editor Walter Sullivan, that was admiring but mixed.

Sullivan started off appreciatively, mentioning the debt owed to this "gifted writer" for having brought the wonderment and beauty of the oceans to millions of readers. *Silent Spring,* however, was a departure for Carson that was likely to shock her many fans—a book that Sullivan likened to an earlier American classic: "In her new book she [Carson] tries to scare the living daylights out of us and, in large measure, succeeds. Her work tingles with anger, outrage and protest. It is a 20th-century *Uncle Tom's Cabin.*"

Sullivan wasn't the only reviewer to make this comparison, nor was he alone in saying that the one-sidedness of *Silent Spring* opened Carson to attack from people who would claim she had not told the whole story. But Sullivan thought the book's "drawbacks" were actually part of its appeal. After all, he said, "*Uncle Tom's Cabin* would never have stirred a nation had it been measured and 'fair.'" Sullivan said that considering world events, *Silent Spring* could not be more timely. "If our species cannot police itself against overpopulation, nuclear weapons, and pollution, it may become extinct."

Sullivan also previewed one of the more ambitious responses coming soon from pesticide makers—a parody of the opening fable from Carson's book. Titled "The Desolate Year," it had been written, according to Sullivan, by "some unsung hero of the chemical industry." It appeared in the October issue of *Monsanto Magazine*—which had a surprising circulation of 140,000 among business leaders, educators, and government officials. Even Carson must have grudgingly thought the piece well done. Flipping Carson's depiction of a dead and brown world devastated by pesticides, "The Desolate Year" pictured one *without* chemical controls—a world where the springtime brings not renewal but revulsion, as ravaging hordes of insects and vermin lay waste to the countryside. The plague moves north with the warming weather, wreaking havoc on crops and spreading disease to humans suddenly defenseless against their ancient and fearsome enemies:

> Genus by genus, species by species, sub-species by innumerable sub-species, the insects emerged. Creeping and flying and crawling into the open, beginning in the southern tier of states and progressing northward. They were chewers, and piercer-suckers,

spongers, siphoners and chewer-lappers, and all their vast progeny were chewers, rasping, sawing, biting maggots and worms and caterpillars. Some could sting, some could poison, many could kill.

Sullivan offered the dubious observation that the luridness of "The Desolate Year" amounted to an "imitation of Miss Carson's poetic style." But, of course, it wasn't meant to be literature. Several times longer than Carson's opening chapter, "The Desolate Year" left no grotesque assault from the insect kingdom unexplored. By the end the crops are destroyed, famine is imminent, and millions are succumbing to malaria and yellow fever. Could anyone wish for *that* world? Helpfully, the article included an appendix of factual findings that supported the plausibility of everything it claimed—plus a selection of public statements by various governmental and academic experts testifying to the need for pesticide use and to their safety when applied properly.

One of Carson's most determined attackers was a New York–based organization called the Nutrition Foundation, whose president, C. G. King, issued a formal rebuttal to *Silent Spring* as an accompaniment to the negative reviews the Nutrition Foundation collected and redistributed far and wide. King said that most scientists held the view that Americans had never been safer, better fed, or healthier—facts that, on their face, refuted any claim of general poisoning and declining health as a result of pesticide use. Government and industry worked tirelessly, King insisted, to make pesticides safe and to inform users how to apply them. Besides, King added, the charges made in *Silent Spring* were obviously the ravings of a poorly informed and probably deranged person.

The problem is magnified in that publicists and the author's adherents among the food faddists, health quacks, and special interest groups are promoting her book as if it were scientifically irreproachable and written by a scientist.

Neither is true. The book presents almost solely selected information that is negative and uses such bits from a period of many years, building a vastly distorted picture. The author is a professional journalist—not a scientist in the field of her discussion—and misses the very essence of science in not being objective either in citing the evidence or in its interpretation.

Reading this, Carson could not help but feel it represented the more or less official reaction to *Silent Spring* from everyone in industry, academia, and government with a commitment to pesticide use. Among the members of the Nutrition Foundation board were the heads and senior executives of the National Biscuit Company, H. J. Heinz, General Foods, General Mills, Standard Brands, the Borden Company, and others. Also on the board was the surgeon general of the United States and the presidents of Columbia, Johns Hopkins, Notre Dame, and MIT.

The love/hate split response to *Silent Spring* continued for months after it was published as it climbed onto the bestseller lists. A few reviewers managed to be in both camps. Writing in the journal *Science,* I. L. Baldwin, an agriculture professor at the University of Wisconsin, called *Silent Spring* "beautifully written" and likened Carson to a prosecuting attorney who concentrated on the evidence that supported her case while sidestepping facts that did not. Baldwin argued—not unfairly—that the widespread use of chemical pesticides was the result of the "obvious benefits" they produced. But he said those same benefits in agricultural production and public health might have created an attitude of complacency that ignored the fact that synthetic pesticides are poisons and therefore present serious hazards. The right course, Baldwin argued, was greater care in the safety testing and use of pesticides. Backing away from them entirely was not an option:

Modern agriculture, with its high-quality foods and fibers, could not exist without the use of pesticides. Weeds, disease, and insect pests would take an extremely heavy toll if these chemicals were not used. The yields per acre, the yields per man-hour, and the quality of the product would all suffer materially if these chemicals were withdrawn from use. One cannot do more than guess about the changes that would be necessary in American society if pesticides were banned. An immediate back-to-the-farm movement would be necessary, and this would involve many millions of people. It is hoped that someone with Rachel Carson's ability will write a companion volume dramatizing the improvements in human health and welfare derived from the use of pesticides.

The editors at *Chemical Week* judged correctly that press reactions to *Silent Spring* were likely to "come out pretty squarely on Miss Carson's side" and were not going to be nearly so judicious or so knowledgeable as Baldwin had been in the pages of *Science*. The trade magazine reported that the Manufacturing Chemists' Association and the National Agricultural Chemicals Association had devised an industry response different from that offered by the Nutrition Foundation. The idea was to avoid a direct attack on Carson's book and instead emphasize the benefits of pesticide use. Paul Brooks heard the campaign had a $250,000 war chest.

But *Chemical Week* also noted that Monsanto had already broken ranks in going at Carson head-on with "The Desolate Year," reprints of which had been sent by the company to newspapers and radio and television stations across the country. Pesticide makers thought sales of products intended for homes and gardens would probably experience little impact from *Silent Spring,* as the book had come out in the fall and consumers were likely to forget about it come spring when the pesticides market bloomed. But companies with heavy sales in agriculture and forestry prepared for a protracted siege. More worrisome than *Silent Spring* itself for the industry was President Kennedy's pesticide commission, which *Chemical Week* doubted had the scientific depth among its members to properly evaluate pesticide safety.

Carson's critics in the chemicals industry pointed to the term "toxic chemicals" as unfair and misleading, as almost any chemical in the right dose and through the right exposure can be toxic. The counterargument, of course, was that pesticides were formulated to be toxic and, unlike other chemical compounds, were lethal when used as intended. Another common complaint against *Silent Spring* was that Carson portrayed a universal contamination of the environment—of the soil and water and all living things—based on examples of poisonings and circumstances that were actually rare and isolated. *The Economist* thought this and argued in a long, critical piece that the pesticides industry would probably survive *Silent Spring* with little damage, as American farmers weren't going to pay the book any heed. The magazine thought Carson had probably "damaged seriously her professional reputation as a reliable scientific journalist."

Financial World magazine took much the same position in an article examining the high stakes for American pesticide makers and the efforts they were launching to fight back against *Silent Spring*. According to the magazine, Monsanto's agricultural chemicals division had been growing 20 percent annually for a decade. No wonder their vision of a world without pesticides was a "desolate" one. Sales growth rates for most other manufacturers were lower, but pesticides were still a robust segment of the business for many of them. Pesticides were a big business worth protecting for the manufacturers. American Cyanamid, for example, derived nearly a fifth of its total revenues from pesticide sales. No one was surprised when a pompous man named Robert H. White-Stevens, who worked in the research and development section of American Cyanamid's agricultural chemicals division, began barnstorming the country, giving speeches and debating Carson supporters while extolling the virtues and necessity of chemical pest control.

White-Stevens overnight became the anti-Carson. With his slicked-back hair, thin mustache, and black horn-rimmed glasses he was a dead ringer for the horror actor Vincent Price. He seemed to be everywhere, unctuous and sour, rolling his r's and speaking in echoey, Shakespearian cadences. White-Stevens's defense of pesticides always

circled around two assertions. One was that if you looked dispassion-
ately at the world you would see that starvation and disease tended to
occur in places where pesticides were not available. Unhitch modern
society from pesticides and you invite malnutrition and sickness back
into the picture. The other repeated claim was that the government
and the chemicals industry took more than adequate care in licensing
pesticides and instructing users in their safe application.

Although few reviewers in the press agreed with the pesticide industry's take on *Silent Spring,* the handful who did were puzzled by what
they considered Carson's strident, unbalanced portrayal of products
that had done so much to improve the world. A notable critique came
from *Time* magazine, which in an unusually long and sharp-elbowed
review—it ran in the magazine's Science section—called the book an
"emotional and inaccurate outburst." *Time* said the drama in *Silent
Spring* was high but based on a distortion of reality:

> There is no doubt about the impact of *Silent Spring;* it is a real
> shocker. Many unwary readers will be firmly convinced that most
> of the U.S.—with its animals, plants, soil, water and people—is
> already laced with poison that will soon start taking a dreadful
> toll, and that the only hope is to stop using chemical pesticides
> and let the age-old "balance of nature" take care of obnoxious
> insects.
>
> Scientists, physicians and other technically informed people
> will also be shocked by *Silent Spring*—but for a different reason.
> They recognize Miss Carson's skill in building her frightening
> case; but they consider that case unfair, one-sided, and hysteri-
> cally overemphatic. Many of the scary generalizations—and there
> are lots of them—are patently unsound.

Time, relying on the several-years-old study of DDT effects in
convict volunteers by the U.S. Public Health Service's Dr. Wayland J.

Hayes, called DDT "harmless." The magazine conceded that other, more toxic pesticides posed potential threats to human health—but reported that so far there wasn't any evidence of such effects. And while it was true that DDT was dangerous to fish and that robins had been killed in DDT programs against Dutch elm disease, none of these impacts on the natural world were "complete." Not even Miss Carson, *Time* said, could point to a place where "no birds sing" as a result of pesticide use.

Many months after the reviews of *Silent Spring* had ceased—in fact, a full year after the book was published—Carson was savaged in a long, sarcastic essay in the *Saturday Evening Post* written by her jilted would-be collaborator Edwin Diamond, to whom Paul Brooks had so casually sent an advance copy of the book. Diamond agreed with the *Silent Spring* detractors who called the book unfair and said that Carson greatly overstated the risks from pesticide use—but he was more concerned with exploring why the book had been such a success, the implication being that there can be no good reason for a bad book to sell so well.

Diamond drew the obvious conclusion that Carson's reputation and stylish prose had something to do with it—though he said *Silent Spring* had none of the beauty of her earlier books beyond a measure of "expository gloss." Diamond also thought the thalidomide scandal had primed the public for scary stories about chemicals—the more exaggerated the better. In an odd partial inversion of the claim Velsicol had made that Carson was in league with Communist influences, Diamond said he thought *Silent Spring* appealed to the sort of person who might believe that pesticide pushers were Communists. Rather than consign Carson to the lunatic fringe as Velsicol had, Diamond thought she was instead playing to the nuts out there. To love this book was to be at least a little bit crazy:

> *Silent Spring,* it seems to me, stirs the latent demons of paranoia that many men and women must fight down all through their lives. At one time or another, all of us have been affected by the

feeling that some wicked "they" were out to get "us." In recent years the paranoid among us could be observed in the ranks of such cultists as the antifluoridation leaguers, the organic-garden faddists and other beyond-the-fringe groups. And who are the "they" intent on poisoning or tricking "us"? In the rough hand-bills passed out on street corners by the antifluoridationists, the plotters turn out to be Communists—scientists and dentists who want to soften, literally, the brains of the American citizenry to prepare them for Russian takeover by adding an insidious chemical to the drinking water.

Showing some expository flair of his own, Diamond also wondered if Carson's bestseller was not the product of the same venal motivations that drove pesticide makers in their heedless quest to earn millions:

What, finally, is *Silent Spring*'s game? If we are to believe Miss Carson's own description of our times—an era when the right to make an irresponsible dollar is seldom challenged—then the answer would be an easy one.

None of this criticism slowed down *Silent Spring.* In February 1963 it was published in England, where it was a huge success, and soon after that in France, Germany, Italy, Sweden, and a host of other countries. In London, Lord Shackleton—member of the House of Lords and son of the famed Antarctic explorer Ernest Shackleton—wrote an introduction for the book. A couple of months after the English edition was published, Shackleton told the House of Lords that cannibals in the South Pacific now preferred the flesh of Englishmen over Americans—as Americans had higher body burdens of DDT. Shackleton dryly added that his comments were strictly "in the interests of the export trade."

• • •

By Christmas 1962 *Silent Spring* had climbed to number one on the *New York Times* bestseller list, fallen back, then returned to the top spot. Houghton Mifflin prepared a ten-page, 5,500-word booklet rebutting Carson's critics, and continued sending out regular press releases updating the book industry on sales and endorsements from important persons. That same month, Carson got a letter from a girl named Elsie Baier, a high school senior in North Kingstown, Rhode Island. Baier said she'd been assigned to defend the "thesis" of *Silent Spring* in an upcoming debate at school. The enterprising teenager told Carson she was worried that her opponent was likely to have a pile of material from the critics of *Silent Spring*. Baier asked if Carson could send her examples of support for the book from "reputable authorities."

Carson, who routinely said no to prominent people and institutions asking for her time or help, gave careful thought to Baier's naive request before writing her back at length and enclosing materials Baier could use in making her argument. Carson's advice to Baier provided a rare insight into how she perceived much of the criticism directed at *Silent Spring*:

> One thing that fascinates me is this: Has "the thesis of Rachel Carson" been defined with precision as a preliminary to the debate? If it has not, you will probably find that you and your opponent are talking about entirely different things. I say this because a great many people who are talking about the book have not read it; they are arguing, not about what I have said, but about what the pesticide industry wants people to *believe* I said. Therefore, if you find your opponent saying my "thesis" is to abandon controls and "let nature take over," I hope you will bring him back to reality by quoting from my concluding chapter.

Carson probably found her correspondence with Baier a pleasant diversion from the noise that had enveloped *Silent Spring*—and from her continuing health problems. In late October 1962, Carson had gone to Cleveland for the dual purpose of attending a reception in her honor at the Museum of Natural History and a checkup at the Cleveland Clinic. Carson's cancer was thought to be under control for the time being—more X-rays a few weeks later seemed to confirm this—but Carson told Dorothy Freeman she'd had a terrible premonition. She said she could write letters as though a "menacing shadow" did not exist, but that just before she'd left for Cleveland she had a moment when she felt time stop and it had occurred to her that "there might even be no tomorrow."

In December, Carson made her most thorough public response to the attacks on *Silent Spring*. It was in a speech to the Women's National Press Club, and in it Carson's frustration with critics who had twisted or ignored her meaning—as well as her amusement at those who attacked the book without having read it—came out at last. After being introduced as "Silver Spring's Joan of Arc," Carson told the audience that the industry response to *Silent Spring*—what she called the "unquiet autumn" following its publication—was something she and Houghton Mifflin had anticipated all along, and that it had employed "all the well-known devices" for weakening a cause, which included claims the book said things it did not.

Carson quoted an editorial from Vermont's *Bennington Banner* that said, "The anguished reaction to *Silent Spring* has been to refute statements that were never made." Another line of attack had been the effort to discredit the person behind the book. Carson, bemused, said she had been branded a bird lover, a cat lover, a fish lover, and—heavens—a "high priestess of nature." To her detractors, Carson belonged to "a mystical cult having to do with the laws of the universe which my critics consider themselves immune to."

She offered a number of examples that demonstrated continuing problems with pesticides, and she specifically challenged *Time* magazine's claim that accidental poisonings from pesticides were rare. California—one of the few states with accurate records, Carson said—was reporting as many as one thousand accidental poisonings a year. Carson also warned that the chemicals industry protected its interests among academic researchers and government regulators in ways that were often invisible to the public. She said pesticide makers routinely underwrote the cost of studies that reported favorably on pesticide safety. Not even the prestigious National Academy of Sciences, which had recently reviewed the pesticide issue, was immune—the NAS committee behind its latest report, Carson said, included no fewer than nineteen chemical companies representing the interests of the pesticides industry.

Carson's voice that day was firm and clear. But only days later she was flattened with crippling back pain. Her doctors assured her this was the result of "normal" joint deterioration from her arthritis. Dorothy sent her some exercises designed to relieve back problems. Carson told Dorothy she was looking forward to having a couple of weeks off. She said she'd just enjoyed a performance of the annual Christmas pageant at Roger's school in which he at last had the role of King after playing smaller parts in previous years. As the year came to a close, Carson told Dorothy she wouldn't have appreciated the impact *Silent Spring* was having or been able to endure her deepening health problems without Dorothy's constant support.

Then, on New Year's Day 1963, Carson wrote to Dorothy with a grim update that canceled many of the hopes they had maintained about her condition. Carson admitted to "holding out" on Dorothy "a little" before remembering that they had promised each other not to conceal anything.

Carson said that about a week before Christmas she'd complained to her doctor again about back pain—wondering if there wasn't something more that could be done for it. When the doctor reexamined her X-rays he unexpectedly suggested they begin a course of radiation treatment on her spine right away. Checking with Barney Crile in Cleveland, Carson was told this was a wise course, as when cancer invades the vertebrae the patient may experience pain before anything shows up on X-rays. The sooner radiation treatments began, the better the chance they would stop the spread of cancer if that's what it was. The good news was that this time the treatments were with a smaller, less frightening machine that made the sessions more bearable, Carson said. The radiation had again caused severe nausea, but now it was over and the hard part was behind her. Carson was told to expect it would take several weeks before her pain subsided, but she told Dorothy there seemed to be little change.

Carson tried to reassure Dorothy that there was no definite diagnosis that cancer was the cause of her back problem and that perhaps there was not a malignancy after all. But she preferred to assume it was exactly that. And if it was, the good news was that it had been caught early. "So there's much reason for optimism," Carson said.

But her back was not Carson's only problem now. In the same letter she told Dorothy that one day while she'd been out Christmas shopping for Roger she started to feel funny. Suddenly everything went black, and when she came to she found that she had collapsed and toppled over a record display. Once her head cleared, Carson realized she was close to her regular clinic and went over to have her fainting spell evaluated. Everything seemed okay, she said, except for a racing heart. Now her doctors wanted her to see a heart specialist, as she had also recently complained of chest pains. Her symptoms pointed to angina on top of cancer. Carson tried to laugh it off for Dorothy's benefit. "Well, I may do something about it one of these days, but if it is angina it is certainly a mild case and I'm not running up hills or anything like that." But four weeks later she did see a cardiologist—who said it was unmistakably angina, "a classical case."

The changes this meant for Carson were significant. A hospital bed was sent to her home in Silver Spring and she was ordered to stay in the house. There was to be no stair climbing. Carson told Dorothy she was henceforth forbidden to do anything that someone else could do for her. The reason for these dramatic restrictions, Carson said, was that it turned out she had a well-understood but rare form of angina that most often struck while she was sleeping and not as the result of any exertion. At the same time, Carson's doctor said exercise probably wouldn't help her condition, either. She told Dorothy she now expected her life to be "pretty tame."

In early February 1963, Carson told Dorothy her new routine was to go back to bed as soon as Roger was off to school each day—and that she often stayed there without bothering to get dressed, although this tended only to increase her weariness. Dorothy wrote back, wondering how Carson managed to take it all. Carson reminded her that it was Dorothy who made things easier, though she also hinted at more difficult times ahead. "Because of you there has been far more joy in the happy things," Carson wrote, "and the hard spots have been more bearable. And so it will be in time to come, I know."

Inevitably, Carson began to think about her legacy, as it now seemed undeniable that her time was growing short. Like any writer, she hoped that her work would outlive her. She told Dorothy that the past decade—the time when they had known each other—had been crowded with sorrow and illness, but also with "everything I shall be remembered for."

Less than two weeks later, Carson had more bad news. Two new tumors had appeared, one by her collarbone and another higher up on her neck. She tried to reassure Dorothy that radiation usually knocked out these kinds of tumors—but she allowed that this latest setback was not likely to be her last. She said she could not pretend to be "lighthearted" about any of this and mainly tried not to think about it. This wasn't easy, as the discovery of new cancer had been accompanied by an increase in her chest pains. She said her confinement to bed was "strange." She was afraid to do so much as pull up the blinds or even pick up the cat. Carson said she had told almost nobody how ill she was and, as a result, wasn't getting the kind of attention she would have received in the hospital. Being home this way, not knowing how to decrease her physical activity any further, was dreadfully lonely.

Only days after this, Carson wrote to Dorothy again, telling her that the "arthritis" she'd been complaining about in her left shoulder for two months now looked like more cancer in the latest round of X-rays. The new radiation treatments were extended to include this area. Her doctor warned her that any similar pain she felt in other joints in the future needed to be looked at promptly.

Carson tried to stay upbeat: "The main thing I want to say, dear, is that we are not going to get bogged down in unhappiness about all this," she wrote. "We are going to be happy, and go on enjoying all the lovely things that give life meaning—sunrise and sunset, moonlight on the bay, music and good books, the song of thrushes and the wild cries of geese passing over."

Houghton Mifflin and Carson had worked out arrangements for her appearance on *CBS Reports*. Carson got plenty of advice from the publicity people at Houghton Mifflin about how she should present herself on television. Don't allow yourself to be shot at an angle "from the knees down," she was told, and wear little or no makeup, especially lipstick, as it tended to look black on black-and-white film. The publisher's main concern, though, was that Carson avoid looking "too stern." Even though the subject was a serious one, she should smile a little now and then, as it would "relax" her face and keep her from appearing as grim as her message. Of course, it was the message that was most important to Houghton Mifflin, but the publisher also wanted their much-loved author to reveal a little of her naturally gentle nature. Her scientist self would come through on its own.

But months after interviewing Carson, CBS rescheduled the program several times and everyone got nervous again, wondering if CBS, which was also talking to Carson's critics, might be allowing the program to tip in the direction of the pesticides industry. In November 1962 the publicity department at Houghton Mifflin warned Carson she should brace herself for harsh treatment on the show. The program's producer, a man named Jay McMullen, had a reputation for being slow and methodical—and Houghton Mifflin thought that could mean their "friends in the chemical business" might in the end make a strong defense of pesticides.

Privately, Carson had reason to think CBS reporter Eric Sevareid was favorably disposed to the case she'd made against pesticides in *Silent Spring,* as she believed he shared her views on the sometimes careless nature of human progress. Carson had clipped and saved a newspaper account of a CBS Radio news broadcast Sevareid had done in 1958 about proposals for sending rockets—and someday men—to the moon. Sevareid believed that "winning" the moon would mean losing that magical relationship humanity had always had with it—though he understood that many people younger than himself would not share his feelings. "There must come a time in every generation," Sevareid said on the broadcast, "when those who are older secretly get off the train of progress, willing to walk back to where they came from, if they can find the way."

While an ailing Carson waited for *CBS Reports* to air—it was finally scheduled for the evening of April 3, 1963—she was showered with accolades, winning awards from the Garden Club of America, the American Geographical Society, and the National Audubon Society. The Geographical Society's prize, called the Cullum Medal, had never before been presented to a woman. Carson was also elected to the American Academy of Arts and Letters. But she confided to Paul Brooks that of all the honors she'd been given, the one that had been the most touching was being elected the first member of a newly formed chapter of Phi Beta Kappa at her alma mater, the Pennsylvania College for Women—which was now called Chatham College.

In early March 1963, Carson and Dorothy began to feel their time together was running out. Carson said her days were now unremittingly difficult. Any movement at all caused her pain—in her back and ribs mainly—and she was beset with constant nausea that made working all but impossible. Torn between wanting Dorothy to know everything and wanting to protect her from the worst news, Carson confided that she'd held on to a letter she'd written about a month before after a night of such intense chest pains that she'd thought she might not live until morning. The thought of Dorothy, bereft and having had no chance to say goodbye, caused her to write down "what is in my heart" so that Dorothy might have something of her if the end came without warning.

In the weeks since, Carson thought her angina improved enough that she was not likely to die suddenly after all. Now she wanted to make sure they were completely honest with each other: "All that is most wonderful in our relationship has been based on that spontaneous outpouring of thoughts and feelings. We both know that my time is limited, and why shouldn't we face it together, freely and openly?"

Carson said it was ironic that other people had to accept the many honors being bestowed on her, and that all her opportunities to travel to interesting places had to be turned down. Idly she thought about getting away to Myrtle Beach—Roger would love it—though it would mean flying down and renting a car, as the drive from Silver Spring now seemed unimaginable. Carson, whose moods were becoming more erratic, said it was often hard to keep going from one day to the next, but as long as she could stay at least a little busy she could manage—maybe even get well.

"I shall feel better soon, I'm sure," she wrote. "The present great weariness is due to the very heavy radiation I've had, undoubtedly. And the 'misery' in my side will presumably disappear. Sometimes I wish I had nothing to do, but probably it is better to keep my mind occupied."

Carson tried to keep up with scientific and environmental news. In December 1962 she'd been pulled into a fight over the use of dieldrin against the white-fringed beetle in Norfolk, Virginia. Earlier in the fall, larval grub worms of the beetle—a voracious and indiscriminate plant eater—had been discovered in the area, and the Virginia Agriculture Department responded with a plan to spread nine thousand pounds of granular dieldrin over three thousand acres of mostly residential lawns and gardens. Stories about the program in the *Virginian-Pilot* ignited public outrage. The news that dieldrin was already being heavily applied to golf courses and private lawns in Norfolk deepened divisions in the community.

Norfolk's new city library said it could not keep up with demand for *Silent Spring*. Eventually, Virginia's governor, Albertis S. Harrison, Jr., got involved. He said he'd read *Silent Spring,* but that weighing the risk of going ahead with the dieldrin program against the economic damage that could result if the beetle went unchecked, the treatment plan should proceed. Even Carson's old outfit, the U.S. Fish and Wildlife Service, agreed, telling the *Virginian-Pilot* that dieldrin was "extremely destructive to wildlife" but stopping the white-fringed beetle was essential and there was nothing else to be done.

After a lawsuit failed to obtain an injunction, the program began in March when a turbine blower towed behind a jeep started spreading dieldrin throughout the city. Interviewed by the *Virginian-Pilot,* Carson said an application rate of three pounds per acre for dieldrin was "quite heavy." She was dismissive of official claims that the treatments were safe and would be carefully supervised. "They always say that," she said. Carson reminded everyone that many of the most egregious misuses of pesticides she'd uncovered in researching *Silent Spring* had occurred in government-run programs.

Carson took a more academic interest in another below-the-radar environmental issue in early 1963. It was a subject she'd been concerned about for years—a pattern of warmer temperatures and rising sea levels. In March, a group called the Conservation Foundation convened a small, private scientific conference to consider the possibility that the burning of fossil fuels was causing a rise in heat-trapping atmospheric carbon dioxide. A report from the conference was moderately alarming—and a preview of things to come.

"It seems quite certain," the report read, "that a continuing rise in the amount of atmospheric carbon dioxide is likely to be accompanied by a significant warming of the surface of the earth which by melting the polar ice caps would raise sea level and by warming the oceans would change considerably the distributions of marine species including commercial fisheries."

The report said the "biogeochemical" regulation of the earth's climate was not well understood but that in general the climate was stable over long periods of time. The natural "buffering mechanisms" that made it so now appeared to be inadequate to moderate the effects of changes to the atmosphere caused by human activity. This was reason for serious concern, maybe not at the moment but in the years to come: "The effects of a rise in atmospheric carbon dioxide are world-wide. They are significant not to us but to the generations to follow. The consumption of fossil fuel has increased to such a pitch within the last half century that the total atmospheric consequences are matters of concern for the planet as a whole."

CBS Reports: "The Silent Spring of Rachel Carson" aired on April 3, 1963. Among those watching was President Kennedy, who was urged to catch the program by his science adviser Jerome Wiesner. Kennedy and Wiesner were both doubtless interested in how the government's reaction to *Silent Spring* would be represented by their often-wavering Secretary of Agriculture Orville Freeman. Carson, too, was curious about how she'd come off on the show—she told Dorothy she hoped not to seem like an "utter idiot." She said she'd been in a state of exhaustion during the two days of filming in Silver Spring, and that her voice had been unnaturally husky.

But while Carson looked to be in less than vigorous health, her even, unemotional delivery was brilliant and a stark contrast to the performance of her primary opposite number in the program's point-counterpoint format—the supercilious Robert H. White-Stevens. The program opened with shots of pesticides being sprayed on trees and crops and through neighborhoods as children trailed along in the fog from the trucks, while Carson read from *Silent Spring* the passage calling pesticides "biocides." Then came White-Stevens:

The major claims in Miss Rachel Carson's book *Silent Spring* are gross distortions of the actual facts, completely unsupported by scientific experimental evidence and general practical experience in the field. Her suggestion that pesticides are in fact biocides, destroying all life, is obviously absurd in light of the fact that without selective biological activity these compounds would be completely useless. The real threat, then, to the survival of man is not chemical but biological—in the shape of hordes of insects that can denude our forests, sweep over our croplands, ravage our food supply, and leave in their wake a train of destitution and hunger, conveying to an undernourished population the major diseases and scourges of mankind.

If man were to faithfully follow the teachings of Miss Carson we would return to the Dark Ages, and the insects and diseases and vermin would once again inherit the earth.

White-Stevens, who evidently tended to talk that way all the time, was dressed for the occasion in a white lab coat that was meant to emphasize his expertise against "Miss Carson's" hysterical foolishness. But as CBS intercut White-Stevens's comments with shots of bubbling beakers and chemical-company smokestacks, the line between sober researcher and mad scientist blurred. White-Stevens's claim that a registered pesticide used in accordance with label directions posed *no* hazard to humans or wildlife was, as he might have said it, a gross distortion of the actual facts. The more he talked, the more his defense of pesticides seemed an over-the-top cover story. Sevareid, meanwhile, piled on statistic after statistic about pesticide use, totaling up crop damage and pesticide consumption and the sheer volume of new poisonous products for farm, home, and garden. It was numbing after a while. But it sounded like *way too much*.

White-Stevens was not the program's only pesticide proponent. Luther Terry, the U.S. surgeon general, said insecticides had been vital in controlling diseases such as malaria—in America, but also more extensively abroad. George Larrick, head of the FDA, denied that pesticide residues in food were a problem. Larrick took the position—and was encouraged to do so by Jay McMullen, who did much of the interviewing—that pesticides at small enough doses were not toxic. The ever-reliable pesticide defender Wayland Hayes, from the U.S. Public Health Service, agreed that there was no evidence that the amounts of pesticides Americans now regularly consumed were dangerous—though he conceded that one, DDT, was stored at measurable levels in the fatty tissues of people. He said this storage of DDT "has not caused any injury that we can detect."

This was all a familiar story to Carson. "We've heard a great deal about the benefits of pesticides," she said. "We've heard a great deal about their safety. But very little about the hazards, very little about the failures, the inefficiencies—yet the public was being asked to accept these chemicals, the public was being asked to acquiesce in their use and did not have the whole picture. So I set about to remedy the balance."

Carson was asked to read selected passages from Silent Spring— including her all-important disclaimer that nothing she wrote should be construed as a call for the end to all pesticide use. These excerpts covered several of Carson's most frightening revelations—the magnification of pesticides through the food chain, the collateral damage to nontarget species, the silencing of the birds, and the patently offensive idea that these poisonous substances were now readily available for purchase everywhere, by anyone, for any purpose—even though they were, in general, far more toxic than medicines requiring a written prescription. And there was no escape from this toxic new environment. "We have to remember," Carson said, "that children born today are exposed to these chemicals from birth. Perhaps even before birth. Now what is going to happen to them in adult life as a result of that exposure? We simply don't know. Because we've never before had this kind of experience."

Balance being a thing hard to achieve but easy to perceive where it exists, Carson won the debate, handling herself with poise and coming across as a voice of reason and reasonable concern—in no way appearing to be a raving member of the lunatic fringe or a front for Communist seditionists.

Carson, predictably, did better than the spokesmen for the federal government in part because they could not decide what position to take. After saying that pesticide residues in food were not a problem, the FDA's George Larrick added vaguely that *Silent Spring* had caused the agency to "take a new look at our responsibilities to the general public." Larrick expressed doubt about the government's ability to regulate pesticides, given the rapid pace of innovation that was flooding the market with new products. Larrick also conceded that mass sprayings over large areas with airplanes were all but impossible to confine within their intended boundaries, and that it was hard to limit their effects to only the targeted species.

Even White-Stevens admitted that large-scale spraying had some negative effects on wildlife—though he insisted that "in general" wildlife numbers quickly recovered. A spokesman for the FDA said it was true that pesticide residues were being found in drinking water— and Larrick confirmed this was also the case with milk. No tolerance level for DDT or any other pesticide had ever been established for milk, Larrick said, though the objective was to keep pesticides out of milk because of its "very special" importance in the diets of children and infants.

An FWS man—perhaps not surprisingly given the agency's history of pesticide testing—took the harshest view of pesticide use, saying that damage to wildlife was widespread and that sublethal doses of DDT had been demonstrated to cause reproductive and developmental problems in birds. He said not nearly enough was known about pesticide contamination of the total environment, but that it had become all but impossible to find animals that did not have some body burden of pesticides. Speaking for humans, Surgeon General Luther Terry said the main question was what the consequences of long-term exposure to low levels of pesticides might be. Everyone understood that people accumulated pesticide residues in their bodies just as wildlife did; whether that was harmful was an open question.

But it was Orville Freeman—almost daring anyone to take him seriously—who best captured the government's confused, impotent response to Carson's portrait of official ineptitude and inaction. Trying his best to characterize the impact of *Silent Spring* on official policy, Freeman could not get his bearings on camera:

> Let's say the book I believe will have helped the American people in alerting them that we need to do more work but we also need to be personally conscious—this is like anything else. The government is not going to do it for you. Somebody else is not going to do it for you. Basically you're going to have to do it for yourself. And that means to protect yourself and that means to see to it that your government protects you when you can't protect yourself.

What Freeman meant by "do it" wasn't clear, though he seemed to be talking about the regulation and proper use of pesticides—which the public had been assured in every other context was, in fact, under the able control of the government. When Freeman was asked if he thought the public had been sufficiently informed about the potential hazards of pesticides he was more sure of himself. "The answer I can say very quickly," he said, "is no." Asked why that was, Freeman said he thought the public had not been "receptive" to such information. Smiling incongruously at one point, Freeman said the issue of wildlife being harmed in spraying programs was one that he could speak to "with relative, shall we say, detachment" because all of the examples Carson reported had occurred before he was secretary of agriculture. When he was asked how much the USDA was spending to develop biological insect controls, Freeman said about $1.5 million a year—which was, as Jay McMullen pointed out, less than the $2 million the chemical industry said it invested in developing just one synthetic pesticide.

During the course of the program both Sevareid and McMullen described its subject as "the pesticides problem." McMullen, in a long speech to the camera near the end of the show, lamented the general lack of knowledge about the depth of the problem among most of the experts he'd interviewed. McMullen also questioned the delays in a report from President Kennedy's pesticide committee. He said CBS had learned the committee was riven with dissension and that disagreements among various government agencies over what if anything to do about pesticides had stalled the report.

Sevareid brought the program to a close on a philosophical note—saying the real difference between Rachel Carson and her critics wasn't so much an argument over pesticides as a duel between competing views of nature and our place in it. White-Stevens, taking the bait, said that man—with his cities and roads and airports and exploding population—had already undone the so-called balance of nature, and that his survival thus depended on the continuing control of natural processes that worked against his interests. Carson, almost but not quite smiling at this, sat up a little straighter and said:

> Now to these people apparently the balance of nature was something that was repealed as soon as man came on the scene. Well, you might just as well assume that you could repeal the law of gravity. The balance of nature is built on a series of relationships between living things, and between living things and their environments. You can't just step in with some brute force and change one thing without changing many others. This doesn't mean we must never interfere, never tilt the balance of nature in our favor. But when we make the attempt we must know what we're doing. We must know the consequences.

This neat and modern definition of ecology rang true—and Carson was allowed to continue her thought on the point at length. Understanding and respecting the balance of nature had become even more important, she said, with our recently acquired capacity to destroy all of nature. Even short of total annihilation, we now caused the "deadly products of atomic explosions" to rain down on the earth regularly. Unless we could learn that we were part of nature, not its overlord, we weren't going to see the foolishness of a war against nature.

"I truly believe that we in this generation must come to terms with nature," Carson concluded, "and I think we're challenged as mankind has never been challenged before to prove our maturity and our mastery not of nature, but of ourselves."

For Carson and for her publisher, the program was a victory. Houghton Mifflin bought a copy of it for a man in the Massachusetts Department of Fish and Game who wanted to show it at meetings. Carson, relieved it had gone well, went back to thinking about her health and the future. She enjoyed a letter from one of the sponsors of *CBS Reports,* the Kiwi shoe polish company. The president of its American division wrote to her directly, telling Carson the company had been flooded with letters commending it for bringing "such an important program" to the public. He said that in fifteen years of advertising in the United States they'd never had "such a fine reaction" to a program they'd sponsored.

Carson got more support for *Silent Spring* when—as Paul Knight had predicted—the U.S. Department of the Interior committed itself to working harder on the pesticide problem by opening a new pesticides lab at what was now the Patuxent Wildlife Research Center. Carson was invited but couldn't attend the opening ceremony— though Interior Secretary Stewart Udall made sure her presence was felt. In his speech, Udall said the government's first-ever facility dedicated to studying pesticides and wildlife was really meant to take on questions that went beyond chemicals and animals:

> This laboratory is dedicated to Man—to his search for knowledge about the natural world around him—to his wise use of the tools for controlling that world. The work done here may prevent or halt the threat of the "silent springs" that stalk the earth—for this laboratory marks the beginnings of a new national awareness of the present and potential dangers we have almost thoughtlessly brought to the world in which we live.

A great woman has awakened the Nation by her forceful account of the dangers around us. We owe much to Rachel Carson.

The Interior Department, through the U.S. Fish and Wildlife Service, was actually already in the middle of a two-year review of pesticide data that would appear in a massive report a few months later. The findings included evidence of pesticide contamination in wildlife living hundreds or even thousands of miles away from where the chemicals were being used. The researchers determined that although 75 percent of the United States had *never* been treated with insecticides—and only about 5 percent of the country was treated in any given year—DDT and other insecticides were found in the bodies of three of every four animals and birds collected across a broad swath of North America. For some species—notably the bald eagle—it was hard to find any specimen that didn't have DDT in its tissues.

Still to come that spring, however, was the report of the president's pesticide committee—which was finally released on May 15, 1963. Seen by almost everyone as a vindication of *Silent Spring,* the forty-three-page report prompted CBS to broadcast a follow-up to "The Silent Spring of Rachel Carson" saying as much. Eric Sevareid reported that *Silent Spring,* the "most controversial book of the year," had now sold more than five hundred thousand copies and started a "national quarrel." The CBS report noted that pesticides, used properly, were important in fighting disease, as during an outbreak of mosquito-transmitted encephalitis in the St. Petersburg area of Florida in the fall of 1962. But it also acknowledged the many risks that came with pesticide use.

Carson, interviewed for her reaction to the committee's report, noted that it went further than she had in claiming that pesticides contaminated vast portions of the landscape, even when applied to much smaller areas. Sevareid wrapped up the report saying that both *Silent Spring* and now a presidential commission had confirmed that there was "danger in the air, and in the waters and the soil, and the leaves and the grass." Carson, he said, had two objectives in *Silent Spring.*

One was to alert the public to the hazards of pesticide misuse—which she had done. The other was to "build a fire" under the government. The findings of President Kennedy's pesticide commission, Sevareid said, were "prima facie" evidence that she'd accomplished this, too.

The *New York Times* ran an editorial two days after the report's release calling for a "serious re-examination" of pesticides such as DDT, heptachlor, aldrin, and dieldrin, as public controls over the use of these "potent substances" were inadequate. Without mentioning Carson by name, the *Times* said the report of the president's pesticide committee confirmed the dangers from an "unchecked proliferation" of synthetic pesticides that she had warned about. There was no longer any doubt, said the *Times,* that "these chemicals, even when properly used, have killed large numbers of birds, fish and other usefully living organisms, thus upsetting the ecological balance.

"Furthermore," the *Times* wrote, "the committee makes it clear that there is a great deal that we still do not know about the long-range effects upon human beings of continued ingestion of even small quantities of these chemicals, which can enter the human body through the food we eat, through inhalation, and through skin absorption. The dire effect of ingesting large amounts of the chemicals has never been in doubt." In the same issue of the paper, the *Times* reported that Jerome Wiesner, the president's science adviser and head of the pesticides committee, was urging Congress to establish a "large environmental health center" that would study the effects of pesticides on wildlife and human health. Wiesner said that while the extent of the danger was still unknown, pesticides were a potentially greater hazard than radioactive fallout.

Dorothy wrote to Carson to say how "powerfully happy" she must be and that May 15, 1963, would "go down in history as Rachel's triumph." Dorothy marveled again at the perfect note struck by the title *Silent Spring* and the satisfaction she took that a woman had written it. She said Rachel Carson's name would be remembered long after Gordon Cooper's—the Mercury astronaut who was at the time orbiting the earth.

The committee report made a number of recommendations for studying the effects of pesticides and measuring the extent to which they had contaminated the environment. It said hazards to wildlife should be considered in registering pesticides under the Federal Insecticide, Fungicide, and Rodenticide Act. And it pointedly called for funding to determine what harm the government's own spraying programs might be doing, noting that those projects had received about $20 million in 1962, while no money at all had been allocated for concurrent field studies of their effects on the environment. The report made specific reference to Rachel Carson when it concluded by saying that federal agencies involved in the regulation or use of pesticides should launch programs to educate the public about their potential dangers and their "toxic nature," a reality that should have been self-evident, but that now required reinforcement following the publication of *Silent Spring*. President Kennedy issued a statement along with the report, ordering the "responsible agencies" to implement its recommendations and to begin preparing legislation that could make that happen.

But as the report was more carefully considered it became apparent that internal divisions among the committee members had rendered it balanced to the point of being ineffectual. There was nothing in the report that required or even suggested an immediate reduction in pesticide use. On the contrary, the report stated flatly that "The panel believes that the use of pesticides must be continued if we are to maintain the advantages now resulting from the work of informed food producers and those responsible for control of disease." With this premise, all of the recommendations for more studies of pesticides—necessary as they might be—hinted that the actual view of the government was that pesticides were innocent until proven guilty.

Joseph Alsop, the Washington columnist for the *New York Herald Tribune*, took the position that the report was all talk and no action. "If Rachel Carson is right—and the chances are that she is largely right—something ought to be done about it," Alsop wrote. "Furthermore, the something done needs to be considerably sterner than the report of the President's scientific advisers, which had the approximate power of an old lady's moral lecture to a confirmed drunk."

Carson told Dorothy Freeman she'd bought a new car that was so easy and pleasant to drive that riding in it was like floating. Plus, it had seat belts and, in a concession to Roger, a radio. In early May 1963 she said she was desperate to talk to Dorothy in person, as there were "things I need to say to you, but they should be said with my arms around you." This would be difficult, as Stan Freeman, whose health had been in decline in recent years, was ill again, and Carson had to tell herself that having a visit from Dorothy was impossible for now. "I think we must drift for the present," she said. The hardest truth was that Carson wasn't sure she could make it to Maine for the summer. There were rumors—Dorothy said she didn't know how they started—that Carson might even rent out her cottage that year.

But at the end of May, Carson and Roger flew to Maine and stayed five days with the Freemans. Carson had decided to go up for the summer at Southport Island after all, but first she had to return home for an appearance before Congress, where Connecticut senator Abraham Ribicoff's committee on government operations had summoned her for hearings on how to coordinate a federal response to the environmental hazards of pesticides. Carson appeared on June 4, 1963, and found Ribicoff plainly on her side and spoiling for a fight over pesticides.

One recommendation of the president's pesticide panel had been that the U.S. Department of Agriculture end a practice called a "protest registration" through which a pesticide found to be unsafe by the department could be put on the market for a period of time anyway, without informing anyone it had been disapproved. Secretary of Agriculture Orville Freeman had already told Ribicoff's committee that he supported getting rid of protest registrations—but when the press had asked for a list of such disapproved products currently on the market, Freeman's agency had said no. Furious, Ribicoff said the USDA had until the end of the day to release the list—otherwise he'd read it on the floor of the Senate the next day.

Carson entered a long, prepared statement into the record, rehearsing the widespread environmental contamination by pesticides—and noting the growing evidence that living organisms everywhere on the planet were accumulating pesticides in their bodies. Carson also made a number of specific recommendations, including endorsing the pesticide committee's call for more research, but also arguing that citizens needed recourse when the areas where they lived were being sprayed against their wishes and that much greater restrictions on the sale and use of pesticides were needed. Ribicoff questioned Carson closely as to whether she advocated a ban on pesticide use. She said she did not—and she agreed with Ribicoff that this had been a false charge made against *Silent Spring*.

Carson also took questions from Senator Ernest Gruening of Alaska—who a year later would distinguish himself by being one of only two senators to vote against the Gulf of Tonkin Resolution expanding U.S. involvement in Vietnam. Gruening wanted to know whether Carson supported the idea of creating a new federal agency—he thought it might be called the Department of Ecology—that would take over the regulation of pesticides and other environmental matters. Carson said she thought that would be a good thing to do.

Carson and Roger—accompanied by Carson's assistant Jeanne Davis—got up to Southport Island on June 25, 1963, arriving in time for Roger to start a month-long summer camp. Carson told Dorothy one reason she was determined to go to Maine that summer was that she so disliked the idea of being an invalid. She thought she could manage on her own if she was careful. Her heart condition was one consideration. Another was her back, in which she'd recently suffered a compression fracture. Her doctors warned that this meant any kind of fall could have serious consequences. Even so, Carson sent Dorothy a note that read: "Would you help me search for a fairy cave on an August moon and a low, low tide? I would love to try it once more, for the memories are precious."

One day in early September 1963, Carson and Dorothy drove to the southern tip of Southport Island, to the village of Newagen where the lovely Newagen Seaside Inn was surrounded by lush gardens and a wide lawn that looked west, toward Griffith Head on the other side of Sheepscot Bay. After lunch they walked outside, taking in the view. The sky was blue and it felt like summer still, and they listened to the sound of the wind threading through the spruces and the surf falling against the rocks along the shoreline. There were monarch butterflies drifting over the grounds, all heading in the same direction, one after another, each pulled onward by the invisible force of the migratory instinct. Carson and Dorothy talked about the butterflies, and their complex life cycle, in which several generations live and die over the course of thousands of miles of travel in the space of a single year.

Back home in Silver Spring a few days later, Carson wrote to Dorothy, mentioning the butterflies and saying what a happy memory they were. They had realized on that fine, warm day that none of the ones they saw then would return. Remarkably, this hadn't seemed sad at the time. Carson thought it was because both of them knew that every living thing must come to the end of its days, and that it was only natural that it should be this way. The monarch's life cycle is measured in only months, Carson said. "For ourselves, the measure is something else, the span of which we cannot know. But the thought is the same: when that intangible cycle has run its course it is a natural and not unhappy thing that a life comes to its end."

Carson's cancer was spreading quickly now. After a long day at the hospital, X-rays showed lesions had invaded the entire left side of her pelvis—which accounted for the new pain and lameness Carson had experienced over the summer. Dorothy, still in Maine and hoping to cheer Carson, wrote letter after letter describing her days at Southport Island, telling Carson about the birds and the plants and sometimes imagining the two of them walking together under the moonlight along Sheepscot Bay. Dorothy recalled that after one such walk long ago she'd told Carson she looked like alabaster.

In October 1963, Carson started a course of testosterone and phosphorus treatments her doctors thought would reduce her discomfort and difficulty walking. This mattered to Carson, as she was scheduled to give a speech at the Kaiser Medical Center in San Francisco later that month. But she was losing confidence that she was up to it, as every day her pain—which now moved randomly from one part of her body to another—increased. Sometimes she couldn't walk at all. Dorothy commiserated, saying she wished Carson could make the trip to California without pain and fear for how she would hold up. She mentioned some of the things she and Carson had seen and done together when they first met. She said she knew now they'd never see or do those things again, but that she was content that it must be so.

The trip to San Francisco was arduous, though Marie Rodell went along to help Carson manage. A local newspaper account of her speech described Carson as a "middle-aged, arthritis-crippled spinster" whose earth-shaking book on the dangers of pesticides had produced a packed house at the Fairmont Hotel.

Carson told Dorothy how exciting it had been to fly over the Grand Canyon. She loved San Francisco and said if she had another life to live she'd happily spend at least a few years of it there. Somehow she managed a visit to the redwood forest at Muir Woods the morning before her talk, though it was frustrating to see such a place from a wheelchair. The sightseeing was exhausting but not nearly so bad as Carson imagined it would have been to sit all day through the presentations that preceded hers. She told Dorothy she wasn't sorry she'd gone, but that it had been foolish to travel all the way across the country when her physical condition was so poor. When she got home, Carson told Dorothy she had no further obligations and could "afford to be dopey." She had begun taking sleeping pills regularly and was spending most of her time in bed. She said she looked forward to staying awake long enough to read the autographed copy of *The Quiet Crisis* that Stewart Udall had sent her.

Some days were better than others, though Carson said her routine now rarely changed. She got up sometimes, depending on how she felt and whether she could make her way around the house with a walker. She assured Dorothy that she was not in constant pain and maybe even feeling a little better—though in one letter she said she had to stop writing, as her hand would not work any more that day.

Carson had agreed to donate her personal papers to Yale University, and in November 1963 she began digging through old manuscripts and correspondence with publishers. She said it was quite an experience—happy in a way she hadn't anticipated. She told Dorothy she wished they could have done the task together, as there was an air of "dewy freshness and innocence and wonder" that brought back not only memories of her first literary efforts, but also of the early times with Dorothy in Maine. Later that month, Carson found it hard to write to Dorothy for several days after the assassination of President Kennedy on November 22, 1963. Carson said she felt as if she'd lost a member of her family and that his killing brought on feelings of "shock, dismay, and revulsion at the black aspects of our national life—the bigotry, intolerance and hatred preached by so many."

Although she now had severe, continuous pain in her neck—and had more trouble making her hands work—Carson went to New York in early December to accept the Cullum Medal from the American Geographical Society. Worried about shipping a portion of her papers to New Haven, she brought them instead to New York so Marie Rodell could later deliver them to Yale. Stan and Dorothy Freeman went down to the city for the event and spent a few hours with Carson. Dorothy wrote to Carson afterward and said she had never imagined she would see Carson out of bed again after she'd left Maine that fall, and that seeing her up on the dais "looking so fresh and lovely" had brought her near tears.

A week before Christmas 1963, Carson's much-loved cat, Jeffie, died. Carson was devastated, but said she was in one way relieved as she had been concerned for some time about what was to become of both Jeffie and Roger when she died. She thought it was unlikely that whoever would raise Roger—a question for which she had no concrete answer—would also take the cat. Now, she told Dorothy, she had one less worry. A few days later, Carson said how much she was looking forward to a visit from Dorothy over the holidays. Now that the solstice had arrived the days would be getting longer, and maybe—against all odds—they would yet have another summer together at Southport Island.

After Dorothy made a four-day visit to Silver Spring—they both agreed it had been wonderful—Carson more objectively assessed her future. She felt that she'd talked too much about her illness and how little time she likely had left. There was scarcely a place anywhere on her body that didn't hurt now. One of her doctors had lately reminded her that she'd lived with cancer for three years. Carson said she thought he wanted to add—but didn't—that she shouldn't expect much more time now. Only a few days after Carson told Dorothy this, Stan Freeman died of a heart attack at the kitchen table in West Bridgewater as he watched birds come to a feeder he'd just filled.

Carson was crushed by the news. She said she regretted burdening Dorothy with her own health worries. She added that she was "going to be around for quite a while" and planned to spend as much of that time as possible taking care of Dorothy. Carson went up to West Bridgewater for the funeral. One ray of happiness during this somber visit was getting better acquainted with Stanley, Jr., and his wife, Madeleine. Carson told Dorothy how impressed she was that the father's "sweetness and gentleness" lived on in his son. When Stanley, Jr., took Carson to the airport to go home, he told her that whatever his father would have done for her, he was now prepared to step in and do. She told Dorothy she was fortunate to have such a fine son.

Two months later, it was early spring in Maryland when one of Carson's doctors stopped in at the house for what he said was "just a social call." He endorsed Carson's plan to go soon to see Barney Crile at the Cleveland Clinic. The cancer had spread to Carson's liver, and during the several weeks she was hospitalized in Cleveland she was near death. She told Dorothy about an out-of-body experience she had that was pleasant. In early April she was strong enough to go home, though hardly well. Dorothy came down for a visit. When she got home after a couple of days she told Carson she was glad that she could now picture what the days were like for her. On the morning of April 14, 1964, Dorothy wrote to Carson, telling her that she felt "a great sense of peace" and that her first thought every morning was to wonder how Carson had slept the night before. She said how nice it was that birds sang every morning outside the house in Silver Spring. Later that same day, Carson's heart stopped. She died before the sun went down. She was fifty-six years old.

Among the things Carson left behind was the letter for Dorothy that she had written over the course of several days about a year earlier. It was full of goodbyes and Carson's wish that Dorothy remember not the sadness of their last times together, but the many joys that had come before. "I think you must have no regrets in my behalf," Carson wrote. "I have had a rich life, full of rewards and satisfactions that come to few, and if it must end now, I can feel that I have achieved most of what I wished to do."

Carson was cremated. Her brother, Robert, insisted on burying some of her ashes next to their mother's grave and reluctantly agreed to let Dorothy Freeman spread the remainder on the ocean at Southport Island.

On May 4, 1964, the tide at Newagen was high at five in the morning. Dorothy drove down to that end of the island at six thirty to catch the ebbing tide. The day was calm and clear, and the ground swell broke against the rocks like the pulse of the ocean. Dorothy found a cleft in the granite where the water rose up with each wave and she poured the ashes into the edge of the sea, followed by a white hyacinth. She realized she had no idea what to do next. It was so lovely. Dorothy sat down and stayed there a long time, watching the birds and the blue ocean, until the tide turned again.

Epilogue

I n the half century since the publication of *Silent Spring,* America has embraced the book's central message unevenly—the country's efforts to protect the environment have been a mix of progress, partisanship, and pigheadedness that Rachel Carson would find familiar. It's hard to imagine her in this world now. She would like writing on a computer—there's nothing like Microsoft Word for an obsessive reviser—and she would find the ability to retrieve almost any kind of information from the Internet a joy. The great breakthroughs in biology that have unlocked the inner workings of the cell and the genome at the molecular level would astonish and delight her. Other changes would be less comfortable. It's likely she would be dismayed by e-books and smartphones and social networking and that she'd be mortified by the steady demise of the great newspapers and magazines that were so large a part of the culture of her times. She would struggle to comprehend the newly virulent resistance to science that now clouds issues such as evolution and climate change— which she would surely see not as "issues" at all, but as facts not open to disbelief.

While compiling information for Carson's obituaries, Anne Ford—who was head of publicity at Houghton Mifflin—wrote down her recollections of the author. She remembered Carson once being described as a "nun of nature." It was an odd thought, but one that matched up with Ford's memory of Carson's bedroom, an "austere" cell in which she said it was easy to see that its occupant craved simplicity and order—and the peace and quiet that came in the bargain.

Because the environmental movement survived the end of the

Cold War, the context in which it was born, Carson can be credited not only with putting the movement into motion but for doing so in a way that would allow it to eventually stand on its own. *Silent Spring* was many things—plea and polemic and prayer—but most important it was right. This was eventually conceded even by some early skeptics. In the fall of 1963, Secretary of Agriculture Orville Freeman invited Carson to join President Kennedy in dedicating the Pinchot Institute for Conservation Studies in Milford, Pennsylvania, at the ancestral home of Gifford Pinchot.

Carson declined.

During the Pinchot Institute's first year of operation in 1963, experiments at another facility, the new wildlife pathology lab at Patuxent, demonstrated that sublethal doses of pesticides in the food supplies of waterfowl and upland game birds caused drops in reproductive success and led to mortality. The researchers at Patuxent were also studying the long-term, multigenerational effects of pesticides in fish and were monitoring "serious" accumulations of pesticide residues in the tissues of ducks, geese, bald eagles, deer, and other wildlife.

In the spring of 1964—just days before Rachel Carson died—Secretary of the Interior Stewart Udall told Senator Ribicoff's committee that evidence of such widespread pesticide contamination was so compelling that a nationwide pesticide monitoring program was needed. Udall also said it was time to end the use of highly toxic chemical pesticides in applications that could not be controlled. This was an acknowledgment that, despite the claims of manufacturers and government regulators, some pesticides were unsafe even when used as directed. Udall said his department had mounting evidence that episodes of pesticide contamination in wildlife—including some of the appalling fish kills on the lower Mississippi—were the result of "normal" pesticide use. Udall said ways had to be found to limit the movement of persistent toxic compounds everywhere throughout the environment, or there was no alternative but to stop using them altogether.

This, of course, was the point Carson had made in *Silent Spring*—

poison one corner of the environment and you risk poisoning the whole thing. In the fall of 1964, Udall exercised his considerable authority over most federal lands and issued tough new rules for pesticide use on more than 550 million acres under the jurisdiction of the U.S. Department of the Interior. In general, the guidelines made chemical pesticides a last resort control method and called for the most limited applications and the lowest possible doses whenever they were used. He instructed all the agencies involved to avoid using pesticides—including DDT, chlordane, dieldrin, and endrin—that were known to accumulate in living organisms. Two months later, the FWS issued a notice declaring the agency's serious concern for bald eagles, which were building up alarming body burdens of DDT wherever they were studied.

For a decade and more, the dangers of pesticides were the focal point of a broadening environmental movement that led to the enactment of the Clean Air Act (1963), the Clean Water Act (1972), and the Endangered Species Act (1973). On April 22, 1970, environmental activists organized by Wisconsin senator Gaylord Nelson—a fan of Aldo Leopold's *Sand County Almanac* and Rachel Carson's *Silent Spring*—held the first Earth Day, and millions attended rallies across the country. Later that spring, Secretary of the Interior Walter Hickel formalized Stewart Udall's earlier policy on pesticide use on federal lands, formally banning the use of DDT, aldrin, dieldrin, heptachlor, lindane, and several others.

Shortly after his inauguration in 1969, President Richard Nixon established the Council on Environmental Quality in his administration. In April 1970—as the Earth Day rallies were being organized—Nixon was advised to create a new agency with formal regulatory control over environmental matters, including the registration and use of pesticides under FIFRA. In July, Nixon asked Congress to authorize the Environmental Protection Agency—which opened for business the following December. Among the first orders of business for the new agency was the removal of many pesticides from general use, starting with DDT. A young, eager legal staff took on the mission of canceling pesticide registrations and during the 1970s the EPA ended the domestic use—but not the manufacture for export—of DDT, aldrin, dieldrin, chlordane, heptachlor, and endrin. The United States thus joined Sweden—where Paul Müller had received his Nobel Prize—as one of the first countries to ban DDT.

Those early days of swift, aggressive action against environmental contaminants gave way to a slower, softer EPA in the years since, under both Democratic and Republican administrations. More sophisticated chemical and biological assay techniques have made it possible for pesticide makers to game the system by overwhelming the EPA with study after study, dragging out renewal registrations for suspect chemicals for years while they stay on the market. That may change as the agency begins looking more closely at chemicals that interfere with or mimic hormones.

In 1996, the field of toxicology was turned upside down with the publication of a book called *Our Stolen Future,* which described emerging evidence that some chemicals—including pesticides such as DDT and their by-products—bind to specialized receptors in cells that are meant to recognize hormones like estrogen, but which can be fooled by a chemical mimic. The result can be disease, reproductive problems, and birth defects—the same problems that now turn up in epidemiological studies of people living in areas with high exposures to pesticides. For many people, *Our Stolen Future* was seen as a sequel to *Silent Spring.* The same year it was released, Congress directed the EPA to develop new assays to detect endocrine-disrupting properties in chemicals.

It took until the fall of 2009 for the first of those test procedures to be approved—and when they were, one of the first chemicals that tested positive as an endocrine disrupter was the pesticide atrazine, a weed killer that for many years was the most heavily used herbicide in the world. Banned in the European Union in 2003, atrazine had a long, long history of continued use in the United States while the EPA went in circles with the manufacturer over whether it was safe. In 1988, Congress ordered the EPA to reregister older pesticides, including atrazine. Atrazine was then selected for "special review" in 1994. Twelve years and one million pages of documents later, the EPA ignored evidence that atrazine was an endocrine disrupter and issued the new registration. Three years later, after its own new assays confirmed potential problems with atrazine, the EPA reopened the case.

In 2006, the World Health Organization announced its endorsement of the use of DDT to combat malaria, mainly in Africa. The WHO had never lifted its approval of DDT for this purpose, but that year the agency decided an affirmative commitment to the insecticide was needed. The move was backed by most environmental groups—as it certainly would have been by Rachel Carson had she been alive to do so. But the myth that Carson wanted a total end to the use of chemical pesticides persists.

Carson would be less tolerant of the lack of action to reverse or at least slow global warming caused by fossil fuel consumption. George W. Bush had promised during his campaign for the presidency in 2000 that he wanted carbon dioxide emissions regulated by the EPA as a greenhouse gas pollutant. Within weeks of taking office in 2001 he reversed his position. Bush also announced the United States would not sign on to the Kyoto Protocol, an international agreement intended to limit greenhouse gases. In June 2001, the National Academy of Sciences—which Bush had asked to look into the global warming question—reported to the president that global warming was real, that human activity was the main cause, and that things were getting worse. Bush did nothing then, and little—apart from improvements in automobile fuel consumption—has happened since. Rachel Carson would find nothing new in the unwillingness to confront this problem. Human arrogance and disregard for the collateral damage we inflict upon the environment was a story she knew well.

Roger Christie went to live with Paul Brooks and his wife, whom Carson had named in her will as prospective guardians—along with

Stanley Freeman, Jr., and his wife. Inexplicably, she had never discussed this with either family.

In 1968 Dorothy Freeman married a longtime family friend who lived year-round on Southport Island. Her second husband died two years later, but Dorothy remained at Southport, dividing her time between the house and the cottage at Dogfish Head. In 1975 she gave a talk about Carson at the University of Southern Maine in Gorham. She told the audience that Rachel Carson had been her "closest friend" and that she believed Carson felt the same about her. "Because of the eleven years that I knew her," Dorothy said, "I feel that my whole life was enriched beyond understanding." Dorothy Freeman died in 1978 at the age of eighty.

Acknowledgments

M y deepest thanks to Stanley Freeman, Jr., and Martha Freeman, and to their spouses, the late Madeleine Freeman and Richard Barringer—an accomplished and gracious family who spent a lovely summer morning showing me the Freeman cottage at Dogfish Head on Southport Island in Maine, where we sat on the deck overlooking Sheepscot Bay as they shared their recollections of Rachel and Dorothy. My conversations continued with Stan and Martha for many months thereafter, and I appreciate their help, their openness, and their encouragement more than I can say.

Thanks, also, to Roger Christie and Wendy Sisson for allowing me to spend a week at the Carson cottage on Southport Island, where I wrote portions of Chapter 7 at Rachel's desk as the sounds and smell of the sea came to me through an open window.

I started work on this book by asking Linda Lear whether she thought I should, and I am grateful to her for encouraging me to do so. Linda's essential biography, *Rachel Carson: Witness for Nature,* and her collection of research materials at Connecticut College were invaluable sources of fact and inspiration. I am also indebted to my friend Mike Lannoo, of the Indiana University School of Medicine, who read the manuscript and offered valuable suggestions for its improvement. Mike's own fine book, *Leopold's Shack and Ricketts's Lab,* was essential to my understanding of both of these men. Many thanks to Mark Madison, David Klinger, and Anne Post at the U.S. Fish and Wildlife Service's National Conservation Training Center. Mark, an early and enthusiastic adviser on this book, opened the Fish and Wildlife archives to me, while David and Anne helped with personnel and publication records from Carson's time at the agency.

Special thanks to my longtime friend and prose mentor, Dan Kelly, who read the manuscript and made me make it better, as I knew he would.

Thank you to Fran Collin and Sarah Yake of the Frances Collin literary agency, trustee of the Rachel Carson literary estate, for reviewing quoted passages from Carson's writings and granting permission for their use. Thanks to Brian Goldberg of the Department of English at the University of Minnesota for a helpful interpretation of "Locksley Hall" and to Mark Edlund of the St. Croix Watershed Research Station for a tutorial on diatoms. Thanks also to Simon Ratsey and Gwyneth Campling in England for their help with terminologies peculiar to the countryside and waterways of Devon. And thank you to William H. Calvert for information on the migration and life cycle of monarch butterflies.

Thank you to Nell Baldacchino of the Patuxent Research Refuge for showing me around that sprawling facility and to Greg Piniak for doing the same at the Center for Coastal Fisheries and Habitat Research at Beaufort. Thanks as well to lab director David Johnson for his historical perspective on the Beaufort station and the region. Thank you to Ron Orchard of the Southport Historical Society and Hendricks Hill Museum for the local lowdown on Carson's summertime destination. Thanks to Patricia M. DeMarco, former executive director of the Rachel Carson Homestead Association, for showing me Carson's childhood home in Springdale. And thank you to Diana Post, president of the Rachel Carson Council, and to her husband, Clifford C. Hall, who showed me Carson's last house in Silver Spring.

Special thanks to my good friends Paul Lombino and Leslie Schultz in Boston, and Karl Vick and Stacy Sullivan in New York for putting me up and keeping me fine company when I was doing research in those cities.

Acknowledgments

I would have been lost without the capable and friendly assistance of the librarians and archivists who guided me through the long written record of Carson's life and work. Most sincere thanks to Elaine Ardia at the Edmund S. Muskie Archives and Special Collections Library at Bates College; to Rachel M. Grove Rohrbaugh, archivist at the Jennie King Mellon Library at Chatham University; to Benjamin Panciera and Nova M. Seals at the Linda Lear Center for Special Collections and Archives at Connecticut College; to Lynda Garrett at the Patuxent Wildlife Research Center library; to Thomas Lannon of the New York Public Library Manuscripts and Archives Division; to Stephen Plotkin, reference archivist at the John F. Kennedy Presidential Library; to Maureen Booth, law librarian, U.S. Department of the Interior Library; and to Ann Roche of the Southport Memorial Library. Thanks also to the dedicated staffs at the National Archives and Records Administration in College Park, at the Washington Historical Society, at the Historical Society of Old Newbury, and at the Hennepin County Central Library, my hometown go-to resource for odd books and obscure articles.

Apart from some of the early letters from Dorothy Freeman—which regrettably are lost to history—Rachel Carson never threw away anything written by or to her, and through good fortune her personal papers ended up in New Haven. The Beinecke Rare Book and Manuscript Library at Yale University houses one of the world's great literary collections in one of the world's most beautiful buildings. It was for many weeks my home away from home. I am deeply indebted to the entire staff there, especially to those on the front desk who retrieved materials, answered my questions, and in general made my research a pleasure from start to finish. Very special thanks to Karen Nangle, who did all that and so much more.

Sincere thanks to Domenica Alioto at Crown, for her many suggestions and close attention to the manuscript and in helping me with permissions and other essential details. Rachel Klayman, my editor at

Crown, and Chuck Verrill, my agent, have been full partners in this endeavor. I thank them for their wise counsel and unflagging support, though I cannot actually thank them enough. Thanks, also, to John Glusman for his early and ardent support, and for finding me a home at Crown.

Finally, thank you to my wife, Susan, and to our children, Joe, Martha, Tom, and Liz, for letting me do this again.

Notes

Rachel Carson lived in the age of words and print. To say that she wrote professionally understates the case. Carson wrote nonstop, leaving behind four books, many newspaper and magazine articles, and, just as important, thousands of letters that tell the story of her work and her life. She corresponded regularly with scientists, doctors, colleagues, publishers, editors, publicists, agents, friends, students, politicians, and her legions of admirers. Carson's letters were models of lean prose that exhibited the author's knack for saying exactly what she meant.

Carson's correspondence with Dorothy Freeman is held in the Dorothy Freeman Collection at the Edmund S. Muskie Archives and Special Collections Library at Bates College. Most of the balance of Carson's letters, along with an extensive inventory of personal papers and records—including notebooks, manuscripts, research materials, speeches, and unpublished writings—make up the Rachel Carson Papers, which are in the Yale Collection of American Literature at the Beinecke Rare Book and Manuscript Library at Yale University. The original documents from these two collections, or in some instances facsimiles of originals, are the primary sources for this book.

I also found important source materials in other archival collections. These included the John F. Kennedy Presidential Library and Museum; the Linda Lear Collection of Rachel Carson Books and Papers, held in the Linda Lear Center for Special Collections and Archives at Connecticut College; the Rachel Carson Collection in the archives of the Jennie King Mellon Library at Chatham University; the *New Yorker* records and the National Audubon Society records in the Manuscripts and Archives Division of the New York Public Library; the archives of the U.S. Fish and Wildlife Service at the National Conservation Training Center Museum and Archives; the Historical Society of Old Newbury; the National Archives and Records Administration in College Park, Maryland; the library of the U.S. Geological Survey Patuxent Wildlife Research Center; the Historical Society of Washington, D.C.; the Southport Historical Society and Hendricks Hill Museum; and the Southport Memorial Library.

I have also drawn on many secondary published sources, including newspaper and magazine articles, industrial and trade publications, and peer-reviewed papers from scientific journals. Books, cited in detail in the accompanying bibliography, were also vital sources, and three deserve special mention: *Rachel Carson: Witness for Nature,* Linda Lear's seminal biography and the essential road map for all subsequent Carson scholarship; *Always, Rachel: The Letters of Rachel Carson and Dorothy Freeman 1952–1964,* edited and annotated by Dorothy's granddaughter Martha Freeman and that includes most of the letters from the Muskie collection; and *The Voyage of the Lucky Dragon,* Ralph E. Lapp's superb account of the Castle Bravo incident and its aftermath.

In the interests of economy, I have dispensed with source citations for factual information of a general and easily retrievable nature—geographical details, name and place spellings, dates of major events, routine biographical accounts of prominent persons, and so on—as well as for broad assertions that are my own conclusions based on having read the record. All other factual statements are derived from the sources that follow in the notes below.

Over time, copies of documents have migrated among various archives, so that some are now found in more than one place. Where possible I have indicated the location I believe to be the primary repository; otherwise I cite the location where I found the document. For frequently mentioned collections, the following abbreviations are used:

Beinecke   Rachel Carson Papers, Yale Collection of American Literature, Beinecke Rare Book and Manuscript Library, Yale University, New Haven, Connecticut

Chatham   Rachel Carson Collection, archives of the Jennie King Mellon Library, Chatham University, Pittsburgh, Pennsylvania

JFK Library   John F. Kennedy Presidential Library and Museum, Boston, Massachusetts

Lear Collection   Linda Lear Collection of Rachel Carson Books and Papers, Linda Lear Center for Special Collections and Archives, Connecticut College, New London, Connecticut

Muskie   Edmund S. Muskie Archives and Special Collections Library, Bates College, Lewiston, Maine

NARA   National Archives and Records Administration, College Park, Maryland

NCTC   U.S. Fish and Wildlife Service National Conservation Training Center Museum and Archives, Shepherdstown, West Virginia

Patuxent   Library of the U.S. Geological Survey, Patuxent Wildlife Research Center, Laurel, Maryland

CHAPTER ONE: MISS CARSON'S BOOK

3   *Late in the summer of 1962: Washington Post,* August 29, 1962.

3   *That same day, President John F. Kennedy appeared:* News Conference 42, JFK Library.

5   *Although not yet actually a book:* Carson, "Silent Spring," *New Yorker,* June 16, 23, and 30, 1962.

6   *Although it had been first synthesized: New York Times,* October 29, 1948.

7   *When the U.S. Army sprayed:* Ibid.

7   *At the award ceremony:* The Nobel Prize in Physiology or Medicine 1948, Presentation Speech, http://www.nobelprize.org/.

7   *On June 5, 1945:* Clarence Cottam and Elmer Higgins, "DDT: Its Effect on Fish and Wildlife," U.S. Fish and Wildlife Service Circular 11, 1946, Patuxent.

8   *Further laboratory studies:* Ibid.

8   *On August 22, 1945:* U.S. Fish and Wildlife Service press release, August 22, 1945, NCTC.

8   *By 1947, Patuxent had a staff biologist:* Patuxent Research Refuge Field
    Program and Economic Investigations Laboratory, Quarterly Report,
    March 1947, NARA. The biologist was Joseph P. Linduska, then near
    the beginning of a long and storied career as a government scientist and
    conservationist. In 1950, Linduska warned that the aerial application of
    DDT over large areas would lead to "dire effects" on the balance
    of nature.

8   *That same year:* Patuxent Research Refuge Field Program and Economic
    Investigations Laboratory, Quarterly Report, June 1947, NARA.

8   *In July 1945:* Carson to Harold Lynch, July 15, 1945, Beinecke.

9   *The uses for DDT seemed endless:* "DDT: How to Use It," *Mechanix
    Illustrated,* December 1945, Beinecke.

10 *and in 1955 the World Health Organization launched:* Packard, *Making of a
    Tropical Disease,* pp. 151–52.

10 *By 1959, some eighty million pounds of DDT:* "DDT Regulatory History:
    A Brief Survey (to 1975)," U.S. Environmental Protection Agency,
    September 10, 2009, http://www.epa.gov/.

10 *In early 1958, Carson:* Carson to DeWitt Wallace, January 27, 1958,
    Beinecke.

10 *About that same time:* Carson to E. B. White, February 3, 1958,
    Beinecke.

10 *Carson, disinclined:* Ibid.

10 *By spring, Carson had signed a contract:* Carson to Paul Brooks, April 20,
    1958, Beinecke. Brooks was the editor in chief of Houghton Mifflin.

10 *In 1945, as the U.S. Fish and Wildlife Service:* Miller, *Under the Cloud,*
    pp. 34–57.

10 *A moratorium was agreed to:* U.S. Department of Energy, Nevada
    Operations Office, "United States Nuclear Tests: July 1945 through
    September 1992," December 2000, p. vii.

10 *Over the course of the next three months:* "JFK in History: Nuclear Test Ban
    Treaty," JFK Library.

11 *Between April and November: New York Times,* June 1, 1963.

11 *When a comprehensive ban:* National Research Council, "Exposure of the
    American Population to Radioactive Fallout from Nuclear Weapons
    Tests: A Review of the CDC-NCI Draft Report on a Feasibility
    Study," 2003, pp. 9–11. While it would seem easy to keep track of

things as noticeable as nuclear explosions, the counting of atmospheric nuclear tests has not been precise, and different sources disagree about totals. Some tests involved more than one device at a time. Others used low-yield devices intended only to test safety features or new trigger mechanisms and did not result in large explosions or produce fallout. But the number of tests that did both—and the widespread radioactive contamination that resulted—is appalling.

11   *A by-product of these tests:* Ibid.

11   *In 1957 a group of prominent scientists:* Mead and Hager, *Linus Pauling,* pp. 212–13.

11   *Carson recognized an "exact and inescapable" parallel:* Carson, *Silent Spring,* p. 208.

12   *Some compared the book: New York Times,* September 27, 1962.

12   *A major pesticide manufacturer:* Louis A. McLean to Houghton Mifflin, August 2, 1962, Beinecke. McLean was secretary and general counsel for the Velsicol Chemical Corporation.

12   *The U.S. Department of Agriculture meanwhile: New York Times,* July 22, 1962.

13   *The Book-of-the-Month Club announced:* Lovell Thompson to Carson, June 14, 1962, Beinecke.

13   *A newspaper in London reported: London Evening Standard,* September 5, 1962.

13   *Along with the possibility of:* Carson, *Silent Spring,* p. 8.

13   *In 1959, just days before: New York Times,* November 10, 1959.

13   *Then, in 1961, came devastating news:* Gilbert, *Developmental Biology,* pp. 18–19, 666–67.

14   *The U.S. maker of thalidomide:* Lear, *Rachel Carson,* p. 412.

14   *When a reporter questioned: New York Post,* September 14, 1962.

14   *In October 1962, just after* Silent Spring *arrived:* Chief of Naval Operations, "The Naval Quarantine of Cuba, 1962," Naval Historical Center, http://www.history.navy.mil/.

15   *The day after his press conference: New York Times,* August 31, 1962.

15   *Meanwhile, the FBI:* U.S. Department of Justice, FBI investigative report, December 11, 1962, NCTC. The contents of this two-page document are, regrettably, lost to history. A severely redacted version, in which all but a handful of words were blacked out, was released in 1995 in

response to a Freedom of Information of Information and Privacy Act request from Linda Lear. In May 2010, I initiated a second FOI/PA request for an unredacted version of the report. In August 2010, the FBI informed me that the record had been destroyed in a routine file clearing in 1997. I appealed this response in October 2010, asking the FBI to look for it in backup files. I also asked the FBI if it could determine who requested the investigation and who received the report. In March 2011, the FBI answered again, reaffirming its earlier finding that the report had been destroyed. The agency said it could not respond to my request for a "cross reference" search of other files or for additional information about the report unless I could provide, among other things, the dates, locations, and "specific circumstances" of contact between Carson and the FBI—the very information blacked out on the report—and at that point I gave up. All that can be gleaned from the redacted version is that the investigation was launched at least as early as August 30, 1962, the day after President Kennedy's press conference, that it in some way involved the U.S. Immigration and Naturalization Service, and that Carson's phone was either tapped or a record of her incoming calls was obtained. The report was marked "Confidential." The date "December 11, 1962," was corrected by overtyping and could alternatively be December 14.

15 *Immediately following the* New Yorker *serialization:* Orville Freeman, USDA internal memo, July 16, 1962, JFK Library.

15 *Beleaguered over what to do:* Ibid., July 18, 1962, JFK Library.

16 *What did surprise her was how well:* Paul Brooks to Carson, October 16, 1962, Beinecke.

16 *And the Book-of-the-Month Club edition: Book-of-the-Month Club News,* September 1962, Beinecke.

16 *from U.S. Supreme Court justice William O. Douglas:* Ibid.

16 *Carson complained of "drowning":* Carson to Anne Ford, October 22, 1962, Beinecke.

16 *One notable request:* Ibid., September 17, 1962, Beinecke.

17 *But Carson was hiding:* Paul Brooks to Carson, March 18, 1960, and Carson to Paul Brooks, March 21, 1960, Beinecke.

17 *a minor procedure ten years earlier:* Carson to Marie Rodell, September 10, 1950, Beinecke.

17 *Carson required a radical mastectomy:* Carson to Marjorie Spock, April 12, 1960, Beinecke.

17 *Carson eventually discovered:* Lear, *Rachel Carson,* pp. 378–79. Carson finally discovered the truth after visiting Dr. Barney Crile at the Cleveland Clinic in early December 1960—though she perhaps suspected she'd been misled after her mastectomy. She told Paul Brooks in late December 1960 that she had asked her doctors "directly" after her surgery if there was a malignancy (Carson to Paul Brooks, December 27, 1960, Beinecke). Linda Lear illuminates the situation by explaining that in the 1950s and '60s it was common for doctors to discuss a cancer diagnosis with a woman's husband and not with the patient herself—a disturbing practice that left the unmarried Carson in the dark about her condition (Lear, *Rachel Carson,* p. 368). Dorothy Freeman, who'd been desperately worried about Carson's health, said at the end of 1960 that she was relieved Dr. Crile had set things straight (Dorothy Freeman to Carson, December 31, 1960, Muskie).

17 *When the* Life *magazine piece came out:* Life, October 1962, pp. 105–10.

18 *Earlier that year Carson had been approached:* Houghton Mifflin internal memo, April 27, 1962, Beinecke.

18 *Carson and Houghton Mifflin thought:* Anne Ford to Carson, November 9, 1962, Beinecke. Ford worked in the publicity department at Houghton Mifflin.

18 *When a producer and cameraman:* Lear, *Rachel Carson,* p. 421. Lear fleshed out the story of the CBS production by way of an interview with *CBS Reports* producer Jay McMullen.

18 *In late November:* Ibid., p. 425.

18 *Carson looked terrible:* Personal observation. Just as she had in the *Life* magazine piece, Carson looked old and unwell in front of the camera for *CBS Reports:* "The Silent Spring of Rachel Carson" (Beinecke).

19 *Afterward, Sevareid confided:* Lear, *Rachel Carson,* p. 425.

19 *Carson had already told Freeman:* Carson to Dorothy Freeman, June 27, 1962, Muskie.

19 *"I'm just beginning to find out":* Ibid., December 12, 1962, Muskie.

CHAPTER TWO: BRIGHT AS THE MIDDAY SUN

21 *Since the stock market crash:* "Timelines of the Great Depression,"
http://www.huppi.com/.

21 *Among the dispossessed:* "The Legacy of the Bonus Army," *Washington History* 19 and 20 (2007–8): pp. 87–95.

21 *The veterans ended up:* Ibid.

22 *One of Ickes's first orders of business:* Look, *Interior Building*, pp. 11–17. I visited the Interior Building in the summer of 2010. Although Carson's office is preserved, it is in an area that was closed for construction at the time.

23 *In May 1942:* Department of the Interior personnel records, promotion and transfer form, April 18, 1942, NCTC.

23 *Colleagues, most of them men:* Lear, *Rachel Carson*, p. 124. Lear gleaned this from her interviews with Bob Hines.

23 *Like all federal employees:* Department of the Interior personnel records, signed oath, May 29, 1940, NCTC. The Hatch Act became law on August 2, 1939. More broadly it also prohibits federal employees of the executive branch, other than president and vice president, from engaging in partisan political activities.

23 *When she moved to the Interior Department:* Department of the Interior personnel records, promotion and transfer form, April 18, 1942, NCTC.

24 *Carson's employment file did include:* Department of the Interior personnel records, application for federal employment personal history form, April 20, 1943, NCTC.

24 *In 1918, at the age of eleven:* Carson, "A Battle in the Clouds," *St. Nicholas,* September 1918, p. 1048, Beinecke.

24 *News of this accomplishment:* Personal observation. I visited the Rachel Carson Homestead, which is preserved as such, in spring 2010. Although the surrounding neighborhood is now fully developed, the house and its grounds are essentially unchanged since Carson's girlhood.

24 *Rachel Louise Carson entered the world:* Maria Carson account, Lear Collection. Carson's mother recorded observations about her daughter on three handwritten undated pages.

25 *The Carson house was crowded:* Lear, *Rachel Carson*, pp. 15–26.

25 *The family's financial situation:* Ibid.

25 *In 1910 he advertised:* *Springdale Record,* February 5, 1910, Lear Collection.

25   *Rachel continued submitting stories:* Carson, *St. Nicholas,* January 1919, p. 280; *St. Nicholas,* August 1919, p. 951; *St. Nicholas,* July 1922, p. 999, NCTC.

25   *Springdale's school went only:* Gail Williams, "Rachel Carson: Marine Biologist," November 3, 1995, Chatham. Williams went to high school with Carson and wrote out this eight-page script for a speech she delivered to the Delta Kappa Gamma Society in Sun City, Arizona, on October 25, 1995.

26   *Rachel's like the mid-day sun:* Ibid.

26   *Rachel's senior thesis:* Carson, "Intellectual Dissipation," senior thesis, Parnassus High School, 1925, Beinecke.

27   *Pennsylvania College for Women:* Dysart, *Chatham College,* p. 1. Pennsylvania College for Women—PCW as it was known when Carson attended—has undergone several name changes since its founding. It was originally Pennsylvania Female College, then PCW, later Chatham College, and now Chatham University.

27   *The base of the high ground:* Personal observation. I visited Chatham University in March 2010 to work in the Carson collection at the Jennie King Mellon Library and to see the campus, which retains its former charm.

27   *The college itself comprised:* Dysart, *Chatham College,* pp. 19, 86–87. Dysart's book also includes a number of photographs of the college and its students.

27   *She arrived on September 15, 1925:* Pennsylvania College for Women, "Handbook," 1925–26, p. 9, Chatham.

27   *in a borrowed Ford Model T:* Lear, *Rachel Carson,* p. 26.

27   *Carson had won a $100 scholarship:* Ibid., p. 25.

27   *Tuition in Carson's freshman year was $200:* Pennsylvania College for Women, "Announcements," 1925–26, p. 82, Chatham.

27   *Later, tuition rose:* Ibid., p. 78.

27   *The Carsons managed to keep up:* Legal agreement between Carson and PCW putting up two of her father's lots as collateral, January 28, 1929, plus various notes, invoices, and correspondence between Carson and PCW, including two pleading letters to Margaret Stuart, the college's secretary and assistant treasurer, on February 27, 1931, and August 26, 1932, Chatham.

28   *When one of Rachel's classmates:* Dorothy Thompson Seif, "Letters from
      Rachel Carson," p. 13, Chatham. Dorothy Thompson, later Dorothy
      Thompson Seif, attended PCW with Carson. Her one-hundred-
      page monograph about Carson's college and postgraduate experiences
      includes Seif's detailed recollections of PCW as well a number of letters
      between Carson, Seif, Mary Scott Skinker, and another student, Mary
      Frye. Seif's monograph is unpublished but copyrighted by the Rachel
      Carson Council. The copyright on the letters from Carson reproduced
      in the Seif monograph is owned by Roger Christie. Copies of the Seif
      monograph seem to be in a number of archival collections.

28   *There were eighty-eight women:* Arrow, September 18, 1925, p. 2, Chatham.
      The *Arrow* was a twice-monthly campus magazine at PCW.

28   *Students were not allowed:* Seif, "Letters from Rachel Carson," pp. 9–10,
      Chatham.

28   *There were regular teas:* Ibid., p. 11.

28   *and a formal prom that was:* Pennsylvania College for Women,
      "Handbook," 1925–26, p. 9, Chatham.

28   *Students were expected:* Pennsylvania College for Women,
      "Announcements," 1925–26, p. 78, Chatham.

28   *though it was understood that the main aim:* Seif, "Letters from Rachel
      Carson," p. 10, Chatham.

28   *Students at PCW studied:* Ibid., p. 9; and Dysart, *Chatham College,*
      pp. 176–81.

28   *Carson, dressed in blue bloomers:* Seif, "Letters from Rachel Carson,"
      p. 8, Chatham.

28   *At one game the cheering students:* Arrow, December 16, 1927, p. 6,
      Chatham.

28   *Carson suffered from acne:* Linda Lear, interview with Helen Myers Knox,
      February 11, 1992, Lear Collection. Knox was friends with Carson at
      PCW. See also Lear, *Rachel Carson,* p. 30.

29   *Like most of the other girls:* Seif, "Letters from Rachel Carson," p. 17,
      Chatham.

29   *Never shy in class:* Linda Lear, interview with Dorothy Thompson Seif,
      January 31, 1991, Lear Collection.

29   *A few girls who got to know her:* Ibid., p. 13.

29   *Maria Carson made:* Ibid., p. 12.

29   *One of Rachel's friends:* Linda Lear, interview with Dorothy Thompson
       Seif, January 31, 1991, Lear Collection.

29   *Mrs. Carson spent so much time:* Ibid.

29   *Carson's assignment to write:* Carson, "Who I Am and Why I Came to
       PCW," Beinecke. Carson kept everything she ever wrote, including all
       of her college assignments.

30   *What seems more probable:* Oxenham, *Vision Splendid,* p. 17.

31   *For her next theme:* Carson, "Field Hockey," Beinecke.

31   *Carson entered college as an English major:* Seif, "Letters from Rachel
       Carson," p. 16, Chatham.

31   *In the fall of 1925:* Pennsylvania College for Women, "Announcements,"
       1925-26, pp. 28–29, Chatham.

31   *By Carson's senior year:* Pennsylvania College for Women,
       "Announcements," 1928–29, pp. 24–27, Chatham.

31   *The force behind this change:* Seif, "Letters from Rachel Carson,"
       pp. 22–25, Chatham.

32   *A dynamic and demanding teacher:* Ibid., pp. 18, 22–25.

32   *As a junior, she found herself:* Ibid., p. 19.

34   *In 1925, the National Academy:* Personal communication with Janice F.
       Goldblum, National Academy of Sciences Archivist.

34   *Even the gifted Miss Skinker:* Dysart, *Chatham College,* p. 179.

34   *She worked as a reporter for the* Arrow: *Arrow,* January 13, 1928, p. 11,
       Chatham.

35   *In 1928, she published:* Ibid.

35   *One night in the lab:* Seif, "Letters from Rachel Carson," p. 35, Chatham.

35   *In late February 1928:* Carson to Mary Frye, February 22, 1928, in Seif,
       "Letters from Rachel Carson," pp. 33–34, Chatham. The after-party for
       the sledding outing would have taken place in the first-floor common
       room of Woodland Hall, the newer dormitory Carson moved into for
       her junior year. Woodland Hall, though expanded since Carson's time,
       is still there.

35   *Carson and another girl in biology:* Carson to Mary Frye, March 6, 1928, in
       Seif, "Letters from Rachel Carson," pp. 37–38, Chatham.

36   *She amused herself by dissecting a dogfish:* Ibid.

36   *In March 1928, friends arranged:* Ibid., and Carson to Mary Frye, March
       14, 1928, in Seif, "Letters from Rachel Carson," pp. 39–40, Chatham.

36   *Carson saw Bob Frye at least one more time:* Carson to Mary Frye, March 14, 1928, in Seif, "Letters from Rachel Carson," p. 40, Chatham.

36   *And then she never dated again:* At least that is the best that can be surmised. Nowhere in the long written record is there even a hint of Carson going out with anyone after leaving PCW. Shirley Briggs, in a filmed interview, suggested—unpersuasively—that Carson might have had "gentlemen friends" who took her to concerts or plays and that she had a "perfectly normal social life" when they worked together in Washington in the 1940s. But there is no other evidence of this. Carson's relationship with Dorothy Freeman will be fully discussed later on.

36   *Not long after Carson finalized her decision:* Carson to Mary Frye, March 14, 1928, in Seif, "Letters from Rachel Carson," p. 39, Chatham.

36   *A few weeks later, Carson learned:* Carson to Mary Frye, April 23, 1928, in Seif, "Letters from Rachel Carson," p. 42, Chatham.

37   *Disconsolate, Carson:* Ibid., and Carson to Mary Frye, July 23, 1928, in Seif, "Letters from Rachel Carson," p. 43, Chatham.

37   *She applied for admission:* Carson to Mary Frye, April 23, 1928, in Seif, "Letters from Rachel Carson," p. 41, Chatham; and Lear, *Rachel Carson,* p. 46.

37   *By the middle of her senior year:* Legal agreement between Carson and PCW putting up two of her father's lots as collateral, January 28, 1929, plus various notes, invoices, and correspondence between Carson and PCW, including two pleading letters to Margaret Stuart, the college's secretary and assistant treasurer, on February 27, 1931, and August 26, 1932.

37   *Skinker was replaced by:* Seif, "Letters from Rachel Carson," p. 45, Chatham.

37   *Whiting held a PhD:* Dysart, *Chatham College,* p. 179.

37   *But Whiting turned out:* Lear, *Rachel Carson,* pp. 48–49.

37   *To keep their spirits up:* Carson to Mary Frye, July 23, 1928, in Seif, "Letters from Rachel Carson," p. 44, Chatham.

37   *Carson's thoughts about life after PCW:* Carson to Dorothy Freeman, November 8, 1954, Muskie.

38   *When the poem was published in 1842:* In an email exchange with Brian Goldberg of the University of Minnesota English department, Goldberg

explained for me the darker, more militaristic themes of "Locksley Hall." He said Carson could certainly have read those lines as a call to adventure but only by contemplating them outside of the poem's overall context.

CHAPTER THREE: BIOLOGIZING

41 *The Marine Biological Laboratory at Woods Hole:* Maienschein, *100 Years Exploring Life, 1888–1988,* pp. 19–25, 51–71.

41 *During her time at PCW, Mary Scott Skinker:* Mary Scott Skinker to Mary Frye, July 11, 1928, in Seif, "Letters from Rachel Carson," pp. 26–30, Chatham.

41 *At Woods Hole, students collected:* Maienschein, *100 Years Exploring Life, 1888–1988,* p. 134.

42 *And the immersion in biology there:* Mary Scott Skinker to Mary Frye, July 11, 1928, in Seif, "Letters from Rachel Carson," p. 30, Chatham.

42 *Skinker sent Carson clippings:* Carson to Mary Frye, August 6, 1928, in Seif, "Letters from Rachel Carson," p. 45, Chatham.

42 *Carson, with a recommendation from:* Lear, *Rachel Carson,* p. 50.

42 *In June, she graduated magna cum laude:* Seif, "Letters from Rachel Carson," p. 55, Chatham.

42 *She went first to Baltimore:* Carson to Dorothy Thompson, August 4, 1929, in Seif, "Letters from Rachel Carson," pp. 56–58, Chatham. Carson's long, detailed account of this trip, including her first encounter with the sea, was almost dreamlike. For a young woman who had never been anywhere but who was smitten with the world and all its wonders—from the great ocean to the divine Miss Skinker—it was an unforgettable passage.

43 *Carson wrote to a friend that Woods Hole:* Carson to Dorothy Thompson, August 25, 1929, in Seif, "Letters from Rachel Carson," pp. 58–62, Chatham.

43 *Carson particularly liked exploring:* Seif, "Letters from Rachel Carson," p. 62, Chatham.

43 *The U.S. Bureau of Fisheries:* Ibid.

44 *Carson also enjoyed collecting trips:* "Memo for Mrs. Eales on Under the Sea-Wind," Beinecke. Linda Lear, who included Carson's ten-page memo about the origins of *Under the Sea-Wind* in the anthology *Lost*

Woods: The Discovered Writing of Rachel Carson, believes it was written as part of Carson's response to a standard author's questionnaire requested by a Mrs. Eales in the marketing department at Simon and Schuster. But in a letter to her editor at Simon and Schuster, Carson explained that Mrs. Eales was, in fact, a radio book reviewer in Washington, D.C., on whose program Carson had been interviewed. The memo, then, was background information Carson provided in advance for the interview (Carson to Maria Leiper, March 15, 1942, Beinecke).

44   *But Carson's two months of study:* Carson to Dorothy Thompson, August 25, 1929, in Seif, "Letters from Rachel Carson," pp. 58–62, Chatham. Carson also declared her intention to study the terminal nerve in reptiles on her application to the Marine Biological Laboratory, NCTC.

45   *"We thought we realized":* Ibid.

46   *Of the twenty-three students:* Maienschein, *100 Years of Exploring Life, 1888–1988,* p. 91.

46   *Ann Haven Morgan:* Morgan, *Field Book of Ponds and Streams.*

46   *But Carson had never shared:* Carson to Dorothy Thompson, November 10, 1929, in Seif, "Letters from Rachel Carson," p. 70. I'm extrapolating backward here from Carson's statement in this letter that at Johns Hopkins she was "getting used to tearing through the experiments as fast as the men do." Since her visit to the MBL a couple of months earlier was the first time she'd shared lab space with men, it seems she must have been impressed by their skills from the outset.

46   *At Johns Hopkins she briefly:* Seif, "Letter from Rachel Carson," p. 83, Chatham.

47   *Her days were long, beginning just after seven:* Carson to Dorothy Thompson, November 10, 1929, in Seif, "Letters from Rachel Carson," p. 70, Chatham.

47   *She told a friend that she liked living in Baltimore:* Ibid., p. 73.

47   *In her second year at Hopkins:* Carson to Dorothy Thompson, October 16, 1930, in Seif, "Letters from Rachel Carson," p. 81, Chatham. Carson admitted to Thompson that "impecuniousness" was for her a "constant affliction."

47   *and to help support her family:* Seif, "Letters from Rachel Carson," p. 74.

48   *In 1932, after many missed payments:* Carson to Margaret Stuart, August 26, 1932, Chatham.

48   *Much later, a neighbor:* Personal communication. I was told this anecdote, which has a ring of Depression-era truth, by Diana Post, president of the Rachel Carson Council, and her husband, Clifford C. Hall. They spoke to the neighbor in question on a visit to Stemmers Run.

48   *She gave up on snakes:* Carson to Dorothy Thompson, August 23, 1931, in Seif, "Letters from Rachel Carson," p. 92, Chatham.

48•   *"I don't have time to think any more":* Carson to Dorothy Thompson, October 16, 1920, in Seif, "Letters from Rachel Carson," p. 82, Chatham.

48   *Eventually Carson's adviser:* Carson to Dorothy Thompson, August 23, 1931, in Seif, "Letters from Rachel Carson," p. 92, Chatham.

48   *The pronephros is an embryonic precursor:* Carson, "Development of the Pronephros During the Embryonic and Early Larval Life of the Catfish (Ictalurus punctatus)," master's thesis, Johns Hopkins University, 1932, Beinecke.

48   *When Carson later received letters:* Lear, *Rachel Carson,* p. 76.

49   *She started teaching biology:* Carson to Dorothy Thompson, August 23, 1931, in Seif, "Letters from Rachel Carson," p. 91, Chatham.

49   *which was a long ride:* Seif, "Letters from Rachel Carson," p. 93, Chatham.

49   *but she did fall in love with an animal:* Ibid., pp. 94–95.

49   *In the same lab where she studied:* Ibid., p. 94.

50   *Carson thought another way:* Ibid.

50   *Robert Carson collapsed and died:* Lear, *Rachel Carson,* p. 77.

50   *At the urging of Mary Scott Skinker:* Ibid., p. 78; and Department of the Interior personnel records, Application for Federal Employment, April 20, 1943, NCTC.

50   *In October she was hired as a:* U.S. Department of the Interior personnel records, Personal History Statement, August 17, 1936, NCTC.

50   *Her job entailed:* U.S. Department of the Interior personnel records, Application for Federal Employment, April 20, 1943, NCTC.

50   *These duties consisted mainly of:* Carson, "The Real World Around Us," Beinecke. This was a speech Carson delivered on April 21, 1954 to the Theta Sigma Phi Matrix Table Dinner in Columbus, Ohio, in which she recounted some of the events of her early career.

50   *The job was, as Carson later reported:* U.S. Department of the Interior personnel records, Personal History Statement, August 17, 1936, NCTC.

50   *The Bureau of Fisheries had come into existence:* "Historical Note," U.S. Bureau of Fisheries, records ca. 1877–1948, Smithsonian Institution Archives, http://siarchives.si.edu/.

51   *The* Fish Hawk, *a 157-foot:* U.S. Department of the Navy, Naval Historical Center, http://www.history.navy.mil/.

51   *The* Albatross, *a majestic, white-hulled behemoth:* National Oceanic and Atmospheric Administration, Northeast Fisheries Science Center, http://nefsc.noaa.gov/history/.

51   Oceanic Ichthyology, *the 1895 classic:* "Historical Note," U.S. Bureau of Fisheries, records ca. 1877–1948, Smithsonian Institution Archives, http://siarchives.si.edu/.

51   *The commission continued to grow:* "Administrative History," National Archives Finding Guide to Records Group 22, and "Records of the U.S. Fish and Wildlife Service, Record Group 22," NARA.

52   *Carson's boss was Elmer Higgins:* U.S. Department of Commerce, Bureau of Fisheries, "Progress in Biological Inquiries," report of the U.S. commissioner of fisheries, 1936 and 1937, NARA.

53   *Carson's first newspaper story:* Baltimore Sun, March 1, 1936, Beinecke. Filed with the story clipping is a check receipt for twenty dollars.

54   *Carson also sold a couple of stories:* Richmond Times-Dispatch, March 20, 1938, Beinecke.

54   *In July 1936, Carson was appointed:* Department of Commerce, Appointment Division, personnel records appointment notice, July 13, 1936, NCTC.

CHAPTER FOUR: THE ENGLISH CONNECTION AND THE OCEAN DEEP

55   *Christmas Eve 1914 was clear and cold:* Weintraub, *Silent Night.* This condensed account is derived entirely from Stanley Weintraub's superbly detailed book about the Christmas Truce.

56   *Among the participants:* Anne Williamson, *Henry Williamson,* p. 42.

56   *The son of a stern bank clerk:* Ibid., p. 17.

56   *Williamson had been at the front:* Ibid., p. 44.

56   *Williamson had shaken hands:* Ibid., p. 42.

57   *The trenches on the front:* Ibid.

57   *Only a few weeks after:* Ibid., pp. 46–48.

57   *By March he was better:* Ibid., p. 49.

57   *That spring Williamson got accepted:* Ibid.

57   *and in March 1917:* Ibid., p. 54.

57   *Williamson again saw heavy fighting:* Ibid., pp. 56–57.

57   *He recovered and was returned to the war:* Ibid., p. 58.

57   *Williamson had begun a novel:* Ibid., p. 60.

57   *tearing around the countryside on a Norton motorcycle:* Ibid., p. 63.

57   *Sometime in the summer of 1919:* Ibid., p. 65.

58   *Lying down on the grass:* Jefferies, *Story of My Heart,* pp. 3–4.

58   *"Human suffering," he wrote:* Ibid., p. 119.

58   *His natural companions:* Ibid., p. 103.

59   *"I burn life like a torch":* Ibid., p. 95.

59   *Reading the book was a transforming experience:* Anne Williamson, *Henry Williamson,* p. 65.

59   *He'd also been intrigued:* Ibid., p. 96.

59   *Williamson began spending time:* Ibid., p. 94.

59   *A vivid and at times brutal:* Henry Williamson, *Tarka the Otter.*

60   *A few months after* Tarka *was published:* Lawrence, *Correspondence with Henry Williamson,* pp. 11–33. Lawrence's letter was written in Karachi in 1928 and forwarded to Williamson by their mutual friend, the writer and critic Edward Garnett.

60   *Their long, affectionate correspondence ended:* Ibid., pp. 179–81.

60   *The new book had been inspired:* Henry Williamson, *Clear Water Stream,* p. 189.

60   *It was a cottage named Shallowford:* Anne Williamson, *Henry Williamson,* p. 127. A "deer park" is a private hunting reserve on which deer are maintained. At one time there were hundreds of such hunting parks in England (*New York Times,* January 23, 1887).

61   *He wondered if anything in ordinary life:* Henry Williamson, *Clear Water Stream,* pp. 20–21.

61   *The Williamsons moved to Shallowford:* Anne Williamson, *Henry Williamson,* p. 129.

61   *So I rediscovered the delights of water:* Henry Williamson, *Clear Water Stream,* p. 31.

62   *Finally, in January 1935:* Anne Williamson, *Henry Williamson*, p. 179.

62   *Williamson would later recall:* Henry Williamson, *Goodbye, West Country*, p. 18.

62   *In his last letter to Lawrence:* Lawrence, *Correspondence with Henry Williamson*, p. 177.

62   *And yet by August 1935 the book:* Henry Williamson, *Goodbye, West Country*, p. 19.

63   *Salar knew of neither the fisherman:* Henry Williamson, *Salar the Salmon*, p. 154.

63   *Anita Moffett wrote a long, adoring review: New York Times*, June 21, 1936.

63   *Exhausted but happy to be done:* Henry Williamson, *Goodbye, West Country*, pp. 225–57. My version of this trip is based wholly on Williamson's lengthy account, which is coolly told and, of course, harrowing in hindsight.

64   *"He was very quick in his head movements":* Ibid., p. 244.

66   *Williamson had been favorably disposed:* Ibid., p. 9.

66   *He even thought it possible:* Ibid.

66   *The One to rule a better world:* Jefferies, *Story of My Heart*, pp. 120–21. In a passage that seems at odds with Jefferies's solitary nature, he argues that all human affairs would be better managed if "a man of humane breadth of view were placed at their head with unlimited power."

66   *There was a renewal in Germany:* Henry Williamson, *Goodbye, West Country*, p. 226. Williamson said that everywhere he went in Germany he met people who seemed to be breathing "extra oxygen" and who were firm in their belief that there would not be another war.

66   *In the spring of 1936, the* Dorset County Chronicle: Anne Williamson, *Henry Williamson*, pp. 190–91. Anne Williamson is Henry Williamson's daughter-in-law. In both her biography, *Henry Williamson*, and in an epilogue for T. E. Lawrence's *Correspondence with Henry Williamson*, she argues convincingly that Williamson's infatuation with Hitler and his appreciation for Germany between the wars were mainly the result of his experiences in the trenches in World War I and during the Christmas Truce, when he became convinced that the Germans were not a natural enemy. Less convincingly, she also contends that Williamson was never truly a fascist except in his belief that fascism in Germany would prevent another war. She concedes that Williamson's

wholesale invention of a planned radio program with Lawrence was inexplicable, though it was, she insists, made without "malicious intent" and probably in the genuine belief that, had he lived, Lawrence would have agreed to the idea.

67 *Whatever temporary luster this myth:* Anne Williamson, *Henry Williamson,* p. 22.

67 *In the spring of 1936:* Carson, "The Real World Around Us," Beinecke.

67 *This she did not do right away:* Carson, "Memo for Mrs. Eales on *Under the Sea-Wind,*" Beinecke.

67 *In the spring, Carson entered:* Carson to *Reader's Digest* contest editor, April 30, 1936, Beinecke.

67 *Then, in early 1937:* Lear, *Rachel Carson,* p. 84.

67 *In June, Carson finally sent:* Edward Weeks to Carson, July 8, 1937, Beinecke.

67 *In August, she received a check:* Statement from the *Atlantic Monthly,* August 2, 1937, Beinecke.

67 *Carson had the magazine:* Carson to Edward Weeks, July 18, 1937, Beinecke.

68 *The ocean is a place:* Carson, "Undersea," *Atlantic Monthly,* September 1937.

68 *Even the largest pair of hands:* Personal communication with diatom expert Mark Edlund of the Science Museum of Minnesota's St. Croix Watershed Research Station, who provided this estimate of how many diatoms two human hands might hold.

69 *If the underwater traveler might:* Carson, "Undersea," *Atlantic Monthly,* September 1937.

70 *As early as 1521, while exploring:* Murray and Hjort, *Depths of the Ocean,* p. 2.

70 *Early in 1840, during the British Antarctic Expedition:* Ibid., p. 5.

70 *But this was soon disproven:* Ibid., pp. 9–10.

70 *The picture of the world's oceans:* Corfield, *Silent Landscape,* pp. 2–13.

71 *By the time she returned to England:* Ibid., p. xiii.

71 *On March 23, 1875:* Ibid., p. 204.

71 *"In the silent deeps a glacial cold prevails":* Carson, "Undersea," *Atlantic Monthly,* September 1937.

72 *Individual elements are lost to view:* Ibid.

72   *Van Loon conveyed his enthusiasm:* Quincy Howe to Hendrik van Loon, September 9, 1937, Beinecke.

72   *Howe wrote to Carson:* Ibid.

73   *While the September issue of the* Atlantic: Hendrik van Loon to Carson, September 10, 1937, Beinecke.

73   *Carson, feeling unprepared:* Carson to Hendrik van Loon, October 14, 1937, Beinecke.

73   *In December 1937, van Loon told her:* Hendrik van Loon to Carson, December 18, 1937, Beinecke.

73   *finally went north in mid-January:* Mrs. Hendrik van Loon to Carson, January 7, 1938, Beinecke.

73   *Van Loon—a great man, she realized:* Carson, "Real World Around Us," Beinecke.

74   *Explaining her plan to van Loon:* Carson to Hendrik van Loon, February 5, 1938, Beinecke.

74   *A delighted van Loon wrote back:* Hendrik van Loon to Carson, February 6, 1938, Beinecke.

74   *whose editors were initially receptive:* Edward Weeks to Carson, June 7, 1938, Beinecke.

74   *But when she sent a sample:* Ibid., July 20, 1939, Beinecke. The date is correct; Carson had been toiling away for more than a year since she first proposed selling parts of the book to the *Atlantic*.

75   *Carson and the editors discussed:* Ibid., August 9, 1939, Beinecke.

75   *Meanwhile, she wrote some book reviews:* Statement from *Atlantic Monthly,* April 18, 1938, Beinecke.

75   *In April 1938, Carson implored the* Atlantic: Carson to A. G. Ogden, April 26, 1938, Beinecke.

75   *The magazine declined:* A. G. Ogden to Carson, April 27, 1938, Beinecke.

75   *But a month later they relented:* Ibid., May 23, 1938, Beinecke.

75   *I have been more impressed with Mr. Williamson's:* Carson to A. G. Ogden, April 26, 1938, Beinecke.

75   *In 1936, feeling dispirited with his life:* Williamson, *Goodbye, West Country,* pp. 100–105.

76   *When most of the line was out:* Ibid.

76   *A photograph of Williamson's eventual triumph:* Anne Williamson, *Henry Williamson,* p. 181.

76 *Carson's review of* Goodbye, West Country*:* Carson, "Nature through English Eyes," *Atlantic Monthly,* December 1938.

77 " *'I am all with you when it comes to' ":* Williamson, *Goodbye, West Country,* p. 10.

78 *As early as 1933, in a review: New York Times,* October 11, 1933.

78 *Writers in Germany were required:* Evans, *Third Reich in Power,* p. 158.

79 *Under National Socialism, German literature:* Ibid., p. 155.

79 *In 1937, Hitler had decreed: New York Times,* July 19, 1937.

79 *observed that city-dwelling modernists:* Williamson, *Goodbye, West Country,* p. 53.

79 *Carson wrote to van Loon that:* Carson to Hendrik van Loon, February 5, 1938, Beinecke.

80 *She asked van Loon to introduce her to:* Ibid.

80 *He believed that:* Beebe, *Half Mile Down,* p. 3. This entertaining book about William Beebe's underwater exploits is a page-turning classic.

80 *Staring down into the depths:* Ibid., p. 87.

80 *In 1929, Beebe met a man:* Ibid., pp. 87–137.

82 *On another occasion:* Ibid., pp. 153–54.

83 *Here, under a pressure:* Ibid., pp. 134–35.

83 *Between their deepwater dives:* Ibid., pp. 138–45.

84 *But as Carson began:* Carson to Hendrik van Loon, February 5, 1938, Beinecke.

84 *The business of an advance:* Ibid., June 2 and June 3, 1939, Beinecke.

85 *"I suspect the best thing is just to":* Ibid., June 2, 1939, Beinecke.

85 *Van Loon told her that:* Hendrik van Loon to Carson, June 25, 1939, Beinecke.

85 *Behind in his own work and testy:* Ibid., June 21, 1939, Beinecke.

85 *Carson meanwhile completed an outline:* Carson to Hendrik van Loon, June 20, 1939, Beinecke.

86 *Carson eventually agreed to:* Ibid., April 5, 1940, Beinecke. Carson explained all this to van Loon because she was worried at not having heard anything from Simon and Schuster after sending them well over twenty thousand words of the book. Now she hoped that van Loon might intercede and find out what was happening. But Carson never sent this letter, as on the same day she composed it she finally got a letter from Quincy Howe saying that everyone at Simon and Schuster

had read her manuscript and loved it. A day later she again wrote to van Loon, this time with the good news and a subtler plea that he might remind Howe of the promised additional advance, which Carson said she needed desperately (ibid., June 6, 1940, Beinecke).

86 *In the summer of 1939:* Department of the Interior personnel records, transfer Order, July 1, 1939, NCTC.

86 *which had recently increased to $2,300:* Department of Commerce personnel records, administrative promotion, June 16, 1939, NCTC.

86 *A year later, the bureau was merged:* Department of the Interior personnel records, consolidation order, June 27, 1940, NCTC.

86 *Carson was transferred from Baltimore:* Department of the Interior personnel records, station change, July 19, 1940, NCTC.

86 *In the fall of 1938, Carson:* Carson, field notes, Beinecke. There are a number of uncertainties surrounding Carson's research at Beaufort in 1938. Her surviving field notebooks indicate she was there in mid-September. However, Linda Lear writes that Carson's first visit was in July and that she evidently made more than one trip to Beaufort that year (Lear, *Rachel Carson,* pp. 93–94). The Bureau of Fisheries station at Beaufort, which is still there, now operating as the Center for Coastal Fisheries and Habitat Research for the National Oceanic and Atmospheric Administration, has no record of Carson's visit, though it is an entrenched local legend. Complicating things further—and perhaps showing how fully formed Carson's general scheme for the book was at this early stage—are "observations" included in Carson's field notes concerning spring migrations, which she obviously could not have witnessed in either midsummer or early fall. If Carson could imagine the place at a different season it is perhaps not unreasonable to permit her biographers something less than perfect specificity in deducing from the skimpy record exactly where she was and when that year.

86 *A quiet and for much of the year:* Personal observation. I spent several days in Beaufort and on the Outer Banks in the summer of 2011. I was given a tour of the Coastal Fisheries lab by its deputy director, Greg Piniak. Greg and David Johnson, director of the lab and an old Beaufort hand, also shared their considerable knowledge about Beaufort and its nearby sounds and islands.

87 *In 1899, the U.S. Fish Commission:* Wolfe, *A History of the Federal Biological Laboratory at Beaufort, North Carolina 1899–1999*, p. 1.

87 *Researchers at Beaufort conducted surveys:* Ibid., pp. 18–58.

87 *For several decades the station raised:* Ibid., pp. 65–68.

88 *Carson, who likely stayed:* Carson, "Memo for Mrs. Eales," Beinecke. Carson's staying in Atlantic Beach is conjecture on my part, based on it being the most likely location and also because of Carson's reference in this memo to the way people visiting the shore tend to "stay within sight of the piers and boardwalks of a resort beach," as this would have been a fair description of the scene at Atlantic Beach.

88 *This "lovely stretch of wild ocean beach":* Ibid.

88 *Carson now thought she could give:* Ibid.

89 *She was moved by the words:* Jefferies, *Pageant of Summer*, p. 9.

89 *Carson had a special affection:* Ibid., pp. 48–49. Carson cited this passage in her 1954 speech to Theta Sigma Phi, "The Real World Around Us," Beinecke. She said Jefferies's lines amounted to "a statement of the creed I have lived by."

89 *She made notes and wrote out:* Carson, field notes, Beinecke.

89 *"The crests of the waves":* Ibid.

90 *By the spring of 1940:* Carson to Hendrik van Loon, April 6, 1940, Beinecke.

90 *Shortly before the book's official publication:* Mark S. Watson to Carson, October 31, 1941, Beinecke.

90 *Carson would later admit:* Carson, "Memo for Mrs. Eales," Beinecke.

92 *Between the Chesapeake Capes:* Carson, *Under the Sea-Wind*, p. 105.

92 *She was delighted when the book:* Carson to Hazel Cole Shupp, September 17, 1941, Beinecke. Shupp, who arrived at PCW six years after Carson graduated, was a popular member of the English department faculty (Dysart, *Chatham College*, p. 196). Shupp had asked Simon and Schuster if she could get a photograph of Carson for the school.

92 *In a glowing review:* New York Times Sunday Book Review, November 23, 1941.

92 *A slightly more critical:* Saturday Review of Literature, December 27, 1941.

93 *Toward the end of January:* Maria Leiper to Carson, January 20, 1942, Beinecke. Leiper was Carson's editor at Simon and Schuster.

93 *Carson was gratified when:* Sonia Bleeker to Carson, March 10, 1942,

and Carson to Sonia Bleeker, March 15, 1942, Beinecke. Bleeker worked in the marketing department at Simon and Schuster, and went by the nickname "Sunnie."

93   *In fact, Simon and Schuster's London agent:* Marie Leiper to Carson, January 12, 1942, Beinecke. Leiper apparently enclosed the London agent's harsh assessment, which was dated December 11, 1942.

93   *Two days after the Japanese attack:* Mary Scott Skinker to Carson, December 9, 1941, Beinecke.

94   *but as Carson later put it:* Carson, "The Real World Around Us," Beinecke.

94   *For a while, Carson held out hope:* Carson to Sonia Bleeker, February 8, 1942, Beinecke.

94   *But a mailing to six hundred members:* Maria Leiper to Carson, September 21, 1942, Beinecke. This had been Carson's idea, one of many she sent to Simon and Schuster for marketing the book. The frustration and disappointment that can be read between the lines in Carson's suggestions are palpable.

94   *Carson also discussed:* Maria Leiper to Carson, January 7, 1942, Beinecke.

94   *Around the beginning of March 1942:* Carson to Maria Leiper, March 15, 1942.

94   *with a ten-page memo:* Carson, "Memo to Mrs. Eales," Beinecke.

94   *Shortly afterward, Carson was told:* Maria Leiper to Carson, March 26, 1942, Beinecke.

94   *Sales never reached:* Carson, handwritten note, Beinecke. Carson totaled up the sales for each year since the book's release on the back of the envelope from her January 1948 telephone bill.

94   *In the spring of 1948:* Carson to Tom Torre Bevans, March 27, 1948, Beinecke. Bevans apparently handled author contracts at Simon and Schuster.

95   *She wrote them a letter saying:* Carson to Maria Leiper, March 27, 1948, Beinecke.

CHAPTER FIVE: THIS BEAUTIFUL
AND SUBLIME WORLD

97   *Harold Ickes, Franklin Roosevelt's strong-willed:* Ickes, *Secret Diary of Harold Ickes,* vol. 2, p. 8.

97   *but in the end opposition in Congress:* Ibid., p. 257.

98   *In the early 1930s:* Egan, *Worst Hard Time,* p. 5.

98   *One of the worst swept through:* Ibid., p. 8.

98   *Five days later the storm reached Washington, D.C.:* Ibid., pp. 227–28.

98   *Before the month ended:* Ibid., p. 228.

98   *President Roosevelt, enamored of the idea:* Ibid., pp. 270–71.

98   *Some 220 million trees were planted:* Ibid., p. 310.

99   *The Bureau of Biological Survey:* "Administrative History," National
     Archives Finding Guide to Records Group 22, and "Records of the
     U.S. Fish and Wildlife Service, Record Group 22," NARA.

99   *In 1896, the agency changed its name:* Jenks Cameron, "The Bureau
     of Biological Survey: Its History, Activities and Organization,"
     Service Monographs of the United States Government,
     No. 54, 1929, pp. 1–49.

99   *The Biological Survey advised farmers and ranchers:* Vernon Bailey,
     "Directions for the Destruction of Wolves and Coyotes,"
     Bureau of Biological Survey Circular 55, April 17, 1907.

100 *In 1907 more than 1,800 wolves:* Cameron, "Bureau of Biological
     Survey," p. 46.

100 *In 1922 one of the agency's:* E. R. Kalmbach, Bureau of Biological Survey
     Special Report, No. 13, 1922, NARA.

101 *For wolves, the agency declared:* Cameron, "Bureau of Biological Survey,"
     p. 51.

101 *Despite its best efforts:* Ibid., pp. 177–78.

101 *Less noticed, but having a greater:* Ibid., pp. 55–56.

102 *In colonial America:* Ibid., p. 7.

102 *In the early 1800s:* Souder, *Under a Wild Sky.*

102 *Once, while traveling down:* Ibid., p. 176.

103 *The Boone and Crockett Club began organizing:* Nash, *Wilderness and the
     American Mind,* pp. 152–53. The Boone and Crockett ethos centered
     on the idea that man's true nature emerged and was best improved
     in a primitive environment.

103 *In 1900, Congress passed:* Clepper, *Leaders of American Conservation,* pp.
     194–95.

103 *In 1903, at the urging of:* U.S. Fish and Wildlife Service, Pelican Island
     National Wildlife Refuge, "History of Pelican Island," http://fws.gov/
     pelicanisland/history.html.

103   *Before European settlement of North America:* Isenberg, *Destruction of the Bison,* p. 25.

103   *In the early 1830s:* Ibid., p. 103.

104   *But much greater depredations:* Ibid., pp. 104–9.

104   *The destruction of the bison:* Dary, *Buffalo Book,* p. 127. Dary quotes President Grant's secretary of the interior, Columbus Delano, as saying that he "would not seriously regret the total destruction of the buffalo" as it would hasten the transformation of the nomadic Indians of the west into farmers.

104   *In the late 1860s:* David D. Smits, "The Frontier Army and the Destruction of the Buffalo: 1865–1883," *Western Historical Quarterly* 25, no. 3 (Autumn 1994): pp. 313–38.

104   *By the 1870s:* Isenberg, *Destruction of the Bison,* p. 130.

104   *As early as 1832, the artist George Catlin:* Ibid., p. 164.

104   *But in 1868, Congress approved:* Records of the Secretary of the Treasury Relating to Alaska 1868–1903, Record Group 22, NARA.

104   *Then in 1872, Grant signed:* Nash, *Wilderness and the American Mind,* p. 108, 112–13. Nash quotes the authorizing legislation from the United States Statutes at Large 1872, and notes that Congress seemed more interested in finding a suitable use for land that had little agricultural value than in preserving it in a pristine state, as only specific resources within its boundaries were to be maintained "in their natural condition."

105   *The federal government had also been brought into:* Worster, *Passion for Nature,* p. 403.

105   *In the interim a group of students and professors:* Ibid., pp. 328–29.

105   *In 1905, President Theodore Roosevelt established:* Meine, *Aldo Leopold,* p. 76.

105   *In a span of just four years:* Ibid., p. 77.

105   *In the summer of 1909, Leopold reported:* Ibid., pp. 87–89.

106   *Though inexperienced:* Ibid., pp. 91–94.

106   *In 1915, worried about the vanishing game:* Ibid., p. 146.

106   *Like other recruits to the Forest Service:* Ibid., p. 78.

106   *In 1921, Leopold published a paper:* Ibid., p. 194.

106   *and offered a definition:* Quoted in Meine, *Aldo Leopold,* p. 196.

106   *It had long been the subject of:* Nash, *Wilderness and the American Mind,*
       pp. 44–46. In the mid-1700s, during a period of growing appreciation
       for nature that was central to the Romantic period, Burke's *Philosophical
       Enquiry into the Origin of Our Ideas of the Sublime and Beautiful and Kant's
       Observations on the Feeling of the Beautiful and Sublime* explored the idea
       that wilderness was to be appreciated and experienced, not feared and
       avoided.

106   *eighteenth-century primitivists believed:* Nash, *Wilderness and the American
       Mind,* p. 47.

107   *but when Thoreau traveled into the remote forests:* Ibid., pp. 90–91.

107   *Wilderness, Roosevelt said:* Ibid., pp. 149–50.

107   *as it was thought to be by George Babbitt:* Lewis, *Babbitt.*

108   *Leopold in 1924 helped establish:* Meine, *Aldo Leopold,* pp. 196, 200–201.

108   *In 1929, Leopold gave a series of lectures:* Ibid., p. 266.

108   *Game Management marked the true beginning of:* Lannoo, *Leopold's Shack
       and Ricketts's Lab,* p. 34.

108   *earned Leopold a professorship at the University of Wisconsin:* Ibid., p. 47.

108   *In early 1934, Leopold was named:* Meine, *Aldo Leopold,* p. 315.

109   *The so-called Beck Committee was formed:* Ibid., pp. 315–16.

109   *The deliberations turned contentious:* Ibid., pp. 316–18.

109   *Another month after that:* Ibid., p. 319.

109   *In 1935 Aldo Leopold became:* Ibid., pp. 342–43. Leopold died of a heart
       attack suffered while fighting a brush fire near his Baraboo, Wisconsin,
       country shack in April 1948. He was not to be remembered fondly by
       Rachel Carson. In 1953, Oxford University Press published *Round River,*
       a compilation of essays and remembrances assembled from Leopold's
       journals. Oxford, hoping for something they could use in publicizing
       the book, sent it to their most famous author—Carson—for comment.
       This backfired when Carson discovered the book included hunting
       and trapping escapades in which an assortment of animals were killed
       or tormented. Carson told Oxford they could quote her but that they
       wouldn't want to, as *Round River* was in her opinion "a truly shocking
       book" that had left her in a state of "cold anger." Carson said she had
       until then "believed in the legend of Aldo Leopold" but had now
       been "rudely disillusioned." What Carson saw as "pious sentiments on

conservation" in the book only made Leopold a hypocrite in her mind. Leopold, she said, was a "completely brutal man" (Correspondence between Carson and Fon W. Boardman, Jr., head of advertising and publicity for Oxford University Press, in September 1953, Beinecke and NCTC). In a later irony, the FWS named two of the dormitories at the National Conservation Training Center in West Virginia "Leopold" and "Carson."

110 *when her group was transferred:* Department of the Interior personnel records, change of station notice, August 7, 1942, NCTC. This move was rumored and postponed over some months. Carson did not want to go and told Maria Leiper that every week's delay was a gift.

110 *The relocation was mercifully short:* Department of the Interior personnel records, intratransfer and change in status, April 21, 1943, NCTC.

110 *A year later, FWS created a new:* Department of the Interior personnel records, transfer and promotion, June 1, 1944, NCTC.

110 *after William Beebe had included two chapters:* Beebe, *Book of Naturalists,* pp. 478–95. Beebe combined Carson's two chapters on eel migration into one.

110 *Beebe wrote back that he'd be delighted:* William Beebe to Carson, February 1, 1945, Beinecke. Carson's letter to Beebe in this exchange is not preserved.

110 *Carson wrote to Beebe on a different matter:* Carson to William Beebe, October 26, 1945, Beinecke.

111 *Beebe wrote back to say:* William Beebe to Carson, November 1, 1945, Beinecke.

111 *Osborn answered that if:* Fairfield Osborn to William Beebe, November 5, 1945, and William Beebe to Carson, November 10, 1945, Beinecke.

111 *On November 12, 1944:* FWS press release, November 12, 1945, NCTC. FWS press releases sometimes listed more than one author and/or contact person. In this case the contacts were "Allredge" or "Carson." Whoever drafted the release, both were familiar with its contents.

111 *She promptly proposed:* Merle Crowell to Carson, November 28, 1944, Beinecke. Crowell was a senior editor at *Reader's Digest.*

111 *That same month she published:* Carson, "The Bat Knew It First," *Collier's,* November 18, 1944.

111 *In April 1945:* Jack Goodman to Carson, June 6, 1944, and Carson to Jack Goodman, June 7, 1944, Beinecke. Goodman was a member of the *Transatlantic*'s editorial committee. Carson was able to respond in a single day because Goodman was based in New York.

111 *A few months later, Carson found:* Carson, "Ace of Nature's Aviators," *Coronet,* November 1944; and Merle Crowell to Carson, November 28, 1944, Beinecke.

111 *In early 1946, Carson pitched:* Carson to Maria Caporale, February 20, 1946, and March 10, 1946, Maria Caporale to Carson, February 22, 1946, and Edward M. Stode to Carson, March 24, 1946, Beinecke.

112 *Months before putting out an FWS:* FWS press release, December 21, 1947, NCTC; J. A. Umhoefer to Carson, n.d., Carson to Oscar Dystal, September 23, 1947, and Carson to Merle Crowell, September 9, 1947, Beinecke.

112 *The three of them sometimes lunched together:* Transcript of Shirley Briggs's interview for "Rachel Carson's Silent Spring," an installment of the *American Experience* series on PBS, February 20, 1992, Lear Collection.

112 *Briggs found Carson outwardly:* Ibid.

112 *Howe thought she seemed:* Linda Lear interview with Kay Howe Roberts, June 22, 1994, Lear Collection.

112 *Briggs, in a letter to her mother:* Shirley Briggs to her mother, December 13, 1945, Lear Collection.

112 *In the fall of 1945, she and Shirley Briggs:* Ibid., October 16, 1945, Lear Collection.

113 *One of these papers:* Oscar Elton Sette, "Biology of the Atlantic Mackerel (Scomber scombrus) of North America," U.S. Department of the Interior Fishery Bulletin 38, 1943, NCTC.

113 *On August 10:* FWS press release, August 10, 1945, NCTC.

113 *A couple of weeks later:* Ibid., August 22, 1945, NCTC.

114 *Nine months later:* Ibid., May 18, 1946, NCTC.

114 *In the spring of 1946:* Transcript of Shirley Briggs's interview for "Rachel Carson's Silent Spring," an installment of the *American Experience* series on PBS, Lear Collection.

114 *The series, titled Conservation in Action:* Lear, *Rachel Carson,* p. 132.

114 *Over the course of several days:* Ibid., p. 133.

115 *The government had purchased its nine thousand:* Carson, *Chincoteague: A National Wildlife Refuge,* Conservation in Action 1, 1947, NCTC.

115 *Assateague is one of the barrier islands:* Ibid.

116 *Because Chincoteague was primarily:* Ibid.

117 *Settled by English immigrants:* Randall, *Newburyport and the Merrimack,* p. 7. If the reader detects an affection for and familiarity with Newburyport and Plum Island it is because I lived there once.

117 *Since the earliest settlement:* Weare, *Plum Island,* pp. 43–48.

117 *In 1929 a small, private bird sanctuary:* Ibid., pp. 89–91.

118 *The local residents:* Doyle, *Life in Newburyport 1900-1950,* p. 245.

118 *When Carson and Howe boarded the train:* Kay Howe to Shirley Briggs, September 25, 1946, Beinecke.

118 *The ocean, rising over a level bottom:* Personal observation. The description of Plum Island is based on my experience from when I lived in Newburyport and a subsequent research visit I made to the area in the summer of 2010.

118 *Standing at the water's edge:* Carson, *Parker River: A National Wildlife Refuge,* Conservation in Action 2, 1947, NCTC.

119 *Carson and Howe toured the island:* Carson to Shirley Briggs, September 28, 1946, Beinecke.

119 *They found a restaurant in Newburyport:* Ibid.

119 *Howe hoped the weather:* Kay Howe to Shirley Briggs, September 25, 1946, Beinecke.

119 *There were rumors in town:* Carson to Shirley Briggs, September 28, 1946, Beinecke.

119 *In the end:* Kay Howe to Shirley Briggs, September 25, 1946, Beinecke.

119 *Carson began the second Conservation in Action pamphlet:* Carson, *Parker River.*

120 *A striking fact about the Atlantic flyway:* Ibid.

120 *Parker River was the only:* Ibid.

121 *"As you drive out from the town":* Ibid.

122 *Carson had learned more:* Ibid.

123 *The fifth in the series:* Carson, *Guarding Our Wildlife Resources,* Conservation in Action 5, 1948, NCTC.

124 *"For all the people":* Ibid.

124 *In the spring of that year:* Meine, *Aldo Leopold,* p. 517.

124 *Four publishers had already turned it down:* Ibid., pp. 509, 511, and 517; and Meine, *Correction Lines,* pp. 152–53. Rejections had come from the University of Minnesota Press, Macmillan, Knopf, and William Sloan Associates. The latter didn't literally reject the book but failed to act before Oxford bought it. Knopf, which passed on several versions of the manuscript, remained interested and had continued to discuss how the book might be reworked.

124 *But Leopold died unexpectedly:* Meine, *Aldo Leopold,* p. 520.

124 *Oxford determined the book could still:* Ibid., p. 524.

124 *In one of the book's essays:* Leopold, *Sand County Almanac,* p. 204.

124 *Leopold wrote that of the:* Ibid., p. 210.

124 *When* A Sand County Almanac *was reissued:* Meine, *Aldo Leopold,* pp. 525–26.

125 *"A thing is right," Leopold wrote:* Leopold, *A Sand County Almanac,* pp. 224–25.

125 *"When we see the land as a community":* Ibid., p. viii.

125 *"That land is a community":* Ibid., pp. viii–ix.

126 *In the fifth Conservation in Action booklet:* Carson, *Guarding Our Wildlife Resources,* NCTC.

126 *Carson had managed to take:* Carson to Maria Leiper, November 18, 1946, Beinecke.

126 *They rented a cottage on the eastern shore:* Carson to Shirley Briggs, July 14, 1946, Beinecke.

127 *in a corner of the Pratt Library in Baltimore:* Carson to Henry Beston, May 14, 1954, Beinecke.

127 *Beston was born in 1888:* Wilding, *Henry Beston's Cape Cod,* p. 7.

127 *Beston attended Harvard:* Ibid., pp. 9–10.

127 *Beston was nearly killed:* Ibid., p. 10.

127 *He returned to Massachusetts:* Ibid., p. 12.

127 *In 1923, Beston did a magazine piece:* Ibid., p. 15.

127 *In 1925 he bought thirty-two acres:* Ibid., pp. 1–2, 51–54, and 89.

128 *One night when the surf was churning:* Ibid., pp. 21–22.

128 *Beston stayed at the Fo'castle:* Ibid., p. 18.

128 *Beston, who was over six feet tall:* Ibid., p. 30. Wilding quotes from an interview Beston gave to the *New York Times.*

128 *Outermost cliff and solitary dune:* Beston, *Outermost House,* pp. 5–6.

129 *Night is very beautiful:* Ibid., p. 166.

129 *In 1940, while she was working on:* Lear, *Rachel Carson,* pp. 101–2; and
Dorothy Algire to Paul Brooks, February 15, 1970, Beinecke. Dorothy
Algire, formerly Dorothy Hamilton, was a colleague of Carson's at the
U.S. Bureau of Fisheries and at Woods Hole. She was with Carson on
the day they visited Beston's little house.

130 *Everywhere around the world:* J. B. Hersey and H. B. Moore, "Progress
Report on Scattering Layer Observations in the Atlantic Ocean,"
Transactions 29, no. 3 (June 1948), Beinecke. This paper was in Carson's
research files for *The Sea Around Us.*

130 *Researchers eventually determined:* Tom Garrison, *Oceanography,*
pp. 447 and 449.

130 *She made plans:* U.S. Department of the Interior, records for the
Albatross III, "Instructions for Cruise No. 10," Lear Collection. On
October 1 and 2, 1948, the ship stopped at Boothbay Harbor, Maine,
for the annual meeting of the Atlantic Fisheries Biologists. For some
reason, Carson would later pretend that a cruise she made with Marie
Rodell aboard the *Albatross III* the following year was the first time
any woman had ever done so. But the listed "collaborators" on the
October 1948 trip included Joseph Puncochar, Jean Hartshorne, and
Rachel Carson.

131 *Equipped with sonar:* U.S. Department of the Interior records, "Albatross
III," March 19, 1948, Lear Collection.

131 *Carson began enlisting a group:* Carson to Henry Bigelow, August 22,
1948, Beinecke.

131 *He didn't, but:* Henry Bigelow to Carson, August 26, 1948, and March
14, 1950, Beinecke.

131 *One university professor:* R. G. Hussey to Carson, March 18, 1950,
Beinecke. Hussey was at the University of Michigan. Carson consulted
with him about the geology of the sea floor.

132 *A no-doubt skeptical Carson:* Carson to Thor Heyerdahl, September 23,
1948. Carson's letter is not preserved but is referenced by Heyerdahl in
his reply on October 19, 1948, Beinecke.

132 *Heyerdahl wrote back:* Thor Heyerdahl to Carson, October 19, 1948,
Beinecke.

132   *She waited more than a year:* Carson to Thor Heyerdahl, January 9, 1950, Beinecke.

132   *Heyerdahl, civil but again testy:* Thor Heyerdahl to Carson, February 2, 1950, Beinecke.

133   *Carson had meanwhile signed on:* Lear, *Rachel Carson,* p. 149.

133   *Undaunted, Carson sent Rodell:* Carson to Marie Rodell, December 5, 1948, Beinecke.

CHAPTER SIX: AUTHOR TRIUMPHANT

135   *By February 1949, Carson:* Carson to Marie Rodell, February 23, 1949, Beinecke.

135   *A month later she told Rodell:* Ibid., March 26, 1949, Beinecke.

135   *In April, Rodell:* Marie Rodell to Philip Vaudrin, April 12, 1949, Beinecke.

135   *By May she was in serious discussions:* Marie Rodell, handwritten notes from telephone conversations with Philip Vaudrin on May 4 and May 5, 1950, Beinecke.

135   *On June 3, 1949:* Philip Vaudrin to Marie Rodell, June 3, 1949, Beinecke.

135   *Carson resisted this:* Carson to Marie Rodell, June 8, 1949, Beinecke.

136   *Meanwhile, Carson made plans:* Carson to William Beebe, April 5, 1949, and William Beebe to Carson, July 5, 1949, Beinecke.

136   *Shirley Briggs accompanied:* The account of Carson's diving trip is recorded in a series of handwritten field notes spanning the years 1940 through 1951, Beinecke. Shirley Briggs also took some photographs on this trip, several of which are in the Lear Collection at Connecticut College.

136   *She also unself-consciously wrote to:* Carson to William Beebe, August 26, 1949, Beinecke.

136   *A couple of weeks later Carson was off again:* U.S. Department of the Interior records for the *Albatross III,* "Instructions for Cruise No. 26," Lear Collection; and *Frontiers,* October 1950. Rodell's nicely written magazine piece about the cruise includes the odd claim that she and Carson were the "first women ever to spend more than a few hours aboard" the ship. In a memo Carson wrote for her British publisher on the origins of *The Sea Around Us,* Carson repeats this false history.

In the same memo, Carson also mentions having done "a little helmet diving" as part of her research. Carson—perhaps sacrificing accuracy in the interest of a better story—again overlooked her first cruise on the *Albatross III* in her later speech at a Theta Sigma Phi dinner, "The Real World Around Us."

137 *It was a hot morning:* Ibid.

137 *Not long after returning:* Lear, *Rachel Carson*, pp. 172–73; Philip Vaudrin to Carson, October 4, 1949, and Carson to Philip Vaudrin, October 6, 1949, Beinecke. Lear writes that Carson discussed the Fuertes project with Rodell during the cruise aboard the *Albatross III* in July, and this seems probable. In her October letter to Vaudrin she says she is going to go over the Fuertes paintings with Rodell.

138 *In the summer of 1950:* Paul Brooks to Carson, July 20, 1950, Carson to Paul Brooks, July 28, 1950, and Paul Brooks to Carson, September 1, 1950, Beinecke. In his September 1 letter, Brooks formally asked Carson if she would do the book.

138 *Carson told Marie Rodell:* Carson to Marie Rodell, September 5, 1950, Beinecke.

138 *She applied for a grant:* Carson, application to the Eugene F. Saxton Memorial Trust, n.d., ca. November 1948, Beinecke.

139 *In July 1949:* Amy Flashner to Carson, July 14, 1949, Beinecke. Flashner was the secretary of the Saxton Trust.

139 *Elated, Carson dashed off:* Carson to Amy Flashner, July 24, 1949, Beinecke.

139 *Carson got a letter back:* Amy Flashner to Carson, August 4, 1949, Beinecke.

139 *Furious, Carson pointed out:* Carson to Amy Flashner, August 8, 1949, Beinecke.

139 *They wrote to her again:* Amy Flashner to Carson, August 11, 1949, Beinecke.

139 *Eventually, Marie Rodell stepped in:* Ibid., August 23, 1949, Beinecke.

140 *Carson wrote to the trust:* Carson to Amy Flashner, August 30, 1949, Beinecke.

140 *She also received a courtesy copy of:* Philip Vaudrin to Carson, October 4, 1949, Beinecke.

140 *which she said she looked forward to:* Carson to Philip Vaudrin, October 6, 1949, Beinecke.

140   *She sent seven chapters:* Marie Rodell to Edward Weeks, January 6, 1950, Beinecke.

140   *which turned them down:* Charles W. Morton to Marie Rodell, March 3, 1950, Beinecke. Morton was an associate editor of the *Atlantic.*

140   *More rejections stacked up:* Correspondence between Marie Rodell and various magazine editors, 1950, Beinecke.

140   *Although most of the rejections were polite:* Helen Grey to Marie Rodell, April 20, 1950, Beinecke. Grey was manuscript editor at *Town & Country.*

140   *In April 1950:* Carson to Philip Vaudrin, April 3, 1950, and Marie Rodell to Amy Flashner, April 14, 1950, Beinecke. In fact, Carson confessed that they'd tried out so many titles that she'd lost track as to whether this one had been previously proposed. Evidently it had been, as a letter to Carson from the publicity department at Oxford had referred to the book as *The Sea Around Us* back in January (Catherine S. Scott to Carson, January 3, 1950, Beinecke).

141   *The river is within us:* Eliot, *The Four Quartets.*

141   *"So long ago that we do not know":* Draft fragment, Beinecke. Carson put this down in one of her many small brown spiral notebooks.

141   *and in June 1950, Oxford said:* Carson to Henry Bigelow, July 17, 1950, Beinecke.

141   Science Digest *offered fifty dollars:* G. B. Clementson to Marie Rodell, June 5, 1950, Beinecke. Clementson was the managing editor of *Science Digest.*

142   *She heard from Edith Oliver:* Marie Rodell to G. B. Clementson, June 8, 1950, and Marie Rodell to Carson, June 13, 1950, Beinecke.

142   *By midsummer Oliver had:* Edith Oliver to Marie Rodell, July 11, 1950, Beinecke.

142   *She'd also begun sending the material:* Edith Oliver to Marie Rodell, July 17, 1950, Beinecke.

142   *"Darn the* New Yorker*":* Carson to Marie Rodell, July 17, 1950, Beinecke.

142   *Oliver promised Rodell:* Edith Oliver to Marie Rodell, July 17, 1950, Beinecke.

142   *Rodell, meanwhile, sold:* Paul Pickerel to Marie Rodell, August 18, 1950, Beinecke. Pickerel was the managing editor of the *Yale Review.*

142 *She sold another:* Marie Rodell to G. B. Clementson, July 21, 1950, Beinecke.

143 Reader's Digest *turned down:* Merle Crowell to Marie Rodell, July 27, 1950, Beinecke.

143 *Sometime around the middle of August:* Carson to Marie Rodell, August 17, 1950, Beinecke.

143 *A month later, Carson wrote to Rodell:* Ibid., September 10, 1950, Beinecke.

143 *Carson was going to have a:* Ibid.

143 *"The operation will probably turn out":* Ibid., September 13, 1950, Beinecke.

143 *Carson dashed off:* Ibid., n.d., ca. October 1950, Beinecke.

144 *Carson was impatient with Oxford:* Ibid., October 19, 1950, and December 9, 1950, Beinecke.

144 *Rodell reminded her that:* Marie Rodell to Carson, October 23, 1950, Beinecke.

144 *She recklessly told Rodell:* Carson to Marie Rodell, October 2, 1950, Beinecke.

144 *In October 1950:* Carson, Guggenheim Fellowship application, October 14, 1950, Beinecke.

144 *a $900 advance from Houghton Mifflin:* James F. Mathias to Carson, March 29, 1951, and Guggenheim formal announcement, April 16, 1951, Beinecke.

144 *Beebe told her he couldn't understand:* William Beebe to Carson, November 7, 1950, Beinecke.

144 *Then in early December 1950:* Marie Rodell to Paul Pickerel, December 11, 1950, Beinecke.

144 *Carson mentioned to Rodell:* Carson to Marie Rodell, January 30, 1951, Beinecke.

145 *Carson had been promoted:* U.S. Department of the Interior, personnel records, promotion, February 1, 1950, NCTC.

145 *Carson hated this prospect:* Carson to Marie Rodell, January 7, 1951, Beinecke.

145 *March 1951 brought mixed news:* Lear, *Rachel Carson,* pp. 191 and 193.

145 *a happy development that was partially offset when:* Marie Rodell to Carson, March 21, 1951, Beinecke.

145 *Astonishingly,* Vogue *magazine bought:* Carson to Allen Talmey, March 29, 1951, Beinecke. Talmey was feature editor for *Vogue.*

145 *In April, Carson got:* Carson to Henry Z. Walck, April 6, 1951, Beinecke. Walck was president of Oxford University Press.

145 *In May, William Shawn sent:* William Shawn to Marie Rodell, May 9, 1951, Beinecke.

145 *Rodell deducted her 10 percent:* Marie Rodell to Carson, May 11, 1951, Beinecke.

145 *The next month, Carson applied for:* U.S. Department of the Interior personnel records, request for leave without pay, June 4, 1951, NCTC.

146 *She told Rodell she believed:* Carson to Marie Rodell, n.d., ca. July 1951, Beinecke.

146 *The* New Yorker *reported that:* Washington Star, July 8, 1951. A word about newspaper and magazine citations: For most of her publishing career Carson had a clipping service that routinely sent her copies of articles about her work from across the country and around the world. A great many, but not all, of those I cite in these notes are found in the Rachel Carson Papers in the Beinecke Rare Book and Manuscript Library at Yale. But because such clippings are not unique to this collection I have not given it as the primary repository. Suffice it to say that the thousands of articles at the Beinecke, as well as references to many others I retrieved elsewhere, were invaluable in my research.

146 *Walter Winchell, the prominent:* New York Mirror, June 6, 1951.

147 *"an introduction to oceanography":* Carson to Philip Vaudrin, December 16, 1950, Beinecke.

147 *She began at the beginning:* Carson, *Sea Around Us,* epigraph, p. 3.

148 *Beginnings are apt to be shadowy:* Ibid., pp. 3–4.

150 *Imagine a whole continent of naked rock:* Ibid., pp. 8–9.

150 *Carson said that the "backbone" of the work:* Carson, "Origins of the book *The Sea Around Us,*" 1952, Beinecke. This is the memo Carson prepared for her publisher in London.

150 *Most of man's habitual tampering:* Carson, *Sea Around Us,* pp. 95–96.

152 *Where and when the ocean will halt:* Ibid., pp. 99–100.

153 *Writing in the* New York Herald Tribune: *The New York Herald Tribune,* July 15, 1951.

153 *Leonard wrote that the errors poets make:* New York Times Sunday Book Review, July 1, 1951.

153 *though the reviewer for the* Indianapolis Times: *Indianapolis Times,* July 7, 1951.

153 *The critic at* Newsweek: *Newsweek,* July 16, 1951.

154 *Carson landed on the cover:* Saturday Review of Literature, July 7, 1951.

154 *The* Buffalo Evening News *agreed:* Buffalo Evening News, July 7, 1951.

154 *A week after its review:* New York Times Sunday Book Review, July 8, 1951.

154 *In a publicity piece:* Carson, "Origins of the book The Sea Around Us," 1952, Beinecke.

155 *Proving that everyone seemed to:* Christian Science Monitor, January 3, 1952.

155 *Society columnist Mary Van Rensselaer Thayer:* San Francisco Argonaut, June 29, 1951.

155 *In a short essay she wrote:* New York Herald Tribune Book Review, October 7, 1951.

156 *"In minor ways I am a disappointment":* Ibid.

156 *The* Cleveland Plain Dealer *referred to Carson:* Cleveland Plain Dealer, July 1, 1951.

156 *The* Boston Post *described her:* Boston Post, July 8, 1951.

156 *Among Carson's fans were:* Jane Barkley to Carson, June 22, 1951, Catherine Nimitz to Carson, n.d., ca. May 1951, and Thor Heyerdahl to Carson, May 3, 1951, Beinecke. Jane Barkley was Vice President Alben Barkley's wife. Catherine Nimitz was Admiral Chester Nimitz's wife. Barkley, Nimitz, and Heyerdahl all received advance copies of The Sea Around Us.

157 *Carson also got a generous:* Quincy Howe to Carson, July 30, 1951, Beinecke.

157 *One letter that probably impressed itself:* R. M. Much to Carson, October 20, 1951, Beinecke.

157 *A man named Alfred Glassel:* Alfred C. Glassel, Jr., to Carson, June 11, 1952, Beinecke.

158 *Even Marie Rodell was suddenly:* Washington Daily News, July 4, 1951. The responses, almost always glowing but sometimes strange, continued for years. In 1957, Carson got a letter from a young physician in the pathology department at the University of Michigan Medical School in Ann Arbor. The doctor, who seemed passionate about the subject, wanted more information about bathyspheres and other deep-diving devices. He

wondered if Carson might have access to technical information on such equipment not available to the general public—and, if such details were not "restricted," whether she might share them. He also said how much he liked her book and apologized if his inquiry was an imposition. The letter was signed "Very truly yours, Jack Kevorkian, M.D." (Dr. Jack Kevorkian to Carson, December 4, 1957, Beinecke).

158 *She had insisted that Oxford abandon:* Carson to Philip Vaudrin, December 16, 1950, Beinecke.

158 *Carson and Rodell were angry with Oxford:* Marie Rodell to Henry Z. Walck, August 23, 1951, Beinecke.

158 *Not so believably, Oxford pleaded:* Henry Z. Walck to Carson, August 7, 1951, Beinecke.

158 *she complained even more bitterly:* Carson to Henry Z. Walck, n.d., ca. fall 1951, and Marie Rodell to Henry Z. Walck, August 14, 1951, Beinecke.

159 The Sea Around Us *made the: New York Times,* July 22, 1951.

159 *It was still at number five a week later:* Ibid., July 29, 1951.

159 *In mid-August it was at:* Ibid., August 19, 1951.

159 *and by early September:* Ibid., September 2, 1951.

159 *In November 1951, as sales of:* William M. Oman to Carson, November 9, 1951, Beinecke. Oman was vice president of Oxford University Press.

159 *There was some question:* William M. Oman to Marie Rodell, November 30, 1951, Beinecke.

159 *In December, Rodell sold:* A.B.C. Whipple to Marie Rodell, December 18, 1951, Beinecke. Whipple was an editor at *Life.*

159 *On April 20, 1952: New York Times,* April 20 and 27, 1952.

159 *Sales of* The Sea Around Us: *Chicago Tribune,* February 3, 1952.

159 *One was that more than: Memphis Commercial Appeal,* March 18, 1952.

160 *Still another claim:* Ibid.

160 *Both she and Rodell thought:* Marie Rodell to William M. Oman, August 5, 1952, Beinecke. Carson's dubiousness about the sales figures for *Under the Sea-Wind* were conveyed in an exchange of letters with Rodell that summer.

160 *Carson and Rodell also quarreled:* Carson to Marie Rodell, n.d., ca. August 1952, Beinecke.

160 *The previous October, Carson had spent a strange: New York Herald Tribune,* October 17, 1951.

161 *Carson had campaigned to have:* Carson to Philip Vaudrin, July 10, 1950, and Philip Vaudrin to Carson, July 14 and 26, 1950, Beinecke. Carson's letter is not preserved but is referenced in Vaudrin's of July 14.

161 *In April 1952:* Lear, *Rachel Carson,* pp. 220–21.

161 *she learned she'd won:* Fon W. Boardman, Jr., to Carson, January 8, 1952, Beinecke. Carson had already received a telephone call from Henry Walck with the news.

161 *Although she misplaced the original letter:* Carson to Fon W. Boardman, Jr., January 15, 1952, Beinecke.

161 *as there was a heavy schedule of interviews:* Fon W. Boardman, Jr., to Carson, January 18, 1952, Beinecke.

161 *The award ceremony was held:* Ibid., January 8, 1952, Beinecke.

161 *At the head table with Carson: New York Herald Tribune,* January 30, 1952.

161 *Jones was widely rumored to have been: Boston Herald,* February 10, 1952; and *Providence Journal,* February 17, 1952.

162 *In her acceptance speech:* Carson, acceptance speech, National Book Award for Nonfiction, January 29, 1952, Beinecke.

162 *We live in a scientific age:* Ibid.

162 *"Perhaps if we reversed the telescope":* Ibid.

162 *RKO, the movie company: Publishers Weekly,* January 12, 1952; and Marie Rodell to William M. Oman, August 22, 1952, Beinecke.

163 *When Carson saw a first cut of the movie:* Carson to RKO, January 19, 1952, and Henry Z. Walck to RKO, January 21, 1952, Beinecke.

163 *Marie Rodell complained to Oxford:* Marie Rodell to Henry Z. Walck, January 29, 1952, Beinecke.

163 *In February, Allen and Carson:* Carson to RKO, February 29, 1952, Beinecke.

163 *The finished film:* Personal observation. The film is available on DVD and is, I must say, an unusual period piece.

163 *it would "cheapen and misrepresent":* Carson to Henry Z. Walck, April 12, 1953, Beinecke.

163 *In March 1952:* Marie Rodell to Carson, March 24, 1952, Beinecke.

164 *In the spring of 1952, Carson got away:* Carson to Fon W. Boardman, Jr., March 14, 1952, Beinecke.

164 *On her resignation:* U.S. Department of the Interior, personnel records, resignation, May 12, 1952, NCTC.

164   *Carson bought some land on Southport Island:* Carson to Marie Rodell, September 9, 1952, Beinecke.

164   *It was long and low:* Personal observation. In the summer of 2010, I spent a week at Carson's cottage, which is owned by Roger Christie and his wife, Wendy Sisson. The cottage has changed little in the past half century. The shoreline and its tide pools evolve slowly and continuously, the tides rise and fall, and the long swell running into Sheepscot Bay from the Atlantic is never the same, and so all these things, too, are just as they were in Carson's time.

165   *"blowing and rolling":* Carson to Marie Rodell, September 9, 1952, Beinecke.

165   *Back in New York, Marie Rodell:* Marie Rodell to Carson, November 17, 1952, Beinecke.

CHAPTER SEVEN: DOROTHY

169   *In 1953, Southport Island had:* "Annual Report of the Town Officers of the Town of Southport," year ended January 31, 1953, Southport Memorial Library.

169   *the actress Margaret Hamilton:* Personal communication with Ron Orchard of the Southport Historical Society and Hendricks Hill Museum.

169   *In the 1880s a Massachusetts Civil War veteran:* Personal communication with Stanley Freeman, Jr.

170   *In 1939, Stan and Dorothy:* Ibid.

170   *On Stan Freeman's birthday, July 15, 1951:* Ibid.; Dorothy Freeman's unpublished account of her early friendship with Rachel Carson, and Dorothy Freeman's "round robin" letter, February 17, 1953, Muskie. The "round robin" letters were periodic updates exchanged among Dorothy Freeman and her friends, whom she often greeted in the letters as "Dear Gals."

171   *But Carson did respond:* Carson to Dorothy Freeman, December 15, 1952, Muskie. This letter, like the great majority in the Dorothy Freeman collection at the Edmund S. Muskie Archives and Special Collections Library at Bates College, was published in *Always, Rachel: The Letters of Rachel Carson and Dorothy Freeman 1952–1964,* edited and annotated by Dorothy's granddaughter, Martha Freeman.

171   *A half year later, on June 2, 1953:* Dorothy Freeman diary entry, Muskie.

171   *called on Rachel Carson at her new cottage:* Ibid.

172 *Carson advised them to wear sneakers and pants:* Carson to Dorothy Freeman, September 3, 1953, Muskie.

172 *It was a happy affair:* Ibid.

172 *Dorothy was startled by the wealth of sea life:* Dorothy Freeman's "round robin" letter, September 21, 1953, Muskie. This account of the collecting party also includes Dorothy's initial impression of Carson.

173 *Stan had given Carson a picture:* Carson to Dorothy Freeman, September 10, 1953, Muskie.

173 *The Freemans had also commiserated:* Ibid., September 3, 1953, Muskie.

173 *She sent Dorothy a farewell note:* Ibid., September 10, 1953, Muskie.

174 *Carson sent off a long letter:* Ibid., September 28, 1953, Muskie. Dorothy (whose early letters to Carson are not preserved) had apparently mentioned that she and Stan hoped to see Irwin Allen's movie version of *The Sea Around Us.* Carson expressed her dislike of the film and said she'd been gratified when a reviewer for the *Washington Post* had "roasted" the script. Carson said, however, that she would be "quite prepared to forgive" her new friend if Dorothy saw the movie and somehow enjoyed it.

174 *A week later, Carson wrote again:* Carson to Dorothy Freeman, October 5, 1953, Muskie.

175 *Carson went off to Myrtle Beach:* Ibid., November 5 and 6, 1953, Muskie. Letters that ran on from one day to the next or that started in one part of a day and were continued at a later hour became a fixture in the Carson-Freeman correspondence.

177 *In mid-November, Dorothy proposed that:* Carson to Dorothy Freeman, November 19 and 20, 1953, Muskie.

177 *She told Dorothy she liked to imagine:* Ibid., December 11, 1953, Muskie.

177 *Carson admitted that Jefferies was:* Ibid., November 19 and 20, 1953, Muskie.

177 *"I am sure that my own style":* Ibid.

177 *Cryptically, Carson added:* ibid.

178 *In early December, Carson wrote:* Ibid., December 11, 1953, Muskie.

178 *And, as you must know in your heart:* ibid.

178 *Carson's AAAS talk:* Alfred C. Redfield to Carson, April 15, 1953, Beinecke. The theme of the meeting was "The Sea Frontier."

178 *Carson was listed on the program:* From the printed text of her talk,

December 29, 1953, Beinecke. The title of Carson's talk was "The Edge
of the Sea."

179   *The edge of the sea is a laboratory:* Ibid.

179   *As Carson was leaving the hall:* Dorothy Freeman to Carson, n.d., ca.
Christmas 1954, Muskie. This unpublished letter summarizing their first
extended time alone with each other survives only as a draft. Carson
apparently destroyed most of the letters she received from Dorothy in
1953 and 1954. Martha Freeman reports in *Always, Rachel* that on one
occasion at Carson's home the two women burned some of Dorothy's
letters to Carson. Although they often discussed the special nature of
their friendship and the need to keep some of their correspondence
completely private, Dorothy was evidently less diligent in destroying
letters from Carson than Carson was in getting rid of hers.

179   *Carson slept fitfully on the train:* Carson to Dorothy Freeman, January 1,
1954, Muskie.

180   *A thing of beauty is a joy forever:* Ibid. Carson is quoting the famous
opening lines from John Keats's 1818 epic poem "Endymion." Although
those lines endure, the poem was widely panned when it was published.

180   *Carson was already imagining:* Carson to Dorothy Freeman, January 25,
1954, Muskie.

180   *Carson thought it was going to be difficult:* Ibid.

180   *Eventually they began referring to:* Carson, *Always, Rachel*, p. xvii.

181   *Just when it was hard to imagine:* Carson to Dorothy Freeman, February
6, 1954, Muskie. This long, tender letter is surely one of the most
unguarded professions of love ever composed. It was almost certainly
one of the private "apples" that Carson and Dorothy sent inside
letters that might be shared with friends or family, as it was intimate
and Carson sent another more newsy letter on the same date. Even
so, Dorothy apparently decided to share the "Hyacinth Letter" with
Stan anyway—and reported to Carson that Stan had been completely
understanding. The parable of the white hyacinth seems to have
originated with a thirteenth-century Persian poet named Mosleh od-
Din Saʻdi. Carson may have read a reference to it in the description
of the Italian village of Correggio in *Little Journeys,* by the obscure
American writer Elbert Hubbard.

181 *I don't suppose anyone really knows:* Carson to Dorothy Freeman, February 6, 1954, Muskie.

182 *Brooks envisioned something practical:* Paul Brooks to Carson, September 1, 1950, Beinecke.

182 *Brooks said he didn't have any:* Ibid., September 22, 1950, Beinecke.

182 *Carson, unwilling to be rushed:* Marie Rodell to Paul Brooks, October 4, 1950, Beinecke.

182 *Carson and Brooks decided on:* Paul Brooks to Carson, May 1, 1951, and Carson to Paul Brooks, May 14, 1951, Beinecke.

183 *He told Carson her reports:* Paul Brooks to Carson, December 12, 1951, Beinecke.

183 *Lovell Thompson, Houghton Mifflin's publisher:* Carson to Paul Brooks, July 6, 1952, Beinecke. The imperious tone of this letter probably didn't surprise Brooks, who had watched Carson become a superstar over the course of the past year—a fact Carson herself was never shy about pointing out in her letters to him. Knowing that the seashore guide was now certain to be a bestseller—regardless of how she wrote it or when she turned it in—contributed hugely to his inexhaustible patience.

184 *This set off alarms at Houghton Mifflin:* Memo from Paul Brooks to Lovell Thompson, July 8, 1952, Beinecke.

184 *Thompson, not entirely satisfied:* Thompson jotted this response on the memo Brooks had sent to him on July 8, 1952, Beinecke.

184 *Around Christmas 1952:* Note from Carson to Paul Brooks, n.d., Beinecke.

184 *At New Year's, she got off a portion:* Ibid.

184 *She also proposed a title:* Paul Brooks to Carson, January 7, 1953, Beinecke.

184 *Brooks was pleased with the copy:* Ibid.

184 *Rodell asked Houghton Mifflin to:* Marie Rodell to Paul Brooks, February 5, 1953, Beinecke.

184 *In March, Carson and Brooks:* Carson to Paul Brooks, March 3, 1953, Beinecke.

185 *Brooks, hoping to ease:* Paul Brooks to Bob Hines, March 10, 1953, Beinecke.

185 *Relieved, Carson thanked Brooks:* Carson to Paul Brooks, March 11, 1953, Beinecke.

185 *Not long after the Hines discussions:* Marie Rodell to Paul Brooks, March 13, 1953, Beinecke.

185 *Only a few days later:* Carson to Paul Brooks, March 17, 1953, Beinecke.

185 *Brooks, diplomatically changing the subject:* Paul Brooks to Carson, March 27, 1953, Beinecke.

186 *Carson responded that:* Carson to Paul Brooks, April 1, 1953, Beinecke.

186 *Carson was ill in May 1953:* Telegram from Carson to Paul Brooks, May 26, 1953, and Carson to Paul Brooks, May 28, 1953, Beinecke.

186 *Then her mother suffered:* Carson to Paul Brooks, July 29, 1953, Beinecke.

186 *In late June:* Ibid., June 24, 1953, Beinecke.

187 *In July, Bob Hines was finishing up:* Bob Hines to Paul Brooks, July 5, 1953, Beinecke.

187 *who promised to deliver:* Carson to Paul Brooks, July 29, 1953, Beinecke.

187 *He even visited Carson:* Paul Brooks to Bob Hines, September 21, 1953, Beinecke.

187 *In October, Carson told him:* Carson to Paul Brooks, October 13, 1953, Beinecke.

187 *Carson and Brooks agreed:* Ibid., March 5, 1954, Beinecke.

187 *March came:* Ibid.

187 *because she told Dorothy:* Carson to Dorothy Freeman, January 25, 1954, Muskie.

187 *One day she spoke to:* Ibid.

188 *But just two weeks after telling Brooks:* Carson to Paul Brooks, March 20, 1954, Beinecke.

188 *This time, Brooks pushed back:* Memo from Paul Brooks to Lovell Thompson, April 4, 1954, Beinecke.

188 *Brooks then wrote to Carson:* Paul Brooks to Carson, April 6, 1954, Beinecke.

188 *One editor told Brooks:* Memo to Paul Brooks from "ACW," April 15, 1954, Beinecke. ACW was evidently Ann Wyman of the editorial staff at Houghton Mifflin.

188 *Brooks took this criticism to heart:* Paul Brooks to Carson, April 20, 1954, Beinecke.

188 *To Brooks's relief:* Carson to Paul Brooks, April 27, 1954, Beinecke.

189 *but she also reminded him:* Carson to Paul Brooks, May 4, 1954, Beinecke.

189 *He told her she'd managed:* Paul Brooks to Carson, May 4, 1954, Beinecke.

189 *calling Carson's latest efforts "wonderful":* Memo to Paul Brooks from "ACW," May 4, 1954, Beinecke.

189 *The editor who had:* Ibid.

189 *Carson was happy to hear this:* Carson to Paul Brooks, May 5, 1954, Beinecke.

189 *but she urged Brooks to hold:* Ibid., May 16, 1954, Beinecke.

189 *everyone involved was overjoyed:* Paul Brooks to Carson, August 25, 1954, Beinecke.

189 *In August 1954, Brooks again visited:* Ibid.

189 *But back in Maryland in November:* Carson to Paul Brooks, November 2, 1954, Beinecke.

190 *Brooks wrote back to say:* Paul Brooks to Carson, November 4, 1954, Beinecke.

190 *But in early January:* Carson to Paul Brooks, January 10, 1955, Beinecke.

190 *At the end of January she told Brooks:* Ibid., January 30, 1955, Beinecke.

190 *A month later she said:* Ibid., February 8, 1955, Beinecke.

190 *Then, on March 15, it was done:* Paul Brooks to Carson, March 17, 1955, Beinecke.

190 *Brooks wrote to tell Carson:* Ibid. In an act of exceeding gallantry, Brooks added that the manuscript had arrived on March 15 "as promised."

190 *which Dorothy described as "The Revelation":* Carson to Dorothy Freeman, February 20, 1954, Muskie.

190 *Carson's only regret was:* Ibid., February 13, 1954, Muskie.

191 *Dorothy said they were caught up in:* Ibid.

191 *Carson said it was a process of "discovery":* Ibid., February 20, 1954, Muskie.

191 *In late March 1954:* Ibid., March 20, 1954, Muskie.

191 *Carson met with Paul Brooks:* Ibid., and Carson to Dorothy Freeman, April 3, 1954, Muskie.

191 *Dorothy had promised to bring:* Carson to Dorothy Freeman, March 20, 1954, Muskie.

191 *She also admitted to Dorothy:* Ibid., March 1, 1954, Muskie. Carson had earlier told Dorothy that part of what made work on *The Edge of the Sea* so difficult was the not knowing whether she could "do it again." She said—far too grandly—that her work was a matter of "destiny" and that she had a hard-to-explain feeling that she was merely "the instrument" though which something fine had been created, a process that had

"little to do with" herself (Carson to Dorothy Freeman, February 20, 1954, Muskie).

191 *In April, Carson delivered two speeches:* Carson to Dorothy Freeman, February 21, 1954, Muskie.

191 *Carson thought it odd that:* Ibid., May 3–4, 1954, Muskie.

192 *Carson told Dorothy she didn't like:* Ibid., May 1, 1954, Muskie.

192 *Then, for five days in May 1954:* Carson, *Always, Rachel,* p. 41. Editor Martha Freeman gives the dates for this retreat as May 17–21, 1954.

192 *They stayed mostly at Carson's cottage:* Carson to Dorothy Freeman, May 3–4, 1954, Muskie.

192 *They had lazy, laughter-filled:* Dorothy Freeman to Carson, n.d., ca. Christmas 1954, Muskie.

192 *Carson, who was happy that:* Carson to Dorothy Freeman, April 11–12, 1954, Muskie.

192 *One day they heard:* Dorothy Freeman to Carson, n.d., ca. Christmas 1954, Muskie.

192 *Another time Dorothy surprised Carson:* Carson to Dorothy Freeman, May 23, 1954, Muskie.

192 *Carson briefly returned to Silver Spring:* Ibid.

193 *Carson bought a "terribly sporty looking":* Ibid., June 22, 1954, Muskie.

193 *Carson told Dorothy she loved:* Ibid., May 27, 1954, Muskie.

193 *Dorothy enjoyed exploring the shoreline:* Dorothy Freeman to Carson, n.d., ca. Christmas 1954, Muskie.

193 *One time Carson took Dorothy to a special place:* Dorothy Freeman to Paul Brooks, June 21, 1971, Muskie. Brooks had asked Freeman to read and comment on the manuscript for his book about Carson, *The House of Life.*

194 *Under water that was clear as glass:* Carson, *Edge of the Sea,* p. 3.

194 *Dorothy seemed to remember everything:* Dorothy Freeman to Carson, n.d., ca. Christmas 1954, Muskie.

194 *Months earlier, the woman who:* Carson to Dorothy Freeman, February 6, 1954, Muskie.

194 *Then, on the day of their cruise:* Ibid., July 28, 1955, and Dorothy Freeman to Carson, n.d., ca. Christmas 1954, Muskie.

194 *Carson and Dorothy agreed to think:* Carson to Dorothy Freeman, May 30, 1954, Muskie.

195 *In a candid, almost elegiac letter:* Dorothy Freeman to Carson, April 15, 1956, Muskie.

195 *Suddenly, at one of the most dramatic moments:* Ibid.

196 *One time, as Carson and Dorothy lounged:* Dorothy Freeman to Carson, n.d., ca. Christmas 1954, Muskie.

196 *"Darling," she wrote to Carson:* Ibid.

196 *Carson had finally written a letter:* Carson to Henry Beston, May 14, 1954, Beinecke.

196 *Beston invited her to come over:* Elizabeth Beston to Carson, May 30 and September 25, 1952, Beinecke.

197 *At the end of the season:* Carson to Dorothy Freeman, November 8, 1954, Muskie.

197 *And so, as you know:* Ibid.

197 *Carson had recently discovered:* Ibid., November 27, 1954, Muskie.

197 *They debated over which hotel:* Ibid., December 2, 1954, Muskie.

198 *Could they, Carson wondered:* Ibid., December 26, 1954, Muskie. There is a frisson in the correspondence both before and after this escape to New York—but no proof that it was an occasion for physical intimacy. Carson and Dorothy spoke about their longing for each other often, but had few occasions to be alone together in this way. So what might be taken more than a half century later for sexual tension may have been only happy anticipation.

198 *Carson and Dorothy spent two nights:* Dorothy Freeman to Carson, January 6, 1955, Muskie.

198 *A day later Dorothy again wrote:* Ibid., January 7, 1955, Muskie.

198 *"Darling, again let me tell you":* Ibid.

199 *She said they'd had:* Carson to Dorothy Freeman, January 6, 1955, Muskie.

199 *Dorothy could cook:* Personal communication. This is how Madeleine Freeman remembers it.

199 *what the classicist Allan Bloom called:* Bloom, "Commentary" in *Plato's Symposium*, p. 55. Bloom first published this essay as "Love and Friendship" in 1993. The inevitable question as to whether Carson and Dorothy had a sexual relationship cannot be answered. But the weight of the circumstantial evidence is that they did not. My own view is that their love was much like that shared between the writers Martin Amis

and the late Christopher Hitchens. In an interview, Amis explained that their relationship was like an "unconsummated gay marriage," in which the bond was not sex but rather in each of them knowing with certainty exactly how the other thought and felt about everything. Martha Freeman, with whom I have discussed this issue at length, would argue for an additional consideration: the ability possessed by women, but not by men, to form deep, loving attachments that involve emotional and physical closeness, but not sex.

200 *A few weeks after:* Dorothy Freeman to Carson, January 31, 1955, Muskie.

200 *Oh, darling, live over those days:* Ibid.

201 *Darling, I'm sure now:* Ibid.

201 *When Carson finished:* Carson to Dorothy Freeman, April 12, 1955, Muskie.

CHAPTER EIGHT: THE ENDURING SEA

204 *In the spring of 1951:* Carson to T. A. Stephenson, April 5, 1951, Beinecke.

204 *I am at work on a:* Ibid.

205 *Ricketts was originally from:* Lannoo, *Leopold's Shack and Ricketts's Lab,* pp. 8–13.

205 *he fell under the influence of:* Ibid., pp. 22–23.

206 *Ricketts had gotten married:* Ibid., pp. 13 and 22.

206 *He opened a biological supply company:* Ibid., p. 22–24.

206 *Ricketts operated out of a dilapidated house:* Ibid., pp. 59–73.

206 *He believed there was:* Ibid., pp. 29–31.

206 *Free in his thoughts:* Ibid., pp. 24–31 and 59–73.

207 *He failed to stop:* Ibid., pp. 1–2.

207 *They chartered a seventy-six-foot fishing vessel:* Steinbeck, *Log from the Sea of Cortez,* p. 8.

208 *We have looked into the tide pools:* Ibid., p. 15.

209 *Many years ago:* Ricketts and Calvin, *Between Pacific Tides,* p. 196.

210 *her favorite being St. Simons Island:* Carson, field notes, and Carson to Marie Rodell, October 26, 1957, Beinecke.

211 *The tides following the recent:* Carson to Dorothy Algire, n.d., Beinecke.

212 *Writing of the sand dollars:* Carson, *Edge of the Sea,* p. 140.

212 *Walking back across the flats:* Ibid.

212 *Carson called the edge of the sea:* Ibid., p. 1.

213 *In a draft of* The Edge of the Sea*:* Carson, manuscript draft, Beinecke.

213 *Then in my thoughts:* Carson, *Edge of the Sea,* pp. 249–50. This is perhaps the loveliest passage in all of Carson's work, a reach for deeply felt emotion and cosmic significance that actually catches hold of both.

213 *In May 1955:* Carson to Paul Brooks, May 8, 1955, Beinecke.

214 *Just before the Fourth of July:* Carson to Sanderson Vanderbilt, July 3, 1955, Beinecke.

214 *The speech she mentioned:* Undated newspaper clipping, Beinecke.

214 *Ignoring the fact that:* Carson to Henry Laughlin, July 19, 1955, Beinecke. Laughlin was the president of Houghton Mifflin.

215 *Laughlin was out of the country:* Lovell Thompson to Carson, July 21, 1955, Beinecke.

215 *A week later he wrote:* Ibid., July 29, 1955, Beinecke.

215 *When Henry Laughlin got back:* Henry Laughlin to Carson, August 2, 1955, Beinecke.

215 *Charles Poore caught the:* New York Times, October 26, 1955.

216 *Apparently Miss Carson:* Ibid.

216 *Earl Banner, writing in the:* Boston Globe, October 30, 1955.

216 *Freely mixing its: Time,* November 7, 1955.

216 *Jacquetta Hawkes said: New Republic,* December 23, 1955.

216 *And Farley Mowat wrote: Toronto Telegram,* December 3, 1955.

217 *Good writing, Langdon said: Books and Bookmen,* February 1956.

217 *It is not an accident:* Ibid.

217 *Four weeks after: New York Times Sunday Book Review,* November 20, 1955.

217 *In mid-December:* Ibid., December 11, 1955.

218 *She told Dorothy Freeman:* Carson to Dorothy Freeman, October 29, 1955, Muskie.

218 *"I'll be happy that it is":* Ibid., November 20, 1955, Muskie.

218 *Carson told Dorothy that:* Ibid., January 10, 1956, Muskie.

218 *"many flaws":* Ibid., November 27, 1955, Muskie.

218 *Not surprisingly, Dorothy felt:* Dorothy Freeman to Carson, November 24, 1955, Muskie.

219 *Carson had recently been approached:* Carson to Dorothy Freeman,

December 2, 1955, Muskie. Carson confessed that she really ought to watch television once in a while so she would have some idea what such programs were like.

219 *She told Marie Rodell that:* Carson to Marie Rodell, November 29, 1955, Beinecke.

219 *But as she got further:* Carson to Dorothy Freeman, February 6, 1956, Muskie.

219 *Carson felt herself:* Ibid., February 4, 1956, Muskie.

219 *Dorothy, hoping to calm:* Ibid., February 9, 1956, Muskie.

219 *Dubious, Carson wrote back:* Ibid.

219 *She decided that television people were:* Ibid., February 25, 1956, Muskie.

219 *Carson saw the atmosphere:* Draft outline of Carson's script, n.d., Beinecke.

219 *Afterward, one of Carson's neighbors:* Carson to Dorothy Freeman, March 15, 1956, Muskie.

220 *In a letter to one of:* Carson to Sally Cist, April 14, 1956, Beinecke.

220 *In August 1955, Rodell discussed:* Marie Rodell to J. Robert Moskin, August 29, 1955, Beinecke.

221 *I remember a summer night when:* Carson, "Help Your Child to Wonder," *Woman's Home Companion,* July 1956.

221 *When Dorothy read a draft:* Dorothy Freeman to Carson, April 11, 1956, Muskie.

221 *That year at Christmas:* Carson to Dorothy Freeman, n.d., ca. December 1956, Muskie.

222 *But now Oxford University Press:* Ibid., December 8, 1956, Muskie.

222 *Dorothy, who for a long time:* Dorothy Freeman to Carson, n.d., ca. Christmas 1956, Muskie.

222 *A month later, after a hospitalization:* Carson, *Always, Rachel,* p. 216.

CHAPTER NINE: EARTH ON FIRE

223 *On the morning of January 22, 1954:* Lapp, *Voyage of the Lucky Dragon,* pp. 1–54. Except as noted in citations to follow, this recounting is based entirely on Ralph E. Lapp's extraordinary book.

227 *But as early as 1922:* Hansen, *U.S. Nuclear Weapons,* p. 43.

227 *There were uncertainties:* Ibid.

228 *During World War II:* Ibid., pp. 43–44.

228 *The first explosive hydrogen device:* Ibid., pp. 58–60.

229   *As impressive and frightening:* Ibid., pp. 60–61.

229   *A year and a half later:* Ibid., pp. 61–66.

229   *The firing center for:* Ibid. A post-test report said that "everyone and everything in the northern Marshall Islands had become radiologically contaminated."

230   *On its return to port:* Lapp, *Voyage of the Lucky Dragon,* pp. 55–171.

232   *The* New York Times *reported that:* New York Times, March 17, 1954.

232   *Then, not quite two weeks after:* Ibid.

232   *On March 24, 1954:* Ibid., March 25, 1954.

232   *One immediate step:* Ibid., March 28, 1954.

232   *Then on March 28:* Ibid.

233   *Another hydrogen bomb was exploded:* Hansen, *U.S. Nuclear Weapons,* p. 64.

233   *In early April:* New York Times, April 1, 1954.

233   *U.S. officials started negotiating:* Ibid.

233   *In July 1954, a team of:* Ibid., July 5, 1954.

233   *This was the same conclusion:* Ibid., September 28, 1947.

233   *Even so, the scientists seven years later:* Ibid., July 5, 1954.

234   *Three months later:* Ibid., October 14, 1954.

234   *Most were confident:* Miller, *Under the Cloud,* pp. 33–34.

235   *Between 1951 and 1955:* "United States Nuclear Tests: July 1945 through September 1992," U.S. Department of Energy, Nevada Operations Office.

236   *In his top-secret report:* Williams and Cantelon, *American Atom,* pp. 47–55.

236   *The cloud traveled to a great height:* Ibid.

237   *A few months after:* Miller, *Under the Cloud,* pp. 58–59.

237   *The far-reaching effects:* Ibid., pp. 84–106.

238   *Dr. Einstein explained:* Williams and Cantelon, *American Atom,* pp. 12–14.

239   *Ethel's execution was:* Philipson, *Ethel Rosenberg,* pp. 351–352.

239   *President Truman all but shut down:* Wayne Blanchard, "American Civil Defense 1945–1984: The Evolution of Programs and Policies," National Emergency Center, Monograph Series 2. no. 2, 1985.

240   *Just one month after:* New York Times, April 1, 1954.

240   *A year later:* Ibid., June 10, 1955.

240   *In the early 1950s:* "Survival Under Atomic Attack," Office of Civil Defense, October 1950.

241 *In 1955, the Civil Defense Administration:* Garrison, *Bracing for Armageddon,* p. 60.

242 *In 1958, a high-ranking:* New York Times, September 25, 1958.

242 *But the cost of such a system:* Blanchard, "American Civil Defense 1945–1984."

242 *In 1957, President Eisenhower rejected:* Garrison, *Bracing for Armageddon,* pp. 86–87.

243 *By the 1960s, the question:* This quote is generally attributed to Soviet premier Nikita Khrushchev, *Pravda,* July 20, 1963. Others surely shared the thought.

243 *None of this was lost on:* Personal recollection. I will never forget the "flash" drills I performed (they were, after all, play-acting farces) or the fact that when I moved from elementary school to junior high I no longer lived close enough to home to go there in the event of an attack. The idea that I would not be able to find my two younger brothers in the chaos of a school evacuation as the missiles began to rain down was a torment I tried not to think about.

245 *In 1943, a sample of:* William B. Deichmann, "The Debate on DDT," *Archives of Toxicology* 29, no. 1 (1972), Patuxent.

245 *In 1950, about 12 percent:* "DDT Regulatory History: A Brief Survey (to 1975)," U.S. Environmental Protection Agency, July 1975.

245 *Domestic DDT use peaked in 1959:* Ibid.

246 *These included lindane:* Deichmann, " Debate on DDT."

246 *In 1952:* James B. DeWitt, and John L. George, "Pesticide-Wildlife Review," U.S. Fish and Wildlife Circular 84, 1959, Beinecke.

248 *The first tests were inconclusive:* Clarence Cottam and Elmer Higgins, "DDT: Its Effect on Fish and Wildlife," U.S. Department of the Interior Circular 11, 1948, Patuxent.

249 *"As soon as DDT was taken outdoors":* Arnold L. Nelson and Eugene W. Surber, "DDT Investigations by the Fish and Wildlife Service in 1946," U.S. Department of the Interior Special Scientific Report No. 41, Patuxent.

249 *The nature of complications:* Joseph P. Linduska, "The Effects of DDT on Wildlife," *Shade Tree* 20, no. 12 (December 1947), Patuxent.

250 *Some effects of DDT spraying:* Joseph P. Linduska, and Eugene W. Surber,

"Effects of DDT and Other Insecticides on Fish and Wildlife: Summary of Investigations During 1947," U.S. Department of the Interior Circular 15, 1948, Patuxent.

251 *In one orchard:* Ibid.

252 *"Although the immediate advantages":* C. H. Hoffman, and Joseph P. Linduska, "Some Considerations of the Biological Effects of DDT," *Scientific Monthly* 69, no. 2 (August 1949), Patuxent.

252 *A year later:* Joseph P. Linduska, "DDT and the Balance of Nature," Proceedings and Papers, International Technical Conference on the Protection of Nature, 1950, Patuxent.

252 *Many types of control projects:* Ibid.

253 *By 1951, the Patuxent pesticides project:* Chandler S. Robbins, et al., "Effects of Five-Year DDT Application on Breeding Bird Population," *Journal of Wildlife Management* 15, no. 2 (April 1951), Patuxent.

253 *Meanwhile, an ever-widening:* Allen H. Benton, "Effects on Wildlife of DDT Used for Control of Dutch Elm Disease," *Journal of Wildlife Management* 15, no. 1 (January 1951), Patuxent.

253 *The 1948 spraying:* Ibid.

254 *Only a relative handful:* Ibid.

254 *In one test, hatchlings:* Robert T. Mitchell et al., "The Effects of DDT upon the Survival and Growth of Nestling Songbirds," *Journal of Wildlife Management,* no. 1 (January 1953), Patuxent.

255 *Experiments at Patuxent:* James B. DeWitt et al., "DDT vs. Wildlife: Relationships Between Quantities Ingested, Toxic Effects and Tissue Storage," *Journal of the American Pharmaceutical Association* 44, no. 1 (January 1955), Patuxent.

255 *Another "subtle" effect of DDT:* John L. George, "Effects on Fish and Wildlife of Chemical Treatments of Large Areas," *Journal of Forestry* 57, no. 4 (April 1959), Patuxent.

255 *By 1956 there were:* Paul F. Springer, "DDT: Its Effects on Wildlife," *Passenger Pigeon* 19, no. 4 (winter 1957), Patuxent.

256 *its best guess at a "safe" concentration:* John L. George, "Effects on Fish and Wildlife of Chemical Treatments of Large Areas," *Journal of Forestry* 57, no. 4 (April 1959), Patuxent.

256 *The threat to aquatic species:* Ibid.

256 *A campaign to eradicate gypsy moths:* Ibid.

257 *Immediate mortality of individuals:* Ibid.

257 *In 1950, the American Medical Association's:* "Report of the Council," *Journal of the American Medical Association* 142, no. 13 (April 1, 1950).

258 *The committee said that:* "Report to the Council," *Journal of the American Medical Association* 144, no. 2 (September 9, 1950).

258 *Organophosphate poisoning:* Ibid.

259 *The AMA was worried:* "Insecticide Storage in Adipose Tissue," *Journal of the American Medical Association* 145, no. 10 (March 10, 1951).

260 *the AMA was advising physicians:* "Aldrin and Dieldrin Poisoning," *Journal of the American Medical Association* 146, no. 4 (May 26, 1951).

260 *In 1952, the Committee on Pesticides:* "Report to the Council: Health Hazards of Electric Vaporizing Devices for Insecticides," *Journal of the American Medical Association* 149, no. 4 (May 24, 1952).

261 *Although cases of:* Ibid.

261 *categorically opposed the use of insecticide vaporizers:* "Report to the Council: Abuse of Insecticide Fumigating Devices," *Journal of the American Medical Association* 156, no. 6 (October 9, 1954).

261 *Two years earlier the AMA:* "Report to the Council: Toxic Effects of Technical Benzene Hexachloride and Its Principal Isomers," *Journal of the American Medical Association.* 147, no. 6 (October 6, 1952).

261 *In one case an eighteen-month-old:* "Report to the Council: Abuse of Insecticide Fumigating Devices."

262 *"Insecticidal poisons that":* Ibid.

262 *By the spring of 1957:* Thompson Chemicals Corporation press release, May 1, 1957, Beinecke.

262 *In 1954, Dr. Wayland J. Hayes, Jr.:* "Present Status of Our Knowledge of DDT Intoxication," *American Journal of Public Health* 45, April 1955.

263 *The safety of DDT was also official policy:* USDA press release, May 10, 1957, Beinecke.

264 *In 1956, Carson served on:* Committee roster, August 23, 1956, Beinecke.

265 *Attentive as always:* Carson to Paul Brooks, February 25, 1956, Beinecke.

265 *Polite but understandably defensive:* Paul Brooks to Carson, February 29, 1956, Beinecke.

265 *Life magazine invited her:* Carson to Marie Rodell, April 14, 1956, Beinecke.

265 *One idea that never went:* Marie Rodell to Carson, July 25, 1956, Beinecke.

266 *and confessed to Dorothy Freeman:* Carson to Dorothy Freeman, March 27, 1957, Muskie.

266 *"Sometimes I think I* can't *go on":* Ibid., May 18, 1957, Muskie.

266 *Carson told Dorothy it had been a year:* Ibid., November 5, 1957, Muskie.

266 *Her biggest challenge:* Carson to Marie Rodell, October 26, 1957, Beinecke.

266 *The undisturbed shore is:* Ibid.

267 *Early in 1956, Carson got into:* Carson to Leon Powers, February 15, 1956, Beinecke. Powers was the comptroller of the Musical Masterpiece Society.

267 *In case my name is not:* Ibid. The National Institute of Arts and Letters is not to be confused with the more prestigious American Academy of Arts and Letters, to which Carson was later elected.

268 *She thought everyone now faced:* Carson to Dorothy Freeman, November 7, 1957, Muskie.

269 *Tell us something, they said:* Matheson, *Incredible Shrinking Man,* p. 118.

271 *which she described as:* Carson to Dorothy Freeman, December 2, 1957, Muskie.

271 *One time she stumbled upon:* Ibid., December 31, 1957–January 1, 1958, Muskie.

272 *The nonnative pest:* I. B. Bird, "What Are the Side Effects of the Imported Fire Ant Control Program?" Presented to Second Seminar on Biological Problems in Water Pollution, 1959, Beinecke.

272 *By 1958, reports from the field:* Ibid.

273 *A report from the Alabama Division of Game and Fish:* Ibid.

273 *banned the use of heptachlor on food crops:* FDA press release, October 27, 1959, Beinecke.

273 *Congress had authorized the FDA:* Winton B. Rankin, "Control of Pesticides on Food," *Public Health Reports* 71, no. 6 (June 1956), Beinecke. The law was known generically as the "Miller Amendment."

273 *It had been discovered that heptachlor:* FDA press release, October 27, 1959, Beinecke.

273 *It is rank folly for the government:* *New York Times,* January 8, 1958.

274 *Later that year, three Harvard biologists:* Edward O. Wilson et al. to Ezra Taft Benson, n.d., ca. 1958, Beinecke.

274 *Broadcast application of insecticides:* Ibid.

274 *Meanwhile, in the fall of 1957:* *New York Times,* December 3, 1957.

275 *just days after Carson had heard from:* Marjorie Spock to Carson, February 5, 1958, Beinecke.

275 *Spock had been contacted by:* Ibid.

275 *She told White about the lawsuit:* Carson to E. B. White, February 3, 1958, Beinecke.

276 *White wrote back at once:* E. B. White to Carson, February 7, 1958, Beinecke.

CHAPTER TEN: COLLATERAL DAMAGE

277 *She wrote to Paul Brooks:* Carson to Paul Brooks, February 21, 1958, Beinecke.

277 *"lively as seventeen crickets":* Carson to Dorothy Freeman, January 24, 1957, Muskie.

278 *When Dorothy had offered to have Roger:* Ibid., March 23, 1957, Muskie.

278 *But I have been mentally blocked:* Carson to Dorothy Freeman, February 1, 1958, Muskie.

279 *"shut her mind":* Ibid.

279 *"space age universe":* Ibid.

279 *On April Fools' Day 1958:* Ibid., April 2, 1958, Muskie.

279 *In the spring of 1945:* New Yorker, May 26, 1945.

280 *In April she agreed:* Carson to Paul Brooks, April 20, 1958, Beinecke.

280 *She at this point saw it as:* From Paul Brooks's internal Houghton Mifflin memo, "Report to the Executive Committee," April 1, 1958, and Marie Rodell to Lovell Thompson, March 21, 1958, Beinecke.

280 *Diamond signed a letter agreeing:* Marie Rodell to Edwin Diamond, April 18, 1958, Beinecke.

280 *But two days later:* Marie Rodell to Edwin Diamond, May 5, 1958, Beinecke.

280 *a few days later was again told:* Joan Daves to Edwin Diamond, May 9, 1958, Beinecke. Daves was Rodell's partner in the agency.

280 *In mid-May, Paul Brooks stepped in:* Paul Brooks to Edwin Diamond, May 26, 1958, Beinecke.

281 *A few weeks later:* Joan Daves to Miss Minahan, June 11, 1958, Beinecke. Minahan was Paul Brooks's secretary.

281 *Diamond, meanwhile, ignored:* Edwin Diamond to Paul Brooks, June 24, 1958, Beinecke.

281 *Brooks, who was on vacation:* Paul Brooks to Edwin Diamond, July 21, 1958, Beinecke.

281 *In June, Carson met with:* Carson to Dorothy Freeman, June 12, 1958, Muskie.

281 *"actually happy and excited":* Carson to Dorothy Freeman, October 20, 1958, Muskie.

282 *On November 22, 1958, she suffered:* Carson to Marjorie Spock, December 4, 1958, Beinecke.

282 *By the end of the day:* Carson to Dorothy Freeman, December 4, 1958, Muskie.

282 *"half-baked at best":* Carson to Paul Brooks, February 14, 1959, Beinecke.

283 *She told Brooks she was intrigued by:* Ibid.

283 *"not be so rash as to predict":* Ibid.

284 *Over the course of the sixteen-day trial:* New York Times, March 5, April 26, and June 24, 1958.

284 *A surprise witness who appeared:* Ibid., February 14, 1958.

284 *The key witness for the government:* Ibid., February 22 and 25, 1958.

285 *Before the judge could issue:* Ibid., April 26, 1958.

285 *In June, the court issued a broad ruling:* Ibid., June 24, 1958.

285 *Although the plaintiffs contend:* Ibid.

286 *Wallace and his graduate students:* George J. Wallace and Richard F. Bernard, "Tests Show 40 Species of Birds Poisoned by DDT," *Audubon,* July–August 1963.

288 *Locating and dealing with infected trees:* New York Times, November 10, 1957.

288 *Anthroposophy was the underlying principle:* Spock, *Eurythmy.*

289 *a woman named Mary Richards:* Spock wrote to Carson on stationery engraved "Marjorie Spock–Mary T. Richards, Whitney Lane and Norgate Road, Glen Head Post Office, L.I., NY."

289 *Spock wrote to Carson immediately afterward:* Marjorie Spock to Carson, June 6, 1958, Beinecke.

289 *stopped in to meet Carson:* Ibid., August 16, 1958, Beinecke.

289 *Carson insisted they address each other:* Carson to Marjorie Spock, September 29, 1958, Beinecke.

289 *"I can hardly wait until":* Marjorie Spock to Carson, May 11, 1959, Beinecke.

289 *She mentioned an interview:* Carson to Marjorie Spock, June 30, 1958, Beinecke.

290 *Schneiderman said it was still unknown:* Howard Schneiderman to Carson, October 13, 1958, Beinecke.

290 *Carson told Spock she thought:* Carson to Marjorie Spock, October 17, 1958, Beinecke.

291 *Penicillin was first used:* Henry Welch, "Problems of Antibiotics in Food as the Food and Drug Administration Sees Them," *American Journal of Public Health* 47, no. 6 (June 1957).

291 *It should be emphasized that:* Ibid.

292 Time *magazine reported that:* Time, September 26, 1960.

292 *Carson wrote a long letter to the editor:* Carson to DeWitt Wallace, January 27, 1958, Beinecke. Wallace was the editor of *Reader's Digest.*

292 *Carson got an immediate answer:* Walter B. Mahoney to Carson, January 30, 1958, Beinecke. Mahoney was a senior editor at *Reader's Digest,* who answered because Wallace was out of the office when Carson's letter arrived.

293 *She wrote to the author:* Carson to Robert Strother, June 19, 1959, Beinecke.

293 *which he graciously agreed to do:* Robert Strother to Carson, June 24, 1959, Beinecke.

293 *In the spring of 1959:* New York Times, August 24, 1959.

294 *In 1958, a group called:* Williams and Cantelon, *American Atom,* pp. 197–202.

294 *A half century later:* New York Times, December 13, 2010.

295 *"virtually certain that genetic effects":* "Estimates and Evaluation of Fallout in the United States from Nuclear Weapons Testing Conducted Through 1962," Report of the Federal Radiation Council, Report No. 4, May 1963 (JFK Library).

295 *presented the United Nations with a petition:* Mead and Hager, *Linus Pauling,* p. 213.

295 *"Each nuclear bomb test":* Ibid.

296 *Teale and his wife had visited Carson:* Edwin Way Teale to Carson, September 12, 1954, Beinecke.

296 *The Teales also shared:* Ibid., March 18, 1956, Beinecke. The subject of cats came up in numerous letters between Teale and Carson.

296 *Carson urged Teale to find a way:* Carson to Edwin Way Teale, March 25, 1956, Beinecke.

296 *Teale wrote to encourage her:* Edwin Way Teale to Carson, May 26, 1958, Beinecke.

296 *Paul Brooks shared this view:* From Paul Brooks's internal Houghton Mifflin memo, "Report to the Executive Committee," April 1, 1958, Beinecke.

297 *When Paul Brooks asked Carson about:* Paul Brooks to Carson, February 13, 1959, Beinecke.

297 *"I hate to advise you":* Carson to Paul Brooks, February 14, 1959, Beinecke.

297 *Sometime in early 1959:* Paul Brooks to Carson, May 25, 1959, Beinecke. Exactly when this title was proposed, or whose idea it was, can't be determined.

297 *Carson again felt only lukewarm:* Carson to Paul Brooks, June 3, 1959, Beinecke. Carson seemed caught off-guard by Brooks's reference to the new title. Although she said it "seems to wear pretty well" now that she had lived with it for a few weeks, Carson sounded less than enthusiastic, admitting only that her initial doubts "seem" to have disappeared.

297 *In May, Brooks told Carson:* Paul Brooks to Carson, May 25, 1959, Beinecke.

298 *Carson wrote back to assure him:* Carson to Paul Brooks, June 3, 1959, Beinecke.

298 *Carson and Marie Rodell were alarmed:* Marie Rodell to Paul Brooks, June 24, 1959, Beinecke.

298 *Carson wrote to the publicity department:* Carson to Anne Ford, July 6, 1959, Beinecke. Ford worked in the publicity department at Houghton Mifflin.

298 *Filed away alongside:* Carson's undated handwritten notes for the book, Beinecke.

299 *Both Carson and Roger were laid low:* Carson to Anne Ford, August 7, 1959, Beinecke.

299 *Carson did make time to:* Ibid., August 27, 1959, Beinecke.

299 *their car was hit by a truck:* Carson to Paul Brooks, September 17, 1959, Beinecke.

299 *In December 1959, Carson wrote:* Ibid., December 3, 1959, Beinecke.

300   *Carson also apologized:* Ibid.

300   *Brooks wrote back:* Paul Brooks to Carson, December 21, 1959, Beinecke.

301   *Lead, the other metallic residue:* Kallet and Schlink, *100,000,000 Guinea Pigs,* p. 56.

301   *"milk you give your children":* Longgood, *Poisons in Your Food,* p. 2.

302   *One factor that makes DDT so effective:* Ibid, p. 79.

302   *Osmundsen accused Longgood of:* New York Times, May 1, 1960.

302   *Carson was aware of the controversy:* Carson to Marjorie Spock, March 14, 1960, Beinecke.

303   *It is a great problem to know how:* Ibid.

303   *In early November 1959:* New York Times, November 10, 1959.

303   *Grocers across the country:* Ibid., November 11, 1959.

304   *Aminotriazole had initially been tried:* Ibid., November 12, 1959.

304   *In Massachusetts, a crowd of nearly:* Ibid., November 16, 1959.

304   *In Wisconsin:* Ibid., November 15, 1959.

305   *One senior chemical executive complained:* Ibid., November 22, 1959.

305   *"wildlife and conservation groups":* Ibid.

306   *Carson's progress slowed:* Carson to Paul Brooks, March 16, 1960, Beinecke.

307   *who had expressed sympathy:* Paul Brooks to Carson, March 18, 1960, Beinecke.

307   *She said she was going to have surgery:* Carson to Paul Brooks, March 21, 1960, Beinecke.

307   *He told her that, unlike a historian:* Paul Brooks to Carson, March 18, 1960, Beinecke.

307   *Carson wrote back to say:* Carson to Paul Brooks, March 23, 1960, Beinecke.

307   *Carson also told Brooks:* Ibid.

308   *In my flounderings I keep asking:* Ibid.

308   *Carson said she also wanted to consider:* Ibid.

308   *A couple of weeks later:* Carson to Marjorie Spock, April 12, 1960, Beinecke.

309   *Carson, worried about Roger:* Ibid.

309   *Spock, desperate to help:* Marjorie Spock to Carson, July 20, 1960; and September 29, 1960, Beinecke.

309   *Carson tactfully avoided:* Carson to Marjorie Spock, July 11, 1960; and January 4, 1961, Beinecke.

309 *Paul Brooks, who apparently did not know:* Paul Brooks to Carson, March 29, 1960, Beinecke.

310 *Weak and in pain:* Carson to Marjorie Spock, July 1, 1960, and Carson to Paul Brooks, June 1, 1960, Beinecke. Carson told Brooks her recovery was progressing but that her doctors had told her it would be midsummer before she regained full strength.

310 *She and Brooks arranged for him:* Paul Brooks to Carson, July 27, 1960, Beinecke.

310 *In September she offered:* Carson to Paul Brooks, September 5, 1960, Beinecke.

310 *Brooks wrote back and told Carson:* Paul Brooks to Carson, September 13, 1960, Beinecke.

310 *When Marie Rodell heard about it:* Marie Rodell to Carson, December 2, 1960, Beinecke.

310 *in his dissenting opinion:* "Dissenting Opinion, March 28, 1960, of Mr. Justice Douglas, Upon the Denial of Petition for Writ of Certiorari to the United States Court of Appeals, Second Circuit," Supreme Court of the United States, October Term, 662; *Robert Cushman Murphy et al. v. Butler et al.,* Beinecke.

311 *During the past 15 years:* Ibid.

311 *Based on her latest:* Paul Brooks to Carson, November 10, 1960, Beinecke.

311 *Carson said she would come up:* Carson to Paul Brooks, November 27, 1960, Beinecke.

312 *But at the last minute she canceled:* Paul Brooks to Carson, December 6, 1960, Beinecke.

312 *Carson had found a swelling:* Lear, *Rachel Carson,* p. 378.

312 *She told Dorothy Freeman there was:* Carson to Dorothy Freeman, November 25, 1960, Muskie.

312 *"even though I asked directly":* Carson to Paul Brooks, December 27, 1960, quoted in Brooks, *House of Life,* p. 265.

312 *Carson consulted with Dr. George "Barney" Crile, Jr.:* Ibid., and Lear, *Rachel Carson,* pp. 378–79.

312 *She wrote a letter to Dorothy:* Carson to Dorothy Freeman, December 14, 1960, Muskie.

313 *Carson relayed this news:* Dorothy Freeman to Carson, December 16, 1960, Muskie.

313 *She told Carson it would be so easy:* Dorothy Freeman to Carson, December 16, 1960, Muskie.

313 *In January 1961, the radiation treatments:* Carson to Dorothy Freeman, January 4, 1960, Muskie.

313 *The mass in her chest seemed to be:* Ibid., January 3, 1960, Muskie.

313 *On a cold late afternoon:* Dorothy Freeman to Carson, January 31, 1961, Muskie.

314 *In mid-January 1961:* Carson to Paul Brooks, February 10, 1961, and March 25, 1961, Beinecke.

314 *She kept up a brave mood:* Carson to Dorothy Freeman, February 12, 1961, Muskie.

314 *She told Paul Brooks she hated:* Carson to Paul Brooks, March 25, 1961, Beinecke.

314 *In May 1961, Marie Rodell visited Carson:* Marie Rodell to Paul Brooks, May 23, 1961, Beinecke.

315 *Carson now planned a total of:* Ibid.

315 *Brooks, elated at this:* Paul Brooks to Carson, May 25, 1961, Beinecke.

315 *Carson said she was eager:* Carson to Paul Brooks, June 5, 1961, Beinecke.

315 *In June 1961, after he'd seen Carson:* Memo from Paul Brooks to Lovell Thompson, June 23, 1961, Beinecke.

315 *in July the publisher sent:* Katharine Bernard to Carson, July 6, 1961, Beinecke. Bernard worked at Houghton Mifflin.

315 *She thought the Darlings' drawings were:* Carson to Katharine Bernard, July 14, 1961, Beinecke.

315 *Both Brooks and Lovell Thompson thought:* Memo from Paul Brooks to Lovell Thompson, September 15, 1961, Beinecke. Brooks told Thompson he thought Carson was wrong about the Darlings. Thompson scrawled his concurrence on the bottom of Brooks's memo and sent it back.

316 *Olaus Murie, a prominent naturalist:* Olaus Murie to Carson, January 11, 1962, Beinecke.

316 *But in the fall of 1961:* Carson to Frank Egler, September 14, 1961, Beinecke.

317 *Chastened, Egler wrote back:* Frank Egler to Carson, September 20, 1961, Beinecke.

317 *Still, Carson had enough confidence:* Carson to Frank Egler, January 17, 1962, Beinecke.

317 *Eight days later Carson was floored:* Frank Egler to Carson, January 25, 1962, Beinecke.

317 *She told Egler she would:* Carson to Frank Egler, January 29, 1962, Beinecke.

317 *Although he thought she offered:* George Crile to Carson, January 30, 1962, Beinecke.

317 *In the spring of 1961:* Carson to Malcolm Hargraves, March 31, 1961, Beinecke.

317 *Hargraves concurred with:* Malcolm Hargraves to Carson, April 7, 1961, Beinecke.

318 *In October, Carson wrote to Brooks:* Carson to Paul Brooks, October 6, 1961, Beinecke.

318 *Brooks patiently asked her:* Paul Brooks to Carson, October 9, 1961, Beinecke.

318 *In late October, Rodell told Brooks:* Marie Rodell to Paul Brooks, October 24, 1961, Beinecke.

318 *A few days later:* Paul Brooks to Carson, October 27, 1961, Beinecke.

318 *Brooks privately told Rodell:* Paul Brooks to Marie Rodell, October 30, 1961, Beinecke.

318 *One evening toward the end:* Carson to Dorothy Freeman, January 23, 1962, Muskie.

CHAPTER ELEVEN: HIGH TIDES AND LOW

319 *issue of pesticide use into "literature":* Carson to Dorothy Freeman, January 23, 1962, Muskie. Shawn backed up his assessment with a contract that was to pay Carson $25,000 for a "multi-part long fact piece" on insecticides. This was increased to $28,000 when the *New Yorker* ended up serializing more of the book than anticipated (internal memos from the records of the *New Yorker,* February 12 and August 13, 1962, Manuscripts and Archives Division, New York Public Library).

319 *Carson told Brooks this felt almost:* Brooks, *House of Life,* p. 270.

320 *On April 3, Brooks wrote her:* Paul Brooks to Carson, April 3, 1962, Beinecke.

320 *Marie Rodell asked Brooks:* Marie Rodell to Paul Brooks, February 16, 1962, Beinecke.

320 *In a rare moment of:* Memo from Anne Ford to Paul Brooks, February 23, 1962, Beinecke. Brooks's advice to send Diamond a copy of the book was handwritten across the bottom of the memo and returned to Ford.

320 *In early April, Carson outlined:* Carson to Paul Brooks, April 6, 1962, Beinecke.

320 *chemical pesticides with "broad lethal powers":* Carson, *Silent Spring,* p. 162.

321 *Houghton Mifflin was nervous about:* Anne Ford to Marie Rodell, April 13, 1962, Beinecke.

321 *Marie Rodell pooh-poohed these worries:* Marie Rodell to Anne Ford, April 20, 1962, Beinecke.

321 *As Marie Rodell reminded:* Marie Rodell to Anne Ford, April 6, 1962, Beinecke.

321 *In late April 1962, Paul Brooks asked:* Memo from Diane Davin to Anne Ford, April 27, 1962, Beinecke. Davin worked at Houghton Mifflin.

322 *She said she could still work:* Carson to Dorothy Freeman, March 28, 1962, Muskie.

322 *new mass in her armpit:* Ibid., April 10, 1962, Muskie.

322 *Among the attendees was:* Ibid., May 20, 1962, Muskie.

323 *A number of people had been:* Ibid.

324 *There was a strange stillness:* Carson, *Silent Spring,* p. 2. For simplicity, I am citing the book, as everything published in the *New Yorker* is found in it, but not vice versa.

325 *When Dr. Albert Schweitzer wrote:* John F. Kennedy to Dr. Albert Schweitzer, June 6, 1962, JFK Library.

326 *The latest round of tests:* *New York Times,* June 1, 1963.

326 *But fallout from Soviet testing:* Draft Presidential Statement, n.d., JFK Library.

326 *"We cannot say with certainty":* Ibid.

327 *President Kennedy's science adviser:* Memo from Jerome Wiesner to the President, June 26, 1962, JFK Library. Science adviser Wiesner would soon be tapped to head Kennedy's special commission looking into the

use of pesticides, making him the government's point man on the twin environmental menaces of the time.

327 *Meanwhile, the administration requested:* Memo from Jerome Wiesner to the President, August 9, 1962, JFK Library.

327 *In mid-July 1962, Secretary of Agriculture:* Memo from Orville Freeman to Bob Lewis, July 18, 1962, JFK Library. Like Wiesner, Freeman would become embroiled in the controversies around nuclear fallout and pesticides that summer.

327 *A month later, having been appointed to:* Memo from Orville Freeman to the President, August 21, 1962, JFK Library. The subject of milk contamination was only one of several subjects addressed in this regular report to President Kennedy.

328 *Freeman was briefed on this angle:* Memo from Walter Mondale et al. to Orville Freeman, August 18, 1962, JFK Library.

328 *By November 1962:* Memo from Samuel Botsford to Pierre Salinger, November 23, 1962, JFK Library. Botsford was acting director of public information at the U.S. Public Health Service. Salinger was President Kennedy's press secretary.

329 *The most alarming of all man's assaults:* Carson, *Silent Spring,* p. 6.

330 *The Michigan Department of Agriculture:* C. A. Boyer to Carson, July 11, 1962, records of the *New Yorker,* Manuscripts and Archives Division, New York Public Library. Boyer was in the Plant Industry Division of the Michigan Department of Agriculture.

330 *In a sarcastic letter:* Ibid.

331 *One salty citizen:* Henry J. Davidson to the editor of the *New Yorker,* n.d., ca. 1962, Beinecke. Attempting to gauge the overall reaction contained within the flood of mail prompted by the articles, the staff at the *New Yorker* counted up the letters on both sides and determined that the mail was running a little better than fourteen to one in favor of Carson (editorial department tracking memo, 1962, records of the *New Yorker,* Manuscripts and Archives Division, New York Public Library).

331 *Another angry letter writer:* Austin W. Merrill, Jr., to the editor of the *New Yorker,* July 17, 1962, Beinecke.

331 *"Who would want to live":* Carson, *Silent Spring,* p. 12.

331 *"Yet such a world is pressed":* Ibid.

332 *"It is not my contention that":* Ibid.

332 *In 1958, Congress passed:* Shah, *Fever,* p. 207.

333 *The early years of the:* Ibid., pp. 207–8.

333 *One irate reader wrote:* P. Rothberg to the editor of the *New Yorker,* June 18, 1962, records of the *New Yorker,* Manuscripts and Archives Division, New York Public Library.

334 *This, Carson wrote:* Carson, *Silent Spring,* p. 266.

335 *"Together let us explore the stars":* John F. Kennedy Presidential Statement on the Malaria Eradication Program and related postage stamps, n.d. Manuscripts and Archives Division of the New York Public Library.

335 *In 1963, faced with questions:* Shah, *Fever,* p. 212.

335 *Six years later:* Ibid., p. 216.

336 *She told Dorothy Freeman she was:* Carson to Dorothy Freeman, June 11, 1962, Muskie.

336 *Carson began by telling the students:* Carson, "Of Man and the Stream of Time," Scripps College, Claremont, California, June 12, 1962. Scripps had Carson's speech bound as a pamphlet, noting that it had fulfilled "a hope that had been cherished for a decade."

337 *The once beneficent rains:* Ibid.

338 *The radiation to which we:* Ibid.

338 *Relaxing the next day, she got word:* Carson to Dorothy Freeman, June 13, 1962, Muskie.

338 *Glad but underwhelmed:* Ibid.

339 *Carson and Roger left:* Carson to Dorothy Freeman, June 27, 1962, Muskie.

339 *Among the first to weigh in:* New York Times, July 2, 1962.

339 *But the president was alerted:* Irving Goldman to John F. Kennedy, July 9 1962, JFK Library.

340 *Within days, Kennedy's special assistant:* Draft response to Judge Irving Goldman from Orville Freeman's office, July 20, 1962, JFK Library.

341 *Shirley Briggs warned Carson:* Shirley Briggs to Carson, July 26, 1962, Beinecke.

341 *Freeman told his senior staff:* Memo from Orville Freeman to senior staff, July 16, 1962, JFK Library.

341 *The lid is about to blow off:* Newsday, August 20, 1962.

342 *The truth about pesticides:* Ibid.

342 *Caro took note of:* Ibid. And, in a small sidebar, Caro reported an

apparent connection between mosquito spraying operations and the near extinction of the bald eagle.

343 *In subsequent installments: Newsday,* August 21, 22, 23, and 24, 1962.

343 *Ridiculously, he told Caro: Newsday,* August 24, 1962.

343 *"strong concerted attention":* Ibid.

344 *The FBI had launched an investigation:* See chap. 1, note *"Meanwhile, the FBI,"* on p. 405.

344 *Knight told Carson he was interested in:* Paul Knight to Carson, May 29, 1962, Beinecke.

344 *In July 1962, after the* New Yorker *series:* Ibid., July 5, 1962, Beinecke.

345 *In October,* Newsday's *Robert Caro: Newsday,* October 10, 1962.

345 *Carson had shrewdly seen:* Carson to Paul Brooks, September 11, 1958, Beinecke.

345 *the DuPont Corporation requested:* Lovell Thompson to Marie Rodell, July 26, 1962, Beinecke.

346 *In early August, Velsicol's:* Louis A. McLean to Houghton Mifflin, August 2, 1962, Beinecke. McLean was secretary and general counsel at Velsicol.

346 *Unfortunately, in addition to the:* Ibid.

347 *Carson sent a note back:* Carson to Paul Brooks, August 8, 1962, Beinecke.

347 *This didn't satisfy Velsicol:* Louis A. McLean to William E. Spaulding, August 14, 1962. Spaulding was the president of Houghton Mifflin. His initial response to Velsicol (William E. Spaulding to Louis A. McLean, August 10, 1962, Beinecke) had made it clear that the publishing house stood by its author and that *Silent Spring* was coming out. Spaulding indicated that Houghton Mifflin wasn't convinced of the supposed inaccuracies in *Silent Spring* but said that if Velsicol wanted to supply proof of any they'd give such evidence due consideration. After reviewing Velsicol's second letter, Paul Brooks wrote to McLean saying that after further consideration, Houghton Mifflin remained convinced that *Silent Spring* was both accurate and fair (Paul Brooks to Louis A. McLean, August 22, 1961, Beinecke).

347 *twenty people in Memphis, Tennessee, New York Times,* January 17, 1965.

348 *Then, in April 1964:* Ibid., April 23, 1964.

348 *an even more alarming discovery:* Ibid., January 17, 1965.

348 *In September 1962, the Department of Health:* Public Statement, U.S.

Department of Health, Education, and Welfare, September 1962, JFK Library.

348 *The fact that they [pesticides]:* Ibid.

349 *The agency said it also monitored:* Ibid.

349 *But just over a month later:* Memo from Jerome Wiesner to John F. Kennedy, November 13, 1962, JFK Library. Wiesner attached the critical report.

349 *At a meeting of the:* New York Times, September 13, 1962.

350 *These sprays, dusts, and aerosols:* Carson, *Silent Spring,* pp. 7–8.

351 *"every human being is now subjected":* Ibid., p. 15.

351 *"If we are going to live so intimately":* Ibid., p. 17.

353 *It was the story of a Swedish farmer:* Ibid., pp. 229–30.

353 *"Like Kuboyama, the farmer":* Ibid.

353 *As crude a weapon as:* Ibid., p. 297.

354 *Carson's closing thought:* Ibid.

354 *On September 25, 1962:* Printed invitation, Beinecke.

354 *Then a few days after:* Carson to Dorothy Freeman, October 4, 1962, Muskie.

354 *"Like all good indignant crusaders":* Life, October 12, 1962.

355 *Writing in the* New York Times: *New York Times,* September 11, 1962.

355 *"The basic fallacy—or perhaps the original sin":* Ibid.

355 *one on the cover of:* New York Times Sunday Book Review, September 23, 1962.

355 *Sullivan started off:* New York Times, September 27, 1962.

356 *"In her new book":* Ibid.

356 *which had a surprising circulation of:* Paul Brooks, Houghton Mifflin internal document, October 17, 1962, Beinecke.

356 *Genus by genus, species by species:* "The Desolate Year," *Monsanto Magazine,* October 1962, Beinecke.

357 *The problem is magnified:* Letter to the public from C. G. King, president of the Nutrition Foundation, Inc., January 1963, Beinecke.

358 *the Nutrition Foundation board:* From a "counter" letter to the public from a Mrs. W. F. Hadley, February 19, 1963, Beinecke.

358 *Writing in the journal:* I. L. Baldwin, "Chemicals and Pests," *Science* 137, September 28, 1962.

358 *Modern agriculture, with its high-quality foods:* Ibid.

359 *The editors at* Chemical Week: *Chemical Week,* October 6, 1962.

359 *Paul Brooks heard the campaign:* Brooks, *House of Life,* p. 294.

360 argued in a long, critical piece: *Economist,* October 20, 1962.

360 Financial World *magazine took much the same: Financial World,* October 10, 1962.

360 *No one was surprised when: Ann Arbor News,* December 12, 1962, Beinecke. The paper reported on two of White-Stevens's stops, in Minneapolis and Grand Rapids.

361 *A notable critique came from: Time,* September 28, 1962.

361 *There is no doubt about:* Ibid.

362 *Diamond agreed with the: Saturday Evening Post,* September 28, 1963. Given his original interest in the subject of pesticides, it is hard to read Diamond's attack on *Silent Spring* without seeing in it a measure of revenge. But, despite being dumped as a coauthor of a major bestseller that would one day be judged one of the most important books of the century, Diamond's uneven career continued. In 1961, he was promoted to general editor at *Newsweek.* In 1964, he published a slim book called *The Rise and Fall of the Space Age,* in which he predicted the Apollo program would not succeed in landing a man on the moon during the 1960s.

362 Silent Spring, *it seems to me:* Ibid.

363 *What, finally, is* Silent Spring's *game:* Ibid.

363 *A couple of months after the English:* House of Lords, Official Report 247, no. 58 (March 20, 1963), Beinecke. Shackleton's comment, made with tongue firmly in cheek but with full-throated sentiment against the dangers of pesticides, was widely reported on both sides of the Atlantic.

364 *That same month, Carson got:* Elsie Baier to Carson, December 21, 1962, Beinecke.

364 *One thing that fascinates me:* Carson to Elsie Baier, December 27, 1962, Beinecke.

364 *In late October 1962, Carson:* Carson to Dorothy Freeman, October 25, 1962, Muskie; and Carson to William E. Scheele, September 17, 1962, Beinecke. Scheele was director of the Cleveland Museum of Natural History. Carson wrote to him to accept his invitation to attend a reception in her honor the following months. It's inconceivable that she would have done so had she not already been planning to see Barney Crile in Cleveland at the same time.

365 *She said she could write:* Carson to Dorothy Freeman, October 25, 1962.

365 *It was a speech to the:* Speech to the Women's National Press Club, December 4, 1962, Muskie. Linda Lear also published the text in *Lost Woods.*

366 *Carson's voice that day:* Personal observation. I listened to a recording of the speech in the Muskie archives.

366 *But only days later she was crippled:* Carson to Dorothy Freeman, December 19, 1962, Muskie.

366 *As the year came to a close:* Ibid., Christmas 1962, Muskie.

366 *Then, on New Year's Day:* Ibid., January 1, 1963, Muskie.

366 *Carson said that about a week:* Ibid.

367 *But four weeks later she did:* Ibid., January 29, 1963, Muskie.

368 *In early February 1963, Carson told Dorothy:* Ibid., February 4, 1963, Muskie.

368 *Dorothy wrote back:* Dorothy Freeman to Carson, February 6, 1963, Muskie. This date marked the ninth anniversary of the "Hyacinth Letter." Dorothy told Carson that she was the "center of my being" and that nothing mattered to her unless Carson was a part of the experience. Dorothy, worried that Carson had been exhausting herself in their correspondence, estimated that they had written to each other nearly 1,500 times. She wondered how many books that would make.

368 *Carson reminded her that:* Carson to Dorothy Freeman, n.d. "Hyacinth Time," Muskie.

368 *She told Dorothy that the past decade:* Ibid.

368 *Two new tumors had appeared:* Ibid., February 14, 1963, Muskie.

368 *Only days after this:* Ibid., February 18–19, 1963, Muskie.

369 *"The main thing I want to say":* Ibid.

369 *Don't allow yourself to be:* Anne Ford to Carson, August 7, 1962, Beinecke.

369 *But months after interviewing:* Ibid., November 9, 1962, Beinecke. The nerves at Houghton Mifflin were understandable but unnecessary; McMullen's thoroughness would ultimately vindicate Carson. Meanwhile, Fred Friendly, who had originally approached Brooks about doing the program, would soon become president of the CBS news division.

370 *Sevareid believed that:* Carson read this in a newspaper account dated April 6, 1958, possibly from the *New York Times,* Beinecke.

370   *"There must come a time":* Ibid.

370   *But she confided to Paul Brooks:* Internal Houghton Mifflin document, Beinecke.

370   *Torn between wanting:* Carson to Dorothy Freeman, March 2, 1963, Muskie.

371   *"All that is most wonderful":* Ibid.

371   *"I shall feel better soon":* Ibid.

371   *Stories about the program: Virginia-Pilot,* December 10, 1962, and January 4 and 5, 1963.

372   *"It seems quite certain":* Conservation Foundation, "Implications of Rising Carbon Dioxide Content of the Atmosphere," March 1963.

373   *"The effects of a rise":* Ibid.

373   *Among those watching was President Kennedy:* Memo from Jerome Wiesner to John F. Kennedy, April 3, 1963, JFK Library.

373   *she told Dorothy she hoped not to seem like:* Carson to Dorothy Freeman, April 1, 1963, Muskie.

373   *But while Carson looked to be:* Personal observation. This account of the broadcast is based on my own viewings of it on a DVD provided by the Beinecke library.

379   *Houghton Mifflin bought a copy of it:* Anne Ford to Jack Woolner, May 23, 1963, Beinecke. Woolner worked at the department.

379   *The president of its American division:* Lawrence Emley to Carson, May 24, 1963, Beinecke.

379   *Carson got more support:* U.S. Department of the Interior press release, April 25, 1963, Beinecke.

379   *This laboratory is dedicated to:* Ibid.

380   *The Interior Department, through the:* U.S. Department of the Interior press release, August 12, 1963. The report itself was 109 pages long.

380   *Eric Sevareid reported that:* "The Verdict on the Silent Spring of Rachel Carson," *CBS Reports,* May 15, 1963, Beinecke.

381   *The* New York Times *ran an editorial: New York Times,* May 17, 1963.

381   *In the same issue of the paper:* Ibid.

381   *Dorothy wrote to Carson to say:* Dorothy Freeman to Carson, May 15, 1963, Muskie.

382   *The committee report made:* "Use of Pesticides: A Report of the President's Science Advisory Committee," May 15, 1963, JFK Library.

382 *"If Rachel Carson is right"*: New York Herald Tribune, May 24, 1963.

383 *Carson told Dorothy Freeman:* Carson to Dorothy Freeman, April 23, 1963, Muskie.

383 *In early May 1963, she said she was:* Ibid., May 2, 1963, Muskie.

383 *Dorothy said she didn't know:* Dorothy Freeman to Carson, May 8, 1963, Muskie.

383 *But at the end of May:* Carson, *Always, Rachel,* p. 464.

383 *Carson appeared on June 4, 1963:* U.S. Senate, Subcommittee on Reorganizations and International Organizations of the Committee on Government Operations,"Coordination of Activities Relating to Use of Pesticides," 88th Cong., 1st sess., May 16, 22, 23, and June 4, 25, 1963.

384 *Carson entered a long, prepared statement:* "Statement of Rachel Carson Before the Subcommittee on Reorganization and International Organizations of the Committee on Government Operations," June 4, 1963, Muskie.

384 *Carson and Roger—accompanied by:* Lear, *Rachel Carson,* p. 456.

384 *Carson told Dorothy one reason she was:* Carson to Dorothy Freeman, June 13, 1963, Muskie.

385 *One day in early September:* Ibid., September 10, 1963, Muskie.

385 *Back home in Silver Spring:* Ibid.

385 *"For ourselves, the measure is":* Ibid.

385 *After a long day at the hospital:* Carson to Dorothy Freeman, September 18, 1963, Muskie.

386 *Dorothy recalled that after:* Dorothy Freeman to Carson, October 2, 1963, Muskie.

386 *In October 1963, Carson started a course:* Carson to Dorothy Freeman, October 3, 1963, Muskie.

386 *Dorothy commiserated, saying she:* Dorothy Freeman to Carson, October 11, 1963, Muskie.

386 *A local newspaper account:* San Francisco News-Call Bulletin, October 19, 1963.

386 *Carson told Dorothy how exciting:* Carson to Dorothy Freeman, October 17, 1963, Muskie.

386 *She loved San Francisco:* Ibid., October 21, 1963, Muskie.

386 *When she got home:* Ibid., October 23, 1963, Muskie.

387 *She assured Dorothy that:* Ibid., October 31, 1963, Muskie.

387 *though in one letter:* Ibid. October 23, 1963, Muskie.

387 *She said it was quite an experience:* Ibid., November 14, 1963, Muskie.

387 *"shock, dismay, and revulsion":* Ibid., November 27, 1963, Muskie.

387 *Worried about shipping a portion:* Ibid.

387 *Dorothy wrote to Carson afterward:* Dorothy Freeman to Carson, December 9, 1963, Muskie.

387 *A week before Christmas 1963:* Carson to Dorothy Freeman, December 18–19, 1963, Muskie.

388 *A few days later:* Ibid., December 21, 1963, Muskie. Despite her optimism about another season at Southport Island, this heartbreaking letter showed that Carson knew the end was coming fast. She said she was writing in front of the fireplace in her study after putting Roger to bed. Now she wished Dorothy was by her side so that they could remember all their most treasured times together. She told Dorothy that in spite of the miles that separated them Dorothy remained her "main comfort and support."

388 *After Dorothy made a four-day visit to:* Carson to Dorothy Freeman, January 2, 1964, Muskie.

388 *One of her doctors had:* Ibid., January 9, 1964, Muskie.

388 *Only a few days after Carson told:* Carson, *Always, Rachel,* p. 515.

388 *She said she regretted:* Carson to Dorothy Freeman, January 14, 1964, Muskie.

388 *Carson told Dorothy how impressed:* Ibid., January 18, 1964, Muskie.

388 *Two months later, it was early spring:* Ibid., March 10, 1964, Muskie.

389 *She told Dorothy about:* Dorothy Freeman to Carson, April 12, 1964, Muskie.

389 *In early April she was strong enough:* Ibid., March 31, 1964, Muskie.

389 *When she got home after:* Ibid., April 14, 1964, Muskie.

389 *Later that same day:* Lear, *Rachel Carson,* p. 480. Marie Rodell phoned Dorothy to say that Carson had died at 6:30 p.m. (Dorothy Freeman diary, April 14, 1964, Muskie.)

389 *Among the things Carson left behind:* Carson to Dorothy Freeman, January 24, 1963, and April 11 and 30, 1963, Muskie.

389 *Her brother, Robert, insisted on:* Lear, *Rachel Carson,* p. 482.

389 *On May 4, 1964, the tide at Newagen:* "Notes on My Experience in

Scattering the Ashes of Rachel," Dorothy Freeman's written account of that day, Muskie.

EPILOGUE

392 *During the Pinchot Institute's first year of operation:* U.S. Department of the Interior press release, August 12, 1963.

392 *In the spring of 1964:* Ibid., April 8, 1964.

393 *Udall exercised his considerable authority:* Ibid., September 4, 1964.

393 *Two months later, the FWS:* Ibid., November 15, 1964.

395 *Roger Christie went to live:* Freeman, *Always, Rachel,* Epilogue.

396 *In 1975 she gave a talk:* Audio recording, Muskie.

Bibliography

Abir-Am, Pnina, and Dorinda Outram, eds. *Uneasy Careers and Intimate Lives: Women in Science, 1789–1979*. New Brunswick, N.J.: Rutgers University Press, 1987.

Adam, Peter. *Art of the Third Reich*. New York: Henry N. Abrams, 1992.

Allee, W. C. *Cooperation Among Animals*. New York: Henry Schuman, 1938.

———. *The Social Life of Animals*. Revised ed. Boston: Beacon Press, 1958.

Allee, W. C., et al. *Principles of Animal Ecology*. Philadelphia: Saunders, 1949.

Allen, Garland E. *Life Science in the Twentieth Century*. New York: Wiley, 1975.

American Chemical Society. *Organic Pesticides in the Environment*. Washington, D.C.: American Chemical Society, 1966.

Beebe, William. *The Book of Naturalists: An Anthology of the Best Natural History*. New York: Alfred A. Knopf, 1944.

———. *Half Mile Down*. New York: Harcourt, Brace, 1934.

Beston, Henry. *The Outermost House*. New York: Henry Holt and Company, 1988.

Bonta, Marcia Myers. *Women in the Field: America's Pioneering Women Naturalists*. College Station: Texas A&M University Press, 1991.

Bowler, Peter J. *The Earth Encompassed: A History of the Environmental Sciences*. New York: Norton, 1992.

Bradley, David. *No Place to Hide: 1946/1984*. Hanover, N.H.: University Press of New England, for Dartmouth College, 1983.

Bramwell, Anna. *Ecology in the 20th Century: A History*. New Haven, Conn.: Yale University Press, 1989.

Briggs, Shirley A., and the staff of the Rachel Carson Council. *Basic Guide to Pesticides: Their Characteristics and Hazards*. Washington, D.C.: Taylor and Francis, 1992.

Brinkley, Douglas. *The Wilderness Warrior: Theodore Roosevelt and the Crusade for America.* New York: HarperCollins, 2009.

Brooks, Paul. *The House of Life: Rachel Carson at Work.* Boston: Houghton Mifflin, 1972.

Carson, Rachel. *Always, Rachel: The Letters of Rachel Carson and Dorothy Freeman 1952–1964.* Edited by Martha Freeman. Boston: Beacon Press, 1995.

———. *Chincoteague: A National Wildlife Refuge.* Conservation in Action 1. Washington, D.C.: U.S. Government Printing Office, 1947.

———. *The Edge of the Sea.* Boston: Houghton Mifflin, 1955.

———. *Guarding Our Wildlife Resources.* Conservation in Action 5. Washington, D.C.: U.S. Government Printing Office, 1948.

———. *Lost Woods: The Discovered Writing of Rachel Carson.* Edited by Linda Lear. Boston: Beacon Press, 1998.

———. *Mattamuskeet: A National Wildlife Refuge.* Conservation in Action 4. Washington, D.C.: Government Printing Office, 1947.

———. *Parker River: A National Wildlife Refuge.* Conservation in Action 2. Washington, D.C.: U.S. Government Printing Office, 1947.

———. *The Sea Around Us.* New York: Oxford University Press, 1951.

———. *Silent Spring.* New York: Houghton Mifflin, 1962.

———. *Under the Sea-Wind.* 1941. Reprint, New York: Oxford University Press, 1952.

Clepper, Henry. *Leaders of American Conservation.* New York: Ronald Press, 1971.

Cloos, Hans. *Conversation with the Earth.* New York: Knopf, 1954.

Coates, Peter. *Nature: Western Attitudes Since Ancient Times.* Berkeley: University of California Press, 1998.

Colborn, Theo, Dianne Dumanoski, and John Peterson Myers. *Our Stolen Future: Are We Threatening Our Fertility, Intelligence, and Survival?* New York: Plume, 1997.

Colby, C. B. *Fish and Wildlife: The Story of the Work of the U.S. Fish and Wildlife Service.* New York: Coward-McCann, 1955.

Colman, John S. *The Sea and Its Mysteries: An Introduction to the Science of the Sea.* New York: Norton, 1950.

Comstock, Anna Botsford. *Handbook of Nature Study.* Ithaca: Cornell University Press, 1911. Reprint, Ithaca: Cornell University Press, 1986.

Corfield, Richard. *The Silent Landscape: In the Wake of HMS* Challenger *1872–1876*. London: John Murray, 2003.

Cousteau, J. Y. *The Silent World: A Story of Undersea Discovery and Adventure, by the First Men to Swim at Record Depths with the Freedom of Fish*. New York: Harper and Brothers, 1953.

Crosby, Alfred W. *Ecological Imperialism: The Biological Expansion of Europe, 900–1900*. Cambridge: Cambridge University Press, 1986.

Crowder, William. *Dwellers of the Sea and Shore*. New York: Macmillan, 1923.

———. *A Naturalist at the Seashore*. New York: Century, 1928.

Cueto, Marcos. *Cold War, Deadly Fevers: Malaria Eradication in Mexico 1955–1975*. Washington, D.C.: Woodrow Wilson Center Press, 2007.

Dary, David A. *The Buffalo Book: The Full Saga of the American Animal*. Chicago: Sage Books, 1974.

Diamond, Edwin. *Rise and Fall of the Space Age*. Garden City, N.Y.: Doubleday, 1964.

Doyle, Jean Foley. *Life in Newburyport 1900–1950: A Collection of News Events, City Affairs, and Memories from the First Half of the Twentieth Century*. Portsmouth, N.H.: Peter E. Randall, 2007.

Dunlap, Thomas R. *Saving America's Wildlife: Ecology and the American Mind, 1850–1990*. Princeton, N.J.: Princeton University Press, 1988.

Dysart, Laberta. *Chatham College: The First Ninety Years*. Pittsburgh: Chatham College, 1960.

Egan, Timothy. *The Worst Hard Time*. Boston: Houghton Mifflin, 2006.

Evans, Richard J. *The Third Reich in Power, 1933–1939*. New York: Penguin, 2005.

Federal Writers' Project/Works Progress Administration. *Washington: City and Capital*. Washington, D.C.: U.S. Government Printing Office, 1937.

Fradkin, Philip L. *Fallout: An American Nuclear Tragedy*. Boulder, Colo.: Johnson Books, 2004.

Gaddis, John Lewis. *The Cold War: A New History*. New York: Penguin, 2005.

Garrison, Dee. *Bracing for Armageddon: Why Civil Defense Never Worked*. New York: Oxford University Press, 2006.

Garrison, Tom. *Oceanography: An Invitation to Marine Science with Additional Readings*. 7th ed. Belmont, Calif.: Brooks/Cole, 2010.

Gartner, Carol B. *Rachel Carson*. New York: Ungar, 1983.

Gilbert, Scott F. *Developmental Biology.* 8th ed. Sunderland, Mass.: Sinauer Associates, 2006.

Gosse, Edmund. *Father and Son.* 1907. Reprint, Oxford: Oxford University Press, 2004.

Gottlieb, Julie V., and Thomas P. Linehan, eds. *The Culture of Fascism: Visions of the Far Right in Britain.* London: I. B. Tauris, 2004.

Gottlieb, Robert. *Forcing the Spring: The Transformation of the American Environmental Movement.* Washington, D.C.: Island Press, 1993.

Graham, Frank, Jr. *Man's Dominion: The Story of Conservation in America.* New York: M. Evans, 1971.

———. *Since "Silent Spring."* Boston: Houghton Mifflin, 1970.

Guralnick, Peter. *Last Train to Memphis: The Rise of Elvis Presley.* Boston: Little Brown, 1994.

Hagen, Joel B. *An Entangled Bank: The Origins of Ecosystem Ecology.* New Brunswick, N.J.: Rutgers University Press, 1992.

Hager, Tom. *Linus Pauling and the Chemistry of Life.* New York: Oxford University Press, 1998.

Halliwell, Martin. *American Culture in the 1950s.* Edinburgh: Edinburgh University Press, 2007.

Hansen, Chuck. *U.S. Nuclear Weapons: The Secret History.* New York: Orion Books, 1988.

Herber, Lewis. *Our Synthetic Environment.* New York: Knopf, 1962.

Humphreys, Margaret. *Malaria: Poverty, Race, and Public Health in the United States.* Baltimore: Johns Hopkins University Press, 2001.

Hynes, H. Patricia. *The Recurring Silent Spring.* New York: Pergamon Press, 1989.

Ickes, Harold L. *The Secret Diary of Harold Ickes.* 3 vols. New York: Simon and Schuster, 1953–54.

Isenberg, Andrew C. *The Destruction of the Bison: An Environmental History 1750–1920.* Cambridge: Cambridge University Press, 2000.

Jager, K. W. *Aldrin, Dieldrin, Endrin and Telodrin: An Epidemiological and Toxicological Study of Long-Term Occupational Exposure.* New York: Elsevier, 1970.

Jefferies, Richard. *After London, or Wild England.* 1885. Reprint, Philadelphia: Press at Toad Hall, 2009.

———. *Jefferies' England: Nature Essays by Richard Jefferies.* Edited by Samuel J. Looker. London: Constable, 1937.

————. *A Life of the Fields*. London: Chatto and Windus, 1899. Reprint, Whitefish, Montana: Kessinger Publishing, n.d.

————. *The Pageant of Summer*. Portland, Maine.: Thomas B. Mosher, 1901. Reprint, Whitefish, Mont.: Kessinger Publishing, n.d.

————. *The Story of My Heart: My Autobiography*. 1883. Reprint, London: Tutis Digital Publishing, 2008.

Kallet, Arthur, and F. J. Schlink. *100,000,000 Guinea Pigs: Dangers in Everyday Foods, Drugs, and Cosmetics*. New York: Grosset and Dunlap, 1933.

Kell, Jean Bruyere. *The Old Port Town: Beaufort, North Carolina*. Morehead City, N.C.: Herald Printing, 1980.

Kline, Benjamin. *First Along the River: A Brief History of the U.S. Environmental Movement*. Lanham, Md.: Rowman and Littlefield, 2007.

Lannoo, Michael J. *Leopold's Shack and Ricketts's Lab: The Emergence of Environmentalism*. Berkeley: University of California Press, 2010.

Lapp, Ralph E. *The Voyage of the Lucky Dragon*. New York: Harper, 1958.

Lawrence, T. E.. *Correspondence with Henry Williamson*. Edited by Peter Wilson. Woodgreen Common Near Fordingbridge, UK: Castel Hill Press, 2000.

Lear, Linda. *Rachel Carson: Witness for Nature*. New York: Henry Holt, 1997.

Leopold, Aldo. *Game Management*. New York: Charles Scribner's Sons, 1939.

————. *Round River: Journals of Aldo Leopold*. New York: Oxford University Press, 1953.

————. *A Sand County Almanac, and Sketches Here and There*. 1949. Reprint, New York: Oxford University Press, 1987.

Leopold, Ellen. *A Darker Ribbon: Breast Cancer, Women, and Their Doctors in the Twentieth Century*. Boston: Beacon Press, 1999.

Levine, Ellen. *Up Close: Rachel Carson*. New York: Viking, 2007.

Lewis, Sinclair. *Babbitt*. 1922. Reprint, New York: Barnes and Noble Classics, 2005.

Light, Michael. *100 Suns 1945–1962*. New York: Knopf, 2003.

Lillie, Frank R. *The Woods Hole Marine Biological Laboratory*. Chicago: University of Chicago Press, 1944.

Longgood, William. *The Poisons in Your Food*. New York: Simon and Schuster, 1960.

Look, David W. *The Interior Building: Its Architecture and Its Art*. Washington, D.C.: U.S. Department of the Interior, National Park Service,

Preservation Assistance Division, 1986. Reprint, University of Michigan
Library.

Lytle, Mark Hamilton. *The Gentle Subversive: Rachel Carson, "Silent Spring,"
and the Rise of the Environmental Movement.* New York: Oxford
University Press, 2007.

Maienschein, Jane. *100 Years Exploring Life, 1888–1988: The Marine Biological
Laboratory at Woods Hole.* Boston: Jones and Bartlett, 1989.

Matheson, Richard. *The Incredible Shrinking Man.* New York: Tor, 1994.
Originally published in 1956 as *The Shrinking Man.*

Matthews, Hugoe, and Phyllis Treitel. *The Forward Life of Richard Jefferies: A
Chronological Study.* Oxford: Petton, 1994.

Matthiessen, Peter, ed. *Courage for the Earth: Writers, Scientists, and Activists
Celebrate the Life and Writing of Rachel Carson.* Boston: Houghton Mifflin,
2007.

———. *Wildlife in America.* New York: Viking Penguin, 1959.

McMilen, Wheeler. *Bugs or People? A Reasoned Answer to Opponents of
Pesticides.* New York: Appleton-Century, 1965.

Mead, Clifford, and Thomas Hager, eds. *Linus Pauling: Scientist and
Peacemaker.* Corvallis: Oregon State University Press, 2001.

Meine, Curt. *Aldo Leopold: His Life and Work.* Madison: University of
Wisconsin Press, 1988.

———. *Correction Lines: Essays on Land, Leopold, and Conservation.*
Washington, D.C.: Island Press, 2004.

Miller, Richard L. *Under the Cloud: The Decades of Nuclear Testing.* New York:
Free Press, 1986.

Monteyne, David. *Fallout Shelter: Designing for Civil Defense in the Cold War.*
Minneapolis: University of Minnesota Press, 2011.

Morgan, Ann Haven. *Field Book of Ponds and Streams: An Introduction to the Life
of Fresh Water.* New York: G. P. Putnam's Sons, 1930.

Muir, John. *Nature Writings.* Edited by William Cronon. New York: Library
of America, 1997.

Murphy, Priscilla Coit. *What a Book Can Do: The Publication and Reception of
"Silent Spring."* Amherst: University of Massachusetts Press, 2005.

Murray, John, and Hjort Johan. *The Depths of the Ocean: A General Account of
the Modern Science of Oceanography Based Largely on the Scientific Researches*

of the Norwegian Steamer Michael Sars *in the North Atlantic*. London: Macmillan, 1912.

Nash, Roderick, ed.. *American Environmentalism: Readings in Conservation History*. 3rd ed. New York: McGraw-Hill, 1990.

———. *The American Environment: Reading in the History of Conservation*. Reading, Mass.: Addison-Wesley, 1968.

———. *Wilderness and the American Mind*. New Haven, Conn.: Yale University Press, 1967.

Oelschlaeger, Max. *The Idea of Wilderness*. New Haven, Conn.: Yale University Press, 1991.

Oxenham, John. *The Vision Splendid*. New York: George H. Doran, 1917.

Packard, Randall M. *The Making of a Tropical Disease: A Short History of Malaria*. Baltimore: Johns Hopkins University Press, 2007.

Parker, Philip M., ed. *Fish and Wildlife Service: Webster's Timeline History 1871– 2007*. San Diego: ICON Group International, 2009.

Philipson, Ilene. *Ethel Rosenberg: Beyond the Myths*. New York: Franklin Watts, 1988.

Plato. *Plato's Symposium*. Translated by Seth Benardete. Chicago: University of Chicago Press, 2001.

Randall, Peter E. *Newburyport and the Merrimack*. Camden, Maine: Down East Books, 1981.

Ray, John. *The Wisdom of God Manifested in the Works of Creation: In Two Parts*. 9th ed. London: William and John Innys, 1727. Reprint, Whitefish, Mont.: Kessinger Publishing, 2010.

Reed, Nathaniel P., and Dennis Drabelle. *The United States Fish and Wildlife Service*. Boulder, Colo.: Westview Press, 1984.

Ricketts, Edward F., and Jack Calvin. *Between Pacific Tides: An Account of the Habits and Habitats of Some Five Hundred of the Common, Conspicuous Seashore Invertebrates of the Pacific Coast Between Sitka, Alaska, and Northern Mexico*. 3rd ed. Revised by Joel W. Hedgpeth. Stanford: Stanford University Press, 1962. Originally published in 1939.

Ritter, William Emerson. *An Organismal Theory of Consciousness*. Boston: Gorham Press, 1919.

———. *The Probable Infinity of Nature and Life: Three Essays*. Boston: Gorham Press, 1918.

Roberts, Donald, and Richard Tren. *The Excellent Powder: DDT's Political and Scientific History.* Indianapolis: Dog Ear Publishing, 2010.

Roberts, Sam. *The Brother: The Untold Story of Atomic Spy David Greenglass and How He Sent His Sister, Ethel Rosenberg, to the Electric Chair.* New York: Random House, 2001.

Rostand, Jean. *Humanly Possible: A Biologist's Notes on the Future of Mankind.* New York: Saturday Review Press, 1970.

Schmitt, Peter J. *Back to Nature: The Arcadian Myth in Urban America.* New York: Oxford University Press, 1969.

Schneir, Walter. *Final Verdict: What Really Happened in the Rosenberg Case.* Brooklyn, N.Y.: Melville House, 2010.

Sewell, Brocard, ed. *Henry Williamson, the Man, the Writings: A Symposium.* Padstow, Cornwall: Tabb House, 1980.

Shabecoff, Philip. *A Fierce Green Fire: The American Environmental Movement.* New York: Hill and Wang, 1993.

Shah, Sonia. *The Fever: How Malaria Has Ruled Humankind for 500,000 Years.* New York: Sarah Crichton Books / Farrar, Straus and Giroux, 2010.

Shelton-Roberts, Cheryl, and Bruce Roberts. *Cape Lookout National Seashore: Exploring the History and Wild Coastal Beauty.* Morehead City, N.C.: Lighthouse Publications, 2005.

Showalter, Elaine. *A Jury of Her Peers: American Women Writers from Anne Bradstreet to Annie Proulx.* New York: Alfred A. Knopf, 2009.

Shute, Nevil. *On the Beach.* New York: William Morrow, 1957.

Siddiqi, Javed. *World Health and World Politics: The World Health Organization and the UN System.* Columbus: University of South Carolina Press, 1995.

Sideris, Lisa H., and Kathleen Dean Moore, eds. *Rachel Carson: Legacy and Challenge.* Albany: State University of New York Press, 2008.

Smallwood, William Martin, and Ida Louise Reveley. *Practical Biology.* New York: Allyn and Bacon, 1916. Reprint, Nabu Press, n.d.

Souder, William. *Under a Wild Sky: John James Audubon and the Making of "The Birds of America."* New York: North Point Press, 2004.

Spock, Marjorie. *Eurythmy.* Spring Valley, N.Y.: Anthroposophic Press, 1980.

Steinbeck, John. *The Log from the Sea of Cortez.* 1951. Reprint, New York: Penguin Books, 1995.

Steiner, Rudolf. *Eurythmy: An Introductory Reader.* Forest Row, UK: Sophia Books, 2006.

Sterling, Philip. *Sea and Earth: The Life of Rachel Carson.* New York: Crowell, 1970.

Strachan, Hew. *The First World War.* New York: Viking, 2003.

Thurlow, Richard. *Fascism in Britain: From Oswald Mosley's Blackshirts to the National Front.* Rev. ed. London: I. B. Tauris, 1998.

Udall, Stewart L. *The Quiet Crisis.* New York: Holt, Rinehart and Winston, 1963.

United States Department of Defense. *Civil Defense Booklets.* Red Dog Nuclear Survival Series. Compiled by Jack Stone. Red Dog Press, 2010.

United States Federal Civil Defense Administration. *Annual Report.* Washington, D.C.: U.S. Government Printing Office, 1957. Reprint, University of Michigan Library.

Van der Post, Laurens. *Venture to the Interior.* London: Hogarth Press, 1952.

Watson, James D. *The Double Helix: A Personal Account of the Discovery of the Structure of DNA.* Edited by Gunther S. Stent. New York: Norton, 1980.

Weare, Nancy V. *Plum Island: The Way It Was.* Newbury, Mass.: Newburyport Press, 1996.

Weintraub, Stanley. *Silent Night: The Story of the World War I Christmas Truce.* New York: Plume, 2002.

Welker, Robert Henry. *Natural Man: The Life of William Beebe.* Bloomington: Indiana University Press, 1975.

Wheat, Frank M., and Elizabeth T. Fitzpatrick. *Advanced Biology.* New York: American Book Company, 1929.

Wilding, Don. *Henry Beston's Cape Cod: The Story Behind a Gallant Vagabond's Search for the Great Truth on Eastham's Outer Beach.* Haverford, Penn.: Infinity Publishing, 2003.

Williams, Robert C., and Philip L. Cantelon, eds. *The American Atom: A Documentary History of Nuclear Policies from the Discovery of Fission to the Present 1939–1984.* Philadelphia: University of Pennsylvania Press, 1984.

Williamson, Anne. *Henry Williamson: Tarka and the Last Romantic.* Stroud, UK: Alan Sutton Publishing, 1995.

Williamson, Henry. *A Clear Water Stream.* London: Faber and Faber, 1958.

———. *Genius of Friendship: T.E. Lawrence.* London: Faber and Faber, 1936.

———. *Goodbye, West Country.* Boston: Little, Brown, 1938.

———. *The Pathway.* London: Jonathan Cape, 1928.

————. *Salar the Salmon*. Boston: Little, Brown, and Company, 1936.

————. *Tarka the Otter: His Joyful Water-Life and Death in the Country of the Two Rivers.*. New York: E. P. Dutton, 1928.

Wilson, Douglas P. *Life of the Shore and Shallow Sea*. London: Ivor Nicholson and Watson, 1935.

Wilson, Mamré Marsh. *A Story of North Carolina's Historic Beaufort*. Charleston, S.C.: History Press, 2007.

Wolfe, Douglas A. *A History of the Federal Biological Laboratory at Beaufort, North Carolina 1899–1999*. Beaufort, N.C.: U.S. National Oceanic and Atmospheric Administration, 2000.

Worster, Donald. *A Passion for Nature: The Life of John Muir*. New York: Oxford University Press, 2008.

Yonge, C. M. *The Sea Shore*. London: Collins, 1949.

Zimmerman, O. T., and Irvin Lavine. *DDT: Killer of Killers*. Dover, N.H.: Industrial Research Service, 1946. Reprint, Repressed Publishing, n.d.

Index

About the Author

William Souder has been a frequent contributor to the *Washington Post* and many other publications. His biography of John James Audubon, *Under a Wild Sky,* was a finalist for the Pulitzer Prize. He lives in Grant, Minnesota.

MORRIS PUBLIC LIBRARY
4 North Street
Morris, CT 06763
(860) 567-7440